ARABIC IN THE FRAY

ARABIC IN THE FRAY

LANGUAGE IDEOLOGY AND CULTURAL POLITICS

◆ ◆ ◆

YASIR SULEIMAN

EDINBURGH
University Press

Edinburgh University Press Ltd
22 George Square, Edinburgh EH8 9LF
www.euppublishing.com

Typeset in KoufrUni by
Servis Filmsetting Ltd, Stockport, Cheshire,
and printed and bound in Great Britain by
CPI Group (UK) Ltd, Croydon CR0 4YY

A CIP record for this book is available from the British Library

ISBN 978 0 7486 3740 9 (hardback)
ISBN 978 0 7486 8031 3 (paperback)
ISBN 978 0 7486 8032 0 (webready PDF)
ISBN 978 0 7486 8034 4 (epub)

Published with the support of the Edinburgh University Scholarly Publishing Initiatives Fund.

CONTENTS

FIGURES

ACKNOWLEDGEMENTS

It gives me great pleasure to thank all those who have contributed to the research on which this monograph is based. Yonatan Mendel offered invaluable help in organising my research trips to Israel and Palestine. He has done so with his usual good humour and great efficiency, drafting Manar Makhoul – a man of many talents – to help on many occasions. My trips through landscapes that are part of my family history were often emotional and educational. Yoni and I stopped at roadside wedding parties in the Galilee, got lost many times together, visited communities none of us could visit separately and had many 'adventures' – or *mughāmarāt*, as Yoni would fondly call them – that brought laughter and sadness to my heart and, I am sure, to his. My research trips will always be etched in my memory as a site of pain and yearning for a non-exclusivist utopia, which, I feel, is forever lost.

I would also like to thank the following writers and critics, Palestinians in Israel and Israeli Jews, who have spent hours answering my questions and giving me their time and knowledge unstintingly to discuss Hebrewphone writings in Israel. I will list them here in alphabetical order: Mahmoud Abbasi, Sami Abu Shehadeh, Naim Araidi, Shimon Ballas, Nasir Basal, Almog Behar, Dan Bnay-siri, Oudeh Bisharat, Altayyib Ghanayim, Marzouq Halabi, Gayil Haraven, Hanan Hever, Ala Hlehel, Sayed Kashua, Mahmoud Kayyal, Tamima Kittana, Nida Khury, Sami Michael, Atallah Mansour, Dror Mishani, Ismail Nashif, Salman Natour, Zahia Qundus, Adel Shakour, Meir Shalev, Yehouda Shenhav, Rueven Snir, Sasson Somekh and A. B. Yehoshua. The interviews I conducted with these writers and critics touched on many topics, not all of which are covered in this monograph. I hope that I have done their views justice. Any errors in representing their positions on topics that excite intense feelings are completely my responsibility. The dates and places of all interviews are noted in the text at the point where these interviews are relevant.

My third set of thanks is due to Yonatan Mendel, Manar Makhoul and Yuval Evri for reading Chapter 4 and providing helpful comments. Hawraa Al-Hassan read the whole manuscript and gave me useful comments, too. The fact that Yonatan, Manar and Hawraa were all my doctoral students at Cambridge makes this part of the acknowledgement a cause of great pleasure for me. Any errors are completely my responsibility. I am also grateful to Continuum for the permission to publish parts of my paper 'Constructing languages, constructing national identities' (in *The Sociolinguistics of Identity*, edited by Tope Omoniyi and Goodith While (2006)) in this volume.

Finally, the greatest help came from Shahla, my wife and long-suffering companion. Her interest in my work has never waned and her material help has always been there whenever I needed it, given generously and lovingly. For these contributions alone, Shahla's name deserves to appear next to mine as an author of this book. Our two sons Tamir and Sinan have always been the inspiration that drives us on. To them, my thanks, in the hope that they will, in the future, if not now, dip into this book to find out what their father has been dabbling in for months on end.

King's College, Cambridge
December 2012

For *Tamir*, on his graduation,

For *Sinan*, in anticipation of his graduation

And for *Shahla*, who deserves full Honours!

INTRODUCTION

This is a book about Arabic in the social world in the pre-modern and modern periods. It deals with identity and conflict in society, showing their continuity as features of social life, as well as the variety of ways in which they are manifested through debates about language in the political, cultural and theological spheres. The book therefore straddles many areas, hence the reference to the 'social world' in characterising the book, rather than framing it under 'sociolinguistics' or the 'sociology of language' as general headings, although it addresses researchers from these two constituencies from multiple perspectives. Owing to this broad framing, the book will be topic based and thematic, rather than chronological. It selects a few productive sites from which to pursue the twin themes of identity and conflict *through*, not in, language and deals with them in reference to the set of principles outlined below. The data utilised for this book are therefore second order perspectives on language, rather than data that are culled from language use, as is customary in formal linguistics. In other words, the data contained within this book are meta-linguistic, rather than linguistic in nature. Owing to this, these data tend to relate to the extra-linguistic world, rather than issues of linguistic structure or how data of this kind directly relate to social variables, such as those that abound in Arabic correlational sociolinguistics.[1]

The book starts from a set of framing ideas / principles, which give it unity of perspective. In doing this, the book recognises the distinction between the instrumental and symbolic roles of language in society and approaches its subject from the latter. Treating *language as a symbolic resource*, the book shows that Arabic has been pressed into service in the pre-modern and the modern worlds to articulate issues of continued relevance in society. In the pre-modern period, the book deals with the fundamental issue in

[1] See Yasir Suleiman, *Arabic, Self and Identity: A Study in Conflict and Displacement* (New York and Oxford: Oxford University Press, 2011a).

Islamic thought of the (in)imitability and, as a corollary, the (un)translatability of the Qur'an and links these to early debates about group identity and the prosecution of inter-group strife/conflict. This interpretation of the symbolic role of language is rooted in competing theological positions, but it goes beyond these positions to place language at the centre of debates that are political (with a small 'p') in nature. Jahiz's (255–868/9) theory of language as a semiology of semiologies is an example of the elaborate ways in which the debate about identity and conflict was articulated through language (see Chapter 2). The symbolic role of language in mediating conflicts is further shown to have played a role in the transition from the pre-modern to the modern world. Al-Jabarti's (1753–1825) critical commentary on Napoleon's proclamation to the Egyptians, following his invasion of Egypt in 1798, provides a clear example of how language was symbolically deployed to resist the discursive power of the French invaders (see Chapter 5). Al-Jabarti does this by pointing out the mistakes in the proclamation and using the technical terminology of Arabic grammar to signal the lies – as he sees them – perpetrated by the French invaders. The fact that language was used as an instrument of discursive resistance at such a critical moment in the history of Egypt – a period that is conventionally taken to mark the transition from the pre-modern to the modern history of the Arab Middle East – points to two things: the symbolic role of language as a unit of meaning in society and the awareness of this role as something that is categorially different from language instrumentality. Here we have an excellent example of how language as an instrument of/for communication is used to comment on language as a symbolic resource that is utilised *to do politics in society*, hence the use of the phrase 'cultural politics' in the subtitle of this book. Doing politics in society through language comes to the fore at times of social or political conflict; this, in fact, being the case in discussions of the inimitability of the Qur'an.

The symbolic role of Arabic is exploited in modern times to the same end. The book examines this by considering representative evidence from paratexts: book titles, dedications, epigraphs, prefaces and jacket copies on subject matters related to Arabic (see Chapter 3). As thresholds that are neither inside nor outside the books that they accompany, paratexts are engaged by members of the public, who may never step inside the book proper as readers. Owing to their telegraphic nature, book titles in Arabic about Arabic exploit metaphors that draw our attention to various aspects of the two themes of identity and conflict which form the subject of this monograph. And they do so in a way that is both enticing and task-orienting. From a pragmatic perspective, book titles denote, connote and orient their recipients towards action in the three tripartite sense of locutionary, illocutionary and perlocutionary speech acts, respectively. They tell the recipients that this is a book about 'X', that 'X' has additional meanings in its contextual setting and that 'X' is intended to promote action of a particular kind among its target readership.

Paratextual metaphors are reiterated in meta-linguistic debates about language in the media and literature. These two sites circulate the metaphors concerned throughout society, for example, the belief that Arabic is in danger because of external intervention or internal neglect among its speakers or that it is in a state of ossification that threatens its efficacy as an instrument of communication. Literature is an important arena through which these metaphors – as formulaic modes of expression – and what they allude to in the extra-linguistic world are canonised. Literature, here, does not provide evidence in the strict sense of the term, but its involvement in discussing language meta-linguistically adds depth to the cultural contextualisation of language as a symbolic resource. Through literature, especially poetry, metaphors develop a life of their own, making them available for appropriation as emblematic expressions in paratextual and textual material in traditional, as well as the ever expanding electronic, media (see Chapter 3). Their currency in society endows them with the status of 'common sense' knowledge in a way that makes them available for use in language ideology. As units of language ideology, metaphors connect language to politics in folk-linguistic conceptualisations of the language.

Hybrid literature provides another site from which to pursue the theme of identity in situations of conflict. The book deals with this theme by focusing on language choice within this literature, as this choice is articulated in meta-linguistic debates on the topic (see Chapter 4). Francophone North African literature and Hebrewphone literature by Palestinian writers in Israel both provide a wealth of material for exploring this theme. The two situations are different from each other, but they reveal how the language of hybrid literature is used as a channel for doing politics intra- and inter-culturally in politically charged situations. Issues of power, domination and resistance are explored in this research to reveal the ideological and political situatedness of language choice. This is most clearly represented in the concept of un-Jewing the Hebrew language, which Anton Shammas, as an ideology broker,[2] sought to pursue through his novel *Arabesques* (1988). Through writing a Palestinian family saga in Hebrew which questions some of Israel's founding narratives, Anton Shammas sought to dismantle the privileged relationship that ties the language exclusively to a Jewish identity that excludes Palestinians in Israel from incorporation as full citizens. The debate that this novel raised among Israeli Jewish writers reveals the importance of language in national self-definition and the resistance of the language-identity link in Israel to include the Palestinian 'Other' in this definition. The Palestinians may use Hebrew, but they cannot claim it as a marker of group identity in a way

[2] Blommaert includes the following in the category of language ideology brokers: 'politicians and policy-makers, interest groups, academicians, policy implementers, the organised polity [and] individual citizens'. See 'The debate is open', in Jan Blommaert (ed.), *Language Ideological Debates* (Berlin and New York, NY: Mouton de Gruyter, 1999), p. 9.

that erases the difference between them and Israeli Jews. Having said this, language choice in hybrid literature is not exclusively motivated by considerations of identity expression in situations of conflict. This choice is further informed by language competence, language attitudes, the intended target readership and the constitution of literature as a cultural market that offers the writer opportunities for public exposure and material gain. In addition, conflicts mutate and change their meanings, leading to re-evaluation in the meaning of language choice in hybrid literature; this is clearly reflected in Francophone North African literature, especially in Algeria.

Meta-linguistic discussions of Arabic invoke its cognitive role in linking thought to reality. Approaching this mediating link from a behaviour- and structure-based perspective – especially the former – the book reveals the socio-psychological load that the language is made to carry in its own cultural milieu and inter-culturally (see Chapter 5). Readings of language behaviour and structure are used to characterise Arabic-based culture as an 'acoustic' phenomenon that is devoid of any real cognitive content; as a desert-bound product that keeps the Arabs rooted in the past and unable to step into modernity with culturally transforming engagement; as an arena of exaggeration, over-assertion and inter-cultural miscommunication that leads to breakdowns in inter-cultural communication for which the Arabs, rather than their interlocutors, are held responsible; and as a site of repetition in its capacity as a mode of rhetorical persuasion that runs counter to the syllogistic method that characterises Western thought and culture. This set of readings of Arab thought and culture through language is provided by Arab and non-Arab linguists and commentators without – at least in the behaviour-based approach – any solid evidence. Non-Arab writers and Arab writers writing in English tend to rely on literal translation to argue their views on the impact of Arabic on thought and reality. Owing to this, discussions of the cognitive role of Arabic may be read as no more than ideological pronouncements that, wittingly or unwittingly, give credence to the stereotype of Arab exceptionalism in popular discourse on Arabs and Arab culture in the West.

I have referred to language symbolism as a basic principle of this study. By enabling language through meta-linguistic debates to express extra-linguistic concerns, language symbolism is linked with the deployment of language as proxy in society. The recognition of *language as proxy* is another principle of this study. This principle is at work in every aspect of the material used in this book: Arabic language standardisation as a form of national/ethnic self-definition in the modern and pre-modern periods; the debate over the (in)imitability and (un)translatability of the Qur'an; the use of Arabic grammar as an instrument of discursive resistance; the view that Arabic is in a state of ossification and/or is facing danger from external and internal forces in society; language choice in hybrid literature in its multiple and changing meanings; and the cognitive framing of Arabic to characterise the Arabs and Arabic culture in ways that explain their supposed backwardness and difference from other people and cultures. The use of language as proxy enables ideological brokers to do politics through language, in the sense that talk about language becomes talk about the extra-linguistic world in fulfilment of Gramsci's view that: 'every time the question of language surfaces, in one way or another, it means that a series of other problems is coming to the fore [in society]'.[3]

A third principle of this study concerns the nature of the data that it explores and the knowledge it generates. I have referred to the data above as second order meta-linguistic views, discussions or debates. These data are constructions which may or may not represent empirically valid descriptions or evaluations of Arabic, but this in no way diminishes their importance in dealing with the role of the language in society. This is particularly applicable to the question of which linguistic codes constitute languages and which do not. By looking at recent examples from this area in a range of diverse political settings and against the background of conflict and nation-building, we can observe the working of construction and the extra-linguistic purposes to which it is put in different parts of the world (see Chapter 1). Construction is a form of purposeful manipulation that actually impinges on linguistic structure by branding certain linguistic features as standard and others as non-standard. Through corpus and status planning, the linguistic frontiers of a language are defined in pedagogical and structural ways that frame language standardisation. Both the oral and scriptal forms of the language fall within the purview of construction. This *constructivist perspective* constitutes the third underlying principle of this study. This perspective further extends to the analyses provided here. These analyses do not aim to capture the truth in the positivist sense by applying a replicable methodology to arrive at empirically warrantable knowledge;[4] they represent readings and interpretations that are subject to contestation. However, these readings have the virtue of accessing fluid terrains of meta-linguistic data that correlational sociolinguistics is prone to declare 'out of bounds', leading to the impoverishment of our understanding of the role Arabic plays in the social world.

The ideological nature of the meta-linguistic data is signalled in the subtitle of this monograph. Language / linguistic ideology is an important topic for any exploration of the role of language in the social world,[5] hence its connection to folk-linguistics, which deals with popular conceptualisations of the language through, among other things, language attitudes and language myths. The idea that the language of the Qur'an is inimitable is part of the belief structure of Arabic-speaking Muslims that is normally not open to debate. The (un)translatability thesis follows with little intellectual rupture from this inimitability principle. Ordinary Arabic-speaking Muslims may

3 Antonio Gramsci, *Selections from Cultural Writings*, trans. W. Boelhower (London: Lawrence & Wishart, 1985), p. 183.

4 See Suleiman, *Arabic, Self and Identity*.

5 See K. A. Woolard and B. B. Schieffelin, 'Language ideology', *Annual Review of Anthropology* (1994), 32: 55–82.

not be aware of the symbolic and proxy nature of these two principles in the past or of their intellectual pathways in Islamic thought, but they need not do so precisely because of the 'common sense' status these principles have acquired in society.[6] The idea that Arabic is in danger is another 'taken for granted' attitude in society. This is also true of the status of *fuṣḥā* Arabic as a standard language: ordinary speakers are not aware of the constructed nature of this variety. In all of these cases, we have data that can be moulded into language ideology in its capacity as a: 'cultural [amalgam] of ideas about social and linguistic relationships, together with their loading of moral and political interests'.[7] This understanding of ideology is displayed to full effect in folk-linguistic views on Arabic as a language in danger and under attack from inside and outside. The ideas of power, domination, external scheming and internal collusion are all examples of what is meant by 'moral and political interests' in the above characterisation of ideology.

I have replaced the original term 'system' with 'amalgam' in the above description of ideology, so as to avoid the strong connotations of the former term as a coherent/internally consistent set of ideas or practices that are linked to each other in an explicit or conscious manner. As an amalgam, ideology consists of different strands of thought and perceptions that are difficult to separate out from each other in a neat way. Furthermore, being more elastic, the term 'amalgam' reflects a strategy of hedging on my part, which is more consistent with the meandering nature of ideology and the constructivist approach that I have adopted here. Clearly, ideology is an ill-defined concept, like the notions of language, dialect, nation, identity and many of the concepts that are routinely used in the humanities and the social sciences when we talk about thought, behaviour and society.[8]

However, the fact that language ideology is ill-defined does not mean that it has little useful content in academic discourse. This is the case, in spite of the fact that language ideology is subject to skewed selection, historical

6 Common sense is placed at the centre of ideology in Verschueren's definition of the concept: 'We can define as ideological any basic pattern of meaning or frame of interpretation bearing on or involved in (an) aspect(s) of social "reality" (in particular the realm of social relations in the public sphere), felt to be commonsensical, and often functioning in a normative way'. See Jef Verschueren, *Ideology in Language Use: Pragmatic Guidelines for Empirical Research* (Cambridge: Cambridge University Press, 2012), p. 10. Describing a pattern as normative here includes its ability to signpost not just how things may be, but 'how things should be' (p. 8).

7 Judith T. Irvine, 'When talk isn't cheap: language and political economy', *American Ethnologist* (1989), 16: 255.

8 McLellan opens his book on ideology by noting its ill-defined and contested nature: 'Ideology is the most elusive concept in the whole of social science. For it asks about the bases and validity of our most fundamental ideas. As such, it is an essentially contested concept, that is, a concept about the very definition (and therefore application) of which there is acute controversy'. See *Ideology* (Buckingham: Open University Press, 1995), p. 1.

distortion, factual error, illusion, myth-making, affective appeal and spurious rationalisation: all of which are aspects of ideology that are consistent with the notion of construction used above. In spite of this, language ideology is, or ought to be, an important subject of study, because of the insights it provides on language in the social world. Language ideology reflects and gives rise to a group consciousness that further acts as a mediating frame among different interests in intra- and inter-nation relations. Issues of belonging, loyalty, patriotism, power, entitlement, development, purity and Othering or differentiation are strong strands in this mediating role of language ideology. The fact that language ideologies are invariably heterogeneous, even contradictory at times, signals that contestation is built into the very structure of language ideology. And the fact that language ideology can signify a variety of meanings enables language to be used as a proxy for talk about extra-linguistic issues when talk about such issues is embargoed in society for political, legal or other reasons. Finally, language ideology is more than just talk: it is usually deployed to act in, and on, society in the promotion of aims which may or may not be well-defined. Motivation and task-orientation are therefore an integral part of language ideology, as of all kinds of ideology.

It is clear from the above that language ideology permeates all spheres of human activity where language is in practice: in education, the media, cultural institutions, legal institutions, the political sphere and especially where language is used to comment or reflect upon language itself, producing a kind of ideologically impregnated meta-language. This, in effect, means that language ideology is everywhere and, because of this, it may, in fact, appear to be nowhere. It is this pervasiveness of language ideology that normalises it to the point of making it covert and barely visible in ordinary discourse. The idea that 'our' language is richer, more beautiful and has a more noble pedigree than other languages is regarded as self-evident in many language communities. It is this self-evident aspect of ideology that conspires to make it look invisible in society. This book aims to show the far reaching ways in which language ideology works in the social world.

In spite of this, ideology tends to have a pejorative meaning in popular and, to a lesser extent, academic discourse.[9] McLellan captures this attitude to ideology well when he states:

> With significant exceptions, the word ideology comes trailing clouds of pejorative connotation. Ideology is someone *else's* thought, seldom our own. That our thought might be ideological is a suggestion that we almost instinctively reject

[9] In the public imaginary, ideology has negative connotations, because it is usually associated with totalitarian regimes. As Thompson observes: 'to characterise a view as "ideological" is *already* to criticise it, for "ideology" is not a neutral term' [emphasis in the original]. See John B. Thompson, *Studies in the Theory of Ideology* (Cambridge: Polity Press, 1984), p. 12.

lest the foundations of our most cherished conceptions turn out to be composed of more shifting sand than we would like.[10]

In spite of this aversion to ideology, McLellan argues that: 'we are all implicated in ideology which is both real and powerful'.[11] Understanding this, McLellan argues, is important to 'prevent us from becoming [the] unconscious victims of [ideology]'.[12] In scholarly practice, this may take the form of declaring our positionality or acknowledging the role of the researcher's subjectivity in conducting research in the social sciences and the humanities – a matter that is more honoured in the breach than compliance.[13] This is particularly important in discussing the role of language in marking identity, especially when this is framed against the background of social and political conflict. As a conflict-ridden area, the Middle East provides an excellent arena for exploring these issues.

In investigating the above topics, a mixture of *traditional scholarship* and aspects of *qualitative investigation* are applied in this research. The latter is most clearly represented in the discussion of Hebrewphone literature by Palestinians in Israel. An extensive set of unstructured interviews were conducted and audio-recorded with Israeli Palestinian and Jewish writers and scholars, in order to understand the politics of language choice and its ideological content. These interviews were conducted over two visits in different locations in Israel: the first with Palestinian writers and scholars during the month of September 2011; the second with Israeli Jewish writers and scholars during June 2012. The interviews were analysed and used in conjunction with library-based research. The interviewees were told about the nature of the research and my background as the researcher: the fact that I am a scholar of Palestinian origin and British nationality at Cambridge. It was important to make this information known to the interviewees, so as to enable them and the researcher to monitor the flow of the conversation against any possible bias. In particular, the researcher used this declaration of subjectivity to signal to the interviewees – Israeli Palestinians and Jews – that he is not, as a scholar, acting as a Palestinian with an advocacy role. This was important because of the political nature of language choice in Israel, as Chapter 4 will reveal. The interviewees expressed a range of political views on matters that, on many occasions, went beyond language choice in Hebrewphone

[10] See McLellan, *Ideology*, p. 1 [emphasis in the original]. The pejorative attitude towards ideology often fails to acknowledge some of its benefits, including, in the case of the much maligned nationalist ideology, its great achievements in art, architecture and other walks of life.

[11] Ibid. p. 2.

[12] Ibid. p. 2.

[13] See Yasir Suleiman, *A War of Words: Language and Conflict in the Middle East* (Cambridge: Cambridge University Press, 2004); Yasir Suleiman, *Arabic, Self and Identity*.

literature. Some of these views were intimately connected with political ideology; a prime example of which was the interview with the leading Israeli writer A. B. Yehoshua, in which a seamless transition from politics to literature was evident.

The use of traditional, text-based scholarship as an investigative approach is not a choice of last resort in this research, but a conscious one. Considering the dominance of the positivist / quantitative approach in investigating social phenomena in the social sciences,[14] it takes some scholarly courage to admit that one is using a traditional approach. An excellent example of this is Michael Billig's argument for using this form of scholarship in studying ideology. Billig's position resonates with this researcher, who has been arguing for the use of non-quantitative methodologies not in place of, but *together with* the quantitative, correlationst method[15] to arrive at richer understandings of Arabic in the social world. Billig points out that, to the 'modern methodologist traditional scholarship seems a haphazard and biased affair. The traditional scholar does not seem obsessed with laying bare the methodological procedures, which can be followed by anyone with sufficient training'.[16]

Here traditional scholarship is different from both quantitative and qualitative methodologies, although it is more akin to the latter in its interest in

[14] In dealing with the debate about quantitative and qualitative research, Bryman characterises this approach as follows: 'Quantitative methodology is routinely depicted as an approach to the conduct of social research which applies a natural science ... approach to social phenomena. [This approach is characterised by] a preoccupation with operational definitions, objectivity, replicability, causality, and the like ... Through questionnaire items concepts can be operationalized; objectivity is maintained by the distance between observer and observed along with the possibility of external checks upon one's questionnaire; replication can be carried out by employing the same research instrument in another context; and the problem of causality [is] eased by the emergence of path analysis and regression techniques to which surveys are well suited'. See Alan Bryman, 'The debate about quantitative and qualitative research: a question of method or epistemology?' *The British Journal of Sociology* (1984), 35: 77. Billig seems to have more quantitative, rather than qualitative, methodology in mind when he writes the following as a prelude to defending traditional scholarship: 'A *methodology* involves presenting rules of procedure about matters such as the collection of data and their analysis. The rules are impersonal, in that they are meant to apply equally to all researchers. It is assumed that any two researchers who approach the same problem should arrive at identical results, as long as neither infringes the methodological rules. Thereby, it is hoped that individual bias is excluded from the research process. In this way, methodology attempts to standardise practice of the social sciences and to eliminate quirkiness'. See Michael Billig, 'Methodology and scholarship in understanding ideological explanation', in Charles Antaki (ed.), *Analysing Everyday Explanation: A Casebook of Methods* (London: Sage Publications, 1988), pp. 199–200.

[15] See Suleiman, *Arabic, Self and Identity*.

[16] Billig, 'Methodology and scholarship in understanding ideological explanation', p. 200.

interpretation. Billig acknowledges the individual, interpretive and therefore contestable nature of traditional scholarship. He points to the importance of wide reading in analysing texts and the ability 'to make connections between seemingly disparate phenomena'.[17] He further adds that:

> traditional scholars are not particularly bothered with the origins of their insights, in the sense that they do not attempt the impossible task of laying bare all the intellectual experiences which lead up to the ability to make a scholarly judgement. Nor do they presume that other scholars will read the same texts in just the same way as they have. In fact, scholars spend a great deal of energy in criticising the reading of their fellow scholars.[18]

Billig concludes by connecting traditional scholarship to ideology research: 'The traditional skills of scholarship have much to offer the study of ideology',[19] not least because of the elusive nature of ideology. This is true in relation to this particular research on language ideology and cultural politics, which is largely based on interpretive readings of a set of disparate texts that relate to language, identity and conflict in the Arabic-speaking milieu. The texts are drawn from a variety of domains and historical periods. They seem to deal with different issues, which relate to Arabic in the social world. What this research does is to connect them to each other by adopting a tripartite perspective consisting of the principles of *language symbolism, language as proxy and constructivism*.

To these principles, we can now add a fourth: *methodological complementarity*. This research is based on a combination of qualitative methodology and traditional scholarship. Underlying this perspective is a wider commitment to methodological complementarity in exploring the role of Arabic in the social world, which includes quantification and its typical manifestation in correlating social variables with linguistic variants.[20] Methodological complementarity is especially important in view of the expansion of data in social research to include second order, meta-linguistic reflections on language in society. This expansion is important for developing a richer understanding of the role of language in the social world and how this role relates to ideology and cultural politics in society. Methodological complementarity further recognises that data pertaining to language in the social world are best investigated using different approaches. Failure to acknowledge this would lead to limiting the empirical domain of language in the social world as a scholarly enterprise to those data that a particular methodology can handle,

[17] Ibid. p. 200.

[18] Ibid. p. 200.

[19] Ibid. p. 200.

[20] For an interesting analysis of the use of the social variable in sociological research, see Herbert Blumer, 'Sociological analysis and the "variable"', *American Sociological Review* (1956), 21: 683–90.

treating what remains outside as, technically speaking, irrelevant. Cutting the empirical fabric of language in society to fit the methodological tools at our disposal is a form of Procrustean scholarship.

Methodological complementarity can also open the door for the use of the results of one method in calibrating the results of other methods or in opening new avenues for new research. For example, qualitative research or traditional scholarship may point to the existence of an expanded repertoire of social variables that can be correlated with linguistic variants in quantitative research. Alternatively, qualitative research may generate results that can be subjected to further interpretation using quantitative methodology or traditional scholarship. My treatment of the language situation in Jordan is an example of this complementarity.[21] Instead of sticking to the results of correlating social variables with language variants in the quantitative approach, language variation was reconceptualised to go beyond 'sex' as the controlling variable to issues of national identity and political conflict using a mixture of qualitative research and traditional scholarship.

Finally, this is the fourth volume in an evolving five-monograph project on Arabic in the social world. The first volume, *The Arabic Language and National Identity: A Study in Ideology*,[22] investigated the use of Arabic in developing pan-Arabist, regionalist and state-centred nationalist ideologies and the interaction between them. The focus here was on the group. Conflict was acknowledged in this enterprise, but it was not given great visibility. The second volume, *A War of Words: Language and Political Conflict in the Middle East*,[23] turned the gaze to conflict between dialects, dialects and the standard language and between standard languages (mainly Hebrew and Arabic). Group identity was invoked as an important background to ethnic and national conflicts in the language domain in this volume, but was treated as secondary to conflict in terms of research focus. The third volume, *Arabic, Self and Identity: A Study in Conflict and Displacement*,[24] brings identity and conflict together. It develops this twin theme in two important ways: by concentrating on individual identity – the Self – and by discussing the effect displacement, as an outcome of conflict, has on individual and, to a lesser extent, group identity in diaspora or diaspora-like situations. The volume also provided an extensive critique of some fault lines in studying Arabic in the social world, including methodological ones. The present volume concentrates on the twin themes of identity and conflict, with reference to language ideology and cultural politics. It therefore interacts with the first two volumes by adding new empirical domains that show the continuity and extensive reach of these two themes in the pre-modern and modern periods. The four

21 See Suleiman, *A War of Words*.

22 See Yasir Suleiman, *The Arabic Language and National Identity: A Study in Ideology* (Washington, DC: Georgetown University Press, 2003).

23 See Suleiman, *A War of Words*.

24 See Suleiman, *Arabic, Self and Identity*.

principles outlined above – those of language symbolism, language as proxy, constructivism and methodological complementarity – underlie these four volumes, giving them a unity of perspective and intellectual coherence that justify including them as constituent members of my project on Arabic in the social world. These same principles will apply in the next, and final, volume in this project, which aims to investigate language policy in this world.

Finally, I have adopted the following conventions in rendering the Arabic materials in the book. All of the items in the bibliography appear in full transliteration and whenever these items are referred to in footnotes. In the text, most items appear in an English form that is nearest to their full transliteration. I have adopted this approach to make the text more accessible to readers with little or no knowledge of Arabic or of transliteration. Most non-bibliographic material in Arabic is rendered without full inflections in transliterated form.

CHAPTER

1

LANGUAGE CONSTRUCTION AND LANGUAGE SYMBOLISM

This chapter provides a comparative perspective on language construction in the non-scriptal and scriptal worlds. It does so by reference to the symbolic function of language.[1] The use of language as proxy in expressing conflict in society reveals its availability for expressing competing narratives of the in-group and the out-group. The chapter deals with these topics by exploring three processes in language construction: *identification, differentiation* and *distanciation*, relating them to issues of national identity and inter- and intra-group political conflict. Language ideology is central to this exploration, as is the use of language to *do politics through culture* in society. A secondary aim of this chapter is to counter the folk-linguistic idea in the Arabic-speaking world that what is called *fuṣḥā* Arabic stands outside this constructivist paradigm, largely owing to its longstanding status as a standard language.

Introduction

Standardisation has the effect of making languages assume the status of *natural* categories of the social world. This is particularly true when language standardisation has deep roots in history, as is the case for Arabic. Most Arabic speakers are unaware of the constructed nature of their language, both at the status and corpus planning levels, or of the ideological factors involved in the complex and multi-layered process that led to its emergence as a marker of identity. The fact that this process is linked to ideas about uniformity, correctness, purity and ethnic election requires excavation,

[1] I am grateful to Continuum for the permission to publish parts of my paper 'Constructing languages, constructing national identities' (in *The Sociolinguistics of Identity*, Tope Omoniyi and Goodith White (eds) (London and New York, NY: Continuum, 2006), pp. 50–71) in this volume.

in order to bring it into the overt discourse about the language in folk-linguistic terms. However, even this may not be sufficient to counter the long-ingrained idea in common parlance that Arabic has not been subject to construction. This ahistorical view of the language writes the processes of status and corpus planning – which are inherent to all languages – out of history, thereby giving the impression that the language was the result of an almost miraculous birth. Therefore, challenges to aspects of Arabic emerge as challenges to a fact of the social world which, through its association with Islam and high culture, has been consecrated as a God's truth principle of the Arab intellectual tradition.

I have dealt with the ideological dimension of the standardisation of Arabic in an earlier paper, in which I highlighted the forces running through the corpus-planning measures that permeated the setting up of the language as a medium of learning and religious practice.[2] There is therefore no need to rehearse the arguments for this position here: the reader can refer to this paper directly. It is, however, instructive to consider a variety of cases in debates about language and identity in modernity, in which ideological construction is not lost in the mist of time. This comparative perspective will provide compelling evidence, especially for Arabic and the Arabs, of the constructed nature of standard languages and of some of the forces at play in the process of standardisation. Against this background, talk about the constructed nature of Arabic would not be considered as an aberration, as it might, in fact, be construed in folk-linguistic conceptualisations of the language, but rather as an integral part of the linguistic profile of any group. For this purpose, I will deal below with examples that shed light on the interplay of ideology, politics and conflict in constructing languages as identity markers at the group level.

The deployment of languages as markers of identity is another arena, in addition to standardisation, in which construction rules supreme. The same language may be constructed to support different or conflicting conceptions of identity. This shows the potential of languages for ideological manipulation, as I will explain below by examining the variety of ways in which Arabic was constructed to articulate different identity repertoires in the modern period. In this case, construction is context-bound, with politics being one of the determining factors. Thus, in Egypt, Arabic was constructed as a marker of an Egypt-bound or, alternatively, an Arab-bound identity at different times in the modern history of the country to suit existing political imperatives. In Lebanon, Arabic was exploited for similar purposes to construct identities that would help resolve the sectarian tensions in the country. Some did this by denying that Arabic signals an Arab identity for Lebanon,

[2] See Yasir Suleiman, 'Ideology, grammar-making and the standardisation of Arabic', in Bilal Orfali (ed.), *In the Shadow of Arabic: The Centrality of Language to Arabic Culture* (Studies Presented to Ramzi Baalbaki on the Occasion of his Sixtieth Birthday) (Leiden and Boston, MA: Brill, 2011), pp. 3–30.

favouring, in this respect, the Lebanese dialect as a marker of a specifically Lebanese identity, by claiming that Lebanon is a multilingual country with many identities or by giving primacy to environment over language as the defining factor in group identity. Others accepted that Arabic can signal an Arab identity for the country, but that this identity inflection does not exclude specifically Lebanese, nation-state or sub-state community bound identities. In each of these cases, the language-identity link is a matter of construction in which historically situated political interests play a defining role.

Standardisation relates directly to both the instrumental (communicative) and symbolic roles of language. The instrumentality of language is most directly relevant to corpus-planning, wherein the prime concern is providing the language with the resources that it needs to discharge its communicative role in society: an orthographic system, dictionaries, style manuals, punctuation manuals and so forth. With time, some of these resources – for example, the orthographic system in the case of Arabic – start to carry a great symbolic load as markers of group identity. Proposals to reform some of these resources are, as a result, not read instrumentally in language debates, but construed symbolically as attempts to alter a marker of group identity. In other words, with time, some corpus-planning resources start to assume ideological meanings (at least more than others), making them subject to contestation in cultural politics.

Language symbolism is most closely linked to status planning. The choice of a language for communication carries with it narratives of group identity that are historically, culturally and politically significant. As a result, proposals to replace one language with another or with one of its dialects are met with stiff resistance in language ideological debates, because they touch a raw nerve of the language community; this is the case in Arabic, as I have shown in my book *A War of Words: Language and Conflict in the Middle East*. Diglossia in Arabic may complicate the symbolic associations of language with identity by creating different, but largely coterminous, language communities in the same body-politic: one associated with behaviour through the dialects as mother tongues; the other associated with shared evaluations through the *fuṣḥā* as a native language.[3] Drawing this distinction between

[3] See Yasir Suleiman, 'Egypt: from Egyptian to pan-Arab nationalism', in Andrew Simpson (ed.), *Language and National Identity in Africa* (Oxford: Oxford University Press, 2008), pp. 26–43. The following quotation articulates the position that I am advocating here. See Robert L. Cooper, *Language Planning and Social Change* (Cambridge: Cambridge University Press, [1989] 1996), pp. 134–5: 'In fact, language standardisation is more likely to be approached with regard to its attitudinal than its behavioural component. People, that is, are more likely to agree that an all-purpose model exists than use it for all the purposes for which they feel it to be appropriate, if in fact they use it at all. Indeed, Labov (1966, 1968) defines a speech community in terms of shared evaluations, not in terms of shared verbal behaviour. According to this view, people belong to the same speech community when they evaluate a given instance of language behaviour similarly . . .'

'mother tongue' and 'native language' is important for capturing the structure of practice and feeling in communities that use Arabic. Language symbolism is further associated with the use of language as a proxy in society to express extra-linguistic views and anxieties, as well as to hint at the political orientations of a group or an individual. I will give examples of this role of language later in this book. At this stage, suffice it to say that the proxification of language is not possible without its symbolism: the former goes hand-in-hand with the latter. Attending to language symbolism in the spoken and scriptal domains, as I will be doing in this book, is one important way in which to access the dominant language ideology / ideologies as a form of cultural politics.

Since language is related to identity through symbolism, we must begin by providing a sketch of what identity stands for in this work. Instead of employing heavy duty scholarly discourse on the topic, I will invoke a common sense and self-reflective discussion of the concept by the Lebanese-French writer Amin Maalouf, author of the bestselling novel *Leo the African*. In his book *On Identity*, Amin Maalouf begins as follows:

> How many times since I left Lebanon in 1976 to live in France have people asked me, with the best intention in the world, whether I felt 'more French' or 'more Lebanese'? And I always give the same answer: 'Both!'
>
> To those who ask the question, I patiently explain that I was born in Lebanon and lived there until I was 27; that Arabic is my mother tongue; and that it was in Arabic translation that I first read Dumas and Dickens and *Gulliver's Travels*; and that in my native village, the village of my ancestors, that I experienced the pleasures of childhood and heard some of the stories that were later to inspire my novels. How could I forget all that? How could I cast it aside? On the other hand, I have lived for 22 years on the soil of France; I drank her water and wine; every day my hands touch her ancient stones; I write my books in her language; never again will she be a foreign country to me.
>
> So am I half French and half Lebanese? Of course not. Identity can't be compartmentalized. You can't divide it up into halves or thirds or any other separate segments. I haven't got several identities: I have just got one, made up of many components combined together in a mixture that is unique to every individual.[4]

Maalouf is primarily interested in personal identity, but he is aware that this identity is socially located by virtue of being at the crossroads of many of life's currents and social categories of self-definition. First, personal identities, according to Maalouf, are both complex and unique pluralities. They are not single malts, but blends for which there is no single recipe. Second, personal identities also invoke an assumption of alterity, pointing to the fact that it is not possible to posit identity without speaking of difference, of

4 Amin Maalouf, *On Identity*, trans. Barbara Bray (London: The Harvill Press, 2000), p. 3.

Otherness, as will be shown throughout this work. This assumption of difference/Otherness has often been held responsible for the excesses of identity-politics in intra- and inter-group conflicts. In response, it is pointed out that identities are neutral constructs: it is how they are deployed in our social lives that brands them as a force of good or conflict in society. 'A sense of identity', as Sen points out, 'can be a source not merely of pride and joy, but also of strength and confidence';[5] however, problems start to surface when these positive aspects of identity give way to an exaggerated and intolerant sense of categorical difference with the Other. Third, personal identities, as Maalouf also tells us later in his book, are both stable and changeable.[6] Maalouf emphasises the potential for identity mutation – the fact that identity is always in a state of becoming – and he links this to the different configurations in the 'hierarchy' of elements that make up identity.[7] Fourth, Maalouf recognises that the components of personal identity may clash with each other under certain conditions, yet these same components can exist in harmony under other, less inciting conditions.

This is one of the paradoxes of identity: it has the capacity to combine the forces of relative harmony and fragmentation, fusion and fission, and inclusion and exclusion into a single, but complex unit that manifests itself in different ways under different conditions. Owing to this, some scholars prefer to speak of an identity repertoire, rather than just identity on its own. This concept of identity as repertoire is close to how Amartya Sen describes himself in his book *Identity and Violence: The Illusion of Destiny*:

> I can be, at one and the same time, an Asian, and Indian citizen, a Bengali with Bangladeshi ancestry, an American or British resident, an economist, a dabbler in philosophy, an author, a Sanskritist, a strong believer in secularism and democracy, a man, a feminist, a heterosexual, a defender of gay and lesbian rights, with a nonreligious lifestyle, from a Hindu background, a non-Brahmin and a nonbeliever in an afterlife.[8]

Context acts as the determinant for which aspect/s of identity assume(s) relevance in a particular situation, as well as the intensity at which this aspect is/are deployed. Finally, personal identities are used as a resource with which to do things, and, in discursive terms, they are projects of the self that are inscribed in discourse as performance. They can be deliberately deployed

[5] Amartya Sen, *Identity and Violence: The Illusion of Destiny* (London: Allen Lane, 2006), p. 1.

[6] I take the view that a totally constructivist or postmodernist view which denies stability as an aspect of identity is untenable.

[7] Maalouf's use of the term 'hierarchy' in this context is not helpful, as I will explain later. I personally prefer to talk in terms of the poly-centricity of identity instead.

[8] Sen, *Identity and Violence*, p. 19.

and actively manipulated to achieve utilitarian or other objectives in social life.[9]

These features of personal identity apply to group identity – one of the main concerns of this book – although their mode of operation will differ in each case. Whether at a group or individual level, identities assume great visibility and force under conditions of stress, anxiety, conflict and insecurity, which is often the case for group identity at times of historical, social or political crisis or upheaval. As Zygmunt Bauman states, in a figurative turn of phrase that will be invoked in different guises in Chapter 3: 'a battlefield is identity's natural home. Identity comes to life only in the tumult of battle; it falls asleep and silent the moment the noise of the battle dies down'.[10] And while recognising that identities are negotiable, this study does not subscribe to the view that they are fleeting or easily discardable, not least because of their intersubjectivity, which implies that even if we shed an identity, others may continue to ascribe it to us. Identities are categorically different from lifestyles, from the fact that people eat falafel, use extra-virgin olive oil, holiday in Spain, wear designer clothes, listen to jazz or drive BMWs.[11] Identities have an element of liquidity, but they are not entirely liquid in all domains of definition. Speaking metaphorically, some aspects of identity – for example, religious identity – tend to be more solid than liquid at the macro-level. At the micro-level, the level of detail or the individual identities show variation, but without, in most cases, orbiting excessively outside their macro-formations.

Yet in spite of the importance of language in constructing identity, it tends to be given short shrift in discussions of how it marks the individual and, especially for our purposes here, the group. In his book *National Identity*, Anthony Smith, a leading scholar of nationalism, states, not unsurprisingly, that: 'national identity and the nation are complex constructs composed of a number of interrelated components – ethnic, cultural, territorial, economic and legal-political'.[12] Anthony Smith does not name language *per se* as a

[9] See Suleiman, 'Ideology, grammar-making and the standardisation of Arabic', pp. 44–76, for an extensive discussion of this aspect of identity.

[10] Zygmut Bauman, *Identity* (Cambridge: Polity, 2004), p. 77.

[11] I find the following comments on identity by Sen to be apt here: 'Not all of the categories that can be consistently generated would serve as a plausible basis for an important identity ... People who wear size 8 shoes are typically not linked with each other with a strong sense of identity on that shoe-size ground ... [However], whether a particular classification can plausibly generate a sense of solidarity or not must depend on social circumstances. For example, if size 8 shoes became extremely difficult to find for some complicated bureaucratic reason ... then the need for shoes of that size may indeed become a shared predicament and give reason enough for solidarity and identity'. See Sen, *Identity and Violence*, p. 26. I prefer solidarity to identity as a way of describing this kind of voluntary association.

[12] Anthony D. Smith, *National Identity* (London: Penguin, 1991), p. 15.

maker of national identity, although we can assume from the arguments that he makes that it is one of the most important markers, at least in the cultural definition of the nation. In fact, language in this book is the *absent–present* of the nation in definitional terms. But even when scholars – for example, Ernest Gellner,[13] Eric Hobsbawm[14] or Benedict Anderson[15] – highlight the role of language in national identity and nation-building, they tend to treat language as a given of nationalism, hardly ever discussing its constructedness in sufficient detail or in a way that responds to the interests of professional linguists. In fact, I found myself slipping into this mode of thinking and then correcting myself when writing my book *The Arabic Language and National Identity: A Study in Ideology*. The practice, if not the theory, in nationalism studies that languages are more or less self-evident categories must therefore be subjected to critical analysis. Referring to Benedict Anderson's well-known book *Imagined Communities*, Susan Gal points out that: 'not only communities but also languages must be imagined before their unity can be socially accomplished'.[16] Imagined communities go hand-in-hand with imagined languages in the nationalist or ethnic enterprise. This constructivist perspective is one of the main principles of this study. The main aim of this chapter is to elucidate this principle.

As we shall see below, languages are constructed units of the social world. In this context, we may point out that whether two or more varieties are established as different languages or as dialects of the same language will depend on a variety of contextual factors that are related to the history, politics, culture and demography of any given community. The ideas that languages are discursive projects and standard languages are the products of ideological processes are two further guiding principles in this research, as the next section will reveal.[17]

Constructing Languages, Constructing National Identities

Starting with Scandinavia, we can talk about the constructed nature of Swedish, Danish and Norwegian as distinct national languages. These languages are historically related, exist on a continuum and are mutually intelligible, although each has its special linguistic characteristics and regional

[13] Ernest Gellner, *Nations and Nationalism* (Oxford: Basil Blackwell, 1983).

[14] Eric Hobsbawm, *Nations and Nationalism since 1870* (Cambridge: Cambridge University Press, 1990).

[15] Benedict Anderson, *Imagined Communities: Reflections on the Origin and Spread of Nationalism* (London and New York: Verso, 1991).

[16] Susan Gal, 'Multiplicity and contention among language ideologies', in Bambi B. Schieffelin, Kathryn A. Woolard and Paul V. Kroskrity (eds), *Language Ideologies: Practice and Theory* (New York and Oxford: Oxford University Press, 1998), p. 325.

[17] See K. A. Woolard and B. B. Schieffelin, 'Language ideology', *Annual Review of Anthropology* (1994), 32: 64.

flavour.[18] In purely instrumental terms, they can be treated as varieties of the same overarching language. The differences between them seem to be less than those between the Arabic dialects at the end points of the Arabic language continuum from East to West, which, in contrast, are treated as varieties of the same language, rather than as distinct languages. Swedish, Danish and Norwegian are treated as three distinct languages for reasons that are intimately linked to political history and nation-building. In fact, the relative linguistic proximity of Danish and Swedish has been a factor in the conscious marking of their difference through specific scriptal symbols.[19] Script and script variations are an effective way of making visible – of constructing – differences between languages, as I will discuss in the next section.[20]

Within the Scandinavian sphere, Norway provides further evidence of identity driven language construction – what may be called linguistic constructioneering (by analogy with engineering) – to signal the largely conscious and target-oriented character of the process of fashioning the language-identity link. Now generally perceived as two standard varieties of the same language, although for a long time during the nineteenth and twentieth century, they were construed and promoted as distinct and competing standards, Nynorsk (New Norwegian) and Bokmål (Book or Literary Language) represent two different national imaginaries of Norwegian identity. Nynorsk, which was originally called Landsmål (the language of the countryside), sought to anchor Norwegian national identity to the dialects of the countryside, particularly those in the west and the mountains of the south-east, in the romantic conception that it is these dialects that link Norwegian to its authenticating traditions and folk culture and, ultimately, through these, to Old Norse. But, not unusually in nationalism, this was a hard-headed romanticism: it had the intention of putting sufficient distance between the emerging Norwegian language and Danish – the old official language – by suggesting that Landsmål/Nynorsk belonged to a different Scandinavian sub-family (Old Norse) from Danish. The construction of Nynorsk is therefore an integral part of an attempt to create a Norwegian national identity that is as different as possible from Danish. Alterity or significant Otherness, which we encountered in commenting on personal identity, was the main impulse here. Within the Norwegian body-politic, Nynorsk, as hinted above, was an expression of regional identity, which, to this day, is a strong feature of the life and politics of modern Norway. In contrast, the construction of Bokmål sought to fashion a Norwegian national identity that is urban based and that sought to give expression to existing

[18] See Lars S. Vikør, 'Northern Europe: languages as prime markers of ethnic and national identity', in Stephen Barbour and Cathie Carmichael (eds), *Language and Nationalism in Europe* (Oxford: Oxford University Press, 2000), pp. 105–29.

[19] Ibid. p. 109.

[20] Ibid. p. 109. Note that the Danish letters *æ* and *ø* were rendered as *ä* and *ö* in Swedish.

continuities with Danish, so as to serve the interests of a class-based culture and elite. However, in turn, Bokmål, as can be expected, gradually acquired Norwegian peculiarities of speech, which marked it as different from Danish.

A similar situation obtained in post-independence Greece of 1832, lasting until the second half of the twentieth century and involving Katharevousa (purifying Greek) and Dhimotiki (demotic) as the two variants of Greek.[21] Each of these varieties was constructed to respond to a different repertoire of national values and express a particular vision of Greece as a national unit. In the popular imagination, Katharevousa accumulated symbolic meanings that linked it to the ancient past, Hellenism, Orthodox Christianity, the monarchy and to the zeal to purify the language from borrowed, especially Turkish, words to symbolise the eradication of centuries-long foreign domination. In contrast, Dhimotiki became associated with republicanism and democracy, with its origins firmly rooted in dialect mixing in the Peleponnese – the area that formed the early nucleus of independent Greece. However, unlike in Norway where Bokmål seems to have gained the upper hand in education and the media, Dhimotiki in Greece seems to have won the protracted struggle against Katharevousa at least since 1976, following the overthrow of the military junta in 1974. Also, unlike in Norway, the struggle between Katharevousa and Dhimotiki led to open conflict on the streets in Greece. The translation of the gospels into Dhimotiki in 1901 led to riots in Athens and the subsequent deaths of eight people. In 1903, the performance of Aeschylus' *Orestia* in Dhimotiki led to further riots and to the death of one person.[22] If this tells us anything, it is that, in some cases, people are prepared to pay with their lives for different constructions or imaginings of their linguistic-based identities, whether these are linked to religion or not.

Sadly, in some cases, people pay with their lives for 'acts of linguistic transgression', not because they knowingly or deliberately transgress, but because they unknowingly violate 'lexical border guards' that symbolically act as signs of belonging. In Lebanon, in the early stages of the civil war in the 1970s and 1980s, the Arabic pronunciation of tomato acted as a shibboleth, as a sign of belonging, which helped determine the speaker's identity as Palestinian or Lebanese. Literally, in some cases, pronouncing the word for tomato as '*bandura*' in a Palestinian inflection, rather than '*banadura*', which is the Lebanese pronunciation, was tantamount to signing one's death warrant, because the difference was read as a sign of enemy ethnic-belonging.[23] The fact that a short vowel *a* inter-syllabically in the Arabic pronunciation of

[21] See Peter Trudgill, 'Greece and European Turkey: from religious to ethnic identity', in Stephen Barbour and Cathie Carmichael (eds), *Language and Nationalism in Europe* (Oxford: Oxford University Press, 2000), pp. 240–63; Peter Mackridge, *Language and National Identity in Greece, 1766–1967* (Oxford: Oxford University Press, 2009).

[22] Trudgill, 'Greece and European Turkey', p. 250.

[23] The difference between the two pronunciations is less marked than the difference between the American and British English pronunciations of tomato.

tomato meant the difference between life and death is a damning judgement on nationalism.[24] It is a chilling example of how lethal identity-politics can be when it really gets out of hand. It also offers support to Elie Kedouri's well-known condemnation of nationalism, when he says that the 'attempt to refashion so much of the world on national lines has not led to greater peace or stability. On the contrary, it has created new conflicts, exacerbated tension, and brought catastrophe to numberless people innocent of all politics'.[25]

In Scandinavia and Greece, we have seen examples of how national or ethnic identities are used to construct or imagine language as a category of self-definition, and how language, in turn, is used to underpin, symbolise and promote these identities. This ideological constructedness of language along ethnic/national lines is found elsewhere – for example, in the Balkans. Linguistically, the Serbian, Montenegrin, Croatian and Bosnian varieties are similar enough to be classified as varieties of the same language, as reflected by their membership in Serbo-Croatian until the dissolution of Yugoslavia in 1991. In fact, at the point of dissolution, the Serbian, Montenegrin, Croatian and Bosnian varieties were drawing closer and closer to each other, with lexical variation between them ranging between 3 per cent and 7 per cent.[26]

However, the dissolution of Yugoslavia marked a turning point in this process, particularly as far as Croatian and Serbian were concerned, both of which began to be promoted as distinct languages along nationalist lines. The fact that Croatian was written in Roman and Serbian in Cyrillic script no doubt contributed to this process, but the main impetus for the new direction was national in character, and it lost no time in expressing itself in

24 Reactions of this kind apply in the scriptal world, too. Commenting on the Arabic and Devanagari scripts for Urdu and Hindi respectively against the background of inter-communal violence in pre-independence India, King writes: 'Communal hatreds between Muslims and Hindus cannot be simply wished away by pretending that scripts used to write their languages are devoid of evoked meaning. The power of language as icon must never be underestimated. Like it or not, the Urdu script *means* Muslim, and the Devanagari script *means* Hindu. The Urdu script as seen by an angry, inflamed Hindu mob summons up talismanic images from the present and the past: cow-slaughter, temple-bashing, iconoclasm, crescent and star Aurangzeb, green [the Muslim colour]. When Hindus bent on doing violence to Muslims see a shop sign in Urdu, they want to smash it and burn that shop down and vice-versa. The Hindi script conveys to an enraged Muslim mob Vishnu and Shiya and a score of many-handed, many-headed gods and goddesses, cowdung, music before the mosque, dead pigs flung into mosques, Shivaji [a Maratha leader hated by Muslims]. Old sins cast long shadows' [emphasis in the original]. See Robert D. King, *Nehru and the Language Politics of India* (Delhi: Oxford University Press, 1998), p. 84.

25 Elie Kedourie, *Nationalism* (London: Hutchinson University Library, 1966), p. 138.

26 Cathie Carmichael, 'A people exists and that people has its language': language and nationalism in the Balkans', in Stephen Barbour and Cathie Carmichael (eds), *Language and Nationalism in Europe* (Oxford: Oxford University Press, 2000), p. 236.

the political sphere. Thus, it is reported that in the negotiations between the Serbs and the Croatians over Bosnia-Herzegovina in the 1990s, a member of the Croatian team demanded that translation services be provided, which led to huge laughter and consternation in the room, with one member on the Serbian side leaving the negotiations in disgust, never to be seen again. Similar expressions of Croatian identity were found in Yugoslavia before 1991, but these were kept in check through a number of coercive measures. Thus, in 1971, the Croatian [language] Society called for the use of Croatian in commands in the Yugoslav Navy on the grounds that 80 per cent of the navy operated in Croatian waters; the excuse or trigger for this being the use of Serbian as the language of commands in the army.[27] The Croatian demand was totally ignored by the Serbians, who had the upper hand in Yugoslavia.[28]

The Balkans, in the twentieth century, provide data on the coming together of mutually intelligible varieties to form a distinct language and, later, on the parting of the ways between these same varieties, to form distinct languages – a phenomenon replicated in the relationship between Czech and Slovak in the modern period.[29] Issues of ethnic/national identity lie at the heart of these two opposite processes of construction. We may talk here about ideological *fusion* and *fission* in the nation-based linguistic construction of identity in the former Yugoslavia.

Moving the discussion forward, we can further point out that whether a language is constructed as a marker of national identity or not will, to a great extent, depend on the particular strategies of nation-building adopted by the nationalist elite. These strategies are historically contingent, and they depend on the objective features of a given situation and their potency. In Taiwan, Mandarin was promoted as the national language after the collapse of the nationalist leadership in mainland China and the reconsolidation of its government in Tawian in 1949. This policy was motivated by two objectives: fostering linguistic unity and ethnic harmony in Taiwan and maintaining the claim that the nationalists were the legitimate representatives of the whole of China.[30]

In Spain, Basque has traditionally been a weak marker of Basque ethnic/national identity, although this situation started to change towards the end

[27] Ibid. p. 237.

[28] See Greenberg (2004) for the disintegration of Serbo-Croatian after the dissolution of Yugoslavia in 1991.

[29] See Flourian Coulmas, 'Language policy and language planning: political perspectives', *Annual Review of Applied Linguistics* (1994), 14: 34–52; Barbara Törnquist-Plewa, 'Contrasting ethnic nationalisms: Eastern Central Europe', in Stephen Barbour and Cathie Carmichael (eds), *Language and Nationalism in Europe* (Oxford: Oxford University Press, 2000), pp. 183–220.

[30] See A-chin Hsiau, 'Language ideology in Taiwan: the KMT's language policy, the Tai-yü language movement, and ethnic politics', *Journal of Multilingual and Multicultural Development* (1997), 18: 302–15.

of the nineteenth century.[31] When the stirrings of nationalism reached the Basque region in the nineteenth and early twentieth century, the language was mainly spoken in the countryside in a large number of dialects and sub-dialects, some of which were highly differentiated to the point of being mutually unintelligible. In addition, the urban population and middle-class intellectuals had a poor command of the language, and the spoken Basque dialects in the country lacked a rich corpus of literary material to act as the norm or standard in writing. Race, not language, was therefore elected as the primary factor in the definition of the Basque national self,[32] although language started to assume more importance in later iterations of Basque national identity.

Italy provides another interesting example of the place of language in national self-definition. Ruzza argues that language is a 'relatively weak indicator of national identity [in Italy], despite the substantial coincidence of linguistic, national and state boundaries'.[33] To signal this, Ruzza describes Italian as a 'marker' of national identity, rather than a 'source' of it.[34] Strong regional identities, coupled with the existence of mutually unintelligible languages (German, Catalan, Franco-Provencal and Friulian / Romansh) and dialect groups, and the diglossic distance between written and spoken Italian have all conspired to turn standard Italian into a weak marker of the Italian national identity, except perhaps during the fascist period when a new emphasis on language emerged.

Dutch provides further insight into the construction of language and national identity, or, as I pointed out earlier, how imagined communities imagine their languages. In the Netherlands – one of the early nation-states in Europe – Dutch is a marker of national identity, but it is by no means the most important marker. In Belgium, the situation is very different: Dutch is the most important component or 'source', to use Ruzza's terminology, of Flemish national identity. Here we have an example of the same language

31 See Jacqueline Urla, 'Ethnic protests and social planning: a look at Basque language revival', *Cultural Anthropology* (1988), 1: 379–94; Jacqueline Urla, 'Contesting modernities: language standardization and the production of an ancient / modern Basque culture', *Critique of Anthropology* (1993), 13: 101–18.

32 See Clare Mar-Molinero, 'The Iberian Peninsula: conflicting linguistic nationalisms', in Stephen Barbour and Cathie Carmichael (eds), *Language and Nationalism in Europe* (Oxford: Oxford University Press, 2000), pp. 83–104; Cameron Watson, 'Folklore and Basque nationalism: language, myth, reality', *Nations and Nationalism* (1996), 2: 17–34.

33 Carlo Ruzza, 'Language and nationalism in Italy: language as a weak marker of identity', in Stephen Barbour and Cathie Carmichael (eds), *Language and Nationalism in Europe* (Oxford: Oxford University Press, 2000), p. 168.

34 Ibid. p. 172. This is an interesting distinction, because it points to different ways in which language participates in the construction of national identities, hence the use of the terms marker, ingredient, component and constituent to designate this phenomenon, although the difference between the last three is ill-defined.

being constructed, imagined or conceptualised in two different ways in nationalist terms, owing to different historical factors, and this in spite of the fact that the areas where the language is spoken are compact and contiguous. In Belgium, the status of Flemish/Dutch as an instrument of national self-definition has always been constructed in relation to a significant Other – the French language and its Walloon speakers.[35] For most of the nineteenth and twentieth century, Flemish/Dutch had to fight for equality with the French language in education and the public sphere. This struggle for equality has turned the language into a potent symbol of Flemish national identity. However, internally, Flemish national identity manifested itself in two conceptions of the language. The first, Flemish-oriented, stressed the differences between the Dutch spoken in Flanders and that spoken in the Netherlands and sought to establish the former as the norm. Proponents of this position espoused a view of Flanders as part of Belgium, but with strong ties to the Netherlands. The second, a Dutch-oriented movement, considered the standard Dutch of the Netherlands as the norm and espoused as its political objective a union with the Netherlands.[36]

As in Scandinavia and Greece, issues of language and national identity in the Netherlands and Belgium show the nuanced nature of construction or imagination. On one level, Dutch has different symbolic meanings in the Netherlands and Belgium. In the latter, it is highly ideologised as a component of national self-definition. This ideologisation derives its meaning from the opposition of Dutch to French. *Alterity* is a prime force of definition here, with French and the Walloons being the significant Others. On another level, Dutch is ideologically differentiated in Flanders between the Flemish-oriented and the Dutch-oriented movements. I am sure that other differentiations do exist in Flanders, but the point I wish to emphasise here is that of the complex and contextual nature of construction of the language-identity link. One may be tempted to describe this situation in terms of layers of self-definition or by reference to archaeology of construction in line with Maalouf's use of the term 'hierarchy', as mentioned above. As I stated at the beginning of this chapter, I prefer to talk about poly-centricity instead for three reasons: (1) the arbitrary ordering of the strata of definition in the archaeological model; (2) this arbitrariness is bound to be compounded when we factor in categories of individual and collective self-definition – for example, those pertaining to gender, class, religion or lifestyle; and (3) an archaeological model would be ill-suited to account for the intersecting and context-dependent repertoire of identities, be they individual or collective in nature.

[35] See Robert B. Howell, 'The low countries: a study in sharply contrasting nationalisms', in Stephen Barbour and Cathie Carmichael (eds), *Language and Nationalism in Europe* (Oxford: Oxford University Press, 2000), pp. 130–50.

[36] See Jan Blommaert, 'Language and nationalism: comparing Flanders with Tanzania', *Nations and Nationalism* (1996), 2: 235–56.

Swahili provides an interesting case of how vernaculars develop into national languages in emerging (postcolonial) nation-states. In the territories comprising present day Kenya, Swahili, historically, served as *lingua franca* in trade and culture among linguistically and ethnically diverse populations.[37] Its status as the pre-eminent language of East Africa derived from its association with Islamic civilisation and literacy before colonialism and, in the colonial period, from being used in missionary activity to spread the Christian gospel. The colonial administration also used Swahili to communicate with the local population: for pragmatic reasons, it was better to use one language, rather than a multiplicity of languages, when administering the affairs of the country. These new functions of the language added to its already considerable prestige as the medium through which pan-ethnic culture was encoded. In the struggle for independence, Swahili was used as the medium for communicating the nationalist message, encoded in memorable slogans, in a way that enhanced its role as an instrument of solidarity across ethnic boundaries. Added to this, the elite considered Swahili to be an unmarked African language that was not linked to any of the dominant tribal ethnicities.[38] Although this view was contested by those who wished to promote their languages in the national arena, Swahili was supremely qualified, owing to the coalescence of the above mentioned factors, to serve as the national language in post-independence Kenya. In a similar vein, although English plays an important role in Kenya in the fields of education, business, the media and the political sphere, it has not been able to dislodge Swahili from its position as the national language par excellence. And since independence (1963), Swahili has developed a national inflection that brands it as a marker of a specifically Kenyan identity that is different from the Swahili-bound identity of neighbouring Tanzania, where the language also serves as a marker of nationhood. As in Scandinavia, small differences in language assume a great role in identity differentiation across state boundaries.

In Tanzania, Swahili was pressed into the service of the nation as a pan-ethnic language to overcome tribal divisions with even greater vigour than in Kenya under the leadership of the first President, Julius Nyerere.[39] Swahili had pedigree as the language of culture and learning – a fact that

[37] See Chege Githiora, 'Kenya: language and the search for a coherent national identity', in Andrew Simpson (ed.), *Language and National Identity in Africa* (Oxford: Oxford University Press, 2008), pp. 235–51.

[38] See Ali A. Mazrui and Alamin M. Mazrui (*The Power of Babel: Language and Governance in the African Experience* (Oxford: James Currey, 1998)) for the status of Kiswahili as an African language, against the charge of hybridity levelled at it as an African–Arab language.

[39] Nyerere was not a native speaker of Swahili, but he had an excellent command of the language, which he used in his poetry and political speeches. See Farouk Topan, 'Tanzania: the development of Swahili as a national and official language', in Andrew Simpson (ed.), *Language and National Identity in Africa* (Oxford: Oxford University Press, 2008), pp. 252–66.

made it amenable for use as an anti-colonial language that could carry the voice of the independence movement to the ethnically diverse members of the putative nation. After independence (1961), the Tanzanian leadership adopted a socialist programme of national development, whose messages had to be communicated to the mostly agrarian people of Tanzania. As an ethnically neutral language, Swahili was the natural choice for this nation-building task. The position of Swahili as a national language was further enhanced through its use in education and the media, with concomitant status-planning measures, such as the production of dictionaries, word lists of new terminologies and school textbooks building, in this respect, on the earlier work of German missionaries[40] and the British colonial administration, who, for pragmatic reasons, used the language in their work. Although English has a strong presence in Tanzania, it has not posed a challenge to the symbolic and instrumental role of Swahili as the pre-eminent national language.

Names as signs of national and ethnic identity are important in labelling languages or varieties. Naming a variety or language gives it recognition and legitimacy and helps make it a site of identity formation in the ideological sphere, mainly through the exercise of alterity. In Flanders, it matters whether the language is called Dutch, Flemish or Flemish Dutch. Jan Blommaert comments on this aspect of language ideology as follows: 'Naming the language(s) in Flanders is, in general, a very sensitive issue, and every option one may choose, however well-motivated sociolinguistically or anthropologically, quickly becomes the object of controversy'.[41] Following the demographic upheaval of the division of the Indian subcontinent in 1947, the Hindus of the Punjab called their language variety Hindi, not Punjabi, to differentiate themselves from the Sikhs, who spoke Punjabi.[42] However, the attempt to gain recognition and legitimacy in the public domain tends to be undermined when a variety receives a multiplicity of names or goes by many aliases. An example of this is African American English (AAE), which has been referred to by a variety of names (for example, 'Black Talk', 'Black

[40] It is interesting to note here that Christian missionaries in both Kenya and Tanzania considered the cultural affinity of Swahili to Arabic as a 'liability', because of the religious connotations of some of the vocabulary that the former borrowed from the latter. See Githiora, 'Kenya: language and the search for a coherent national identity'; Topan, 'Tanzania: the development of Swahili as a national and official language'.

[41] Jan Blommaert adds: 'My own choice to identify the language of Flanders as "Flemish Dutch" would be seen by some to imply that Flemish is seen as a dialect (substandard, inferior) variety of Dutch. They would suggest . . . "Flemish / Dutch", a term stressing the identity and equivalence of Flemish to Dutch' (See 'Language and nationalism', p. 254).

[42] See R. B. Le Page and A. Tabouret-Keller, 'Models and stereotypes of ethnicity and language', *Journal of Multilingual and Multicultural Development* (1982), 3: 161–92.

English Vernacular', 'Ebonics' and 'African American Vernacular English'). Wassink and Curzan argue that the use of multiple names for this variety has compromised its legitimacy as a marker of identity and has given 'potential ammunition for those who choose to disregard or denigrate AAE'.[43] It is suggested that one step towards stopping this lack of recognition would be the adoption of one name / label to designate this variety.

Not just languages, but names of countries can also be a site of construction and national identity contestation. In 1990, a debate took place in Czechoslovakia concerning the new name of the country. Known as the 'great hyphen debate', the Slovaks insisted on inserting a hyphen in the name of the newly reformed country, *Czecho-Slovakia,* in order to give visibility to their national identity, which will be marked by an uppercase, rather than a lowercase, 'S' in the proposed name. The proposal was rejected in the legislature in favour of a new name with two versions: Czechoslovak Federative Republic in Bohemia and Moravia (the Czech-speaking part) and Czecho-Slovak Federative Republic in Slovakia.[44] The hyphen disappeared when the two parts of pre-1990 Czechoslovakia went their separate ways politically in January 1993.

Greece provides another revealing example of the interest in names as signs of national identity. Coulmas reports how the Greek Government was able to persuade other European Community members that the 'former Yugoslav republic of Macedonia would be granted EC recognition only on condition that it used another name'.[45] Coulmas explains the reason behind this move as follows:

> Any association of [the republic of Macedonia] with the Macedonians of northern Greece, whose language enjoys no official status, had to be avoided. Greece considers the name 'Macedonian' to be part of its heritage and fears it would imply territorial claims by the new state on the northern Greek province of Macedonia.[46]

43 Alicia Beckford Wassink and Anne Curzan, 'Addressing ideologies around African American English'. *Journal of English Linguistics* (2004), 32: 177.

44 See Coulmas, 'Language policy and language planning: political perspectives'.

45 Ibid. p. 39.

46 Ibid. p. 39. In this context, ethnic labels are particularly interesting because of their ability to stereotype, inferiorise and exclude, as I have shown for Jordan through the use of the term *Beljīk* (Belgians) to refer to Jordanians of Palestinian origin (Suleiman, *A War of Words: Language and Conflict in the Middle East*, pp. 116–9), linking this to the linguistic construction of sub-state identity. In Lebanon, during the civil war (1975–90), the term *ghurabā'* (lit. strangers) was used to brand non-Lebanese Arabs, mainly Palestinian refugees and Syrian workers, as the 'Other', in spite of the fact that this 'Other' had thick ties of religion, language and culture with the Lebanese. See Marlyne Nasr, *al-Ghurabā' fī khiṭāb al-lubnāniyyīn 'an al-ḥarb al-ahliyya* (Beirut: Dār Al-Sāqī, 1996). In some cases, a group may not accept the name used to designate it. For example, in recent years, the Greek Orthodox

In the above discussion, I dealt with a range of issues that are at the heart of the linguistic construction of national identity. These include the historically contingent nature of the construction of national identity or what I have called the language-identity link; the role of the elites in formulating this identity; how alterity is invoked as an instrument of national self-definition; how language standardisation is exploited as a site of conflict between different models of national identity in the same polity (urban-based versus countryside-based, as in Greece and Norway, or civic versus cultural conceptions of the nation, as in Flanders); how languages are constructed to express different visions of national identity in a given country; how names of languages, countries and ethnicities feed into the construction of the language-identity link; how fission and fusion operate in constructing language-based national identities; and how language-based identity-politics can be enmeshed in strife in, and between, nations.

These are not the only themes in investigating the links between language and national identity within the constructivist model.[47] Others include how identity is marked in discourse,[48] dictionary-making,[49] linguistic landscapes,[50] language policy and language planning,[51] bilingual education

community in Palestine and Jordan has objected to the term 'Greek' in its name, arguing for it to be replaced by 'Arab' (See Wajīh al-Faraḥ, 'Khaṭa' dārij yajib taṣḥīḥuh: li-mādhā kalimat al-rūm wa-naḥnu 'arab urdhudux?', *Al-Nashra* (2004), 32: 30–2 (The Royal Institute of Religious Studies, Jordan)). The voices calling for this change have become more and more vociferous over the past few years as a result of the sale or lease of Church land by the Greek leadership of the Church to the Israeli authorities in the Palestinian occupied territories and Israel.

47 See John Edwards, *Language and Identity* (Cambridge: Cambridge University Press, 2009).

48 See Ruth Wodak et al., *The Discursive Construction of National Identity*, trans. Richard Mitten (Edinburgh: Edinburgh University Press, 1999); Paul Chilton, *Analysing Political Discourse: Theory and Practice* (London and New York, NY: Routledge, 2004).

49 See Phil Benson, *Ethnocentricism and the English Dictionary* (London and New York, NY: Routledge, 2001).

50 See E. Ben-Rafael et al., *Linguistic Landscape and Multiculturalism: A Jewish-Arab Comparative Study* (Tel Aviv University: The Tami Steinmetz Centre for Peace Research, 2004); R. Landry and R. Y. Bourhis, 'Linguistic landscape and ethnolinguistic vitality: an empirical study', *Journal of Language and Social Psychology* (1997), 16: 23–49; Tim Jon Semmerling, *Israeli and Palestinian Postcards: Presentations of National Self* (Austin, TX: University of Texas Press, 2004); Elena Shohamy and Durk Gorter, *Linguistic Landscape: Expanding the Scenery* (New York and London: Routledge, 2009); Yasir Suleiman, *A War of Words: Language and Conflict in the Middle East* (Cambridge: Cambridge University Press, 2004).

51 See Robert L. Cooper, *Language Planning and Social Change* (Cambridge: Cambridge University Press, [1989] 1996); Elena Shohamy and Elena Goldberg, *The Hidden Agendas of Language Policy: An Expanded View* (New York, NY: Routledge, 2006).

and minority rights,[52] language and postcoloniality,[53] language and anxiety,[54] gender politics and code-switching.[55]

The above discussion reveals the variety of ways in which the language-identity link is constructed, which we will summarise under three headings: *distanciation*, *differentiation* and *identification*. In some cases – for example, Flanders, the Netherlands, Kenya and Tanzania – the same language may be constructed to designate different identities across nation-state lines. This is a case of distanciation. In other cases, the same language is conceptualised in different ways to signal different inflections of identity within the boundaries of the same nation-state. This is a case of differentiation. This is true of Norwegian and Greek where different national imaginaries are assigned to different forms of the language. Old Yugoslavia provides another example of how different forms of the same language can be constructed as sub-state inflections, this being a process of identification, but are later treated as different languages following the dismantling of the state, presenting a case of distanciation between nation-states (between Bosnia and Herzegovina and Serbia) or a case of differentiation between Bosniacs, Croats and Serbs inside Bosnia and Herzegovina. All of these examples and processes signal the power of construction in conceptualising languages and how each construction is tied to its specific historical and political context. Italy and the Basque Country do not give the same prominence to language as the above examples do, in terms of indexing national identity. This is, again, a matter of construction. Each nation has a repertoire of symbols that it can use to index itself in identity terms. Language is one of those symbols, but this symbol – strong in some cases – may be downgraded when it proves to be a weak index. The choice of names to designate languages is but an outward expression of this process of language construction, in addition to being a reflection of the politics surrounding this construction. Anxiety and conflict are inherent in each act of construction above, signalling the potent force of language as a cultural symbol. And at no point is instrumentality an issue of concern – a fact that points to the logical separation in categorial terms between instrumentality and symbolism, which justifies devoting most of this monograph to the latter.

52 See Stephen May, *Language and Minority Rights: Ethnicity, Nationalism and the Politics of Language* (Harlow: Longman, 2001).

53 See Dennis Ager, *'Francophonie' in the 1990s: Problems and Opportunities* (Cleveland, OH: Multilingual Matters, 1996).

54 See Tim William Machan, *Language Anxiety: Conflict and Change in the History of English* (Oxford: Oxford University Press, 2009).

55 Monica Heller, 'Code-switching and the politics of language', in Lesley Milroy and Pieter Muysken (eds), *One Speaker, Two Languages: Cross-disciplinary Perspectives on Code-Switching* (Cambridge: Cambridge University Press, 1995), pp. 158–74; Suleiman, *A War of Words: Language and Conflict in the Middle East*; Yasir Suleiman, *Arabic, Self and Identity: A Study in Conflict and Displacement* (New York and Oxford: Oxford University Press, 2011a).

Arabic and the Construction of the Language-Identity Link

The three discursive strategies of identification, distanciation and differentiation were at play in constructing the language-identity link in the Arabic-speaking world in the nineteenth and twentieth centuries. In Israel, a different strategy of erasure applied to Arabic-speaking Jews, as I explain below. Identification applied in different degrees in the nineteenth and twentieth centuries in arguing against the Ottoman policy of Turkification that Arabic is the primary marker of national identity and that this marker cuts across faith-based ties of ethnicity. This identification strategy was particularly relevant in the Levant, especially Lebanon, where faith-based ethnic identities dominated. Its relevance in this context further resided in the attempt to alter the identity gaze of Muslim Arabs away from identification with the Turkish Ottomans – their co-religionists – who started to develop a Turkish-inflected Ottoman identity, which gave scant regard to the Arab members of the Empire. Pan-Arab nationalism in the post-Ottoman world built on this identification strategy, but, under Sati' al-Husri and Zaki al-Arsuzi, explicitly expanded the reach of the pan-Arab nationalist idea to include all speakers of the language, not just those in the Arab heartland of the Middle East. Al-Husri expressed this view in different renditions at different times over the course of his career; the following is one of these renditions:

> Every individual who belongs to the Arab countries and speaks Arabic is an Arab. He is so, regardless of the name of the country whose citizenship he officially holds. He is so, regardless of the religion he professes or the sect he belongs to. He is so, regardless of his ancestry, lineage or the roots of the family to which he belongs. He is an Arab, and that's that . . . Arabness is not restricted to those who can trace their origin back to the Arabian Peninsula; nor is it restricted to Muslims alone. It encompasses every individual who belongs to the Arab countries: whether he is Egyptian, Kuwaiti or Moroccan; whether he is Christian or Muslim; whether he is Sunni, Twelver Shi'i or Druze; and whether he is Catholic, Orthodox or Protestant. [Regardless of what he is,] he is a son of the Arab nation as long as he belongs to the Arab lands and speaks Arabic.[56]

Unlike identification, distanciation applies in differing degrees. The Lebanese linguist and jurist Abdullah al-'Alayli[57] considered Arabic as a marker of identity among all those who share it, but he did not raise it to the status of a sufficient condition of nation-building. Other factors, such as common interests, history, customs and traditions are also important in common identification within the nation. These factors can apply at both the macro-level of all Arabic speakers, as well as the micro-level of smaller units of

[56] Ṣāṭi' al-Ḥuṣrī, *al-'Urūba awwalan* (Beirut: Markiz Dirāsāt al-Waḥda al-'Arabiyya, 1985), pp. 14–15.

[57] 'Abdullah al-'Alāylī, *Dustūr al-'arab al-qawmī* (Beirut: Dār al-Jadīd, [1938] 1996).

identification – the nation-states – provided that the latter are treated as a step towards achieving the former. In holding this intermediate position between the macro- and micro-levels of identification, al-'Alayli steers a middle course between his pan-Arab nationalist leanings and the political reality of Lebanon, wherein different ethnic trends of nationalist identification existed. In other words, al-'Alayli was prepared to recognise the nation-state as a unit of national identification, only insofar as it is regarded as a transitory step towards pan-Arab nationalism as a political ideal. Al-'Alayli considers this ideal to be important in contesting what he calls geological-archaeological nationalisms in the Arabic-speaking world, such as Phoenicianism in Lebanon, Pharaonism in Egypt and Assyrianism in Iraq as fossils of a very distant past.

A greater degree of distanciation applies when *fuṣḥā* (Standard Arabic) is treated as a marker of the nation-state as a political entity, but without severing the cultural ties that the language engenders with other nation-states, in which Arabic is used as a nationalist emblem. This is the view of Arabic taken by some Lebanese nationalists – for example, 'Abdallah Lahhud[58] and Kamal al-Hajj,[59] who refused to surrender the Lebanese nation-state to the pan-Arabist political ideal, while at the same time refusing to endorse the narrow interpretation of Lebanese nationalism that seeks to de-establish any links with other Arabic-speaking countries in the nationalist realm. A similar position obtained in Egypt. Taha Hussayn[60] believed that Arabic was Egypt's national language and that it created cultural ties between this country and other Arabic-speaking countries, but he did not treat the language as constituting a legitimate bond of nationalist identity between Egypt and these countries. An earlier expression of this view was advocated by Ahmad Lutfi al-Sayyid (1872–1963), who called Arabic the Egyptian language (*al-lugha al-miṣriyya*).[61] As Egyptian nationalists, these two important figures believed in the integrity of Egypt as a nationalist unit, which they were unwilling to secede to the rising tide of the pan-nationalist ideal in the first half of the twentieth century. But they were also determined to fight the extreme Egyptian nationalists, who wanted to dislodge *fuṣḥā* Arabic from its status as the language of culture and religious expression in

[58] See 'Abdallah Laḥḥūd, *Lubnān: 'arabiyy al-wajh, 'arabiyy al-lisān* (Beirut: Dār al-'Ilm li-l-Malāyīn, 1993).

[59] Kamāl Yūsuf al-Ḥājj, *Difā'an 'an al-'arabiyya* (Beirut: Manshūrāt 'Uwaydāt, 1959a); Kamāl Yūsuf al-Ḥājj, *Fī al-qawmiyya wa-l-insāniyya* (Beirut: Manshūrāt 'Uwaydāt, 1959b); Kamāl Yūsuf al-Ḥājj, *al-Qawmiyya laysat marḥala* (Beirut: Manshūrāt 'Uwaydāt, 1959c); Kamāl Yūsuf al-Ḥājj, *Fī ghurrat al-ḥaqīqa* (Beirut: Manshūrāt 'Uwaydāt, 1966); Kamāl Yūsuf al-Ḥājj, *Fī falsafat al-lugha* (Beirut: Dār al-Nahār, [1956] 1978).

[60] Taha Ḥusayn, *Mustaqbal al-thaqāfa fi miṣr* (Cairo: Maṭba'at al-Ma'ārif, [1938] 1944).

[61] See Aḥmad Luṭfī al-Sayyid, *al-Muntakhabāt* (Cairo: Maṭba'at al-Anglū al-Miṣriyya, 1945), volume 1, p. 247.

Egypt, as well as weaken the linguistic basis of cross-state identification in the Arabic-speaking world. An example of this extreme expression of state nationalism is offered by Tawfiq 'Awwan in 1929 in the weekly newspaper *al-Siyāsa al-usbū'iyya,* in which he argued for complete differentiation among Arabic-speaking countries on the basis of the differences between their colloquials:

> Egypt has an Egyptian language; Lebanon has a Lebanese language; the Hijaz has an Hijazi language; and so forth – and all of these languages are by no means Arabic languages. Each of our countries has a language which is its own possession: so why do we not write as converse in it? For the language in which the people speak is the language in which they also write.[62]

Differentiation applies in two ways. First, it aims to shift the basis for national identification from *fuṣḥā* to the colloquials of each nation-state. This shift, as the above quotation shows, provides a greater rupture in the role of the language in creating cross-state ties of national identity. It is further reflected in the names suggested for the newly constructed languages. Differentiation, in this case, downgrades the role of the existing standard language as a medium of national identification. In addition, differentiation may be based on a view of the language which treats it as secondary to the environment as the organising principle for national identification: language as a mode of identification, in this case, is the result of people coming together in the first place, rather than as the reason for their coming together to form a unit of identification. Under this argument, language is acknowledged as a social fact, but is denied a defining role in national definition. This is the position advocated by Antun Sa'ada (1904–49) – leader of the socialist Syrian Nationalist Party – who opposed pan-Arab nationalism and narrow Lebanese nationalism in equal measure (1994). Sa'ada advocated a form of nationalism based on geography / environment, which first included all the countries of the Levant, but was later expanded to include Iraq and a slice of Cyprus where Greek is the dominant language. The inclusion of the latter is significant in the present context, because it signals in no uncertain terms that language cannot serve as a principle of national identification. It is neither a necessary nor a sufficient condition in symbolic terms in constructing the nation, although it plays a strong and instrumental part in fostering links between members of the nation.

Let us now consider *erasure* as a strategy of nation-building in the Middle East. Arabic among Mizrahi Jews (Jews of Arab culture) provides an excellent illustration of this process in ethnic terms. The Zionist movement in Palestine promoted Hebrew as the language of all Jews in the country before and after

[62] See Israel Gershoni and James Jankowski, *Egypt, Islam and the Arabs: The Search for Egyptian Nationalism 1900–1930* (New York and Oxford: Oxford University Press, 1986), p. 220.

the establishment of Israel in 1948. Although the official norm of this language followed the Mizrahi, Arabic-oriented form, the de facto status norm was, and still is, Ashkenazi inflected in prestige terms. This fact created its own dynamic in society. For early Mizrahi immigrants from Arabic-speaking lands, their Hebrew speech, if it existed, was stigmatised in two important ways: first, as the language of a less developed segment of the Jewish diaspora and, second, as that which most resembled the speech of the Arabs as the archetypal enemy of the state of Israel into which the early immigrants had to integrate. To make the transition and gain full Israeli identity, Mizrahi Jews tried to modify their speech by adopting the Ashkenazi form of the language, erasing, in the process, their own idiosyncratic speech habits. This erasure is not an erasure of Arabic, but of what was perceived as the Arabic flavour of Mizrahi Hebrew speech.

A second kind of erasure was also expected of Mizrahi immigrants to the newly established country: the loss of Arabic as the language of a stigmatised Jewish diaspora as the language of the enemy outside Israel and as the symbolic marker of the Palestinians in Israel, who were constructed as a potential fifth column and considered members of the lowest socio-economic stratum of Israeli society. Therefore, Mizrahi Jews had many incentives to erase Arabic as part of their repertoire in symbolic and instrumental terms, both horizontally, in conversing with each other in public, and vertically, in passing it from one generation to the next.[63] In this case, the acquisition of a new Israeli identity for Mizrahi Jews in the newly established state involved the double process of identification with the Ashkenazi form of Hebrew and maximising differentiation with Arabic by, in fact, actively trying to lose it as an ethnic language. The latter process, in particular, was in direct response to the Ashkenazi fear, expressed by Ben Gurion (Israel's first Prime Minster), that the 'primitive Arab mentality' of the Mizrahi Jews would, in the words of Abba Eban (his Education Minister), 'drag Israel into "unnatural Orientalism"'.[64] In this connection, Seliktar mentions the use of what she calls '*approbrium controls* (a societal mechanism of disapproval, ridicule or ostracism) . . . against any display of Arab background by the [Mizrahi] immigrants and especially of their offspring'.[65] In the Zionist ideology, this background was associated with 'laziness, lack of motivation and drive, and excessive individualism'[66], which the new state wanted to dissociate itself from. In a memoir of his life in Israel, Somekh reflects on how this Zionist ideology affected the early Iraqi immigrants to Israel:

[63] Rachel Shabi, *Not the Enemy: Israel's Jews from Arab Lands* (New Haven and London: Yale University Press, 2009).

[64] Ofira Seliktar, 'Ethnic stratification and foreign policy in Israel: the attitudes of Oriental Jews towards the Arabs and the Arab-Israeli conflict', *The Middle East Journal* (1984), 38: 42.

[65] Ibid. p. 43.

[66] Ibid. p. 43.

> The Jews of Iraq did not arrive [in Israel] knowing Hebrew, certainly not the kind of Hebrew that had developed in Israel. Those who studied in Jewish schools [in Iraq], in particular in religious schools, learned a Hebrew that was 'Iraqi' in pronunciation and pre-modern in its linguistics. The meanings of words were not always identical to those existing in Israel, not to mention the different [Ashkenazi] accent. While the pronunciation of the vowels was not significantly different . . . the consonants were quite different. First of all, the Iraqi Jews pronounced the guttural consonants such as Het, Tet, 'Ayin, and Qof; in the 'native' Israeli (or 'Sabra') accent, the guttural 'Ayin was swallowed up in a soft Aleph, which was sometimes indistinguishable from the consonant Heh, making it all the more difficult for Iraqis to understand the Hebrew spoken by a 'Sabra' . . . For the Iraqi newcomers these were not only differences in pronunciation, but veritable distortions which impeded their understanding of important words in the contemporary language. Words which should have been easy for speakers of one Semitic language to understand in another Semitic language were incomprehensible for them [Iraqi Jews as speakers of Arabic] . . . Ultimately, not only was the Hebrew some of the Iraqi immigrants brought with them to Israel not useful for communication; it turned out to be a burden. Thus the outcry against the abandonment of the guttural in standard Israeli Hebrew was not merely a linguistic-'ideological' dispute, trying to preserve one kind of speech over another along the East-West pronunciation (and demographic) divide (Mizrahi-Ashkenazi). Above all, the complaint was against the impediments it caused to the comprehension of 'native' Israeli Hebrew by those with a Middle Eastern accent (*not to mention the fact that the Middle Eastern accent was oftentimes a subject of mockery and parody for veteran Israelis because it was reminiscent of Arabic*).[67]

Constructing Scripts, Constructing Identities

Scripts and script styles in the form of typefaces or fonts are linked with group identity. This link comes to the fore at times of change and conflict in society, in which the past is contested, as we shall see below. Scripts share the two functions of spoken language: instrumentality and symbolism. A script is an imperfect instrument for recording spoken language, but it is also conceived as a marker of the identity of a group, signalling script indexicality in symbolic terms. The link with identity is mainly performed through this symbolic function of script in a manner that justifies talking about a script-identity link that parallels the language-identity link.[68] The constructivist nature of this link is more clearly displayed in the former than in the latter: this is evident by the fact that people may deliberately change or modify the script they use to record their language, but cannot readily do the same with

[67] Sasson Somekh, *Life after Baghdad: Memoirs of an Arab-Jew in Israel, 1950–2000* (Brighton: Sussex Academic Press, 2012), pp. 5–6. Note the added emphasis to highlight the approbium controls noted by Seliktar above.

[68] There are limits to this parallelism, but this will not detain us here.

their spoken language, save in exceptional circumstances, such as the practice of erasure in Israel. In this section, I will examine the script-identity link by dealing with a variety of examples, in order to explain some of the ways in which construction works in this domain. It will be clear from this discussion that the instrumentalist idea that script is peripheral to language and should not draw attention to itself does not get much purchase in the study of nationalism. This instrumentalism prevails in empirical/formal linguistics, but it has little resonance in the study of nationalism. As Woolard and Schieffelin state: 'orthographic systems cannot be conceptualized simply as reducing speech to writing, but rather they are symbols that carry historical, cultural and political meanings'.[69]

Construction in script choice is driven by two factors: identification and distanciation – with differentiation as a sub-type of distanciation – among groups in ways that are contextually determined.[70] Taking Turkey as an example, the change from Arabic to Roman script in 1928 was driven by these two impulses. Following the trauma of the First World War, republican Turkey, under Kemal Atatürk, set out to modernise Turkish culture and the institutions of the state in a Western and secularist inflection.[71] To do this effectively, it was argued that Turkey must cut its roots from its Ottoman past, as well as the legacy that this past carried, in terms of an Islamic identity that would continue to link the new republic to the wider Islamic, mainly Arab, world. As precursors to this new direction, culls of Arabic and Persian words from Turkish and various other language measures were applied as purifying instruments with the aim of giving Turkish its integrity as a non-hybrid language, while, at the same time, distancing it from its past, Islam-dominated history. The change from Arabic to Roman script represented the culmination of this trend in Turkish cultural and political life. It aimed, at one and the same time, to identify Turkey with Europe and distance it from the Islamic scriptal world, which the Arabic script represented.

This script was also justified on instrumental grounds, invoking the lack of fit between the phonemic composition of Turkish and the Arabic syllabary, with its limited vowel distinctions. While this was certainly true, this instrumental motivation might not have been sufficient to carry the day, had it not been for the strong symbolic factor, mentioned above, that pushed the case

[69] Woolard and Schieffelin, 'Language ideology', p. 65.

[70] See Peter Unseth, 'Sociolinguistic parallels between choosing scripts and languages', *Written Language and Literacy* (2005), 8: 19–42.

[71] See Erika H. Gilson, 'Introduction of new writing systems: the Turkish case', in Nancy Schweda-Nicholson (ed.), *Languages in the International Perspective* (Norwood, NJ: Ablex Publishing Corporation, 1986), pp. 23–40; Laurent Mignon, 'The literati and letters: a few words on the Turkish alphabet reform', *Journal of the Royal Asiatic Society* (2010), 20: 11.24; Shlomit Shraybom-Shivtiel, 'The question of the Romanisation of the script and the emergence of nationalism in the Middle East', *Mediterranean Language Review* (1998), 10: 179–96 for Turkish script reforms.

for script change to a high level on the list of national priorities. Without this factor, reforms of the Arabic script, rather than script change, might have been considered an instrumentally viable alternative, as was, in fact, argued by some language reformers in the late Ottoman and early republican periods.[72] The fact that powerful members of the elite did not consider the Arabic script as an indigenous Turkish script made the task of replacing it easier, even though this meant cutting republican Turkey from its Ottoman heritage. In fact, it was argued by extreme reformers that the script change was needed precisely because the break with the past was a prerequisite to the much-vaunted modernisation project in the new state.

This same double strategy of identification and distanciation has been at work in the script changes in the ex-Soviet, Turkish-speaking republics of Central Asia.[73] The 1928 change from Arabic to Roman script in these republics was intended to achieve two objectives: (1) distance these republics from Turkey – which, at the time, was still using the Arabic script – as well as from their Islamic heritage; and (2) encouraging cultural modernisation in aid of the first objective. In 1940, Stalin ordered a change in script in these republics to Cyrillic. Distanciation and identification were, again, the motivating factors behind this policy. Through this measure, Stalin wanted to distance these republics from Turkey, which had switched to the Roman alphabet, and, at the same time, to bring them closer to Russia in its capacity as the dominant power in the Soviet Union, politically and culturally. However, as with Romanisation, the move to Cyrillic contained an element of differentiation internally. This was achieved by developing variations in the Cyrillic script in the different republics to express different national identification. These acts of script construction were deliberate and aimed at political ends: distanciation externally from Turkey, identification with Russia and other Soviet republics internally in the Soviet sphere and internal differentiation regionally among the Turkish-speaking Central Asia republics. These symbolic acts of distanciation, differentiation and identification are some of the most important building blocks in constructing the script-identity link.

Following the dissolution of the Soviet Union in 1991 and the emergence of the newly independent republics of Central Asia, the three Turkish-speaking

[72] See Mignon, 'The literati and letters'.

[73] See Victoria Clement, 'Emblems of independence: script choice in post-Soviet Turkmenistan', *International Journal of the Sociology of Language* (2008), 192: 171–85; Ayça Ergun, 'Politics of Romanisation in Azerbaijan (1921–1992)', *Journal of the Royal Asiatic Society* (2010), 20: 23–48; Jacob M. Landau, 'Alphabet reform in the six independent ex-Soviet Muslim republics', *Journal of the Royal Asiatic Society* (2010), 20: 25–32; Lynley Hatcher, 'Script change in Azerbaijan', *International Journal of the Sociology of Language* (2008), 192: 105–16, Jacob M. Landau and Barbara Kellner-Heinkele, *Politics of Language in the ex-Soviet Muslim States* (London: Hurst, 2001); Mehmet Uzman, 'Romanisation in Uzbekistan past and present', *Journal of the Royal Asiatic Society* (2010), 20: 49–60.

countries of Azerbaijan, Turkmenistan and Uzbekistan[74] opted for a return to Roman script, although the application of this policy exhibited regional differentiation. Again, the strategies of distanciation, identification and differentiation in constructing the script-identity link were at play in the new policy. The return to Romanisation was intended as a de-Russification measure to distance these republics from Russia as the dominant power in the territories of the ex-Soviet Union. It was also intended as a measure of identification with Turkey, which tried to influence the Romanisation policy by championing the adoption of a unified Turkish alphabet for the Turkish-speaking peoples. This aspiration on the part of Turkey was thwarted by the impulses of regional differentiation among the three emerging republics in the script-identity link. It resulted in the adoption of variations in the new orthographies for each republic to express local phonemic variations as symbols of country-specific identities, as, in fact, obtained in Cyrillisation.

The return to Romanisation was further promoted as a modernisation measure, based on the assumption that countries that employ the Roman script in North America and Western Europe are more advanced than Russia, both technologically and culturally. It is interesting that this same argument was used, but in reverse, to justify the shift from the Roman to the Cyrillic script in 1940. Romanisation in the 1990s was also promoted as a return to a past heritage, represented in the use of the Roman alphabet between 1928 and 1940, rather than as a radical break with the past. This projection of cultural authenticity was, in part, intended to counter an earlier past, in which the Arabic script was used to record the languages of these countries. Romanisation may therefore be read as a return to an earlier scriptal world, albeit of short duration, which sought to distance the countries of Central Asia from their Islamic heritage under the banner of modernisation. Romanisation in these republics represents identification with a pre-Cyrillic past and a stance of double distanciation from the post- and pre-Cyrillic past of the Romanisation period between 1928 and 1940.

Thus, it is clear that distanciation, identification and differentiation are intertwined threads in the construction of the script-identity link. Although as individual concepts they are emically unitary at the abstract level, they are etically different at the empirical level, depending on the relevant contextual factors that govern their application in particular situations. It is also clear from the above that a process of mirror imaging obtains in the application of these threads or factors. The same justification, but with different content inflections, is applied differently in different situations. This picture of sameness and variation in constructing the script-identity link is in line with the description of identity I have given above as something that is both stable and changing at one and the same time. The return to the pre-Soviet past in constructing the script-identity link signals the strength of a dormant link,

74 These countries are multilingual, but Turkish is the dominant language in each country.

which, during the Soviet era, was submerged under a sea of seemingly inexorable change on a one-way ticket to unalterable Russification. But this proved to be a false analysis. This is another reason why it is sensible to adopt a constructivist view of the language-identity and script-identity link, in which stability and change are operative partners.

The strategies of distanciation and identification in the script-identity link apply with even more force in digraphic situations. Digraphia, coined by analogy with diglossia, describes the use of two different scripts to write what is, in instrumental terms, the same language. The use of the Roman and Cyrillic scripts to record what used to be called Serbo-Croatian is an example of digraphia,[75] as is the use of the Arabic and Devanagari scripts to write Urdu and Hindi, respectively.[76] In the former Yugoslavia, language politics between the Serbs and Croats was enacted in many arenas, but no more so than through script differentiation to mark the distance – in ethnic and national terms – between the two communities. The scripts acted as boundary setters in the linguistic domain between the two communities, even when this boundary was, to a great extent, absent from the domain of spoken language. Following the break-up of Yugoslavia in the 1990s, the Cyrillic and Roman scripts assumed greater importance as signs of newly configured national identities, not just in Serbia and Croatia, but also in Bosnia-Herzegovina, where Bosniacs, Croats and Serbs share one state.

Hindi-Urdu digraphia is an iconic location of difference. It is overloaded with symbolic meanings that mark the script-identity link with a strong dose of distanciation. Commenting on digraphia, King tells us that:

> script differences in 'typical' cases of digraphia always mark profound differences both linguistic and societal: in grammar and vocabulary, in cultural orientation and often in religious orientation as well, in history, in style and preferences for different literary genres, in way of life and sensibility.[77]

He further adds that: 'digraphia is not unlike the proverbial ten per cent of an iceberg that is visible above the water: the part that is visible – the script – is the least part of it'.[78] The Arabic-based script for Urdu signals an association with Islam and Arabo-Islamic culture. The Devanagari script for Hindi signals an association with Hinduism and Sanskrit-based culture. The two scripts evoke political, social and cultural tensions between the speakers of the two languages, some of which are infused with strong animosity, even hatred. The scripts therefore act as signs of identity, which bound each group

[75] See Thomas F. Magner, 'Digraphia in the territories of the Croats and Serbs', *International Journal of the Sociology of Language*, 150: 11–26.

[76] See Robert D. King, 'The poisonous potency of script: Hindi and Urdu', *International Journal of the Sociology of Language* (2001), 150: 43–59.

[77] Ibid. p. 44.

[78] Ibid. p. 44.

into one unit that stands in a distancing relation of Otherness with the other unit.

It would, however, be unwarranted to link digraphia in absolute terms with animosity and hatred. The use of the Roman and Arabic script to write Kurdish in Turkey and Iraq, respectively, may be a locus of intra-ethnic tension or differentiation in the Kurdish-speaking world, but one cannot speak of intra-ethnic animosity or hatred in the social life of the script-identity link. The same is true of the use of the Roman alphabet and the Tifinagh in writing Berber.[79] This scriptal difference signals intra-ethnic differentiation, but the two scripts signal distanciation from the Arabic-dominated scriptal world, in which Berber is dominated or with which it interacts. Distanciation and differentiation operate within the same domain of boundary setting, but they differ from each other in that distanciation operates in inter-group settings, while differentiation marks intra-group inflections.

One may argue that digraphia does not apply in the Hindi-Urdu case, because Hindi and Urdu are considered two different languages, in spite of mutual intelligibility among their common spoken varieties. The same would be the case for Serbian and Croatian after the break-up of Yugoslavia into separate independent states. It may therefore be interesting to look at a case which answers more precisely to the definition of digraphia given above. Cherokee may be an apt example.[80] Two scripts are used to record the language: a Roman alphabet and an indigenous syllabary invented in the 1820s, but these two scripts have different domain connotations, which mark the script-identity link in a complex way. The use of the Roman script is restricted to education and is associated with secularity and knowledge that is not culture-bound. The syllabary is associated with Christianity, traditional medicine and cultural knowledge that must be preserved and protected from the outsider. The syllabary is also increasingly associated with a revitalised ethnic/national identity, hence its use in tribal spaces to signal ownership and differentiation. Its use on street and shop signs in reservations and on tourist commodities is intended to mark the boundary between the in-group and out-group, which is something that the Roman script cannot achieve. The syllabary thus performs a distanciating function, but, in doing so, it also signals the boundary for group inclusion at the same time.

The script-language link does not have to be associated with complete orthographies; it may also be expressed through typefaces or fonts of a script, as in the case of German before World War II, which was printed in Gothic type (Black Letter), so as to differentiate it from French, which used the regular Roman type. In Ireland until the 1950s, a specific Irish typeface

[79] See Andrew Savage, 'Writing Tuareg: three script options', *International Journal of the Sociology of Language* (2008), 192: 5–13.

[80] See Margaret Bender, 'Indexicality, voice and context in the distribution of Cherokee script', *International Journal of the Sociology of Language* (2008), 192: 91–103.

was used for Irish in print to make the language look different from English, which used the regular Roman type. In the transition from the nineteenth to the twentieth century, there was heated debate in nationalist circles in Ireland as to whether to use the Gaelic or the regular Roman font for Irish. Supporters of the former argued that only the Gaelic font can capture the cultural specificity of the Irish and the peculiarities of their language.[81] However, the main reason they championed this font was political in nature: they wanted to signal that Irish is not English, and Irish-ness is not English-ness. In other words, they aimed at political and cultural distanciation from England.

In some situations, it is not script, typeface or font that is invested with symbolic meaning, but individual symbols in a script. In the debate over devising orthography for kreyòl in Haiti, the symbols /k/ and /w/ were linked to an Anglo-Saxon world, which, in the popular mind, was associated with American imperialism. The equivalent symbols /c/ and /ou/ were linked to French colonialism. The debate over script, including the symbolic meanings of these symbols, revolved around 'competing representations of Haitianness at the national and international level – that is how speakers wish to define themselves to each other, as well as to represent themselves as a nation'.[82] A similar situation obtained in Indonesia after independence from the Netherlands in 1947. Because the symbol /œ/ was considered to be stereotypically Dutch, the Indonesians replaced it with /u/ to signal the break from their colonial past.[83] These examples provide evidence of how the adoption of different typefaces/fonts or symbols within one and the same script is used as a device to construct and symbolise different imaginings of national identity.[84]

Let us now consider how some of the above trends and phenomena pan out in the Arabic-speaking world. There have been a few attempts to reform the Arabic script, but none of these have succeeded, largely owing to the strong, socially embedded symbolic meanings of the script in religious, cultural and national terms. Some attempts were made to replace the Arabic script with a Roman alphabet, but these have also failed. The most important and daring of these attempts was Fahmi's proposal to the Arabic Language Academy

[81] See Brian Conchubhair, 'The Gaelic font controversy: the Gaelic League's (post-colonial) crux', *Irish University Review: A Journal of Irish Studies* (2003), 33: 46–63.

[82] Bambi B. Schieffelin and Rachelle Charlier Doucet, 'The "real" Haitian Creole: ideology, metalinguistics and orthographic choices', in Bambi B. Schieffelin, Kathryn A. Woolard and Paul V. Kroskrity (eds), *Language Ideologies: Practice and Theory* (New York and Oxford: Oxford University Press, 1998), p. 285.

[83] See Suzanne Romaine ('Signs of identity, signs of discord: glottal goofs and the green grocer's glottal in debates on Hawaiian orthography', *Journal of Linguistic Anthropology* (2002), 12: 189–224) for other examples of this kind.

[84] See Tomasz D. I. Kamusella, 'Language as an instrument of nationalism in Central Europe', *Nations and Nationalism* (2001), 7: 235–51.

in Cairo in 1943,[85] which raised a storm of protests in the press, not only in Egypt, but also in various other Arab countries.[86] Fahmi produced a scathing critique of the Arabic script on the grounds that it acted as an impediment to the spread of literacy and development. These arguments related to the instrumentality of the script and hardly engaged its symbolic meanings. Fahmi's proposal failed, not because his critique or solution to the problems posed by the script was deficient in instrumental terms, but because he failed to appreciate the strength of the symbolic power of the script. The same fate met the Lebanese poet Sa'id 'Aql, who called to raise the Lebanese dialect to the status of a national language and for writing it in Roman characters. To give expression to the latter proposal, 'Aql published a volume of poetry, *Yara*, in the Roman script.[87] In spite of the publicity that this experiment received in the press and the public interventions 'Aql mounted in supporting it, *Yara* failed to galvanise enough support in favour of Romanisation. Again, the symbolic meanings of the Arabic script proved to be too strong to overcome, even in a country like Lebanon, where the script does not have the same religious connotations for all segments of the population.

As far as variations within the script are concerned, in the Arabic-speaking world, the different orthographic styles do not carry strong meanings that can produce different modulations of the script-identity link that are country specific, except in Morocco. Even here, the Moroccan style has not been invested with strong symbolic connotations that can rupture the pan-Arab meanings of the script, in terms of its association with religion, culture and nation-state identity. Egyptians do not place dots under the Arabic letter representing the long vowel /ī/, but this Egyptian practice is not read as a sign of difference either by Egyptians or non-Egyptians. In fact, most Egyptians and non-Egyptians are not aware of this peculiarity of the Egyptian style. An observable difference becomes a sign of identity only when it is invested with symbolic meaning. In this case, it does not carry such investment, and, therefore, it is a neutral difference. Finally, we may refer to the attempt by members of the Maronite church to print texts of the liturgy in a Syriac-style typeface following the change in the liturgy from Syriac to Arabic at the beginning of the twentieth century. We may read this as an attempt to signal symbolic continuity between the past and the present, to mark the printed material as Maronite and to distance it from the regular Arabic script in its strong associations with Islam. This, however, proved to be a transitional measure, since the regular Arabic script supplanted the Syriac-looking one in this domain of religious practice.

[85] See also Muḥammad Ṣāliḥ 'Umar, 'Mu'āmarat istibdāl al-ḥurūf al-'arabiyya bi-l-ḥurūf al-lātīniyya fī 'ahd al-ḥimāya fī tūnis', *Al-Mustaqbal al-'Arabī* (1987), 99: 65–76.

[86] See Shraybom-Shivtiel, 'The question of the Romanisation of the script and the emergence of nationalism in the Middle East'.

[87] See Franck Salameh, *Language, Memory and Identity in the Middle East: The Case of Lebanon* (Lanham, MD: Lexington Books, 2010).

The script-identity link works through symbolism, not instrumentality. Scripts are as important for marking group identity as language itself. They are more than visible marks that record spoken language. Scripts are an integral part of language ideology in its folk-linguistic sense. They develop meanings and associations with great cultural and political significance that are hard to dislodge, even with illiterate members of a language community. These meanings are signalled at the level of whole scripts, typefaces or fonts and individual characters or symbols in a script. At the instrumental level, script choice and script reforms are corpus-planning measures. They are intended to record a language or improve the efficiency of a script by producing a better fit between sound and written symbol than the existing one. However, on the symbolic level, script choice and, particularly, script reforms act in some situations as though they were status-planning measures. This is why language policy and language planning must attend as much, if not more, to symbolism as instrumentality in some cases. Instrumentality, in fact, is a lesser hurdle in script reform than symbolism. The former relates to the mechanics of orthography; the latter relates to the emotional charge that orthography carries in the social world. Instrumentality does not carry symbolic capital. Symbolism is capital. The script-identity link is anchored to this ideological capital as much as the language-identity link is. The fact that script is parasitic on language does not seem to matter much here. In fact, the visibility of script may carry greater potency in the identity domain than the orality of language. And in discussing how construction works in linking script and language to identity, script offers data that, in some situations, can be dated and studied in relation to existing historical documents in a way that can display the workings of construction in an unequivocal way.

Language as Proxy: Language as Symbolic Construct

The above discussion shows the complex and contingent nature of construction in relating language and script to national identity. At times, construction can take a convoluted route, using language as a *proxy*, what Coulmas calls 'harbinger of crisis',[88] to articulate issues of politics and identity that one would not, or could not, express openly or directly in the public sphere. The decisions in 1989 to establish Lithuanian, Estonian and Latvian as official languages before the break-up of the Soviet Union was rightly interpreted in Moscow as a political and irredentist assertion of national identity, which, no doubt, was the spirit in which these decisions were made. Similar moves in other Soviet republics (for example, Moldavia, Georgia and Armenia) were read in the same way. In an age of political correctness and anti-discrimination laws, language is sometimes pressed into service as a surrogate channel for expressing views about race, education, power and access to state resources. Carol Schmid provides a well-documented study of

[88] Coulmas, 'Language policy and language planning: political perspectives', p. 36.

how this is done in select circles in the United States in her book *The Politics of Language: Conflict, Identity and Cultural Pluralism in Comparative Perspective*. Dealing with the Americanisation movement in the 1920s and the more recent English-Only movement, Schmid writes:

> Language alone has rarely been the major source of conflict in American society; instead it has been the proxy for other conditions that have challenged the power relations of the dominant group(s). [Thus] bilingual education and the usage of non-English languages in the public realm has become a substitute for tensions over demographic and cultural change, increased immigration from third world countries, new linguistic-based entitlements, and changing attitudes towards racial and ethnic assimilation.[89]

The Toubon Law in France has been read in this vein, too. Promulgated in 1994, the law sets out to regulate aspects of the use of French in the public sphere, in commerce and in scholarly output. The law makes French compulsory in:

> advertising, description and directions of use of products; it also demands that bills and receipts be couched in French . . . that publications, journals and papers which benefit from public funds must at the very least include a summary in French if they have to be written in a foreign language, [and] that contracts must be in French, but a translation in the native language of the employee can be demanded by the latter.[90]

While acknowledging that these are genuine concerns for the Toubon Law, Jacques Durand interprets it as a proxy, an attempt to protect French against the onslaught of English, to help France maintain an influential position in the international arena in the face of the globalisation and Americanisation of culture. Another extra-legal aim of the law is said to be to signal French resistance to the creeping erosion of the power of the nation-state within the European Union (EU), which manifested itself in the 'no' vote over the European constitution in May 2005; the fact that the Toubon Law coincided with French anxieties about the Maastricht Treaty at the time gives credence to this interpretation. Finally, the law has been interpreted metonymically as an attempt to keep the French body-politic free of foreign intrusions, whether they are foreign words or foreign bodies. Jacques Durand expresses this link as follows: 'Plans to send immigrants back to their homelands

[89] Carol L. Schmid, *The Politics of Language: Conflict, Identity and Cultural Pluralism in Comparative Perspective* (Oxford: Oxford University Press, 2001), p. 4.

[90] Jacques Durand, 'Linguistic purification, the French nation-state and the linguist', in Charlotte Hoffmann (ed.), *Language, Culture and Communication in Contemporary Europe* (Clevedon: Multilingual Matters Ltd, 1996), p. 82.

may well not be unconnected to the idea of cleansing a language of foreign elements'.[91]

While I am not in a position to judge the veracity of the claims about the erosion of the power of the nation-state in the EU or the metonymic, anti-immigration reading of the Toubon Law, there is, it seems, some truth in the claim about protecting 'Her Majesty the French language', as 'She' is sometimes referred to,[92] against the threat posed by English. This is ultimately an argument about identity, national worth and international standing in a changing world in which the political power of France and her culture have experienced attacks from the outside and creeping erosion from the inside. Anthony Lodge tells us that, in France, 'it is widely believed that to speak French badly, to break the rules of French grammar or to make frequent use of foreign words is to be in some way unpatriotic'.[93] Returning to Amin Maalouf and his book *On Identity*, we can see a clear link between the Toubon Law and French anxieties about the English linguistic invasion. In his characteristically astute manner, but with some added exaggeration to drive his point home, Maalouf writes:

> In France, when I detect anxieties in some people about the way the world is going, or reservations about technological innovation, or some intellectual, verbal, musical or nutritional fashion; or when I see signs of oversensitivity, excessive nostalgia or even extreme attachment to the past – I realize that such reactions are often linked in one way or another to the resentment people feel about the continual advance of English and its present status as the predominant international language.
>
> This attitude seems in some ways peculiar to France. Because France herself had global ambitions as regards language, she was the first to suffer on account of the extraordinary rise of English. For countries that had no such hope, or had them no longer, the problem of relations with the predominant language doesn't arise in the same way.[94]

Gramsci writes that: 'every time the question of language surfaces, in one way or another, it means that a series of other problems are coming to the fore'.[95] This applies to the above representations of English in America and French in France, which shows how language can be constructed as a proxy to express ideas about issues of identity, politics, immigration and access to resources in education and other spheres. I will deal with this later in

91 Ibid. p. 84.
92 Anthony Lodge, 'French is a logical language', in Laurie Bauer and Peter Trudgill (eds), *Language Myths* (London: Penguin Books, 1998), p. 30.
93 Ibid. p. 30.
94 Maalouf, *On Identity*, p. 112.
95 Antonio Gramsci, *Selections from Cultural Writings*, trans. W. Boelhower (London: Lawrence & Wishart, 1985), p. 183.

this book. In Puerto Rico between 1898 – when the country came under American sovereignty – and 1947 – when it was granted self-government – talk about language policy was a proxy for talk about the political future of the country. The two have been so intertwined since then, that one cannot talk about language policy without talking about politics and vice versa.[96] In Taiwan, support for Tai-yü (Taiwanese language) is read as an assertion of a Hok-lo dominated ethnicity, which is seeking to challenge the dominance of the Mandarin-based national identity promoted by the ruling Nationalist Party (KMT) and its 'wai-shen-jen' (Chinese mainlanders) ethnic base.[97] In Senegal under French colonialism, support for the native language, Wolof, and Arabic by the Murid (Muslim) brotherhood in Touba was a mode of passive resistance against the French colonial language policy, to the extent that, to this day, the use of French is stigmatised in this particular community.[98]

In other cases, language is used as a proxy to avoid pressure from political authorities when talking about the taboo subject of national identity. Thus, discussions of the merits of teaching mathematics and science in Arabic or English in Oman are bound up, to an extent, with issues of ethnicity and access to economic resources. In such discussions, the surface meaning is about language choice, but the deep structure meaning is about the politics of ethnicity and national identity, which Omanis broach with extreme care and normally speak about in code, because of their potentially divisive nature. Shelling Sarajevo in 1993, the Serbs declared that they were doing so to protect their culture and language against the Muslims in Bosnia-Herzegovina, although the Bosnians spoke the same language as the Serbs who were shelling them.[99] In Israel in the 1950s and 1960, talk about language rights by the Arab Palestinian minority was a proxy for talk about the loss of land and other national rights, political discrimination and the right to resist.[100] An interesting repeat of this took place in the mid-1980s, when the residents of Beit Hanina – an occupied Arab suburb outside Jerusalem – tried to recreate, through street names in their neighbourhood, a map of the 420 villages destroyed by the new state of Israel after 1948 to signal resistance towards the Israeli occupation.[101] The following chapters will offer other examples of the use of language as a proxy in the pre-modern and modern Arabic-speaking world. Chapter 5 will present an extended discussion of

96 See Nancy Morris, 'Language and identity in twentieth century Puerto Rico', *Journal of Multilingual and Multicultural Development* (1996), 17: 17–32.

97 See Hsiau, 'Language ideology in Taiwan'.

98 See Fallou Ngom, 'Linguistic resistance in the Murid speech community in Senegal', *Journal of Multilingual and Multicultural Development* (2002), 23: 214–26.

99 Coulmas, 'Language policy and language planning: political perspectives'.

100 Suleiman, *A War of Words: Language and Conflict in the Middle East*, pp. 146–9.

101 A. S. Cheshin et al., *Separate and Unequal: The Inside Story of Israeli Rule in East Jerusalem* (Cambridge, MA: Harvard University Press, 1999), pp. 146–7.

this issue by examining in depth a part of a document chronicling the French invasion of Egypt in 1798.

The ability of language to act as proxy is intimately linked to its symbolic function. Language acts in this capacity in the public sphere, especially in the political domain, because of its ability to express meanings of identification, differentiation and distanciation in inter- and intra-group situations. The fact that language does not seem to be overtly political makes it supremely suitable to express these meanings under the cover of politeness, dissimulation or as a way of escaping censorship or what is politically taboo. Language symbolism is an ideologically impregnated location of social meaning, which, in identity construction, is as important as instrumentality. This is why language can act as a metaphor for events in the social world in a way that can shed light on the politics of these events. The reference to the Syrian uprising in 2011 as a Syrian colloquial of the Arab Spring is intended to suggest, via language as symbol, that this uprising is a variant form of a common political vernacular or idiom.[102] It is also intended to suggest that there is a sphere of Arab affinity of concerns, feelings and aspirations which this vernacular symbolises. The language-based metaphor thus aims at identification and differentiation at one and the same time, just as language and script act in these capacities in their symbolic mode.

Conclusion: The Limits of Construction

Using a comparative approach, the above discussion aimed to shed light, through extrapolation, on the strategies involved in constructing the language-identity and language-script links. Four such strategies have been identified: *identification, distanciation, differentiation* and *erasure*. Although I have not dealt with erasure in terms of the script-identity link, it is, of course, possible to make the claim that differentiation may, in fact, be the result of erasure, as the replacement of Arabic by Roman script in the Turkish orthographic reforms exemplifies. Standardisation, which, with the passage of time, bestows on a language, such as Arabic, the appearance of a *natural* fact of the social world, obscures the workings of construction in status and corpus-planning terms. This obscurity acts as a springboard for the inevitable camouflage of the constructed nature of the language-identity and language-script link. Although the arguments for construction may be supported by instrumentally based claims, such as the suitability of one particular script more than another in rendering a language in writing, the fact remains that the main impulses in this kind of construction derive from the symbolic role of language. It is this role that allows language to act as a proxy for socio-political concerns in society, as this monograph will amply show.

[102] See http://www.jadaliyya.com/pages/index/2377/the-syrian-colloquial_the-uprising-of-the-working-soci (accessed 15 August 2011).

In the literature on nationalism, construction is a loaded term. It is sometimes used to reject the antiquity of the nation (perennialism) or its organic conception as a social given of the natural order of things (primordialism). This double rejection is consistent with Gellner's understanding of the genesis of the nation.[103] Construction, in this sense, is a metaphor for saying that the nation is the outcome of modernity. However, some writers use construction to argue that as a product of modernity, the nation is a discursive artefact – the result of a print community based on the vernacular, literature and the spread of journalism.[104] Yet, others argue, more strongly, that the nation is an invention or creation that involves a high degree of social engineering and manipulation.[105]

In my own research on the Arabic language and national identity, I started as a convinced constructionist in Gellner's sense. In one way, I still subscribe to this view, insofar as it rejects primordialism and extreme forms of perennialism, in which antiquity is writ large in nation-building in modernity. But, in another way, I no longer agree with Gellner's view, insofar as it claims that nations are the exclusive product of modernity. It is, in my view, still possible to accept the modernist interpretation of the nation in its different constructionist interpretations, while subscribing to a position which claims that nations are not divorced from their pasts and that these pasts supply them with material which they can weave into the never-ending process of nation-building. As used here, construction is a complex process, in which fact, myth, invention, deliberate manipulation and discursive elaboration play a part.

An example of myth in the language-identity link is the Sun-Language Theory – a concoction of fantasy and wishful thinking about the origins of Turkish.[106] This is a paradigm example of unbridled invention in a mod-

[103] See Gellner, *Nations and Nationalism.*

[104] See Anderson, *Imagined Communities.*

[105] See Hobsbawm, *Nations and Nationalism since 1870.*

[106] Aytürk ('Turkish linguists against the West: the origins of linguistic nationalism in Ataturk's Turkey', *Middle Eastern Studies* (2004), 40: 16–17) explains the genesis of this theory as follows: 'The rudiment of the Sun-Language Theory appeared . . . in the last months of 1935 and the theory was proclaimed in its final form in 1936, receiving the blessings and active support of the Turkish government at the Third Language Congress in the late 1936. To put it briefly, the Sun-Language Theory was a bewildering combination of historical comparative philology, various elements from psychological theories of the nineteenth century and psychoanalytical themes from . . . Freud and . . . Jung. . . . In prehistoric times, the theory goes, the Turkic peoples of Central Asia had established an illustrious civilization; but as a result of climatic changes and a severe draught they started to emigrate in all directions, transmitting their Neolithic civilization to other peoples of the world. Naturally, it was assumed, the ancient form of the Turkish that these conquering emigrants spoke was also carried with them and contributed to every primitive language the most important concepts necessary for abstract thought

ernisation policy in which language played a central part. It was championed to ascribe to the Turkish language an unrivalled antiquity, but it failed to survive beyond its immediate utility, because it was seen to lack credibility, not just in the eyes of professional linguists, but also with ordinary people. While invention is a recognised process of nation-building, there are limits, no matter how ill-defined, on its application. Survivability is a *post hoc* indication of the efficacy of invention in the nation-building project. The Sun-Language Theory died the death that it did because it belonged to the realm of fantasy, rendering a Turk who believes in it as an object of ridicule, not least in Turkey.

Discussing the role of myth in nationalist thinking, Schöpflin states that invention and imagination have 'clear and unavoidable limits'[107], which, he suggests, are determined by resonance. For a myth to resonate, we are told, it cannot be made out of 'false material', and it 'has to have some relationship with the memory of the collectivity that has fashioned it'.[108] This applies equally to language and script in the domain of identity construction, as the above discussion has amply shown. Resonance is not epistemologically or methodologically problem free; however, by insisting that construction is not made out of material that is patently false or lacks a basis in collective memory, we can put some limits on construction. The symbolic meanings of language and script provide nationalist elites with clues as to how far invention can go in the nation-building project. Arguments from instrumentality can play a part in this project, as in the merits of one script over another, but not the determining part.

My research on the Arabic language and national identity has led me to appreciate some of the merits of the ethno-symbolist conception of the nation. In particular, the fact that this framework allows one to talk about the modernity of the nation – with its socio-political and economic imperatives – while at the same time engaging the cultural and symbolic repertoire of a community to trace its continuity back in history. For a linguist who is interested in national identity, this ethno-symbolism provides a basis for moving the discussion of language from purely instrumental functionality to include the rich terrain of symbolic meanings in which construction is a fact of life.

as loanwords. An interesting component of the Sun-Language Theory was the role of the sun in the birth of the language . . . It was claimed that language was born as an act of worship, as part of an ancient Turkic ritual in the cult of the sun. Those Central Asian worshippers, who wanted to salute the omnipotence of the sun and its life-giving qualities, had done so by transforming their meaningless blabbering into a coherent set of ritual utterings'. See also Geoffrey Lewis (*The Turkish Language Reform: A Catastrophic Success* (Oxford: Oxford University Press, 1999), pp. 57–74).

107 George Schöpflin, 'The functions of myth and the taxonomy of myths', in Geoffrey Hosking and George Schöpflin (eds), *Myths and Nationhood* (London: Hurst, 1997), p. 26.

108 Ibid. p. 26.

But in order to do this, we will need to free construction from attempts to yoke it to the modernist paradigm in an unfettered way.

Freed in this manner, construction can refer to the selection and shaping of relevant material to support a particular view, position or interpretation in the language-identity and script-identity link. This will inevitably involve a degree of manipulation, even arbitrariness, as, for example, in the selection of script or forms of the standard language. However, to be successful, construction will also have to involve a commitment to resonance to commend the view, position or interpretation in question to the target audience, particularly when group mobilisation, as in nation-building, is at stake. The following chapters will explore aspects of construction and language symbolism by considering different sites of meaning involving the Arabic language. It will be shown how Arabic is conceptualised symbolically to fit different contexts, actors and extra-linguistic objectives at different times. The data for these chapters are varied, and they have been chosen to highlight some of the terrains and different ways in which the language-identity link operates in the social world. It is this link that will form the substance of the following chapters. I hope to return to the script-identity link in future research.

CHAPTER

2

(IN)IMITABILITY, (UN)TRANSLATABILITY AND INTER-GROUP STRIFE

This chapter explores the two themes of group identity and inter-group conflict in the pre-modern Arabic-speaking world, in so far as they relate to language as a primary factor in articulating them. To achieve this, the chapter investigates three major sites of discussion and debate in Arab and Islamic theological, cultural and political life: the (in)imitability of the Qur'an, its (un)translatability and the inter-ethnic strife called *shu'ūbiyya*. The chapter develops parallel lines of discussion in each of these three sites, before it draws them together into a unified framework. The figure of Jahiz – one of the most prolific writers in the first four centuries of Islam – constitutes the fulcrum of this unified framework. His theory of language as a semiology of semiologies is interpreted against the socio-political context of the day to reveal its historical situatedness. The chapter emphasises the continued relevance of the notions of construction, language symbolism and language as proxy, which we encountered in Chapter 1, in understanding aspects of the pre-modern world.

Introduction

The association of Arabic with group identity is inscribed in the lexical link between the name of the people, *'arab*, and that of the language, *'arabiyya*, in a way which may not be mirrored with similar transparency or connectedness in other language situations. The root meaning of both names is semantically related to the notions of: (1) speaking clearly, plainly, distinctly or perspicuously in a way that is free of incorrectness, corruption or barbarousness; (2) making a person recoil from foul speech or obscene language; and (3) knowing a horse by his neighing to be of pure Arab blood.[1] These

[1] Edward William Lane, *Arabic–English Lexicon* (Beirut: Librairie du Liban, 1980), Part 5.

meanings embody an aesthetic of correctness, perspicacity, moral character, intuitiveness and purity that, in essentialist ideological paradigms – whether in their old or modern manifestations in the Arabic intellectual tradition – are used to braid a set of myths / traditions concerning the Arabic language and the character of the group whose language it is.[2]

In the eleventh century, the connection between language and people – in the way in which the former is said to reflect the character of the latter – was made explicitly by Ibn Sinan al-Khafaji (d. 466/1073) in his book *Sirr al-faṣāḥa*:

> The superiority of the Arabic language over other languages is an integral part of the superiority of its Arab speakers as a nation / people (*umma*) unsurpassed by other nations in quality of character. It is, therefore, not unreasonable to assume that if the Arabic language is indeed the creation of the Arabs by convention,[3] it is bound to reflect their character.[4] In claiming this, I am not driven by blind allegiance to either the language or its speakers.[5]

Although al-Khafaji subscribes to an essentialist rendering of the language-identity link, his reference to 'blind allegiance' hints at the belief that the link that he posits is not an unproblematic one, rather, it is in need of validation, which, in this case, we assume to be provided by an implicit appeal to social convention or the authority or consensus (*ijmāʿ*) of grammarians and other scholars as a community of practice, who delved into the subject and accepted this essentialist claim, either explicitly or implicitly.

In the twentieth century, Zaki al-Arsuzi, expressed this same essentialist connection in a hyperbolic manner in his famous slogan: 'the genius of the Arab nation inheres in its language'.[6] However, his resort to lexical validation through semantic networking to 'substantiate' his claim, which I explored in *The Arabic Language and National Identity: A Study in Ideology*, challenges its essentialist character by revealing the tenuous ways in which this essentialism works. Substituting assertion for validation by rational proof or

2 For language myths, see Laurie Bauer and Peter Trudgill (eds), *Language Myths* (London: Routledge, 1998).

3 For Muslim views on the origin of language, see Bernard G. Weiss, 'Medieval Muslim discussions of the origin of language', *Zeitschrift der Deutschen Morgenländischen Gessellschaft* (1974), 124: 33–41.

4 Al-Khafājī provides a list of qualities of Arabs, including generosity, hospitality, loyalty, bravery, mental agility, pride and fortitude, but he does not explain how these qualities are reflected in Arabic, that is, whether this marking of people in language is signalled phonologically / phonetically, semantically, lexically or by some other means.

5 Ibn Sinān Abū Muḥammad ʿAbdallah Ibn Muḥammad Ibn Saʿīd, *Sirr al-faṣāḥa* (Beirut: Dār al-Kutub al-ʿIlmiyya, 1982), p. 52.

6 See Yasir Suleiman, *The Arabic Language and National Identity: A Study in Ideology* (Washington, DC: Georgetown University Press, 2003).

empirical corroboration is a hallmark of construction, which, in this case, is ideologically driven.

Another example of this essentialist mode of braiding the present with the past through the language-identity link is provided by Mustafa Sadiq al-Rafi'i in his still popular book *I'jāz al-qur'ān wa-l-balāgha al-nabawiyya* (*The Inimitability of the Qur'an and the Prophetic Eloquence/Rhetoric*), first published in the 1920s during a time of heated debate over national identity in Egypt. In a chapter entitled *al-Jinsiyya al-'arabiyya fī al-qur'ān* ('Arab nationality in the Qur'an'),[7] al-Rafi'i links the inimitability of the Qur'an to the Arabs' 'pristine linguistic intuitions' (*fiṭra lughawiyya*), on the one hand, and, on the other, to the fact that the ultimate aim of this inimitability was to create a 'political unity' (*waḥda siyāsiyya*) among the Arabs to act as the pulsating heart for the nations of the world in the past, just as, no doubt, in the present (*ka-l-nabḍ li-qalb hādhā al-'ālam*). This ideological talk creates an attribute of race of the language-identity link, which the Arabic term *jinsiyya*, as a designation for nationality in modern political discourse, embodied in its earliest terminological deployment in Arab thought – a shade of meaning that it more or less completely lost in contemporary political discourse.

It seems that the Prophet Muhammad was aware of this race-based interpretation of the language-identity link in his time, of which he disapproved, hence the following *ḥadīth*, which, even if fabricated or weak, is consistent with the overall message of equality in Islam, as we shall see later in the discussion of *shu'ūbiyya*:

> Oh men! Verily God is one and the ancestor of all men is the same ancestor, religion is the same religion and the Arabic language is neither the father nor the mother of anyone of you but is nothing but a language. Therefore all who speak Arabic are Arabs.[8]

This *ḥadīth* affirms the language-identity link in Arab thinking; however, it considers it not to be a matter of genealogy or ethnic stock, both of which

[7] See Muṣṭafā Ṣādiq al-Rāfi'ī, *I'jāz al-qur'ān wa-l-balāgha al-nabawiyya* (Beirut: Dār al-Fikr al-'Arabī, n.d.), pp. 82–92.

[8] See Ignaz Goldziher, *Muslim Studies* (Vol. I), trans. C. R. Barber and S. M. Stern (London: Allen & Unwin, 1967), pp. 111–12. This *ḥadīth* is given in different renditions in the literature. Addressing the people of Mecca, Muhammad, in one such rendition, is reported to have said: 'God has removed from you the baseless pride of the period of ignorance [*jāhiliyya*] and its rivalry of boasting of ancestry. The Arabic language . . . is not a father and a mother; it is understandable speech (*lisān nāṭiq*) and whoever speaks it is an Arab'. See Roy P. Mottahedeh, 'The *shu'ūbiyya* controversy and the social history of early Islamic Iran', *International Journal of Middle Eastern Studies* (1976), 7: 179. Mottahedeh comments on this *ḥadīth*: 'To offer men who spoke Arabic recognition as Arabs was an acknowledgement that it was highly desirable to be an Arab; but it was also an invitation to men to vote with their tongues'.

were crucial for the Arabs in pre-Islamic Arabia and the first centuries of the Islamic era, but a matter of language acquisition and cultural membership.[9] In this *ḥadīth*, Muhammad does not seem to restrict his message to the Muslims; his use of the term 'men' (in other versions 'people') implies that he is addressing Muslims and non-Muslims alike, making Arabic a marker of identity in non-racial terms, both through and beyond faith. There is evidence in the literature that Christian Arabs in early Islam felt that Arabic was as much their language, as it was that of Arab Muslims, but this issue will not detain us here.

The name of the Arabic language in the modern period tends to concatenate *'arabiyya* with *fuṣḥā* in the designation *al-'arabiyya al-fuṣḥā*, to oppose this variety to the colloquial varieties, *'āmmiyyāt*, in the diglossic Arabic language situation. This concatenation adds semantic intensification to the root meaning of *'arab* and *'arabiyya*, which, again, links the language to the notions of clarity, eloquence, perspicacity, purity and freedom of impediment in speech or weaknesses of construction in written language.[10] In the Arabic intellectual tradition, these qualities are thought, by common tradition, to apply to the language and people who originally spoke it in Central Arabia during pre-Islamic and early Islamic times, before these people came into intensive contact with other nations following the Islamic conquests, hence the proscription of linguistic data culled from tribes that mixed with non-Arabs in constructing Arabic grammatical theory. In modern discourse, the term *fuṣḥā* substitutes for *'arabiyya* as a name for the language in its 'standard' form and is used as a marker of national identity in pan-Arab political ideology.

One of the best examples of this ideological amalgamation is the portmanteau title of a book by the Lebanese academic 'Umar Farrukh, *al-Qawmiyya al-fuṣḥā*,[11] in which the term *al-fuṣḥā* replaces *al-'arabiyya* in the common appellation *al-qawmiyya al-'arabiyya* for pan-Arab nationalism. This replacement plays on the semantic overlap between the root meanings of *fuṣḥā* and *'arabiyya* as they apply to the language, but they also make pan-Arab nationalism synonymous with that language as a marker of national identity. In addition, the concatenation of *qawmiyya* with *fuṣḥā* in this title demands of

9 Al-Shāfi'ī (d. 204/820) discusses this topic in his *Risāla*, in which he says: 'No one can learn [Arabic] save he who has learnt it from the Arabs, nor can anyone be as fluent [in Arabic] as they unless he has followed them in the way they learned it. He who has learned it from them should be regarded as one of the people of that tongue. Those who have adopted tongues other than the Arabic, have done so because they have neglected this tongue; if they return to it, they will belong to its people . . . And he who has uttered a few words [in Arabic] will be regarded as belonging to the Arabs'. See Majid Khadduri, *Islamic Jurisprudence: Shāfi'ī's Risāla* (Baltimore, MD: The Johns Hopkins University Press, 1961), pp. 89–90.

10 See Lane, *Arabic–English Lexicon*, Part 6.

11 'Umar Farrūkh, *al-Qawmiyya al-fuṣḥā* (Beirut: Dār al-'Ilm li-l-Malāyīn, 1961).

the reader excavating and activating the lexical meanings of both *'arabiyya* and *fuṣḥā*, as I have done above, rather than accepting them as mere terminological appellations and applying these archived meanings, consciously and explicitly, to both the language and Arab nationalism. Under this reading of the title, the root meanings of *'arabiyya* and *fuṣḥā* are imparted to the triad of language, people and identity to signal the unity among them in an essentialist way that is not cognizant of the constructed nature of this triadic relationship.

This concatenating mode of characterising the language-identity link in modern Arab political thought trades on lexically motivated tropes that hark back to debates that took place in the first centuries of Islam (second to fifth/eighth to tenth). Thus, these tropes are animated by the debate about the inimitability of the Qur'an (*i'jāz al-qur'ān*) as the Islamic foundational text, and they are also archaeologically informed by the most important inter-group strife in Muslim society in the early centuries of Islam between Arabs and non-Arabs, mainly the Persians: the *shu'ūbiyya* movement, as will be discussed below. However, we must be careful not to imply that a seamless intellectual and ideological continuity exists between the modern and pre-modern periods as far as the language-identity link is concerned or the facts that are associated with it. Such an assumption would subscribe to a perennialist interpretation of the nation, with which I have some sympathy, but avoid subscribing to it completely, because of the unwarranted antiquity that it attributes to the Arab nation as an expression of modernity.[12] What we have here is not a straightforward genealogy of ideas between past and present, but the existence of a web of language-identity conceptualisations in the past that resonate with similar ones in the present in constructions of the nation as an aspect of modernity. This chapter will expound some of the themes that have been discussed in Chapter 1 by going back in history.

I will deal with some of these ideas below, starting with the notion of the inimitability of the Qur'an as an Arabic revelation, relating this notion to the debate, in the classical sources, of the (un)translatability of this revelation. The chapter will discuss the link between anti-Arab polemic and the inimitability of the Qur'an as a theological principle, by investigating Jahiz's (d. 255/868–9) theory of communication as a semiological construct. The chapter will also link the concern with Arabic as the language of culture to the anti-Arab polemic waged by some non-Arabs, which, as I will try to show, is not divorced from the notion of the inimitability of the Qur'an. This discussion will reveal the deep epistemological links between Arabic, the inimitability of the Qur'an and the defence of the Arabs against anti-Arab polemic.

12 See Yasir Suleiman, *The Arabic Language and National Identity*.

(In)imitability of the Qur'an[13]

The Qur'an makes reference to the fact that it was revealed in Arabic. Qur'an 12:2 states: *'innā anzalnāhu qur'ānan 'arabiyyan'* ('We have sent it down as an Arabic Qur'an'). This message is repeated in Qur'an 52:5 and Qur'an 53:1–2. This Arabic is qualified as *mubīn* (perspicuous) in Qur'an 26:195 and as being free of 'crookedness' ('*ghayra dhī 'iwajin*') in Qur'an 39:29. The rationale for revealing the Qur'an in Arabic is given in Qur'an 41:44 as: (1) making the message of the revelation accessible to the Arabs;[14] and (b) avoiding the anomaly of an Arab Prophet addressing his own people in a foreign tongue: *wa-law ja'alnāhu qur'ānan 'a'jamiyyan la-qālū law lā fuṣṣilat 'āyātuhu 'a'jamiyyu wa 'arabiyyun* (Had We sent this Qur'an [in a language] other than Arabic, they would have said: 'Why are its verses not explained in detail? What! A foreign (tongue) and an Arab Messenger?'). In the ordinary scheme of things, the second point should be obvious and in no need of stating; however, the fact that the Qur'an mentions it signals the importance of the language issue in any consideration of the revelation.

These Qur'anic pronouncements are amplified in the *ḥadīth* literature. In one such *ḥadīth*, the Prophet is reported to have asked his followers, presumably the non-Arabs, to love the Arabs for three reasons: because he was an Arab, the Qur'an was revealed in Arabic and the speech of the people of Paradise is Arabic.[15] This *ḥadīth* reiterates the close link between language and identity through the person of the Prophet in a way that additionally links life on earth with the hereafter. In another *ḥadīth*, it is reported that the angel Gabriel came to Muhmmad and said to him:

> O Muhammad! All things have a master: Adam is [the] master of men; you are the master of Adam's descendants; the master of the Rūm [Byzantines/Greeks] is Ṣuhayb [Ibn Sinān, one of the Prophet's companions of that origin]; the master of the Ethiopians is Bilāl [Ibn Rabāḥ, a companion of Prophet of that origin]; the master of the trees is the lotus (*sidr*); the master of birds is the eagle; the chief of the months is Ramadan; the chief of weekdays is Friday; and, Arabic is the master of speech.[16]

By leaving Arabic until the end, the *ḥadīth* makes the statement about the language as a fitting finale to a venerable list of highly prestigious persons and objects in Islam, including Adam and Prophet Muhammad.

13 See Issa J. Boullata, 'The rhetorical interpretation of the Qur'an: *I'jāz* and related topics', in Andrew Rippin (ed.), *Approaches to the History of the Interpretation of the Qur'ān* (Oxford: Clarendon Press, 1988), pp. 139–57, for a general introduction of the concept of *i'jāz*.

14 Qur'an 52:5 reiterates this point.

15 Suleiman, *The Arabic Language and National Identity*, p. 44.

16 Ibid. p. 43.

In its most abiding articulation, the inimitability of the Qur'an,[17] as I shall explain below, is intimately linked with the highly prestigious position of Arabic in Islam, reflecting its status in pre-Islamic society as the language of the most important cultural product in Arabia, poetry.[18] In dealing with the inimitability of the Qur'an, I will eschew the theological intricacies of this concept and concentrate on those aspects of it that relate to language, this being the focus of this study.[19] Furthermore, my treatment of these aspects will not pay attention to their chronology or incessant reiteration and minute variations in the literature to modern times, since what matters most from our perspective are the major intellectual isoglosses that frame the discussion of inimitability, insofar as it relates to the language-identity link.

As a description of the matchless language of the Qur'an, inimitability refers to the challenge that God issued to the Arabs (and non-Arabs, according to some interpretations) to produce discourse/compositions that can match its eloquence.[20] This challenge is embodied in what is known in the

17 See Berque, *Cultural Expression in Arab Society Today*, trans. Robert W. Stookey (Austin, TX: University of Texas Press, 1978), pp. 154–70, for an interesting discussion of this topic.

18 Ṭaha Ḥusayn's claim in the 1920s that pre-Islamic poetry was fabricated (*manḥūl*) was vehemently attacked for a variety of reasons. One of these treats this claim as an attack on the inimitability of the Qur'an, because it undermines the belief that the Arabs were people of eloquence, who, if they could, would have tried to respond to the challenge posed to them in the Qur'an. This reaction in the twentieth century reveals the abiding nature of both the inimitability principle and the belief in the special position of poetry in Arab culture. See Muḥammad al-Amīn al-Khuḍarī 'al-'i'jāz', *Majallat al-'ulūm al-'insāniyya wa-l-'ijtimā'iyya* (2005), 21: 3–54.

19 Inimitability is linked to a host of factors, including the following: (1) inter-faith polemic involving Christianity and, to a lesser extent, Judaism in the context of the proofs of prophethood (*dalā'il al-nubuwwa*); and (2) intra-faith polemic between Sunnī and Imāmī Shī'a scholars, between Mu'tazilites and Ashs'arite, as well as among Mu'tazilites in Basra and Baghdad (see Richard C. Martin, 'The role of Basrah Mutazillah in formulating the doctrine of the apologetic miracle', *Journal of Near Eastern Studies* (1980), 3: 175–89). In relation to the first, we may refer to a difference between Christianity and Islam, which makes the inimitability of the Qur'an such an important principle. Von Grunebaum expresses this succinctly, as follows (*A Tenth Century Document of Arabic Literary Theory and Criticism* (Chicago, IL: University of Chicago Press, 1950), pp. xiv–v): 'The Christian had his Scriptures in translation and had not been taught to look upon the original as actual discourse in the Lord's own tongue. Besides, the Bible could not escape being judged against the Graeco-Roman literary tradition while the Qur'an stood out in Arabic literature as an unprecedented phenomenon for the critical valuation of which no standard existed'.

20 Although the Qur'an uses derivations of the root *'-j-z*, from which the term *i'jāz* (inimitability) is morphologically constructed 16 times, it is only in the second half of the third century of the Islamic calendar (ninth/tenth) that this term acquires terminological status.

literature on inimitability as the 'challenge verses' (*ayāt al-taḥaddī*), specifying, as the subject of the challenge, an undefined range of discourse in the Qur'an (52:33–4) (*bi-ḥadīthin mithlihi*), to one chapter [*sūra*] in the Qur'an (10:38), through ten chapters in the Qur'an (11:13). This challenge unfolds at different times in Muhammad's mission to respond to the accusations levelled against him as a poet (*shā'ir*), soothsayer (*kāhin*) and madman (*majnūn*) in an attempt to discredit his prophethood (*nubuwwa*) and the divine truth of his message. This language-inflected challenge is best understood as part of a cultural milieu in which poetic response and counter-response (*mu'āraḍa*), fielded in the public domain, sometimes with expert adjudication, was an integral part of the pre-Islamic Arabian system of personal and tribal honour. Qur'an 2:23–4 alludes to this cultural praxis:[21]

> If you are in doubt concerning what we sent down to our servant [i.e. Muhammad], then produce a chapter [*sūra*] the like of it, and call upon your witnesses apart from God. And if you do not [produce one] – and you never will – then fear the hell fire, whose fuel is humans and stones, prepared for unbelievers.

But what makes this a meaningful challenge to the truth of Muhammad's prophethood and his divine revelation? In addition to pointing to Muhammad being illiterate (*ummī*) and thus technically unequipped to produce a Qur'an-like discourse, Muslim scholars specified a set of conditions which make the challenge a reasonable test, to use a modern idiom. This test includes the fact that the subject of the challenge broke the norm by surpassing what was customary (*naqd al-'āda*) – this being the ability of the Arabs to produce discourse of great eloquence and virtuosity – and, in addition, that its prediction of a failure to do so was realised, confirmed in this case by the inability of the Arabs to produce even one chapter that could match the eloquence of the Qur'an. The second condition has great significance, because the Arabs were known to be enamoured by eloquence and to be great masters of it; because they had every reason to try to meet the challenge in the Qur'an out of linguistic pride and material self-interest, owing, in the latter case, to the fact that Islam sought to destroy their system of belief and did succeed in doing so;[22] and, finally, because they were well-versed in the art of linguistic

[21] Goldziher describes this cultural praxis, as follows: 'The purpose of public *mufākhara* [boasting] was to end a quarrel between two people [or parties]. On such occasions impartial umpires were appointed to judge which of the parties was the winner in poetical boasting. Forfeits were deposited with the umpires to ensure adherence to the judgement'. See Goldziher, *Muslim Studies* (Vol. I), p. 59.

[22] Jāḥiẓ expresses this in his discussion of inimitability: 'Knowing what we do, it is unbelievable that words should have been [the weapon] readiest to their hands . . . and yet that the Prophet's opponents should with one accord have refrained from using them, at a time when they were sacrificing their possessions and their lives, and that they should not have said [with one voice] or that not even one of

duelling (*mu'āraḍa*). The fact that the Qur'an was shown to break custom (*amr khāriq li-l-'āda*) and that it was able to withstand refutation (*ṣālim 'an al-mu'āraḍa*) was therefore considered to be sufficient evidence to corroborate the claim that it is miraculous proof (*mu'jiza*) of Muhammad's prophethood and the truth of the divine message that God revealed to him.[23] In all of the debates concerning the meaning of inimitability, the logographic inflection of this concept stands out, surpassing in importance the references to the prediction of future events that the Qur'an mentions or the reports of past events that it incorporates, which some scholars adduced as proof of its inimitability.

However, not all participants in the debate over inimitability accepted the inability claim, at least in the sense outlined above. Some scholars, but by no means the majority, offered the counterclaim that the Arabs had the ability to match the Qur'an's eloquence, but that God deterred/deflected them (*ṣarafahum*) from doing so. This view came to be known as the 'deterrence/deflection' principle (*ṣarfa*), and it was, in part, related to the fact that it had not been absolutely clear what features of the Qur'an as discourse were inimitable. As Vasalou put it, summarising the basis of this argument in the classical sources on the topic: 'if the Arabs did not know what they were challenged to imitate, then the challenge (*taḥaddī*) would hardly be a "valid" one'.[24] One may add that this would have to be the case because of God's justice, exhibited in the reasonable expectation that it would be unfair not to know, in any call for *mu'āraḍa*, what aspects of the revelation to try to match. Proponents of the logographic interpretation of inimitability argued against deflection on the basis that the challenge laid down in the Qur'an loses its power under this perspective. Why, they argued, should the Qur'an set out to be a revelation of matchless eloquence if the Arabs, who were known for their love of *mu'āraḍa*, were a priori deterred from matching it. It was also pointed out that the principle of deterrence attributed the miraculous nature

them should have said: Why do you kill yourselves, sacrifice your possessions and forsake your homes, when the steps to be taken against him are simple, and the way of dealing with him is easy: let one of your poets or orators compose a speech similar to his, equal in length to the shortest *sūra* [chapter] he has challenged you to imitate or the meanest verse he has invited you to copy?'. See Charles Pellat, *The Life and Works of Jāḥiẓ: Translations of Selected Texts*, trans. D. M. Hawke (London: Routledge & Kegan Paul, 1969), pp. 47–8.

23 See Abdul Aleem, 'I'jazul-Qur'an', *Islamic Culture* (1933), 7: 215–33.

24 See Sophia Vasalou, 'The miraculous eloquence of the Qur'an: general trajectories and individual approaches', *Journal of Qur'anic Studies* (2002), 4: 30. *Ṣarfa* is also related to the created-ness of the Qur'an principle, the idea that the Qur'an was created in time and, therefore, is not an attribute of God. See Margaret Larkin, 'The inimitability of the Qur'an: two perspectives', *Religion & Literature* (1988), 20: 31–47, for the links between inimitability and the controversy surrounding the creation of the Qur'an.

of the revelation to deflection, rather than to the Qur'an itself, which, in addition to being a circular argument, is not what the Qur'an states.

The principle of deflection was, however, important in adding further motivation to the impetus to define the logographic content of inimitability in the Qur'an. In spite of some differences among scholars who delved into this topic, there was broad agreement in the literature that the linguistic content of inimitability resides not in the words of the Qur'an per se, but, more importantly, in the way that these words are syntactically ordered or structured to turn what may be ordinary meanings into wonderfully expressive ones of matchless eloquence. This, in essence, is what is meant by the notion of *naẓm* (structure/construction) in discussing the inimitability of the Qur'an. Qur'anic style, therefore, subsists in this indissoluble trinity of words, syntactic structures and meanings, which is, additionally, infused with rhetorical devices, whose excellence surpasses existing norms in exquisiteness and in the extensiveness of their occurrence within the body of the Qur'an.[25]

To this may be added the impact of the Qur'an as oral discourse on the hearers. Al-Khattabi (d. 388/998) expresses this claim by saying that: 'no words, be they poetry or prose, when heard by the ear, produce on the heart sometimes the effect of sweetness and sometimes that of awe as the Qur'an does'.[26] Touching on this point from the perspective of the controversy over the (un)translatability of the Qur'an, Poonawala writes:

> The persuasive sound of melodic recitation (*tajwīd, tartīl*) is basic to a Muslim's sense of his culture and religion even before he can articulate that sense. It is this mysterious power and charm of its inimitable music, the very sounds of which create a captivating effect in the heart of its listener and move him to tears and ecstasy.[27]

The orality of the Qur'an, as discussed above, is at the heart of this consideration as to its impact as inimitable discourse. The orality is the mainstay of the science of recitation (*tartīl*) in the Islamic tradition down to this day.

The impact of the Qur'an is further related to the fact that it was considered a genre-breaking composition, which differed from existing forms of literary expression known to the Arabs at the time of the revelation: poetry,

[25] According to al-Khaṭṭābī (d. 388/998): 'all the different forms of expression, like dilation [*basṭ*] and elision [*iqtiṣār*], collection [*jam'*] and distribution [*tafrīq*], metaphor and explicitness [*taṣrīḥ*] . . . which are found in their [the poets] compositions are to be found also in the Qur'an. [But] these forms in the Qur'an excel their [poets] forms in every respect'. See Aleem, 'I'jazul-Qur'an', p. 226.

[26] See Aleem, 'I'jazul-Qur'an', p. 224.

[27] See Ismail K. Poonawala, 'Translatability of the Qur'an: theological and literary considerations', *Translation and Scripture. A Jewish Quarterly Review Supplement* (1990): 192.

oration [*khuṭba*] and epistle [*risāla*]. Al-Rummani (d. 386/996) expresses this discovery as follows:

> The Qur'an opened a new path, unique and different from the established ones. It has a degree of beauty which surpasses that of all other forms and excels even verse which is the best form of speech. Its analogy to other miracles lay in the fact that it was similar to the parting of the sea and the transformation of the rod into a snake [a reference to Moses], or other miracles of the same kind [an allusion to Jesus], in so far as it broke the established rule and so hindered the creatures from rivalling it.[28]

Upon hearing the Qur'an, the Arabs were said to have been confused, unable to classify it by reference to existing forms of literary composition. It challenged their literary schema, confounding them even more.

But precisely who is the challenge directed at in the Qur'an? Opinions differ on this question. Some scholars believe that the challenge was addressed to all Arabs, because of their pristine linguistic intuitions; what al-Rafi'i called *fiṭra lughawiyya* above. Others restricted the challenge to the elite among the Arabs, who had the necessary qualifications to rise to it. Some believe that the challenge was addressed to the Arabs alone. Others argued that the challenge was addressed to all Muslims (and, in fact, non-Muslims), regardless of whether they were Arabs or not. In this case, the proof that the Qur'an was inimitable would apply to non-Arabs transitively, in the sense that if the Arabs, or the elite among them, were unable to imitate the Qur'an, so they would also prove incapable. Some believe that the challenge was addressed to the Arabs at the time of the revelation or in the early centuries of Islam, before their pristine linguistic intuitions became subject to corruption, largely owing to intensive linguistic contact with non-Arabs. Others argue that the challenge was not time-limited, in the sense that it was open to Arabic speakers to take it up at any time; it had to be that way, in order to give credence to the challenge of a book that claims to speak an eternal truth. The Egyptian scholar 'A'isha 'Abd al-Rahman, better known as Bint al-Shati', advocated this position in the twentieth century: for the challenge of inimitability to be meaningful, it must remain active, even though: (1) present-day Arabs, including the elite, lack the pristine and untutored intuitions of the Arabs at the time of the revelation; (2) the challenge has withstood the test of time; and, therefore, (3) inimitability has become religious dogma, thus militating any attempt to question it.

The logographic nature of inimitability makes sense, in cultural terms, because of the importance of language for the Arabs[29] – its primary addressee constituency – which fact, as has been discussed at length above, is inscribed

[28] Aleem, 'I'jazul-Qur'an', p. 223.

[29] For some interesting reflections on the link between language and inimitability from a modern perspective, see Adonis, *al-Shi'riyya al-'arabiyya* (Beirut: Dār

in the semantic connectivity of language and people through the root *'-r-b*. The link between the semantic import of this root and the notion of eloquence is inscribed in the concatenation of the name of the language with the root meaning of *f-ṣ-ḥ*, through the superlative adjective *fuṣḥā*, which, on its own, is used as a designation of the language.[30] But inimitability, as developed in the third/ninth century, is also linked to the inter-ethnic strife between Arabs and non-Arabs, mainly Persians, during this period of far-reaching social and political change in Islamic history. Martin alludes to this by linking the debate over Muhammad's prophethood and, hence, the inimitability of the Qur'an to *shu'ūbiyya*:

> The so-called heretics who attacked the Qur'an with bitter scepticism were usually from Iran and Iraq, and often they were not of Arab stock. While the evidence does not indicate that the *shu'ūbī* controversy was the cause of doctrinal disputes over prophethood, the social and intellectual ferment of the *shu'ūbiyya* was nonetheless an important constituent of the intellectual climate in which the controversy over Muhammad's prophethood took place.[31]

Vasalou also points to this contextual linkage.[32] I will deal with this further, so as to show the depth of this linkage in Arab linguistic and political thought during the classical period.

(Un)translatability of the Qur'an

The (un)translatability of the Qur'an is related to the tension between the claim that the Qur'anic revelation was universal in character – sent to all mankind – and that it was, at the same time, the speech of God verbatim sent down to Muhammad in Arabic to communicate to his own Arabic-speaking community in the first instance (as previously explained).[33] In its early form, the controversy over (un)translatability may have been related to the notion of inimitability in its embryonic form, before the term *'i'jāz* came to acquire its technical meaning of apologetic miracle in the second half of the third/

al-Ādāb, [2nd printing] 1989b); Adonis, *al-Naṣṣ al-qur'ānī wa-āfāq al-kitāba* (Beirut: Dār al-Ādāb, 1993).

30 Commenting on this, Tibawi says that inimitability 'derives added significance from emotional factors which are at once religious and national. They are bound up with the Arab's pride in his faith and his love of his language. Not only is Islam superior to any religion, but the Arabic language is peerless'. See A. L. Tibawi, 'Is the Qur'an translatable? Early Muslim opinion', *The Muslim World* (1962), 52: 11.

31 Martin, 'The role of Basrah Mutazillah in formulating the doctrine of the apologetic miracle', p. 179.

32 See Vasalou, 'The miraculous eloquence of the Qur'an'.

33 See Abdul-Raof, *Qur'an Translation: Discourse, Texture and Exegesis* (Richmond: Curzon Press, 2001), pp. 37–61, for a discussion of the (un)translatability thesis.

tenth century. This linkage is made by Tibawi,[34] Rahman[35] and Poonawala[36] – a view which I share, as shall become clear at length.

Early discussions of the translation of the Qur'an related to the need to preach God's revelation to non-Arabs, who, upon accepting Islam, could not be expected to perform the ritual prayer in Arabic. The jurist Abu Hanifa (d. 150/767) seems to have permitted the recitation of the Qur'an in a foreign translation in performing ritual prayer for those Muslims who were not competent in the language. There is some discussion as to whether this was an absolute permission that was granted or just a temporary measure until the new Muslim acquired enough Arabic to be able to recite the Qur'an in its original language, but it seems that Abu Hanifa may have given this license without qualification, in other words, as an absolute permission. This permission, in its absolute form, implies that the form of the revelation in Arabic is detachable from its content, wherein the miraculous nature of the Qur'an lies. By breaking the form-content duality in the Qur'an, Abu Hanifa, in effect, seems to say that a translation of the content of the Qur'an would result in a kind of Qur'an, although primacy, we assume, continues to reside in the Qur'an in the Arabic language. Some of Abu Hanifa's followers – for example, al-Sarkhasi (d. 483/1090) – restricted the license given by Abu Hanifa, making it a temporary one, so as to avoid the above implication, while others persisted in legalising the original ruling – for example, al-Kasani (d. 587/1191).[37]

Most Sunni jurists, however, led by al-Shafi'i (d. 204/820), rejected Abu Hanifa's view on using translations of the Qur'an in ritual prayer, to the extent that al-Shafi'i is reported to have given a dispensation to those who do not know the Qur'an in its Arabic form to pray without reciting it. At the basis of this rejection lies the dissolution of the duality of form and content in

34 See Tibawi, 'Is the Qur'an translatable? Early Muslim opinion'.

35 See Fazlur Rahman, 'Translating the Qur'an', *Religion & Literature* (1988), 20: 23–30.

36 See Poonawala, 'Translatability of the Qur'an'.

37 Al-Kasānī argues his point against al-Shāfi'ī's position as follows: 'The [fact of] Arabic being [called the language of] the Qur'an does not negate that a non-Arabic [language] can also be called the language of the Qur'an. There is nothing in the Qur'anic verse ["We have sent it down as an Arabic Qur'an"] to negate [our assumption]. The Arabic [text] is called the Qur'an because it denotes that it is the Qur'an [i.e., recitation], and the word "Arabic" is [used in this verse as] an adjective (*ṣifat*) [qualifying the Qur'an] because it is the essence of speech (*ḥaqīqat al-kalām*). It is for this reason that we maintain that the Qur'an is not created (*ghayr makhlūq*), in the sense that it is an eternal attribute without regard to its language. Persian [translation therefore] does indicate [that it is also the speech of God], hence it is permissible to call it the Qur'an. The Qur'anic statement, "If We had made it a foreign Qur'an," establishes that if [the meaning of the Qur'an] is expressed in a foreign language, it too can be called the Qur'an'. See Poonawala, 'Translatability of the Qur'an: theological and literary considerations', pp. 184–5 [inserts in the original].

Abu Hanifa's theology, which duality is considered by al-Shafi'i as an integral part of the challenge (*taḥaddī*) that God issued to the Arabs to produce even one chapter in the like of the Qur'an. The form-content duality is, therefore, at the very core of the inimitability of the Qur'an principle: rejecting it would be tantamount to rejecting its inimitability and, therefore, the miraculous nature of the revelation that it underpins in Islamic theology. If a translation of the Qur'an is to be treated as the Qur'an, the inimitability principle would be spectacularly breached in a way that makes the challenge (*taḥaddī*) almost meaningless. Poonawala expresses this point clearly by stating that:

> all the objections to translation stem from the [idea of *i'jāz*]. Except for the Hanafi school, all Sunni schools of jurisprudence maintain that the Qur'an ceases to be the word of God and loses its character as the holy Qur'an once it is translated into another language.[38]

To support this conclusion, al-Shafi'i had to argue that the Qur'an was free of foreign words, ascribing the impression that it might have some such words to accidental similarities between languages.[39] However, in arguing this point, al-Shafi'i seems to go further, implying that any impression of similarity is loaded in favour of Arabic as a donor language:

> We do not deny that [there may exist] in foreign tongues certain words, whether acquired or transmitted, which may be similar to those of the Arab tongue, just as words in one foreign tongue may be similar to those in others, although these [tongues are spoken in] separate countries and are different and unrelated to one another despite the similarity in some words.[40]

In addition, al-Shafi'i had to link his views on refusing to treat the Qur'an in translation as revelation to the excellence of the Arabic language.[41] Al-Shafi'i

[38] Ibid. p. 177.

[39] Another, more popular, view is that there are some words of foreign origin in the Qur'an, but that by the time of the revelation to Muhammad, these words were so thoroughly Arabicised that they ceased to be regarded as foreign.

[40] See Khadduri, *Islamic Jurisprudence: Shāfi'ī's Risāla*, p. 90 [inserts in the original].

[41] This view appears in different guises in the literature, without giving overt recognition to the language-identity link. One of the early views on this topic comes from Jāḥiẓ. See Charles Pellat, *The Life and Works of Jāḥiẓ: Translations of Selected texts*, trans. D. M. Hawke (London: Routledge & Kegan Paul, 1969), p. 132: 'The books of the Indians have been construed, the maxims of the Greeks have been translated, and the rules of the conduct of the Persians have been rendered into Arabic. Some of these translations [into Arabic] are superior to the originals, and others have lost nothing in the process; but if the wisdom of the Arabs were to be translated the marvellous rhythm would completely disappear'. Al-Khafājī shares this view, making the link with language clear, as Suleiman explains: 'The Arabic language is characterised by a host of features, including its richness (*si'a*) which enables the

extolls the qualities of Arabic in his *Risāla*: 'Of all the tongues, that of the Arabs is the richest and most extensive in vocabulary. Do we know any man except a prophet who apprehended all of it?'[42] And:

> The Qur'an was communicated in the Arab tongue rather than in another [because] no one who understands clearly the total meanings of the [legal] knowledge of the Book of God would be ignorant of the extensiveness of that tongue and of the various meanings [of its words] to be found [just as] there are various words for a certain meaning. Doubts which occur to one who is ignorant of [the Arab tongue] will disappear from him who knows it.[43]

Al-Shafi'i then links the excellence of Arabic and the exalted position of the Arabs in Islam to the person of the Prophet:

> Since tongues vary so much that different [people] cannot understand one another, some must adopt the language of others. And preference must be given to the tongue which others adopt. The people who are fit to receive such a preference are those whose tongue is their Prophet's tongue. It is not permissible – but God knows best – for the people of [the Prophet's] tongue to become the followers of people whose tongues are other than that [of the Prophet] even in a single letter; but rather all other tongues should follow his tongue, and all the peoples of earlier religions should follow his religion.[44]

This set of ideas shows the extent to which the language-identity link is built into the debates about the inimitability of the Qur'an as a primarily theological principle.

users of the language to express themselves with ease, elegance and brevity. To support this claim [al-Khafājī] refers, among other things, to the view expressed by a Syriac-Arabic translators of the day, Abu Dawud al-Matran, who told him how choice texts from foreign languages lose their beauty and elegance when translated into Syriac, but how these texts gain in these qualities when translated into Arabic'. See Yasir Suleiman, 'The concept of *Faṣāḥa* in Ibn Sinān al-Khafājī', *New Arabian Studies* (1996), 3: 222. This view is shared by Ibn Faris (d. 395/1004), who tells us that: 'Arabic cannot be translated into any other language, as the gospels from Syriac could be translated in Ethiopian and Greek, or the Torah and Psalter and other books of God could be translated into Arabic, because the non-Arabs cannot compete with us in the wide use of metaphorical expressions. How could it be possible to render the 60th verse of the eighth *sūra* in a language with words which reproduce the exact sense; circumlocutions would have to be used, what is summarised would have to be unrolled, what is separated connected, and what is hidden revealed . . .' See Ignaz Goldziher, *Muslim Studies, Volume I*, trans. C. R. Barber and S. M. Stern, S. M. Stern (ed.) (London: Allen & Unwin Ltd), p. 196.

42 Al-Shāfi'ī, *Risāla*, pp. 88–9.

43 Ibid. pp. 93–4 [inserts in the original].

44 Ibid. pp. 90–1 [inserts in the original].

This view of Arabic is, again, held by Ikhwān al-Ṣafā (The Brethren of Purity, fourth/fifth-tenth/eleventh) in the context of their position on the (un)translatability of the Qur'an. They set out their position as follows:

> The perfect language is the language of the Arabs and the eloquent speech is that of the Arabs. [All other languages], except it, are imperfect. Among the languages Arabic [occupies a place] similar to that of a human form in the animal [kingdom]. As the emergence of human form is the final animal form, so too Arabic language is the perfection of human speech and [Arabic] writing is the termination of the art of writing.[45]

Ikhwān al-Ṣafā continue this line of thinking as follows: 'Indeed, because of its [the Qur'an's] brevity and succinctness, it is not possible to translate it. And this [fact, i.e., its untranslatability] is not hidden [any more]'.[46] Ikhwān al-Ṣafā follow what must have been an established view among the theologians, but they take it to a new height of veneration and rhetorical expression.

Scholars who argued against the (un)translatability of the Qur'an were driven by doctrinal considerations, including the fear that if treated as Qur'ans, the translations would become the basis of legal rulings.[47] The idea that these translations will break the indissoluble bond between form and content is related to this fear, but, as is evident from the discussion above, it is also clear that these translations challenge the principle of inimitability in relation to its doctrinal and language-centred meanings in a manner which would, at least indirectly, impinge on the synchronic and diachronic symbolic loadings of the language (as these have been explained above). If so, the discussion of (un)translatability is not merely a discussion about doctrine, but also an ideological one, in which the language-identity link is involved, even though this link may exist deep below the surface of the debate on (un) translatability and inimitability.

Jahiz: The Power of Taxonomy

Jahiz (d. 255/868–9) is one of the most influential thinkers of the third/ninth century, whose writing cuts across multiple fields of intellectual enquiry, to which, as may be expected from such a humanist and polymath, he made

45 Poonawala, 'Translatability of the Qur'an: theological and literary considerations', p. 187 [inserts in the original].

46 Ibid. p. 187.

47 An attempt to do this in Turkey was mooted by Mustafa Kemal Atatürk. As 'part of his bid to "nationalise" and "secularise" Islam in Turkey, intended to produce an "authoritative" Turkish translation of the Qur'an, he asked the famous Islamic Turkish poet Muhammad (Mehmet) Akif to expedite a translation which Akif had already begun on his own. But Akif, sensing the intent of Atatürk, fled to Egypt and abandoned his project'. See Rahman, 'Translating the Qur'an', p. 26.

seminal contributions. Jahiz was close, both in time and professional inclination, to the debates concerning inimitability,[48] (un)translatability and *shu'ūbiyya*, in which he took an active interest. Although he was not a grammarian or linguist in the technical sense, he nevertheless developed a unique communication theory, which treated language as a system of communication among other, albeit less complex, systems. As I will demonstrate, this theory is embedded within the socio-political context of the time, and it will make maximum sense only if it is related it to the language-identity link as it unfolds in the debate over inimitability and the inter-group strife represented by the *shu'ūbiyya* movement.

In constructing his communication theory,[49] Jahiz follows the established view, as we have seen above, that not all languages are equal and that Arabic is a 'cut above the rest', no doubt for many of the reasons mentioned earlier in this chapter. But Jahiz goes further than this and produces a new and unique argument for this position, basing it, at surface level, on what seems like an unproblematic dichotomy between those objects that are inherently unable to communicate via audible means (*ṣāmit*) and those that can (*nāṭiq*).[50] This dichotomy serves as the basis for two further dichotomies, in which the ultimate aim is to separate the Arabs from non-Arabs – the *'ajam*.[51] In accordance with this, the category of *nāṭiq* objects is divided into two sub-categories:

48 As a technical term, *i'jāz* was not in vogue at the time of Jahiz, but he took an active interest in the subject matter, writing an epistle (non-extant) on the topic.

49 The following communication theory and its ideological underpinnings are reconstructed from different parts of Jahiz's oeuvre of works.

50 I use the term 'object' here in its widest sense to refer to animate and inanimate objects, as well as to ostensible (real) and in-ostensible (potential or abstract) objects.

51 See Bernard Lewis, *The Political Language of Islam* (Chicago and London: University of Chicago Press, 1991), p. 118. Lewis gives the following explanation of this and related terms that denote non-Arabs, which I will quote here in full: 'Many terms are used to denote outsiders. Thus Arab is contrasted with *'Ajam*, which originally simply meant non-Arab and was then often specialised to mean the Persians, who were, so to speak, the non-Arabs par excellence on the horizon of ancient Arabia. In later Arabic usage, *'Ajam* is used almost exclusively in the sense of "Persian". In Turkish, by a development of the earlier usage, the adjectival form *'ajemī* (modern Turkish *acemi*) sometimes has the sense of "clumsy" or "inept". The classical Arabic term *'ilj*, plural *'ulūj*, with the meaning, among others, of "gross", "coarse," is sometimes contrasted with *'Arab*, and has the sense, more or less, of "barbarian". It does not necessarily have a religious connotation, as is shown by the fact that a Syrian Christian author like Ibn al-'Ibri uses it when speaking of the Franks. It has disappeared from modern usage [but see Suleiman 2003: 83, and the use of this term extensively by Muhammad Sa'id al-Sahhaf, Iraq's Information Minister under Saddam, in describing the Americans and their allies during the invasion of Iraq in 2003]. The Arabic term *Barbar* or *Barbarī*, akin to the Greek Barbaros, is normally limited to the pre-Arab inhabitants of North Africa and, in Egyptian usage, to the black people of the upper Nile. It is sometimes given to

faṣīḥ objects, of which man is the only example; and *a'jam* objects, to which, by implication, all other members of the animal kingdom that are capable of communication or articulation by oral or verbal means belong.[52]

Man, according to this distinction, is not just a verbalising animal (*ḥawayān nātiq*), as he is often described, but one that can do so intelligibly or with clarity[53] – a fact captured by the term *faṣīḥ*, which makes man, not other members of the animal kingdom within the *nāṭiq* category, the classificatory point of reference in Jahiz's scheme. According to this scheme, the status of being *faṣīḥ* is not tied to a specific language, but relates to all human languages. This implies that speakers of Arabic and other languages enjoy parity in respect to *intelligibility*, as the lowest point of being *faṣīḥ*, as do their languages, which must be accorded technical equality as systems of communication. However, by introducing into this classificatory schema the well-known distinction in Arab intellectual thought between *'arab* and *'ajam* and by defining the latter as those who do not speak Arabic or those whose speech the Arabs cannot understand, Jahiz constructs a parallelism with the earlier distinction between *faṣīḥ* and *a'jam*, which gives classificatory dominance to Arabic and its speakers over other languages and their speakers. We may express this parallelism in categorial terms by saying that *'arab* is to *faṣīḥ* as *'ajam* is to *a'jam*.[54] The following tree diagram reconstructs this set of distinctions:

other unfamiliar neighbours, e.g, the Mongol descended Hazāra in Afghanistan, but it does not carry a connotation of barbarism'.

52 This may be referenced by what Jāḥiẓ says about the language of birds: 'Birds have a language which allows them to understand what they have to say to each other; they do not need a more highly developed tongue, and would have no use for it . . . If someone should say that is not a language, we would reply: The [Qur'an] itself said that it was a language; poetry likewise regards it as a language, and so the Arabs when they discuss it . . . [Languages] are articulated sounds produced by the mouth and tongue: hence are not the sounds uttered by the various kinds of wild and domestic birds also a language and a means of expression, given that . . . they are distinctly articulated and methodically arranged, are produced by the mouth and tongue, and allow these animals to understand one another?' See Pellat, *The Life and Works of Jāḥiẓ: Translations of Selected Texts*, pp. 180–1.

53 The difference between 'intelligibility' and 'clarity' will become clear below. However, it is important to signal here that Jahiz is not totally consistent across his complete oeuvre, as regards this distinction. For this reason, the distinction is offered here with a cautionary note of tentativeness, although, as we shall see later, it continues to hold water in some important ways.

54 The following quotation sets out the distinction between *'a'jam, faṣīḥ, 'ajam and 'arab* in Jāḥiẓ: *wa-insān faṣīḥ wa-law 'abbar 'an nafishi bi-l-fārisiyya aw bi-l-hindiyya aw bi-l-rūmiyya; wa laysa al-'arabiyy aswa' fahman li-ṭamṭamat al-rūmī [min al-rūmī] li-bayān al-lisān al-'arabī. fa-kull insān min hādhā al-wajh faṣīḥ, fa-idhā qālū: faṣīḥ wa 'a'jam, fa-hādhā huwa al-ta'wīl fi qawlihim a'jam; wa idhā qālū: al-'arab wa-l-'ajam wa lam yalfuẓū bi-faṣīḥ wa a'jam, fa-laysa hādhā al-ma'nā yurīdūn, innamā ya'nūn annahu lā yatakallam bi-l-'arabiyya, wa anna al-'arab lā tafham 'anh'*. See Abū 'Uthmān 'Amr Ibn Baḥr al-Jāḥiẓ,

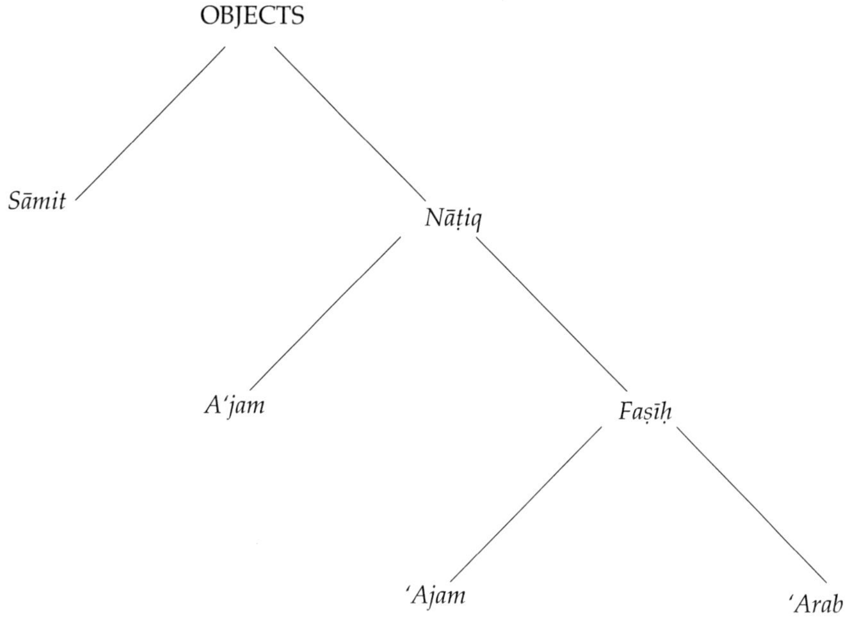

The parallelism mentioned above is signalled in three ways to imply identification and differentiation. The first, implying similarity, is articulated through the obvious lexical relatedness of the two terms *a'jam* and *'ajam* in the above set of dichotomies (through the root *'-j-m*), which constructs the former, *a'jam*, as the superlative form of the latter, *'ajam*, both morphologically and in symbolic or metaphorical terms. A similar relationship between Arab and *a'jam* does not exist. The second, implying difference, is articulated through using the term *bayān* (clarity) to describe the status of being *faṣīḥ*, in the case of the Arabs, and, on certain occasions, the term *ṭamṭama* (intelligibility),[55] when the term *faṣīḥ* is applied to non-Arabs.[56] Third, by establishing 'Arab' as the reference category, in terms of which being *'ajam* is defined as the Other, the Arabs and their language acquire a degree of definitional givenness or metaphorical naturalness that is not available, if not actually denied, to other languages and their speakers. Jahiz tells us that this difference between Arabs and non-Arabs is signalled discursively in the Qur'an, in that when God addresses the Arabs and the Bedouins (*al-'arab wa-l-a'rāb*), He does so with brevity or concision to mark their difference as

al-Ḥayawān (6 Vols), 'Abd al-Salām Hārūn (ed.) (Cairo: Maktabat Muṣṭafā al-Bābī al-Ḥalabī wa-Awlāduh, 1945), pp. i, 32.

55 See Lane, *Arabic–English Lexicon*, Part 5. Part 5 glosses *ṭamṭama* as a 'barbarousness, or vitiuosness, or an impotence, or impediment, in speech, or utterance, so that the speech is not clear, or correct', hence the use of the term 'intelligibility' here.

56 See preceding footnote.

the in-group, as opposed to the Jews, with whom, as the out-group, He uses an elaborate style.[57] It is as though by adopting this communication strategy with the Jews, God is addressing them with the linguistic redundancy that is necessary, so as to compensate for impaired intelligibility on their part, as is the case in ordinary discourse, when one suspects that the interlocutor, for whatever reason, is unable to track the flow of a conversation with ease.

Building on this chain of arguments, it is possible to reconstruct the binary distinctions within the categories of *nātiq* and *faṣīḥ* into a three-point hierarchical classification involving *a'jam*, *'ajam* and Arab. Although the difference between *a'jam*, on the one hand, and both *'ajam* and Arab, on the other, is one of kind (adopting a strategy of differentiation), and although the difference between *'ajam* and Arab is one of degree (adopting a strategy of distanciation) – since both are human and therefore *faṣīḥ* – nevertheless, this way of ranging these objects on a continuum puts *'ajam* in an intermediate position between *a'jam* and Arab in a way that compromises their status as (fully) *faṣīḥ* objects; hence the distinction between 'intelligibility' and 'clarity' in glossing *faṣīḥ* (above) in referring to these two groups.

Categorisation is as much about inclusion as it is about exclusion, since the one cannot exist without the other, whether explicitly or implicitly. Put differently, categorisation, as a form of taxonomy, is ultimately designed to separate groups from each other by reference to some criterion or set of criteria. These criteria may be empirically validated or ideologically constructed, although construction may not be totally absent from the former. Jahiz's taxonomy incorporates both criteria: the difference between *ṣāmit* and *nāṭiq* objects belongs to the empirical world, while that between *'ajam* and Arab is a matter of ideological construction, whose meaning emerges from the socio-political context that frames it, as will become clear. By using language to construct his taxonomic schema in the human domain so early on in his multi-volume book *al-Ḥayawān* (*The Animals*) and by differentiating between the *'ajam* and the Arabs on grounds of communicative intelligibility and clarity respectively, rather than genealogical stock or ethnicity, Jahiz underlines the ability of language to serve as an affiliative bond or marker of group identity.

Furthermore, categorisation, when subject to ideological construction or manipulation, is often deployed to establish differentiation in status

[57] Jāḥiẓ, *al-Ḥayawān*, Part I, p. 94. It is tempting to relate this to Jahiz's preference for concision over prolixity in language as a mark of eloquence, although this preference is circumscribed contextually (see Pellat, *The Life and Works of Jāḥiẓ: Translations of Selected Texts*, p. 112): 'Most often conciseness is admirable and prolixity reprehensible, but sometimes it is the other way round: in the wise man both can be justified, for the choice of the modes of expression depends on the circumstances . . . Economy of words serves for lightening one's speech, prolixity for making oneself understood, repetition for conveying insistence and multiplicity of words for laying stress'. The reference to the speech of the wise man is in conformity with the principle of *muṭābaqa*, which will be dealt with below.

allocation within a community. This is clear from the application of the terms *bayān* (clarity) and *ṭamṭama* (intelligibility) to allocate different degrees of *faṣāḥa* to the Arabs and *'ajam* respectively. In this respect, Jahiz concurs with the well-known Greek tradition, in which those who did not speak Greek were allocated lower status as 'barbarians'. In addition, he seems to conform to a general ideological tendency in group identity construction, whereby one's own group and its cultural products are considered to be more worthy of respect than other groups and their associated cultural products, especially in situations of conflict. Sarup's description of dichotomies, although a little exaggerated, applies in some important respects to Jahiz's taxonomy:

> All visions of artificial order . . . are by necessity inherently asymmetrical and thereby dichotomising. In dichotomies, the second term is but the other of the first, the opposite (degraded, exiled, suppressed) side of the first and its creation. Dichotomies are exercises in power . . . They split the human world into a group for whom the ideal order is to be erected, and another which is for the unfitting . . . and the ambivalent.[58]

Jahiz's scheme consists of three dichotomies and, since the further down on the tree diagram that we move, the greater the artificiality of the dichotomies involved, we must conclude that this figure embodies asymmetrical status allocation, which is intimately related to the inter-group strife between the Arabs and non-Arabs, especially the Persians as the archetypal non-Arabs at the time of Jahiz.

Jahiz and Taxonomy: Further Elaboration

An important aspect of Jahiz's theory of communication revolves around the view that the very existence of the universe and everything within it signifies *ḥikma* (lit. wisdom, knowledge, proof or evidence), in the same way that the Arabic language itself, and Arabic grammar by extension, are said to point to the wisdom of the Arabs (*ḥikamat al-'arab*).[59] The term *ḥikma*, which is used semi-terminologically by Jahiz, is difficult to define; it is, however, safe to assume that it denotes something like 'semantic import' or 'meaning', but only if meaning is used in a very wide sense to refer to a world of infinite messages, which may be encoded, transmitted and decoded through the semiological systems of communication that Jahiz recognises, as I will explain in greater depth.[60]

[58] Madan Sarup, *Identity, Culture and the Postmodern World* (Edinburgh: Edinburgh University Press, 1996), p. 9.

[59] For the notion of the wisdom of the Arabs (*ḥikmat al-'arab*), see Yasir Suleiman, *The Arabic Grammatical Tradition: A Study in Ta'līl* (Edinburgh: Edinburgh University Press, 1999).

[60] Broadly speaking, semiology refers to systems of communication with fixed or semi-fixed conventions that bind the signifier to the signified in a mutual duality.

Jahiz adopts a semiological perspective in dealing with what he calls the means or channels of communication or signification (*wasā'il al-bayān*).[61] In discussing these channels, he starts with perspective that the universe in its totality is the primary signifying object (*al-'ālam al-kabīr*),[62] which, among other things, offers evidence of God's existence and provides proof of His wisdom though His creation; hence the use of the term *ḥikma* by Jahiz. Jahiz makes his position on the status of the universe as the primary signifying object clear when he describes inarticulate objects (*al-ajsām al-khurs al-ṣāmita*) as articulate, with respect to signification (*nāṭiqa min jihat al-dalāla*), and enunciating, with respect to their ability to testify to the existence of a quality, a state of affairs or, most importantly, the existence and infinite wisdom of the Creator (*wa-mu'riba min jihat ṣiḥḥat al-shahāda*), in the same away as being weak or off-colour are taken to signify ill health (*kamā khabbar al-huzāl wa kusūf al-lawn 'an sū' al-ḥāl*) or their opposite pointing to well-being. However, signification in this context is not a matter of fixed or even semi-fixed convention, but one of personal inference in the social world or in the domain of doctrinal belief. This explains the reluctance on the part of Jahiz to treat the universe as a fully-fledged semiological system in *al-Ḥayawān*, although he seems to modulate this position in his *Kitāb al-Byān wa-l-tabyīn* (*The Book of Eloquence and Exposition*) by appending the universe, calling it *niṣba* and *ḥāl*,[63] to the four semiological systems proper: spoken language (*lafẓ*), writing/written language (*khaṭṭ*), calculation/counting (*'aqd*) and body language/gestures (*ishāra*).[64]

This view of *niṣba* (universe) as a boundless source of information,[65] which can be excavated, mined and articulated using the four semiological systems mentioned above, reflects its status as the substance from which meanings

Language is the semiological system par excellence, but it is not the only one. The language of the bees is another semiological system, as are traffic lights and traffic signs in the modern world, in which, I am sure, Jahiz the semiologist would have been interested, if he had lived in modern times. While the conventions characterising these systems, whether natural or manmade, are fixed, those characterising name-giving, for example, are semi-fixed; this is clear from the fact that proper nouns denoting humans can be used to denote animals or other objects – a practice which a system of fixed conventions would militate against.

61 See Jāḥiẓ, *al-Ḥayawān*, Part I, p. 33.

62 Ibid. Part I, pp. 212–15.

63 See Lane, *Arabic–English Lexicon*, Part 6. Part 6 gives the meaning of *niṣba* as: 'a pole, or mast . . . set up to show the way'. The plural, *anāṣib*, is glossed as 'signs, or marks, or stones, set up to show the way'.

64 See Jāḥiẓ, *al-Ḥayawān*, Part I, p. 34. See also Pellat, *The Life and Works of Jāḥiẓ: Translations of Selected Texts*, pp. 102–3.

65 Jāḥiẓ expresses the idea of being boundless as follows: *al-ma'ānī mabsūṭa ilā ghayr ghāya wa-mumtadda ilā ghayr nihāya* (meanings are limitless and infinite). See Abū 'Uthmān 'Amr Ibn Baḥr al-Jāḥiz, *Kitāb al-Bayān wa-l-tabyīn (3 Vols)*, Ḥasan al-Sandūbī (ed.) (Cairo: no publisher, 1932), Part I, 1, 78.

could be culled, rather than as the means for expressing meanings on its own. As Jahiz says: 'if we ask the earth who made the rivers run in their appointed courses, and caused the trees to grow and the fruits to ripen, it will provide us with answers, albeit implicitly not explicitly'.[66] The difference between 'substance' and 'means' is reflected in Jahiz's use of the term *khaṣla* (lit. state or condition), rather than *wasīla* (means, channel), to describe *niṣba* in *al-Ḥayawān*.[67] This difference makes *niṣba* ancillary to the four semiological systems, which act on it to cull and fashion meaning.[68] In some cases, meaning-making is causally determined, as in the occurrence of lightning and thunder, which are governed by the laws of nature. In other cases, meaning is determined by conventional correlation, not causality, as in the setting of the sun and the breaking of the fast in the month of Ramadan. But there are also a myriad of other cases in *niṣba*, where meaning-making is the subject of personal inference, which may not enjoy inter-subjective validity, either by reference to causality or established convention. We may sum up Jahiz's view on *niṣba* by saying that the universe can speak to us,[69] but we are the ones who can make it speak by asking questions of it (as he says in the quotation above) and putting words into its mouth, so to speak, mainly to testify to the Wisdom of the Creator in His infinity, thus turning the universe into a sign (*āya*) that provides proof (*burhān*) of this wisdom;[70] hence Jahiz's discussion of members of the animal kingdom, among other things, in his book *al-Hayawān*.[71]

[66] See Jāḥiẓ, *Kitāb al-Bayān wa-l-tabyīn*, Part I, p. 247: *sal al-arḍ fa-qul, man shaqqa anhāraki wa-gharasa ashjāraki wa-janā thimāraki? fa-in lam tujibka ḥiwāran, ajābtka i'tibāran.*

[67] See Jāḥiẓ, *al-Ḥayawān*, Part I, p. 45.

[68] This ancillary status is implicit in Jāḥiẓ's (*al-Ḥayawān*, Part I, p. 45) statement that *niṣba*: 'falls short of matching the four semiological systems in all their potentialities' (*naqaṣat 'an bulūgh hādhihi al-arba'a fi jihātihā*).

[69] See Jāḥiẓ, *Kitāb al-Bayān wa-l-tabyīn*, pp. 1, 81. *Niṣba* is that: 'state of affairs which speaks without articulation and gestures without using the hand' (*wa ammā al-niṣba fa-hiya al-ḥāl al-nāṭiqa bi-ghayr al-lafẓ wa-l-mushīra bi-ghayr al-yad*).

[70] Jāḥiẓ characterises *niṣba* as follows: 'It is the situation that speaks for itself without the need for words, and is manifest without the necessity for a gesture of the hand. It is everything that is to be seen in the heavens, on earth and in the whole of nature, whether dumb or endowed with speech, animate or inanimate, moving or still. The utterances of an inert object can be as eloquent as the cries of an animal. The dumb man speaks to declare [the existence of God], and the tongue-tied to give the proof of it'. See Pellat, *The Life and Works of Jāḥiẓ: Translations of Selected Texts*, p. 103.

[71] Jāḥiẓ (*al-Ḥayawān*, Part II, p. 109) tells us that his interest, in all aspects of the dog, is intended to signify the capacity of this animal to signal *ḥikma*-bound meanings. In view of the emphasis that Jahiz lays on this aspect of *niṣba* and its intention in the celestial scheme of things, I will quote at length what he says about animals (see Pellat, *The Life and Works of Jāḥiẓ: Translations of Selected Texts*, pp. 141–2): 'It is not the intrinsic worth of the dog and the cock, their price, their looks or the place they occupy in the hearts of the common people that led us to write this dissertation

Jahiz develops his views on *niṣba* by claiming that the universe is divided into objects that can transmit wisdom (*ḥikma*), but do so unknowingly and unintentionally, and those that can transmit wisdom knowingly and intentionally. In absolute terms, therefore, all objects, regardless of the category to which they belong, are *ḥikma*-bearing objects, the difference between them being one of agency: some bear wisdom and others, while bearing wisdom, are capable of transmitting it. Jahiz assigns all animals and inanimate objects to the first category, reserving the second category to humans, who, alone, are capable of generating and processing meaning knowingly and intentionally.

This new dichotomy intersects with the preceding set of dichotomies by collapsing *a'jam* and *ṣāmit* together in a new category, which we may, metaphorically speaking, call *nāṭiq*, in opposition to the category of *faṣīḥ* that accrues to man as the signifying agent par excellence. Jahiz conceptualises man's ability to make meaning as an instrument, which he calls as *bayān*:[72] 'The word *bayān* comprises anything that reveals the sense and brings out the inner meaning, so that the hearer may grasp the reality of it'.[73] In applying this instrument, man employs the semiological systems of spoken language, writing, calculation or counting and body language or gestures to external-

and give it pride of place in our book [*al-Ḥayawān*]. We are not concerned with their price in gold or silver, nor with their value in the eyes of men; rather [we] are thinking about the proofs of His existence that God put into these creatures, the perfection of His art, His wondrous dispositions and His subtle wisdom, the amazing understanding He instilled into them, the mysteries He implanted in them and the tremendous advantages He bestowed upon them, thus demonstrating that He who made all these dispositions for them and vouchsafed them this wisdom wishes us to think on these two creatures and take them for an object lesson and a reason for praising God. He covered the outside of their bodies with His testimony and filled the inside with wisdom, and made us to think and learn the lesson, so that every man endowed with reason may know that God did not create His creation to no purpose, and did not abandon His creatures to their fate; that he overlooked nothing, left nothing without its distinctive mark, nothing in disorder or unprotected; that He makes no mistakes in His wondrous farsightedness and no detail of His disposition fails him, nor yet the beauty of the wisdom and the glory of the powerful proof. All that activity extends to everything from the louse and the butterfly to the seven celestial spheres and the seven climates of the globe'.

72 In this connection, Jāḥiẓ says (*Kitāb al-Bayān wa-l-tabyīn*, Part I, p. 33): *wa-wajadnā kawn al-'ālam bi-mā fīh ḥikma, wa-wajadnā al-ḥikma 'alā ḍarbayn: shay' ju'ila ḥikma wa-huwa lā ya'qil al-ḥikma, wa-lā 'āqibat al-ḥikma, wa shay' ju'ila ḥikma, wa-huwa ya'qil al-ḥikma wa-'āqibat al-ḥikma. Fa-stawā bi-dhāka al-shay' al-'āqil wa ghyar al-'āqil fī jihat al-dalāla 'alā annahu ḥikma; wa-ikhtalafā min jihat anna aḥadahumā dalīl lā yastadill, wa-l-ākhar dalīl yastadill, fa-kullu mustadill dalīl wa-laysa kull dalīl mustadill, fa-shārak kull ḥayawān siwā al-insān jamī' al-jamād fī al-dalāla, wa-fī 'adam al-istidlāl, wa-ijtam' al-insān an kāna dalīlan mustadillan. thumma ju'ila al-mustadill sababan yudall bihi 'alā wujuh istidlālih, wa-wujūh mā nataja lahu al-istidlāl, wa sammū dhālika bayānan.*

73 See Pellat, *The Life and Works of Jāḥiẓ: Translations of Selected Texts*, p. 102.

ise what would otherwise remain dormant. In his *Kitāb al-Bayān wa-l-tabyīn*, Jahiz describes meanings in a series of adjectival couplets, which will be reproduced here in order to convey the flavour of his views on this issue: 'meanings are covert and hidden, remote and untamed, veiled and concealed [and] existent but masquerading as non-existent'.[74] *Bayān* he describes as the instrument which man deploys to 'make what is invisible visible, to render what is absent present and to make what is remote near'.[75] In this sense, *bayān* is a designation for any means that man, as agent, uses to 'unmask meaning and make it available to the receiver'.[76]

Jahiz believes that *bayān* is a necessary attribute of man and a sine qua non of human society. Without *bayān*, human society cannot exist, nor could human beings generate and transmit knowledge (*'ilm*). Jahiz likens *bayān* to vision (*baṣar*) and ignorance (*jahl*) to blindness (*'amā*): without *bayān*, man cannot see, as if he was living in continuous darkness; Jahiz then equates ignorance, as the absence of *bayān*, with *'iyy* / *'ayy* (speech defect or impediment), to signal the importance of language as the primary means of making meaning. Jahiz further describes *bayān* as the translator of knowledge (*turjumān al-'ilm*), its sustainer (*ḥayāt al-'ilm*), and as the pillar which holds knowledge together (*'imād al-'ilm*).[77] This interpretation of *bayān* has far-reaching implications for our understanding of the Arab intellectual tradition, but I will leave these out of consideration in this book.

Jahiz: Two Semiologies, Gestures and Language

There are four semiological systems which make up Jahiz's communication theory: *khaṭṭ* (writing, script), *'aqd* (counting, calculation), *ishāra* (gesture, body language) and *lafẓ* (speech, spoken language). Of these systems, gestures and spoken language are the most relevant to the topic of this chapter, in particular, with reference to *shu'ūbiyya*. I will therefore restrict the present discussion to these two systems. However, it is important in any discussion of Jahiz's views on human communication not to discount the other two systems, as they show the sophistication of Jahiz's thinking on the subject.[78]

74 See Jahiz, *Kitāb al-Bayān wa-l-tabyīn*, pp. 1, 77: *[wa-l-ma'ānī] maṭrūḥa khafiyya, wa ba'īda waḥshiyya, wa maḥjūba maknūna, wa mawjūda fī ma'nā ma'dūma*.

75 Ibid. pp. 1, 77: *[al-bayān] yaj'al al-khafiyy [min al-ma'ānī] ẓāhiran wa-l-ghā'ib shāhidan wa-l-ba'īd qarīban*.

76 Ibid. pp. 1, 77: *wa-l-bayān ism jāmi' li-kull shay' kashafa laka qinā' al-ma'nā . . . ḥattā yufḍī al-sāmi' ilā ḥaqīqatih*.

77 Ibid. Part I, pp. 78–9.

78 For a discussion of these two systems, see Yasir Suleiman, '*Bayān* as a principle of taxonomy: linguistic elements in Jāḥiẓ's thinking', in John F. Healey and Venetia Porter (eds), *Studies on Arabia in Honour of Professor G. Rex Smith: Journal of Semitic Studies Supplement*, 14: 273–95.

Jahiz characterises *ishāra* as follows. First, *ishāra* accompanies spoken language and is used to modulate the meanings conveyed by spoken utterances; he signals this by describing *ishāra* as an aid (*'awn*) to spoken language:[79]

> Speech and gestures are partners, and what a precious helpmate and interpreter gesture is to speech! It often takes its place, or makes writing unnecessary . . . The wink, the movement of the eyebrows and other gestures are priceless adjuncts, and a great help in expressing surreptitious thoughts.[80]

Second, *ishāra* may signify on its own, independently of spoken language, hence the reference to it as the translator (*turjumān*) of this language.[81] Third, *ishāra* is visually mediated, unlike speech, which is mediated through the auditory channel.[82] Fourth – and this is the crucial point, from the perspective of this chapter – *ishāra* may be delivered: (a) through body parts, such as the hands, head, eyes, eyebrows and shoulders; and (b) by other means, as extensions of the body parts – for example, the sword or the staff.

The second category of *ishāra* enables Jahiz to rebut the *shu'ūbī* (anti-Arab) attack that the Arabs cannot be considered masters of *bayān*, because of their use of the *'aṣā* (stick or staff) as an aid in oratory. The basis for this attack, it seems, is the lack of affinity between the *'aṣā*,[83] as an extraneous prop, and spoken language in a way that contravenes the principle of appropriateness (*muṭābaqa*),[84] as will be explained further below. In rebutting this claim, Jahiz points to the privileged place of the *'aṣā* in doctrinal terms, through its association with Moses and Muhammad and by highlighting its utility in real-life situations.[85] What most concerns us here is the view that, as used by the Arabs, the *'aṣā* acts as an extension of the hand and, therefore, belongs to *ishāra* semiologically. Thus the *'aṣā* can be used to signify a variety of meanings, including power, authority or the readiness of the speaker to commence

[79] Jāḥiẓ, *Kitāb al-Bayān wa-l-tabyīn*, Part I, p. 79.

[80] See Pellat, *The Life and Works of Jāḥiẓ: Translations of Selected Texts*, p. 103.

[81] Ibid. p. 103.

[82] Jāḥiẓ, *al-Ḥayawān*, Part I, p. 45. Jahiz expresses this as follows: *al-lafẓ li-l-sāmi' wa-l-ishāra li-l-nāẓir*.

[83] Jāḥiẓ expresses this charge as follows: 'The staff is used for beating rhythm, spears for fighting, sticks for attack, bows for shooting, but there is no relation between speaking and the staff, and none between an address and a bow [on which they lean when delivering an address]. As if such things existed only in order to divert men's minds from the contents of speech'. See Goldziher, *Muslim Studies* (Vol. I), p. 156.

[84] See Jāḥiẓ, *Kitāb al-Bayān wa-l-tabyīn*, Part III, pp. 10–88. In particular, see the expression *wa-laysa bayn al-kalām wa-bayn al-'aṣā sababan* (p. 10).

[85] See Pellat (*The Life and Works of Jāḥiẓ: Translations of Selected Texts*, pp. 106–8) on the story of the Taghlibī lad and his stick, in which Jahiz extols the utility of the stick as an instrument in administering man's affairs.

speaking in formal situations.[86] This understanding of the use of the *'aṣā* is intended to render the *shu'ūbī* attack against the Arabs not just invalid, but also the result of ignorance in regards to how communication works in society.

Let us now turn to spoken language (*lafẓ*). From my perspective, the most important aspect of spoken language as a semiological system is the principle of *muṭābaqa*, expressed by Jahiz in the maxim *muṭābaqat al-kalām li-muqtaḍā al-ḥāl* (the appropriateness of speech or discourse to its context). Applying to all levels of language, *muṭābaqa* rests on the fundamental requirement that an utterance be appropriate to the hearer and the situational context at both the level of expression and content. This implies that different hearers and situational contexts require different forms of address or different kinds of utterance.[87] In pragmatic and sociolinguistic terms, *muṭābaqa* demands that the speaker adjust his speech to suit, among other things, the educational level of the interlocutors, their social backgrounds[88] and the prerogatives of the social context in which a speech act takes place. Thus, a speaker must avoid the use of subject-specific technical terminology with ordinary people and in ordinary everyday situations; conversely, the use of such terminology is a must in communicating with fellow specialists in scientific discourse.[89] The principle of *muṭābaqa* further requires that the speaker avoids the use of obscure or coarse language, unless the topic or situation demands it.[90] Brevity (*ījāz*) or elaboration / prolixity (*ishāb/iṭnāb*) in speech must also conform to the demands of *muṭābaqa*, with brevity acting as the norm in neutral situations: 'The peoples of the world, both Arabs and non-Arabs, admire economy of words, and dislike verbosity, prolixity and undue repetition'.[91] In some cases, silence (*ṣamt* or *sukūt*) may be used as a means of conveying messages in response to the demands imposed by *muṭābaqa*, although silence is a deviation from the norm in *lafẓ* as spoken language.[92] In these and similar

86 See Jāḥiẓ, *Kitāb al-Bayān wa-l-tabyīn*, Part III, pp. 78–9.

87 Jāḥiẓ (Ibid. Part I, pp. 128–9) expresses this as follows: *yanbaghī li-l-mutakallim an ya'rifa aqdār al-ma'ānī wa-yuwāzin baynahā wa-bayna aqdār al-mustami'īn wa-bayna aqdār al-ḥālāt, fa-yaj'al li-kull ṭabaqa min dhālik kalāman, wa-li-kull ḥāla min dhālik maqāman, ḥattā yaqsim aqdār al-kalām 'alā aqdār al-ma'ānī, wa yaqsim aqdār al-ma'ānī 'alā aqdār al-maqāmāt, wa-aqdār al-mustami'īn 'alā aqdār tilka al-ḥālāt.*

88 Jāḥiẓ (Ibid. Part I, p. 133) expresses this point as follows: *wa-kalām al-nās fī ṭabaqāṭ, kamā anna al-nāsa anfusuhum fī ṭabaqāt.*

89 Ibid. Part I, p. 129.

90 Ibid. Part I, pp. 132–3.

91 See Pellat, *The Life and Works of Jāḥiẓ: Translations of Selected Texts*, pp. 111–12.

92 See Jāḥiẓ, *Kitāb al-Bayān wa-l-tabyīn*, Part I, p. 223. Jahiz describes the superiority of speech to silence as follows: 'Talking shows itself to be superior to silence . . . Evidence of the superiority of speech to silence is to be found in the fact that speech makes it possible to expound the virtues of silence, whereas silence does not allow the exposition of the virtues of speech. Were silence superior, the Prophet's mission would have been dumb and the nonexistence of the Qur'an would have been better

examples, the ultimate aim of *muṭābaqa* is to ensure that both the speaker and the hearer cooperate, in order to make communication successful. Jahiz expresses this cooperative principle, to use a Gricean term,[93] by saying that the: 'hearer should not be undermined by the speaker nor should the speaker be undermined by the hearer'.[94]

An interesting application of *muṭabaqa* concerns whether or not to use correct Arabic when recording the speech of others, particularly in literary works. According to Jahiz, the speech of the Bedouins (*kalām al-'a'rāb*) should always be recorded with desinintial inflections (*i'rāb*) to reflect the way that they speak, but that these inflections should not be used to record the speech of those who do not use them.[95] The elision of inflections in the one case or their addition in the other would lead to the distortion of the sociolinguistic meaning of a spoken utterance.[96] This explains why, in his book *Bukhalā'* (*The Misers*), Jahiz incorporated linguistic materials that deviated from the norms of the Arabic language:

> If, in this book, you come across any solecism, or speech wanting in grammatical inflection, or an expression misapplied from its proper sense, you should know that I have left it [in] because grammatical inflection makes this kind of (of story-telling) obnoxious and removes it from its own sphere.[97]

that its existence'. See Pellat, *The Life and Works of Jāḥiẓ: Translations of Selected Texts*, p. 230.

93 See Herbert Paul Grice, 'Logic and conversation', in Peter Cole and Jerry L. Morgan (eds), *Syntax and Semantic 3: Speech Acts*, 41–58 (New York, NY: Academic Press, 1975).

94 This is what Jāḥiẓ Part I, p. 86 says: *yakfi min ḥaẓẓ al-balāgha an lā yu'tā al-sāmi' min sū' fahm al-nāṭiq, wa lā yu'tā al-nātiq min sū' fahm al-sāmi'*.

95 Jāḥiẓ states (Ibid. p 105): 'When you hear a story told in Bedouin dialect, take care only to repeat it with the case-endings and the original pronunciation. If you alter it and get the ending wrong, or use the pronunciation of mongrel Arabs or townsmen, you will spoil the whole flavour of the anecdote and miss the point altogether. Likewise if you hear a plebeian joke or a low class witticism, beware of putting in the final vowels or telling it in correct language or refined accents, for that would spoil the whole point of it, destroy the effect and rob it of spice and flavour'.

96 See Hādī Nahr, *al-Lisāniyyāt al-ijtimā'iyya 'ind al-'arab* (Irbid: 'Ālam al-Kutub al-Ḥadīth, 1998), for a general discussion of sociolinguistic aspects of the Arabic linguistic tradition. See also Muḥammad 'Uways, *al-Mujtama' al-'abbāsī min khilāl kitābāt al-Jāḥiẓ* (Cairo: Dār al-Thaqāfa li-l-Ṭibā'a wa-l-Nashr, 1977), pp. 203–69.

97 See Abū 'Uthmān 'Amr Ibn Baḥr Jahiz, *al-Bukhalā'*, Aḥmad al-'Awāmirī and 'Alī al-Jārim (eds), trans. R. B. Sergeant (Beirut: Dār al-Kutub al-'Ilmiyya, 1983), Part I, p. 78. This extract is taken from R. B. Serjeant's 1997 translation of *al-Bukhalā'* (p. 32). I have replaced the word 'out' in this translation by 'in', noted in square brackets, because this gives a better rendering of the meaning of the original.

Jahiz's interest in *muṭābaqa* is an integral part of his interest in *bayān* and its social meanings. This interest spans speech defects (*'uyūb al-kalām*) as impediments, which compromise a person's ability to display *bayān* at its best. Speech defects cover three major categories: (a) *laḥn*, corrupt speech or solecism; (b) *al-lakna*, mother tongue interference; and (c) speech impairments arising out of physical defects in articulation.[98] *Laḥn* is invariably attributed to inter-group mixing between Arabs and non-Arabs in the new Islamic empire, including inter-marriages between Arab males and non-Arab females, which were responsible for producing a group of people called the *muwalladūn* in Muslim society. So widespread was *laḥn*, that it affected the speech of people from different backgrounds and strata in society, including members of the elite class and the Arab aristocracy. *Kitāb al-Bayān wa-l-tabyīn*, one of Jahiz's most important sources on the subject, is full of references relating to this phenomenon. Mother tongue interference, *lakna*, was also rife in the speech of new converts to Islam.[99] *Lakna* has a negative effect on a person's *bayān*, as do impairments in spoken language, including *'iyy*/*'ayy* (inability to articulate or express oneself clearly), *ḥaṣar* (stammer or stutter) and *lathgha*/*luthgha* (defective pronunciation) affecting the sounds *[sh]*, *[s]*, *[q]*, *[l]* and *[r]* in Arabic.[100]

Jahiz: The Language-Identity Link

Meaning is at the very heart of Jahiz's conception of the universe as *niṣba*. And human language, more than any other semiological system, is the instrument of meaning-making par excellence. Despite the fact that it is not easy to capture all the intricacies of Jahiz's thinking on human communication or his meandering understanding of *bayān*, it is still possible to conclude that Jahiz uses this web of ideas to put forward a hierarchical taxonomy of objects and beings, in which the Arabs stand at its apex; this is why I have dwelt on this

98 For impairments in the Arabic linguistic tradition, see Muḥammad Kashshāsh, *'Ilal al-lisān wa-amrāḍ al-lugha* (Sidon and Beirut: al-Maktab al-'Aṣriyya li-l-Ṭibā'a wa-l-Nashr, 1998); Ya'qūb al-Kindi, 'Risālat ya'qūb al-kindī fī al-lugha', *Majallat majma' al-lugha al-'arabiyya bi-dimashq* (1985), 60: 515–22; Rashīd 'Abd al-Raḥmān al-'Ubaydi, 'Uyūb al-lisān wa-l-lahajāt al-madhmūma', *Majallat al-majma' al-'ilmī al-'Irāqī* (1985), 36: 236–300.

99 Jāḥiẓ gives many examples of *lakna* in his work (see Pellat, *The Life and Works of Jāḥiẓ: Translations of Selected Texts*, p. 101): 'The yokel brought up in the Sawād of Kūfa [in Iraq] speaks standard Arabic, his vocabulary is stylish and well chosen and his ideas are lofty and noble; yet by his speech and pronunciation he is recognisably Nabataean. Similarly with the Khurāsānī: despite all the care he takes over syntax and style, it is obvious from his accent that he is a Khurāsānī. The same is true of the chancery secretaries from Ahwaz'.

100 See Jāḥiẓ, *Kitāb al-Bayān wa-l-tabyīn*, Part I, pp. 44–6. Jahiz uses different terms to designate different types of stammer, but these will not concern us here; see also al-Kindī, *Risālat ya'qūb al-kindī fī al-lugha*.

theory at some length. Below them are the *'ajam*, non-Arab members of the human race, then other members of the animal kingdom (*a'ājim*) and, lastly, mute objects (*ṣāmit*), although, as part of *niṣba*, these objects enunciate silent meanings that testify to God's wisdom through His creation. Man is at the centre of this cosmology, and the Arabs are at its very core. Jahiz points out that each nation has its own characteristics in which it excels, and, accordingly, Arabs have pride of place in a logocentric universe by dint of their pristine linguistic intuitions – compromised by the occurrence of language contact – and their ability to excel in the linguistic arts, such as poetry and oratory. Applying what may be called environmental determinism, Jahiz argues that these qualities of the Arabs are linked to their living conditions. This is how he argues this point:

> [The Arabs] dwelt in the plains, and grew up in contemplation of the desert. They knew neither damp nor rising mist, neither fog nor foul air, nor a horizon bounded by walls. When these keen minds and clear brains turned to poetry, fine language, eloquence and oratory, to physiognomy and astrology, genealogy, navigation by the stars and by marks on the ground . . . to horse-breeding, weaponry and engines of war, to memorizing all that they heard, pondering on everything that caught their attention and discrimination between the glories and the shames of their tribes, they achieved perfection beyond the wildest dreams. Certain of these activities broadened their minds and exalted their aspirations, so that of all the nations they are now the most glorious and the most given to recalling their past splendours.[101]

Under Jahiz's expanded meaning of meaning, the reference to 'physiognomy and astrology, genealogy, navigation by the stars and by marks on the ground' is an allusion to the semanticity of these objects. In other words, while at first glance the reference to these objects may seem to be a deviation from semantics, a closer look reveals that semanticity is maintained extra-linguistically, since each one of these items is the carrier of meaning, whether they are socially constructed or empirically concocted. However, the main concern of the above extract is to point out that the Arabs' pristine linguistic intuitions and their excellence in poetry, eloquence and oratory are a reflection of their uncluttered lifestyle and the open horizons of their physical environment.

Jahiz also tells us that while all nations exhibit *bayān*, among the Arabs, *bayān* as performance is the result of intuition, natural disposition and the enunciation of something akin to revelation.[102] By comparison, among the Persians, the quintessential *'ajam*, *bayān* is said to be contrived, artificial and the result of deliberate study. For these reasons, the common people among the Arabs (*'awāmm*) are said to vie with the elite (*khawāṣṣ*) among other

[101] Pellat, *The Life and Works of Jāḥiẓ: Translations of Selected Texts*, pp. 96–7.
[102] See Jāḥiẓ, *Kitāb al-Bayān wa-l-tabyīn*, Part I, p. 295; Part II, p. 7.

nations in the quality of *bayān*.[103] This is particularly true of the Bedouins who preserved their pristine linguistic intuitions by eschewing mixing with other nations. No wonder Jahiz waxes lyrical about the wondrous linguistic ability of the Bedouins:

> There is nothing on earth more elegant and edifying, pleasanter to the ear, more easily understood by sensible men or better for loosening the tongue and improving the enunciation than the leisurely talk of intelligent, cultured, eloquent Bedouins with a good command of their language.[104]

But by dint of the same quality, the opposite situation, brought about through contact with non-Arabs and in urban spaces, is also true: 'Let me tell you that the most unbearable grammatical errors are those committed by affected people . . . Still worse are those of the Bedouins who pitch their tents in the neighbourhood of main roads and busy markets'.[105] By coming into contact with urban life, characterised as it is with *laḥn* because of ethnic mixing, the Bedouin loses his pristine linguistic intuition and the social status that goes with it.

The language-identity link in Jahiz is embedded in a more sophisticated intellectual framework than is usually the case in other discussions of this link. Whereas in most discussions of the topic the link is stated or asserted with little depth, here is an attempt to put it at the heart of an intellectual edifice that aims to make sense of the problem of meaning in cosmic terms. In this cosmic order, the place of Arabic and the Arabs is endowed with intellectual coherence and theological purpose: they both emerge as part of God's design – a matter of election or selection – rather than being the result of mere historical accident. In this cosmic order, the Arabs are charged, through their language, with the task of bearing witness to the inimitability of the Qur'an and the truth of God's message.[106] This is clear from Jahiz's views on the imitability of the Qur'an:

> Muhammad has one exclusive sign, which affects the mind in the same way that dividing the seas affects the eyes: namely when he says to the Quraishites in particular and to the Arabs in general (and they include many poets and orators,

103 Ibid. Part I, p. 128: *wa ammā al-'awāmm min ahl millatinā wa-da'watinā wa-lughatinā wa-akhlāqinā fa al-ṭabaqa allatī 'uqūluhā wa akhlāquhā fawq tilka al-umam [al-furs, wa-l-hind wa-l-rūm] wa-lam yablughū manzilat al-khāṣṣā minnā, 'alā anna al-khāṣṣa tatafāḍal fī al-ṭabaqāṭ ayḍan.*

104 See Pellat, *The Life and Works of Jāḥiẓ: Translations of Selected Texts*, pp. 104–5. This view is shared by the historian al-Baladhuri (d. c. 279/892), who is of Persian origin. See Harry T. Norris, '*Shu'ūbiyya* in Arabic literature', in Julia Ashtiany, T. M. Johnstone, J. D. Letham, R. B. Serjeant and G. Rex Smith (eds), *'Abbasid Belles-Lettres* (Cambridge: Cambridge University Press, 1990), p. 32.

105 See Pellat, *The Life and Works of Jāḥiẓ: Translations of Selected Texts*, p. 105.

106 This is what counts here, and that is why I had to wait until now to bring all these ideas on (un)imitability, (un)translatability and identity together.

> and eloquent, shrewd, wise, tolerant, sagacious, experienced and farsighted men): 'If you can equal me in a single *sūra*, my claims will be false and you will be entitled to call me a liar'. It is impossible that people like the Arabs, with their great numbers, their diversity of tastes, [the purity of] their language, which is their crowning glory, with eloquence bubbling and overflowing in their breasts, and their outstanding aptitude for fine language – which has enabled them to speak of snakes, scorpions, wolves, dogs, black and other beetles, asses, pigeons and everything that crawls or runs and everything eyes can see or minds imagine – who possess every kind of poetic form ... as well as prose and rhyming prose. ... [it is impossible that among these people] who were fiercest in hatred, the most vengeful, the most sensitive to favour and slight, the most hostile to the Prophet, the quickest to condemn weakness and extol strength, no orator or poet should have dared to take up the challenge; [yet that is what happened].[107]

Therefore, the Arabs' role in history is one of divine destiny: their eloquence, mastery of literary forms and the purity of their language qualify them to stand at the apex of God's creation, as Jahiz's taxonomy of objects and beings aims to demonstrate. It is also this position and the qualities that underpin it that give theological significance to the Arabs' inability to challenge the matchless quality of the Qur'an. This is an argument from people and language to inimitability, but it is also an argument from inimitability to language and people, hence my use of the language-identity link in the title of this particular section. Furthermore, this is an argument about meaning and theology: the list of animals in the above quotation and the references to all ostensible and inostensible objects, 'everything [the] eyes can see or minds imagine', is not accidental; rather, it alludes to *niṣba* and, therefore, to meaning-making in the extra-linguistic world. Even here, language is metaphorically involved by virtue of being the primary means or channel (*wasīla*) for enunciating the covert meanings of *niṣba*. There is little doubt that this web of ideas is related to the anti-Arab polemic of the *shu'ūbīs*,[108] especially to the members of the secretarial class, whom Jahiz accuses of attacking the 'composition of the Qur'an and denouncing its inconsistencies'[109], in addition to giving it short shrift in their professional careers.[110] These attacks are

107 Pellat, *The Life and Works of Jāḥiẓ: Translations of Selected Texts*, p. 47.

108 Goldziher, *Muslim Studies* (Vol. I), p. 191, sums up this web of ideas as follows: 'Competition between anti-Arabs and Arabs expressed itself also in the field of ideas concerning language. The national vanity of the Arabs had bred no more favourite prejudice than that according to which Arabic was the most beautiful sounding, richest and best of all languages of mankind, a belief which was raised to almost religious significance even amongst the orthodox non-Arabs, as it concerned the language in which the divine revelation was expressed in the Qur'an'.

109 Ibid. p. 274.

110 Jāḥiẓ says this about the secretarial class (Pellat, *The Life and Works of Jāḥiẓ: Translations of Selected Texts*, p. 275): 'No scribe has ever been known to take the Qur'an as his bedside reading, exegesis as the foundation of his learning, religious

made against the matchless excellence of the Qur'an and, therefore, both its inimitability and the language-identity link that it invokes. I will now turn to the *shu'ūbī* anti-Arab polemic, insofar as it relates to the language-identity link.

Shu'ūbiyya and Anti-Arab Polemic[111]

Shu'ūbiyya derives its name from the Qur'an 49:13:

> O mankind! We created you from a single pair of a male and a female, and made you into nations/peoples [*shu'ūban*] and tribes [*qabā'ila*], that you may know each other. Verily the most honoured of you in the sight of God is (he who is) the most righteous of you.[112]

knowledge as his escutcheon, or the study of traditions as the cornerstone of his education. If by any chance you come across one quoting passages from the Qur'an or the *sunna*, his jaws seem to stick as he utters the words, and his saliva does not flow smoothly. Should one of them choose to devote himself to *ḥadīth* research, and take to quoting the jurists, his colleagues find him tiresome and perverted: they accuse him of depravity and professional incompetence in attempting to go against nature and pursue a branch of learning for which he was not intended'.

111 *Shu'ūbiyya* has survived well into the modern period, wherein it has retained its negative or pejorative meanings. During the Iran–Iraq War (September 1980 to August 1988) and beyond, it was used by Saddam's Ba'thist regime to designate the Iranians. In the 1950s and 1960s, the term was used to designate some Arabs, as the following illuminating explanation of the term sets out: 'In the modern context, [*shu'ūbiyya*] is an effective term usually used against political movements, groups, or individuals who do not adhere to the principle of Arab nationalism or who affirm local (territorial) or regional nationalism, or who are not actively in favour of total Arab unity. All such parties, groups, and individuals are viewed as enemies of Arab nationalism, traitors of the revolution, and natural allies of neo-imperialism. The term carries with it a profound and deeply wounding insult to anyone who considers himself an Arab, for it separates the "authentic" Arab from the "quasi-Arab" (normally differentiated in terms of religion or ethnic origin). Its particular effectiveness is due to the fact that it can be used indirectly to create suspicion and provide insinuations which need not be clearly stated. The [famous radio station] Voice of the Arabs [broadcasting from Cairo], for example, in attacking Michel 'Aflaq, the founder and intellectual spokesman of the Ba'th [party], would call him *shu'ūbī*, thus indirectly reminding the listener of the fact that he is a Christian, consequently not altogether an Arab, and thus impugning his good faith and national integrity'. See Hisham Sharabi, *Nationalism and Revolution in the Arab World* (Princeton, NJ: D. Van Nostrand Company, 1966), p. 100.

112 For the meaning of the two terms *shu'ūban* and *qabā'il* in this verse, see Roy P. Mottahedeh, 'The *shu'ūbiyya* controversy and the social history of early Islamic Iran', *International Journal of Middle Eastern Studies* (1976), 7: 161–82.

This verse recognises group differences among human beings, considers it the duty of each group to know the other groups (in a positive spirit) and establishes righteousness as the basis of differentiation among people with God. This message of equality was embodied in the Prophet's last address to his followers at the pilgrimage in Mecca, the intention being, in both cases, to counter the Arabs' sense of superiority over non-Arabs in Islam. This call for equality became the rallying cry for non-Arab Muslims – the *'ajam* – who sought to avail themselves of the same rights and privileges as their co-religionist Arabs in the early centuries of Islam. Initially called *ahl al-taswiya* (the levellers), members of this group sought to neutralise the sense of Arab superiority that existed in society, especially among the Arab aristocracy under Umayyad rule (661–750). Under the new dynasty, the 'Abbasids, *shu'ūbiyya* developed into an anti-Arab movement, which sought to show Arab inferiority in comparison to the non-Arabs, especially the Persians and Aramaeans (*Nabaṭ*).

Differences of opinion exist as to the nature of *shu'ūbiyya*. Writing from a nationalist perspective in the modern period, Arab scholars treat *shu'ūbiyya* as a political movement (al-Duri;[113] al-Fikayki;[114] al-Hasani;[115] Qaddura;[116] Sallum[117]).[118] This view is shared by Goldziher in the nineteenth century, who, like Arab scholars in their mid-twentieth century political context, might have been affected by the nationalist spirit of the Austro-Hungarian Empire in which he lived. Gibb disagrees with this interpretation, pointing to the complexity of *shu'ūbiyya*, which was not 'merely a conflict between

113 See 'Abd al-'Azīz al-Dūrī, *al-Judhūr al-tārīkhiyya li-l-shu'ūbiyya* (Beirut: Dār al-Ṭalī'a, [3rd printing] 1981).

114 See 'Abd al-Hādī al-Fikāykī, *al-Shu'ūbiyya wa-l-qawmiyya al-'arabiyya* (Beirut: Dār al-Ādāb, 1961).

115 See Bahīja Bāqir al-Ḥasanī, 'al-Zamakhsharī wa-l-shu'ūbiyya', *Majallat majma' al-lugha al-'arabiyya al-urdunnī* (1989), 37: 177–211.

116 See Zāhiya Qaddūra, *al-Shu'ūbiyya wa-atharuhā al-ijtimā'ī wa-l-siyāsī fi al-ḥayāt al-islāmiyya fi al-'aṣr al-'abbāsī al-awwal* (Beirut: Dār al-Kitāb al-Lunbānī, 1972).

117 See 'Abdallah Sallūm, *al-Shu'ūbiyya ḥaraka muḍādda li-l-islām wa-l-umma al-'arabiyya* (Baghdad: Manshūrat Wazārat al-Thqāfa, 1980).

118 For the use of this term in Iraq under Saddam, see Ofra Bengio, *Saddam's Word: Political Discourse in Iraq* (New York and Oxford: Oxford University Press, 1998), pp. 103–6. Also see Sami Hanna and George H. Gradner, *Arab Socialism: A Documentary Survey* (Leiden: Brill, 1969), pp. 80–97. Hanna and Gradner expand the meaning of the term to cover the period from 657 to 1960s (p. 81) by 'proposing the existence of an actual trend line linking the eighth and the twentieth centuries'. They gloss this as follows (p. 94): 'We are proposing that there have been, since the Arabs emerged as a self-conscious community, a succession of movements, involving both Arabs and non-Arabs, which have threatened to merge the Arab community with a wider non-Arab system or to fragment it, and that in each case this has generated a strong reaction, explicit or implicit, from the Arabs, aimed to preserve their identity'.

two schools of literature, nor yet a conflict between political nationalisms, but a struggle to determine the destinies of the Islamic culture as a whole'.[119] Mottahedeh considers *shu'ūbiyya* to be first and foremost a literary controversy:

> The *shu'ūbiyya* was primarily a literary controversy, and if it was used on rare occasions by political movements with a noticeable 'ethnic' (regional) character . . ., most *shu'ūbīs* were not political and were, as often as not, faithful servants of the caliphate.[120]

Norris is right when he says that the aims of *shu'ūbiyya* cannot be defined clearly.[121]

However, I am of the view that the political (with a small 'p') dimension of *shu'ūbiyya* cannot be discounted, even though *shu'ūbiyya* displayed itself primarily within the realm of literature. The unspoken assumption in some of the previously mentioned views that the literary is not political emerges from a narrow understanding of the political and also runs counter to the established practice in the Arab milieu of reading literature politically. While as literary praxis *shu'ūbiyya* did not aim at what might be called regime change in modern discourse, its practitioners wanted to change the political culture in the Islamic state in a way which tilts or shifts (what modern political scientists call) soft power from one group to another. The fact that some of the defenders of the Arabs against *shu'ūbī* attacks were of non-Arab origin does not mean that there was not a political flavour or flavours to *shu'ūbiyya*. Whenever ethnicity is engaged at any level in society, some form of politics is willy-nilly involved. *Shu'ūbiyya* was an elite phenomenon, not a mass one. Its effects may not have been felt in society at large, but as a form of elite practice using culture as proxy, thus *shu'ūbiyya* could not but be political in the sense outlined above. The following discussion about language in the intra-ethnic fray of the third / ninth and fourth / tenth centuries derives its sociolinguistic meaning from this particular understanding of the political.

Jahiz was one of the combatants against the anti-Arab *shu'ūbī* attacks in the third / ninth century. Even allowing for exaggeration, the following quotation from Jahiz points to a political reading of *shu'ūbiyya* on his part, in which language, ethnic belonging and Islam are not separated:

> The bulk of those who are sceptics in regard to Islam, at the outset, were inspired by the ideas of *shu'ūbiyya*. Protracted argument leads to fighting. If a man hates a thing then he hates him who possesses it, or is associated with it. If he hates [the

[119] Hamilton A. R. Gibb, *Studies on the Civilisation of Islam* (London: Routledge & Kegan Paul, 1962), p. 62.

[120] Mottahedeh, 'The *shu'ūbiyya* controversy and the social history of early Islamic Iran', p. 162.

[121] Norris, '*Shu'ūbiyya* in Arabic literature', p. 31.

> Arabic language] then he hates the [Arabian peninsula], and if he hates the peninsula then he loves those who hate it. Thus matters go from bad to worse with him until he forsakes Islam itself, because it is the Arabs who brought it; it is they who provided the venerable forebears and the example worthy of imitation.[122]

As I read it, this interpretation or accusation by Jahiz has the label of political written all over it: it links language, people, geography and Islam to each other in one fell swoop, and it uses 'hate' as a terminological currency to describe the intensity of anti-Arab feeling among the *shu'ūbī*s.

In spite of our meagre information on *shu'ūbiyya*,[123] most of which derives from *anti-shu'ūbī* rebuttals, we know that the Arabs' pride in their language, oratory and poetry came under attack from the *shu'ūbī*s. This is not surprising, considering the centrality of these cultural constructs in Arab life. The *shu'ūbī*s argued that the Arabs could not match the linguistic skills and literary prowess of the Persians and Greeks. Concerning the claim that the Arabs are the undisputed masters of oratory, the *shu'ūbī*s counter that all nations, even the most vulgar and rough, practice oratory, but that the Persians are the best orators, particularly the people of Marw, who 'speak in the sweetest, most pleasant and captivating manner'.[124] It is in this context that the Arabs are ridiculed for the use of the staff in public address and their speech is said to be 'clumsy' and 'rough' to boot. How could Jahiz fail to read this as an anti-Islamic attack, when the words of the Qur'an were culled from the very linguistic source to which this speech belongs? Jahiz countered this accusation by saying:

> The Persians may have good orators but their eloquence [*bayān*] is always the result of long thought, deep study and counsel . . . [Oratory] is quite different amongst the Arabs. Their eloquence is spontaneous, extempore, as if the result of inspiration.[125]

The distinction between these two styles of oratory plays on a multifaceted dichotomy, in which the artificial versus the natural and the contrived versus the spontaneous play out the differences in linguistic skill and literary flare between the Persians and the Arabs, resulting in favour of the latter. And with great stylistic flourish, Jahiz condescendingly alludes to the *shu'ūbī*s:

> When you take a *shu'ūbī* by the hand and cause him to enter the land of the pure Bedouin Arabs, the source of perfect eloquence, and acquaint him with an accomplished poet or an eloquent orator, he will know that what you say

122 Ibid. pp. 35–6.
123 See José Ignacio Sánchez, 'Ibn Qutayba and Shu'ūbiyya', Masters dissertation, University of Cambridge, 2007.
124 See Goldziher, *Muslim Studies* (Vol. I), p. 157.
125 Ibid. p. 160.

is the truth, an evidence clearly visible to the percipient eye. Understand what I say in this, and know that you have never seen a people more wretched than these *shu'ūbīs*, not more hostile to its religion, nor more vehement in ravaging its honour, nor greater bores.[126]

Shu'ūbī attacks on Arabic included condemning its use of desinintial inflections or, more correctly, the Arabs' belief that Arabic is unique among languages in having these inflections. These attacks were also aimed at the extensive stock of synonyms that Arabic has for, one assumes, culturally significant items, as well as its use of *aḍdād* – homonyms. Abu Bakr al-Anbari (d. 328/939) took the latter attack to be directly aimed against the wisdom of the Arabs, as displayed in their language:

> People who profess false doctrines and condemn the Arab nation wrongly believe that this linguistic phenomenon of Arabic is due to lack of wisdom on the part of the Arabs, to the small measure of their eloquence, and to the many confusions in their verbal intercourse with each other.[127]

Ibn Faris (d. 395/1005) defended synonymy in Arabic, arguing that it is necessary in order to achieve precision of expression, and, on the cultural level, it reflects the Arabs' keen sense of observation, since so-called synonyms are, in fact, only near synonyms, inscribing culturally sensitive differences among the objects that they designate.

Most scholars agree that the embers of *shu'ūbiyya* as a socio-political phenomenon were more or less extinguished sometime during the fifth/eleventh century. However, its linguistic incarnation continued to be a topic of discussion well into the sixth/twelfth century. Like Ibn Faris before him, al-Zamakhshari (d. 538/1143) asserted the superiority of Arabic over other languages, using this claim as the basis for countering the *shu'ūbī* attacks against the language. In the introduction to his very popular book *al-Mufaṣṣal*, al-Zamakhshari says:[128]

> I thank God that He made me busy with Arab philology and has made me fight for (the cause of) the Arabs and has given me enthusiasm for it, and that he did not make me leave their brave helpers and join the band of the *shu'ūbiyya*; that he saved from this part who can do nothing against the former but attack them with slanderous words and shoot at them the arrows of mockery.

It is clear from his extract that al-Zamakhshari speaks as a non-Arab, thus giving his view more credence than if he had spoken as an Arab. It is also clear that he considers the attacks on Arabic to be ultimately an attack on the

126 Norris, '*Shu'ūbiyya* in Arabic literature', pp. 5, 244.
127 Goldziher, *Muslim Studies* (Vol. I), p. 197–8.
128 Ibid. p. 191. Al-Zamakhshari was of Persian origin.

Arabs themselves.[129] Al-Zamakhshari deplores this behaviour on the part of the *shu'ūbī*s in view of the fact that God has sent His 'best revelation' to His 'best Messenger' and that He entrusted this message not to the *'ajam* but to the Arabs', who, one is led to assume, are His best people.[130] Al-Zamakhshari further adds, in a series of rhetorical flourishes, that the *shu'ūbī*s 'deny the excellence [of Arabic], reject its qualities, refuse to respect and glorify it, proscribe learning and teaching it, tear up its fabric and cast aspersions on it',[131] in spite of the fact that knowledge of the language and its grammar is indispensable to the practice of exegesis, jurisprudence and other Islamic sciences. These themes are repeated in some of the poetry that al-Zamakhshari composed in his book *Dīwān al-adab*, which he primarily composed to teach Persians Arabic, using Arabic texts and Persian glosses/explanations.[132] In one poem in his book, al-Zamakhshari mentions that Arabic, spread far and wide, is used in every mosque [*manbar*] and school, is the mainstay of the Arabs, who are unmatched in their excellence, and that when he compares other nations to the Arabs, these nations pale in significance.[133]

It is clear from the above discussion that the language-identity link is at the heart of the *shu'ūbiyya* polemic, in the sense that the superiority or otherwise of Arabic reflects, likewise, upon the superiority of the Arabs. The fight over language was therefore a proxy for a bigger fight about (soft) power, access to resources and who would mould the dominant cultural edifice in society at the highest echelons of the state, even though this fight may have been restricted to the elites on both sides. This is – in line with my discussion of language as proxy in Chapter 1 – a political reading of *shu'ūbiyya*, and it is consistent with the symbolic approach to language that I have advocated in earlier studies and similarly applied in the preceding chapter. As a marker of identity, language plays an important symbolic role in the definition of a group. Praise for a language is praise for that particular group and vice versa. The fact that, as a linguistic phenomenon, *shu'ūbiyya* continued to hold significance well into the twelfth century, even as a rhetorical trope, suggests that *shu'ūbiyya* had not lost its potency as an impulse in society; indeed, there would be no point in deploying a trope, if it had no resonance with its intended audience. It would be anachronistic in the extreme for al-Zamakhshari, as an Arabic grammarian of Persian origin, who is known to have lived, travelled and taught in both Arabic- and Persian-speaking lands

129 See James T. Munroe, *The Shu'ūbiyya in Al-Andalus: The Risāla of Ibn García and Five Refutations* (Berkeley, CA: University of California Press, 1970), for *Shu'ūbiyya* in al-Andalus.

130 See Abū al-Qāsim Muḥammad Ibn 'Umar al-Zamakhshari, *al-Mufaṣṣal fī al-naḥw* (Alexandria: Maṭba'at al-Kawkab al-Sharqī, [1291] 1874), p. 3.

131 Ibid. p. 3.

132 See Bahīja Bāqir al-Hasanī, 'al-Zamakhsharī wa-l-shu'ūbiyya', *Majallat majma' al-lugha al-'arabiyya al-urdunnī* (1989), 37: 177–211.

133 Ibid. p. 203.

and who is the author of a treatise teaching Arabic to Persians, to introduce his book *al-Mufaṣṣal* with a rebuttal of *shu'ūbī* attacks on Arabic, if he felt that this was no longer an issue of some interest to his readers. Al-Zamakhshari is clear about the pedagogic purpose of his book – a book for the here and now. The vehemence of his rebuttal very strongly suggests that he was not doing this from a historical perspective, although this perspective must have been important contextually, but because he was tackling an issue that resonated with those who would use his book.

Reference was made above to the connection between *shu'ūbiyya* and the inimitability of the Qur'an. The literature contains the names of people, mainly of Persian origin, who tried to match the excellence of the Qur'an, seemingly to no avail.[134] Most of these writers were implicated in *shu'ūbiyya* or *zandaqa* – a form of free-thinking, which traces its roots back to pre-Islamic doctrines in Persia. Although we cannot be certain about the truth of these claims, it is still possible to establish a connection between *shu'ūbiyya* and the challenge to inimitability indirectly by pointing out that both the *shu'ūbī*s and those who cast doubt on the inimitability of the Qur'an would, at some point, have intersecting views, in respect to the claims made about Arabic by the Arabs and their supporters – in particular, the claims concerning the superiority of the Arabic language.

Conclusion: The Language-Identity Link

The above discussion puts the language-identity link at the centre of a web of ideas that dominated early Muslim thought and elite competition. These ideas – (in)imitability of the Qur'an, its (un)translatability and *shu'ūbiyya,* all of which came into vogue at roughly the same time, thus justifying the use of the term 'web' – relate to matters of theology and inter-group strife, which have survived to the present day. The persistence of these ideas from past to present, as has been pointed out in several instances, does not imply a continuous intellectual genealogy, but an archived set of themes, which continue to resonate in Arab society to this day. Delving into the past, as I have done in this chapter, helps us understand the depth of the language-identity link in modern Arab political thought. Although this link, in many respects, is a matter of construction and ideological manipulation, its deep historical roots in Arab culture give it a veneer of naturalness, turning it into an essentialist motif of group identity that is hard to dislodge. This naturalness and essentialism are inscribed in Arabic lexically, being, in this respect, part of the very fabric of the language, as it refers to itself and the people who speak it.

This link between language and people has racial overtones, which seem to have barred outsiders from claiming it as their language in the ethnic sense of the term. Why else should the Prophet of Islam remind his followers that a person who speaks Arabic is an Arab? Is not this act of advocacy intended to

134 See Vasalou, 'The miraculous eloquence of the Qur'an'.

break the lock that chains language to people? And why else should al-Shafi'i – one of the most distinguished jurists of Sunni Islam – state that a person who speaks even a few words of Arabic is an Arab? Is not this intended to break the same lock in the language-identity chain? These calls for inclusion were intended to counter linguistic exclusion, on the one hand, and foster the message of equality in Islam, on the other. But this is a slanted form of equality, in the sense that it calls on non-Arabs to 'vote with their tongues', as Mottahedeh puts it,[135] by adopting Arabic as their language. The Arabs stay linguistically put, while others travel in their direction in an additive or subtractive form of bilingualism involving their old or heritage language.

Arabic, in this respect, is not markedly different from other dominant languages and language communities throughout history. However, the principle of inimitability, building on pre-Islamic social practices, gives the language-identity link a strong theological twist, which, as far as I know, is not replicated in other cultures. Unlike in Judaism and Christianity, the truth of the Apostle's prophethood in Islam rests on a miracle whose main substance is language. How could the quotidian become the substance of the miraculous? Language hardly draws attention to itself in ordinary situations. In the Qur'an, the situation is reversed: language is constantly drawing attention to itself as medium, coupled with a challenge at imitation that is predicted to fail. For this new paradigm of apologetic miracle to work, it must resonate with those to whom it was addressed in the first instance. The Arabs seem to have accepted this paradigm and the subsequent challenge that came with it because it resonated with their feeling of pride in their language, as well as with their continued assertions about their excellent linguistic skills and unsurpassable literary flair. Instead of weakening the Arabs' feeling of exclusive belonging to their language in Islam, the inimitability of the Qur'an principle seems to have done the opposite: it entrenched the language-identity link by making the Arabs its primary target, if not, according to some, its only target, as has been pointed out. In other words, inimitability added to the visibility of the language as a cultural marker among the Arabs, rather than detracting from this visibility. And it did so not just among the Arabs, but also among the non-Arab Muslims – the *'ajam* – whom Jahiz considered to occupy a lower rung on the scale of *bayān* / *faṣāḥa* (eloquence) than the Arabs in his elaborate series of dichotomies.

This, I think, is why the Prophet was at pains to advocate a principle of equality in Arabic, much as he did in Islam. Shafi'i did the same, but less successfully, because, in arguing against the translatability of the Qur'an, he felt theologically impelled to: (1) assert the superiority of Arabic over other languages, linking this to the person of the Prophet and to the fact that God chose to reveal the Qur'an in this language; and (2) in an act of erasure, deny that the Qur'an contains any foreign words. For an Arab or

[135] Mottahedeh, 'The *shu'ūbiyya* controversy and the social history of early Islamic Iran', p. 179.

Muslim Arabophile, the fact that God chose to reveal His Qur'an in Arabic – a fact commented upon in several places in the Qur'an – could not but be read as a matter of divine election, which affirmed the existing status of the language and, in the new order, added extra prestige to it. Islam called for ethnic equality through language, but, instead, it added prestige to Arabic in a way which made it a highly prized cultural (and religious) commodity for its original speakers. As is normal in such situations, the language became an even more coveted symbol of identity for these speakers, who, as might be expected in a market of cultural products, wanted to press their advantage through exclusivity. Instead of relaxing the exclusivity of the language-identity link among the Arabs under the banner of equality, Islam seems to have engendered the opposite effect.

It should, therefore, come as no surprise that Arabic was a central plank in *shu'ūbiyya* polemics. The vehemence with which this polemic was pursued (as we have seen in this chapter) testifies, yet again, to the importance of the language-identity link in Muslim and Arab society. The symbolic loadings of language and its associated arts, rather than its instrumentality or the content of those arts, was what mattered most, if not exclusively. This symbolism enabled the language to act as a proxy, through which issues of a non-linguistic nature would be pursued and points would be scored between the combatants in the *shu'ūbiyya* polemic. These combatants were not, however, ranged against each other on strictly ethnic grounds. Some of the defenders of the Arab cause and the Arabic language – for example, al-Zamakhshari – were, in fact, of non-Arab stock. This implies that a degree of acculturation seems to have taken place in Islam, answering to the Prophet's call that a person who speaks Arabic can become an Arab in the cultural sense of the term. However, it is interesting to point out that the literature on *shu'ūbiyya* does not preserve the name of even a single person of Arab stock who supported the claims made by the *shu'ūbīs* on behalf of the *'ajam* in their totality or with the same vehemence[136] or who accepted the 'vile' claims that the *shu'ūbīs* made against the Arabs. It is true that the Arab poet Abu al-'Ala' al-Ma'arri (449/1057) composed a poem in which he praised the Persians and placed them above the Arabs in some respects, but this act remains the exception, not the rule.[137] Furthermore, this position, on his part, may be related to his philosophical sympathies, which saw merit in Pre-Islamic Iranian ideas.

The fact that *shu'ūbiyya* expressed itself through literature does not mean that it was devoid of political content. Divesting *shu'ūbiyya* of political meaning must be based on a narrow understanding of what the political stands for, as well as the entrenched Arab paradigm of reading poetry and other forms of cultural production politically. Literary production is a good

136 Tone was an important aspect of the *shu'ūbiyya* polemic, hence the reference to 'vehemence' here.

137 Goldziher, *Muslim Studies (Vol. I)*, pp. 162–3.

source for reading history from a political angle.[138] In addition, the non-political interpretation of *shu'ūbiyya* ignores the potential of language to act as proxy for extra-linguistic issues, as Gramsci rightly reminds us: 'Every time the question of language surfaces [in society], in one way or another, it means that a series of other problems is coming to the fore'.[139] Having said this, I would like to conclude with a quotation from Norris, which shows the irony in the anti-Arabic attack in *shu'ūbiyya*: 'Even the most fanatical *shu'ūbī* expressed his sentiments in the tongue first spoken by the Arabian lizard-eaters he so despised'.[140]

[138] See David Aberbach, 'The poetry of nationalism', *Nations and Nationalism* (2003), 9: 255–75; David Aberbach, 'Nationalism and the Hebrew Bible', *Nations and Nationalism* (2005), 11: 223–42; Yasir Suleiman, 'Nationalist poetry, conflict and meta-linguistic discourse', in Yasir Suleiman (ed.), *Living Islamic History: Studies in Honour of Professor Carole Hillenbrand* (Edinburgh: Edinburgh University Press, 2010), pp. 252–78; and Ramzi Baalbaki, 'The historic relevance of poetry in the Arab grammatical tradition', in Ramzi Baalbaki, Salih Said Agha and Tarif Khalidi (eds), *Poetry and History: The Value of Poetry in Reconstructing Arab History* (Beirut: American University of Beirut Press, 2011), pp. 95–120.

[139] Antonio Gramsci, *Selections from Cultural Writings*, trans. W. Boelhower (London: Lawrence & Wishart, 1985), p. 183.

[140] Norris, '*Shu'ūbiyya* in Arabic literature', p. 47.

CHAPTER

3

FRAMING ARABIC: PARATEXTS, POETRY AND LANGUAGE IDEOLOGY

This chapter continues the exploration of the notions of construction, language symbolism, language conflict and language as proxy through an examination of paratexts and poetic compositions. Paratexts, such as titles, dedications, epigraphs and jacket copies have received little or no attention in relation to studying Arabic in the social world. This chapter argues that since most encounters with texts are mediated through these thresholds, scholars of language in the social world must pay attention to them for the information they yield on language ideology and the deployment of culture to do politics in society. The same is true of poetic compositions. This chapter further identifies the most productive tropes of language ideology in the modern world, together with their constitutive metaphors, in order to shed light on issues of language conflict and language anxiety. The tropes of crisis, fossilisation and war act as shorthand codes for the promulgation and recursive circulation of Arabic language ideology in society. As a given of this world, Arabic language ideology does its work without drawing attention to itself. Although the terrain dealt with in this chapter is historically and intellectually different from the one dealt with in Chapter 2, the conceptual unities underlying these two terrains reveal infra-structural continuities in the study of Arabic in the social world across time.

Introduction: Language Symbolism in Expanded Domains

In Chapter 1, I argued that although the status of a language as a *national* language may, in retrospect, seem natural or self-evident, it is, in fact, the case that the process leading to this is subject to manipulation and contestation at every stage in its development. It is also the case that manipulation and contestation continue to apply even after a language has acquired the status of national language. This is what is meant by construction in the nationalist canon when talking about language. This process of linguistic consecration is quintessentially ideological in nature: we can track it through extrapolation by looking at recent examples in the creation of national languages from different parts of the world. However, it is paradoxical that the normativisation of language ideology through standardisation makes this ideology – as it coalesces around the national language – appear natural or self-evident, especially when standardisation seems to be historically deep or sanctioned by religious culture. Contesting the status of the national language, as a marker of the nation and its associated culture, may therefore appear to be ideologically driven when judged against standard language ideology, which is considered, in a subterranean kind of way, to be absent, both in terms of the public consciousness or intellectual discourse.[1] The emergence of Arabic and its *fuṣḥā*-linked standard language ideology is a good example of this network of ideas. Challenges to this covert or naturalised ideology are cast as ideologically driven contestations with questionable legitimacy, precisely because they are projected to be concocted for a particular purpose or because they are believed to be the result of external attack, internal collaboration from a fifth column, self-hatred or as misguided attempts at responding to *bona fide* problems.

My discussion of the inimitability of the Qur'an in Chapter 2 fits this framework in many respects. Inimitability is deployed to link Arabic language ideology with theology and, through this, further link language to ethnicity and inter-group strife, although there is a lot more to inimitability than this rendition of it. This web of linkages has deep historical resonances, which are an integral part of the fabric of Arab cultural life in the modern period. The debate over the (un)translatability of the Qur'an is not exclusively a debate about translation, whether in the pre-modern or modern period. It is also a debate about theology, religious doctrine and authenticity, in which the notion of identity is always lurking in the background. Scratch the surface of the (un)translatability debate and the issue of inimitability, in all its aspects, starts to sprout, igniting the full weight of cultural history behind it in the process. While it is indisputable that the Qur'an is in Arabic and that the challenge it poses concerning its own inimitability is equally indisputable, it is also indisputable, or it ought to be, that some of the issues surrounding the inimitability of the Qur'an are subject to interpretation and, therefore, are also subject to construction and (some) ideological framing. The fact that the principle of *ṣarfa* (deterrence/deflection) emerged right from the very beginning of the debate on inimitability in the third/ninth century signals, in no uncertain terms, the constructed nature of this debate

[1] See Yasir Suleiman, 'Ideology, grammar-making and the standardisation of Arabic', in Bilal Orfali (ed.), *In the Shadow of Arabic: The Centrality of Language to Arabic Culture* (Studies Presented to Ramzi Baalbaki on the Occasion of his Sixtieth Birthday) (Leiden and Boston, MA: Brill, 2011b), pp. 3–30, for ideology and the standardisation of Arabic.

and, dare I say, its ideological impregnation as a strand, among others, that make up this debate.

This chapter will therefore consider some of the issues that we encountered before, testifying to the continued relevance of language symbolism as a prism through which to understand aspects of the social world. The political (with a small 'p') impregnation of language is central to this language symbolism. Evidence will be presented utilising paratexts and poetic compositions, in order to argue this thesis. Paratexts, as a site of meaning, have the great advantage, over more extended textual material, of being able to convey their ideological content in a telegraphic manner. Paratexts enlist members of the public, who may not go past them to read the full text or a sizeable portion of it. The public knock on the door of a text, but do not necessarily enter into it. In spite of this cursory encounter with the text, the public act as channels through which the text circulates in society in one form or another, as I will explain below. Poetry serves a similar function. When it attains canonicity in its cultural milieu, it tends to travel synchronically and diachronically to circulate language ideologies that have the force of 'givens' of the social world. Tracking these givens as they coalesce around language through tropes and metaphors helps to reveal extra-linguistic anxieties in society.

Paratexts and Language Ideology

One of the most intriguing and least-studied sites of language ideology is paratexts. Paratexts include such devices as titles, inter-titles, dedications, epigraphs, prefaces, epilogues and the publisher's blurb or jacket copy. Each of these devices has its own function, but they collectively work to signpost and navigate the text – the main body of a work – in addition to mediating the interaction between the text, the reader and the public. Standing on the fringes of texts and acting as 'thresholds of interpretation' – using Genette's phrase – these liminal discourses are framing devices, which are neither fully inside the text, nor completely outside it, hence the use of the expression 'framing Arabic' in the title of this chapter to signal the discursive relationship between interiority and exteriority in interpreting the intent or messages of a text. As for the frame in a picture, these framing devices are both inside and outside at one and the same time. Because of this, they are the subject of minimal engagement between author and recipients: readers rush past them – as viewers normally do with the frame of a picture – without paying due attention to their import and ideological loading. In this chapter, it is my intention to deal with such framing devices to uncover the meanings that they convey about language ideology.

These meanings may be easy to recover without reading the text closely, but this is not always the case. The recurrence of the same meanings justifies treating some paratextual frames or devices as tropes of language ideology – for example, the 'crisis' trope in discussions about Arabic, as we shall see discussed later in detail. However, these tropes may start to lose some of their rhetorical force with overuse in language ideology discourse, resulting in illocutionary leakage. The 'crisis' trope in Arabic language ideology may be an example of this situation, although it is still invested with rhetorical value and can deliver a motivational charge in task-orientation. In other words, the popularisation of a trope of language ideology may signal the onset of a process of shifting its meaning from the illocutionary / perlocutionary domain to the locutionary or propositional sphere of signification. This transition signals, in turn, a move from visibility to invisibility or from the overt to the covert in language ideology.

Acting as a gateway to the text, titles are the most visible, cognitively speaking, of all paratexts; because of this, I will start with a brief discussion of these devices, relying, in this respect, on Genette's exploration of paratexts.[2] Titles, Genette reminds us, perform three functions: designation, description and temptation or enticement. These functions apply to inter-titles, with some variation, but I will restrict the discussion below to titles only. Designation in titles is a matter of naming the text – giving it an onomastic identity of its own that sets it apart from other texts, without, however, necessarily isolating it from them. As received by the audience, a title is a product of a process which may or may not offer clues about its prenatal gestation.[3] However, designation, as an act of baptism, may carry a strong ideological charge, because of the prehistory of the words it uses: the fact that some of the words in a title have their own salient cultural resonances means that titles cannot, in principle, be connotation-neutral. Words, dialogically, recall other words, which recall other words, working to form a network of significations, which acts as the canvas against which the ideological tinting of a title is displayed. In some cases, the tinting is translucent, rendering it hardly noticeable; in others, it is cryptic and opaque, without being completely impenetrable. An excellent example of the latter is Farrukh's book title *al-Qawmiyya al-fuṣḥā* (*The Eloquent/Pure Nationalism*), which I discussed in Chapter 1, calling it a portmanteau title that conflates the 'Arabic language' as a name with 'Arab nationalism' by triggering through co-location the original pair of expressions: *al-qawmiyya al-'arabiyya* (Arab nationalism) and *al-lugha al-fuṣḥā* (the eloquent or pure language) or *al-'arabiyya al-fuṣḥā* (the eloquent or pure Arabic) from which the title is constructed; this process of blending is reminiscent of the creation of terms such as, for example, 'smog' from the two terms 'smoke' and 'fog'. As we shall see below, the term 'crisis' in the title of some books about Arabic recalls a host of meanings related to this term – some medical and some political – that must be activated in deciphering language ideology. Language ideology subsists not only in this term, but also in the way that it is wired to other terms it recalls in the social world.

[2] Gerard Genette, *Paratexts: Thresholds of Interpretation* (Cambridge: Cambridge University Press, 1997).

[3] Ibid. pp. 171–5, for a discussion of process and outcome in naming practice.

The second function of describing the content of the text is the most mundane or quotidian aspect of titles. However, the mundane does not necessarily equate with unimportant: the audience needs some clues as to what the text is about. In this respect, the title may provide a shorthand entrée to the content of the text. A title such as *The Problems of the Arabic Language* tells us that the text is about Arabic and that Arabic is facing problems, which the text aims to diagnose, describe and, perhaps, offer a solution. There is no implication in this title that Arabic is unique in this respect or that it is in a state which calls for immediate or urgent attention. In other words, there is no red alert here. In this formulation, the title is a locutionary speech act that, on the surface, alludes to the propositional meanings that the text carries. However, the same textual prospectus may be designated by the title *The Crisis of the Arabic Language*. While this title describes what the author of the text considers to be problems facing Arabic, it also carries the additional valuation that these problems are in an acute state of being that needs quick intervention, in order to stem the effects of these problems or eliminate them altogether. Here, then, there is a red alert. This indication of acuteness turns the new title into an illocutionary speech act by virtue of adding a connotative colouring to the locutionary meaning that underlies it: the term 'crisis' signals urgency and, therefore, a call for intervention.[4] This is what I meant by motivation and task-orientation, above which, in speech-act terms, constitute the perlocutionary force of the title. Language ideology in titles draws attention to itself in a maximal way when it operates at the illocutionary and perlocutionary levels. At the locutionary level, titles are part of the mundane or quotidian.

Temptation or enticement – the third function – is intended to allure the reader to procure and read the text: 'a good title would say enough about the subject matter [of the text] to stimulate curiosity and not enough to sate it'.[5] However, neither of these intended effects – procuring or reading – may, in fact, take place, but this does not mean that the text loses its illocutionary and perlocutionary force in society, which, in language ideology terms, are what really matters. To explain this, I will invoke Genette's distinction between the reader and the public in the reception of a text. While the reader is a person who reads the text or, at least a significant portion of it, the public includes others who engage with the text, but do not read it. Genette expresses this as follows:

> It seems to me that the public is nominally more far-flung than the sum of its readers because that entity includes, sometimes in a very active way, people who do not necessarily read the book (or at least not in its entirety), but who participate in its dissemination and, therefore, in its 'reception'.[6]

4 For the concept of 'crisis', see Reinhart Koselleck, 'Crisis', *Journal of the History of Ideas* (2006), 67: 357–400.

5 Genette, *Paratexts: Thresholds of Interpretation*, p. 92.

6 Ibid. pp. 74–5.

Genette further adds:

> If the addressee of the text is indeed the reader, the addressee of the title is the public . . . The title is directed at many more people than the text, people who by one route or another receive it and transmit it and thereby have hand in circulating it. For if the text is an object to be read, the title . . . is an object to be circulated – or, if you prefer, a subject of conversation.[7]

This function of the title highlights the importance of endowing it with illocutionary and perlocutionary force in language ideology, in order to reach, for task-orientation purposes, a constituency of addressees that is larger than its readers.

As we shall see below, the title of Shubashi's book on Arabic, *Li-taḥyā al-'arabiyya, yasquṭ Sībawayhi* (*Long Live Arabic!: Down with Sibawayhi!*), aptly illustrates these points. The title seems to imply that for the Arabic language to flourish, Sibawayhi's (d. 180/796) foundational grammatical legacy in the Arabic intellectual tradition needs to be drastically pruned, if not, in fact, 'brought down'. Some of the most critical reactions to the book came not from those who read it (or who read substantial chunks of it), but from members of the public who were enticed by its title and engaged, partly because of this enticement, with its circulation in the media and in public fora, where the book was the subject of discussion and debate.[8] In the process, these members of the public became unwitting, but active, agents in its further circulation, as happened with Salman Rushdie's novel *The Satanic Verses* in the late 1980s, when it received strong public condemnation from British Muslims, most of whom had probably not read it. However, although an enticing title may enhance the circulation of a book, there is no guarantee that this will, in fact, be the case: 'The temptation function [of a title] is always present but may prove to be positive, negative or [neutral] depending on the receiver, who does not always conform to the sender's own idea of the addressee'.[9] This caveat is important in assessing the impact of a title, but it is not so important in terms of understanding the ideology that titles carry: the temptation or allure of a title may not be equalled by the enticement of its

[7] Ibid. p. 75.

[8] Genette calls this circulation of the text as its public epitext, which he describes as: 'any paratextual element not materially appended to the text within the same volume but circulating, as it were, freely, in a virtually limitless physical and social space. The location of the epitext is therefore anywhere outside the book – but of course nothing precludes its later admission to the text' (Ibid. p. 344). Sticking with Shubashi, some of the public reactions to his book were included in the third printing as an epilogue under the title *Qālū 'an al-kitāb* (this is what they said about the book). Epitexts may appear in 'newspapers and magazines, radio or television programmes, lectures . . .' (Ibid. pp. 344–5).

[9] Ibid. p. 93.

text, but this should not matter for our purposes here. A text with an enticing title may not live up to the expectations generated by that title (this is, in fact, the case in regards to al-Shubashi's book), but this does not deem the title an unworthy object of study as to the ideology that it carries and the debates it may ignite and circulate within wider society. In other words, the text may carry mundane or hackneyed meanings, but the title, as a speech act in its own right, may give us important clues about ideology. I say this to warn the reader not to expect that all the books that I cite below match the enticement that their titles seem to promise in terms of their originality or the quality of the arguments they enunciate. Some, in fact, are boringly repetitive – a better term may be reiterative, as I will discuss – as if written to a cultural template or schema, yet their titles offer information on Arabic language ideology that is worthy of scholarly attention.

A second type of paratext is the dedication (*ihdā'* in Arabic). In spite of the fact that dedications do provide information on Arabic language ideology, this paratextual genre has received very little attention, if any at all, in the literature, owing, in the main, to its liminality and inchoate functionality.[10] Readers pay scant attention to dedications, because they consider them to be outside the text. In their traditional role, dedications express a relationship between the author and the dedicatee. Genette declares that:

> the dedication is always a matter of demonstration, ostentation, exhibition: it proclaims a relationship, whether intellectual or personal, actual or symbolic, and this proclamation is always at the service of the work, as a reason for elevating the work's standing or as a theme for commentary.[11]

For our purposes here, we will read dedications in books about Arabic for the ideological information they carry. Most of the dedications of this type that I have come across are addressed to imaginary groups for task-orientation purposes. More specifically, these dedications give us clues about the author's positionality – where he stands in relation to the text – and his intent in authoring it, as the discussion below will demonstrate.

Epigraphs are the third type of paratext that will be utilised here. Epigraphs are quotations that shed light on the text: they may offer clues as to the choice of title, the propositional content of the text, its connotative intent or the kind of affect or task-orientation it is hoped that the text will elicit. Epigraphs can seem enigmatic and their relevance for the text or the title may not be initially possible to decipher until the whole text is read, but this is not always the case. Furthermore, epigraphs may be subject to varying interpretations, and, in some cases, they may be used for decorative purposes only. One of the main functions of epigraphs, however, is to lend support and backing to what the

[10] See Yasir Suleiman, *A War of Words: Language and Conflict in the Middle East* (Cambridge: Cambridge University Press, 2004), p. 49, as an exception.

[11] Genette, *Paratexts: Thresholds of Interpretation*, p. 135.

author wants to say, to his connotative intent or to the affect that he wishes to create. As Genette, quoting Stendhal, concurs: 'the epigraph must heighten the reader's feeling, his emotion, if emotion there be, and not present a more or less philosophical opinion about the situation [it deals with]'.[12] This is why the epigraphs in texts dealing with Arabic language ideology tend to be quotations from the Qur'an, well-known poetry, Prophetic *hadīth* or other compositions that have achieved canonical status in Arab culture. Epigraphs from these sources hold significant religious or cultural weight, which the author intends to marshal in support of his text. Quotations from the Qur'an tend to refer to the supreme status of Arabic in Islam and God's promise to protect it by protecting the Qur'an in which it was revealed. Epigraphic *ḥadīth* materials echo this message or they may refer to the connection between Islam, Arabic and the Arabs. When the Qur'an or *ḥadīth* are invoked in a text, we can be certain that the ideological trope of defending the language from overt or covert dangers, whether they are internally generated or externally injected, is one of the intents of the text concerned.

Poetry performs similar functions, owing to its high status in Arab culture to this day. Hafiz Ibrahim's (1871–1932) poem, in which Arabic speaks to the Arabs directly, blaming them for neglecting it, is one of the most popular sources for culling epigraphic material in texts dealing with Arabic language ideology. I will deal with this poem at some length in this chapter. Prose quotations are less frequently utilised. One of the most famous compositions in the modern period, however, is Gibran's (1883–1931) famous piece, in which he attacks those language defenders / guardians who oppose opening Arabic to modern developments. I will also deal with this composition later in some detail.

The preface, which may or may not be written by the author, is another type of paratext that can give us clues about the language ideology of the text. A text may have more than one preface. The preface may appear under different titles in Arabic books: *iftitāḥ* (lit. opening),[13] *fātiha* (lit. beginning),[14] *istiṭlā'* (lit. probing),[15] *taṣdīr* (lit. putting forward),[16]

12 Ibid. p. 158.

13 See Aḥmad Samīr Baybars, *al-Wāqi' al-lughawī wa-l-huwiyya al-'arabiyya* (Cairo: Dār al-Fikr al-'Arabī, n.d.).

14 See 'Abd al-Ḥaqq al-A'ẓamī, *al-'Arab wa-l-'arabiyya bihimā ṣalāh al-umma al-'arabiyya wa jamī' al-umam al-bashariyya* (Dayr al-Zūr: al-Maktaba al-'Urūbiyya, 1983); Hādī al-'Alawī, *al-Mu'jam al-'arabī al-jadīd: muqaddima* (Latakiyya: Dār al-Ḥiwār, 1983); Amīn al-Khūlī, *Min hady al-qur'ān: mushkilāt ḥayātinā al-lughawiyya* (Cairo: al-Hay'a al-Miṣriyya al-'Āmma li-l-Kiṭāb, 1987); Nihād al-Mūsā, *al-Asālīb: manāhij wa-namādhij fi ta'līm al-lugha al-'arabiyya* (Amman: Dār al-Shurūq li-l-Nashr wa-l-Tawzī', 2003).

15 See Nihād al-Mūsā, *Qaḍiyyat al-taḥawull ilā al-fuṣḥā fi al-'ālam al-arabī al-ḥadīth* (Amman: Dār al-Fikr li-l-Nashr wa-l-Tawzī', 1978).

16 See Muḥammad Kāmil Ḥasan, *al-Lugha al-'arabiyya al-mu'āṣira* (Cairo: Dār al-Ma'ārif bi-Miṣr, n.d.); Maḥmūd Aḥmad al-Sayyid, *Shu'ūn lughawiyya* (Beirut: Dār

taqdīm (lit. presentation),[17] *tamhīd* (lit. paving, as in paving the way),[18] *tawṭi'a* (lit. preparation),[19] *madkhal* (lit. entrance),[20] *muqaddima* (lit. front)[21] and *qabl al-muqaddima* (lit. that which precedes the front/introduction).[22] The main aim of the preface is to put the reader on the right track, as it were, in respect to how to read the text or, as Genette puts it: 'this is *why* and this is *how* you should read this book'.[23] In this respect, the preface acts as a pre-emptive strike against the wrong construal of the illocutionary and task-orientation intent of the author, the implication being that the text may be read in ways that are not intended by the author. A preface is not a road map, but it gives some direction as regards the major routes of interpretation that its author wishes the reader to travel or negotiate.

Paratexts and Language Ideology: An Example

To show how Arabic language ideology is encoded in paratexts, I will discuss this in relation to al-Nahwi's (1998) small, pocket-size book, considering the title, dedication, epigraph and jacket copy, as well as various

al-Fikr al-Mu'āṣir, 1989); Sa'īd Aḥmad Bayyūmī, *Umm al-lughāt: dirāsa fi khaṣā'iṣ al-lugha al-'arabiyya wa-l-nuhūḍ bihā* (Cairo: Maktabat al-Ādāb, 2002); Muḥammad Fawzī al-Mināwī, *Azmat al-ta'rīb* (Cairo: Markiz al-Ahrām li-l-Tarjama wa-l-Nashr, 2003); al-Junaydī Khalīfa, *Naḥwa 'arabiyya afḍal* (Beirut: Manshūrāt Dār al-Ḥayāt, n.d.); Maḥmūd Aḥmad al-Sayyid, *Fī qaḍāyā al-lugha al-tarbawiyya* (Kuwait: Wakālat al-Maṭbū'āt, n.d.).

17 See Aḥmad Bin Nu'mān, *al-Ta'rīb byana al-mabda' wa-l-taṭbīq fi al-jazā'ir wa-l-'ālam al-'arabī* (Algiers: al-Sharika al-Waṭaniyya li-l-Nashr wa-l-Tawzī', 1981); Muḥammad Khalīfa al-Tūnusī, *Aḍwā' 'alā lughatinā al-samḥa* (Kuwait: Dār al-'Arabī, 1985); Usāma al-Alfī, *al-Lugha al-'arabiyya wa-kayfa nanhaḍ bihā nuṭqan wa-ktiābatan* (Cairo: al-Hay'a al-Miṣriyya al-'Āmma li-l-Kitāb, 2004); Ṭālib 'Abd al-Raḥmān, *al-'Arabiyya tuwājih al-taḥaddiyāt* (Qatar: Wazārat al-Awqāf, 2006).

18 See 'Abd al-Karīm Khalīfa, *Taysīr al-'arabiyya bayna al-qadīm wa-l-ḥadīth* (Amman: Manshūrāt Majma' al-Lugha al-'Arabiyya al-Urdunnī, 1986); Aḥmad Darwīsh, *Inqāẓ al-lugha, inqāẓ al-huwiyya: taṭwīr al-lugha al-'arabiyya* (Cairo: Nahḍat Miṣr, 2006); 'Ā'isha 'Abd al-Raḥmān, *Lughatunā wa-l-ḥayā* (Cairo: Dār al-Ma'ārif, n.d.).

19 See Muḥammad Sawwā'ī, *Azmat al-muṣṭalaḥ al-'arabī fi al-qarn al-tāsi' 'ashar: muqaddima tārīkhiyya 'āmma* (Damascus: al-Ma'had al-Faransī li-l-Dirāsāt al-'Arabiyya bi-Dimashq, 1999).

20 See Sa'īd al-Afghānī, *Min ḥāḍir al-lugha al-'arabiyya* (Damascus: Dār al-Fikr, 1971).

21 See 'Adnān 'Alī Riḍā al-Naḥwī, *Limādhā al-lugha al-'arabiyya*? (Riyadh: Dār al-Naḥwī li-l-Nashr wa-l-Tawzī', 1998); Sa'īd Ḥārib, *al-Ta'rīb wa-l-ta'līm al-'ālī* (Sharjah: Jam'iyyat Ḥimāyat al-Lugha al-'Arabiyya, 2000); Hādī Nahr, *al-Lugha al-'arabiyya wa-taḥaddiyāt al-'awlama* (Irbid: 'Ālam al-Kutub al-Ḥadīth, 2010).

22 See Idrīs al-Kattānī, *Thamānūn 'āman min al-ḥarb al-frakūfūniyya ḍidd al-islām wa-l-lugha al-'arabiyya* (Rabat: Manshūrāt Nādī al-Fikr al-Islāmī, 2000). This is not an exhaustive list.

23 Genette, *Paratexts: Thresholds of Interpretation*, p. 197 [emphasis in the original].

other materials of a paratextual nature. Starting with the title, it is cast as a question: *li-Mādhā al-lugha al-'arabiyya*? (*Why Arabic*?), no doubt to arouse the reader's curiosity (see Figure 3.1). Quoting Lessing, Genette concurs that a: 'title must be no bill of fare . . . The less it betrays of the contents, the better'.[24] This description of the title applies to al-Nahwi's book. We may go even further and say that this title conforms to Eco's view, quoted in Gennete, that a: 'title must muddle the reader's ideas, not regiment them'.[25] The main function of this title, therefore, is to allure, entice or tempt: it is used to heighten the reader's interest in procuring the book and reading it to find out what the title means and what answers the text provides to the question that the title poses. However, the reader does not come to this title without pre-existing perspectives. In other words, the process of interpreting the title takes place against a specific cultural and ideological schema that shapes or guides the act of interpreting it, before even starting to read the text. As an aside, and although this is accidental, the author's surname, al-Nahwi (lit. the grammarian), creates a connection between its root meaning and concern with grammar (*naḥw*): in the public imagination, *naḥwiyyūn* (grammarians) are considered to be masters of Arabic grammar, as well as staunch guardians of the language, protecting it against anything or anyone that is thought to threaten it. On the other hand, some consider them old-fashioned, out of touch and maybe even culturally dangerous. In the same vein, the name of the publisher, Dār al-Naḥwī (Nahwi's House for Publication and Distribution), located in the bottom right-hand corner of the front cover (see Figure 3.1), reproduces the surname of the author of the book, who seems to use it (the publishing house) as a vehicle to publish his own work on a variety of religious topics (a list is provided at the end of the book). However, the connection with grammar in the name of the publishing house lurks under the surface. To establish this, I showed a copy of the book's cover, without the author's surname, to ten university-educated Arabic speakers in Jordan and asked them to guess what al-Naḥwī (within the name of the publisher) referred to. They all answered – no doubt extrapolating from the title of the book – it referred to *naḥw* (grammar) as the primary specialisation of the publisher. Five respondents said that it may also refer to the publisher's surname, but this was the second answer they gave. The point I wish to draw from this is to emphasise the meandering method of interpretation that the public and readers apply and how this may relate to language ideology in this case.

Let us continue considering this last point by thinking through what pre-emptive/pre-textual, culturally guided interpretations members of the public may make based on the title before reading the text – that is, before they can be categorised as readers in the sense explained above. To get at this, I asked the same ten informants to guess what the book may be about from its

[24] Ibid. p. 92.
[25] Ibid. p. 92.

title – that is, to read the book from its cover in accordance with the popular English proverb. Their answers fell under two headings. The first referred to the special position of Arabic in Arab and Islamic culture and its excellent properties. These are strongly held beliefs among Arabs and Muslims, owing to the link of language with the Qur'an and the rich cultural heritage it gave rise to, as explained in Chapter 2. The second referred to the belief that Arabic is under attack or is being targeted by its enemies, who wish to weaken it, in order to weaken Islam and the Arabs. These two interpretations of the title – picked up from the jacket copy, as I will demonstrate – are supremely ideological in character, responding to the definition of language ideology that I have adopted in this book as a 'cultural amalgam of ideas about social and linguistic relationships, together with their loading of moral and political interests'.[26] The excellence of Arabic is an integral part of a cultural edifice that seeks to create a reciprocal valuation between language and people, wherein excellence in one implies excellence in the other, as we have previously seen in discussions of the (in)imitability principle in Chapter 2. The moral loading of excellence, both socially and linguistically, need little explanation in this expression of Arabic language ideology: they are ultimately about identity and group worth, and they are taken on trust as (almost) articles of faith.

The reference to 'political interest' in the above definition is displayed to its full effect in the second pre-emptive / pre-textual interpretation of the title. The idea that Arabic has enemies and that these enemies will not rest until they weaken the language and what it stands for is a supremely political idea and one that receives diverse articulations in other walks of life in Arab societies, including the political, economic and military spheres. This part of Arabic language ideology (see below) is therefore but a reflection of a more comprehensive ideology of the same kind in Arab societies, no doubt associated with the colonial experience and maybe earlier encounters that go back to the rise of Islam and the Crusades.[27] One does not have to read the whole book under consideration here or even most of it in order to decipher these aspects of language ideology. As social constructs, these aspects of language ideology are already in circulation in society; because of this, they constitute the text's horizon of expectation, providing it in this way with regimes of interpretation over which there is common, diachronically rooted authorship, which, in an important epistemological sense, transcends the author's copyright over his book. A member of the public does not need to become a reader of the text, in the sense given above, to get at these aspects of Arabic language ideology or their ramifications in other spheres in society. All he needs to do is to infer, generate or construct meaning by tapping his cultural schemas, as these are encoded in what I have referred to above as invisible or

[26] Judith T. Irvine, 'When talk isn't cheap: language and political economy', *American Ethnologist* (1989), 16: 255.

[27] As we shall see below, the war trope in Arabic language ideology makes references to the Crusades.

covert language ideology. The title, in this sense, acts as a spark, effectively setting an internalised ideological tinderbox alight.

The inside cover page (see Figure 3.2) repeats the same information as the outside cover, but adds, in the top right-hand corner, the expression *ilā liqā' al-mu'minīn wa-binā' al-jīl al-mu'min*. Although I am not sure what *ilā liqā' al-mu'minīn* exactly signifies, it may be roughly translated as: 'Working towards/aiding the unity/agreement of the believers and building a [young] believing generation'. This expression cannot be a dedication, because the book contains a clearly marked dedication (which I will discuss below). It may, therefore, be a motto of the publishing house, but this is guesswork on my part, since I have not investigated this issue by looking at other books produced by this publisher. However, regardless of the status of this expression in paratextual terms, there is no doubt as to the strong religious colouring it has: the use of the terms *al-mu'minīn* (believers) and *al-mu'min* (believer) marks this fact clearly. This colouring initiates a process of casting the title in an Islamic hue, thus giving us a clue as to the ideological path or trajectory of the text. This interpretation is consolidated by the ornate rendering in Arabic of the Islamic formula: 'In the Name of God the Compassionate, the Merciful' in Figure 3.3. Figure 3.4 consolidates this interpretation even further: the logo of the publishing house has the name al-Naḥwi perched inside a crescent. The crescent is an Islamic symbol par excellence. It appears in the flags of Algeria, Pakistan, Tunisia and Turkey.

The Islamic impregnation of the title is confirmed and taken to a new level in the dedication (see Figure 3.5). To make the discussion below easy to follow and to give the reader a flavour of the writing, I will provide a translation of the dedication here:

> Dedication
>
> To every Muslim so that he or she will know one of the responsibilities that are incumbent on him or her: the protection of Arabic. This is a duty which God has ordained on all Muslims who will be called to account for it on the Day of Judgement.
>
> To those who call non-Muslims to Islam and to educators so that they know the esteemed place Arabic must occupy in educational curricula to build [a Muslim society], to create a believing generation and to bring about agreement/unity among the believers.
>
> To all Muslim organisations and institutions in the Muslim world, in the East and in the West, and in all corners of the earth so that they assign to Arabic its rightful place in their lectures, publications and publicity.
>
> To all institutions regardless of the work they do so that they assign to Arabic what belongs to it and to confer on it the right status and the dignity it deserves in all their dealings, advertisements, records and such like, all of this in order to defend and support God's religion, the language of God's religion and that of his Prophet, Peace be upon him, in aid of man's future on this earth . . . and for his salvation in the Hereafter.

The dedication is written from a faith perspective, now locating the title in an unquestionably Islamic orbit of interpretation. The audience is defined as a Muslim constituency that has religiously inscribed responsibilities and duties towards Arabic: promoting it in education, public discourse, commercial activity and in official dealings with each other as a prerequisite to defending the faith. By using *fuṣḥā* Arabic in these and other domains, Muslims will not only be giving expression to the status the language has in doctrinal terms and to the status it ought to have as a living medium of expression, but they will additionally be defending it against an unspecified enemy, who seems to want to weaken it, both religiously and culturally. The umbilical cord joining religion to language in the dedication is a matter of faith and ideology, and it occurs in many of the texts I will discuss below. The ideological thrust in this dedication comes through loud and clear in the use of the two terms *ḥimāyat* (protection) and *yudāfiʿū* (to defend), whose aim is to motivate the reader to become active and task-oriented in society, which is conceptualised as a symbolic, if not, in fact, real, battleground between the forces of good and evil. The fact that those addressed in the dedication are an imaginary group adds to the power of this call to symbolic arms: the reader is implicitly enlisted in this group, making him or her personally and morally responsible for defending the language, as suggested by the author. As an expression of language ideology, the dedication combines the ideational with the emotional, but it tilts the balance in favour of the latter. This is why I have described this dedication as a: 'symbolic call to arms'. Task-orientation must therefore be the main focus of this dedication.

This interpretation of the link between language and faith is picked up again in the epigraph (see Figure 3.6), which al-Nahwi calls *iftitāḥ* (lit. opening), reminding us of the first chapter of the Qur'an: *Fātiḥa*. The epigraph contains eight quotations from the Qur'an, which I will give here: 'We have sent it down as an *Arabic Qur'an*, in order that you may learn wisdom' (Qur'an 12:2); 'Verily this is a Revelation from the Lord of the Worlds. With it came down the Spirit of Faith and Truth to your heart and mind so you may admonish, in the *perspicuous Arabic tongue*' (Qur'an 26:192–5 [emphasis added]); 'A Scripture of which the verses are explained, an *Arabic Qur'an* for people who have knowledge' (Qur'an 41:3 [emphasis added]); 'And verily we have coined for mankind in this Qur'an all kinds of similitudes, that perhaps they may reflect; an *Arabic Qur'an containing no crookedness*, that perhaps they may ward off (evil)' (Qur'an 39:27–8 [emphasis added]); 'Those who disbelieve in the Reminder when it comes to them (are guilty), for it is an unassailable Scripture. Falsehood can come at it from before or from behind it. (It is) a Revelation from the Wise, the Owner of Praise' (Qur'an 41:41–2); 'We have not sent you but as a universal (messenger) to men, giving them glad tidings, and warning them (against sin) but most men do not understand' (Qur'an 34:28); 'And We know well that they say, "it is a man that teaches him". The tongue of him who they wickedly point to is notably foreign, while *this is Arabic, pure and clear*' (Qur'an 16:103 [emphasis added]);

and, 'Thus we have revealed it to be a *judgement of authority in Arabic*. Were you to follow their (vain) desires after the knowledge which has reached you, then would you find neither protector nor defender against God' (Qur'an 13:37 [emphasis added]).

Six of the verses translated above refer to the Qur'an directly as an Arabic Qur'an, reminding the reader of the link between faith and language in Islam in an unequivocal way. This epigraph serves two functions here. On the one hand, it provides the strongest possible backing in Arab and Islamic culture to the connection between language and faith. The authority of the Divine Voice is marshalled in aid of the text to give it backing and authority. On the other hand, the epigraph is intended to work on the reader emotionally, so as to heighten the feeling that the defence of the language is a defence of faith. It therefore underlines the author's message that the fate of Arabic is an individual responsibility that each Muslim will have to account for when facing God on the Day of Judgement. Motivation and task orientation are at the heart of this epigraph, revealing its task-orientation purpose as a speech act. We may add another point here. These six verses are the ones that we have come across in discussions of the inimitability of the Qur'an, insofar as it relates to *shu'ūbiyya*. The connectedness of the present with the past will not be lost on some readers, who can discern this link without too much effort or knowledge of past history.

The connection between the past and the present is an aspect of language ideology in most cultures and nationalisms. The connection between faith and language is subject to ideological manipulation in nation-building. The public can access these two ideological impulses easily, because of their normative nature in society. And they – the public – can do so without having to read the text or even any portion of it – that is, without becoming readers in the sense explained above. All the public have to do is to activate the religious, cultural and ideological frames of reference that they have internalised through education and socialisation. It is in this sense that language ideology can be most effective, because it does not draw attention to itself as a covert force in society. Repetition of these and other impulses of Arabic language ideology – some of which I will discuss below – is a matter of recursive circulation or *reiteration*, rather than, strictly speaking, repetition in the technical sense. Reiteration, as a form of self-perpetuating recursivity, gives continued life to a language ideology, while, at the same time, establishing it as a norm similar in its affective force to the predictive power of the laws of nature. Herein exist the basis – epistemologically bogus, no doubt – that normative Arabic language ideology is not construction, but a statement of fact that is self-evident, as if it was a category of nature. Constant reiteration will be needed to ensure that what is thought to be self-evident remains so. Considering the reiterative and recursive as repetitive in language ideology is to miss the point, because it fails to capture the intent behind the formalism of repetition.

Let us now consider the jacket copy in al-Nahwi's book (see Figure 3.7).

This copy consolidates, with some modulations, the above language ideology by expanding on the tropes of protection and defence encountered earlier in the dedication. I will translate this jacket copy below, so as to discuss these tropes further:

> The enemies [of Arabic and Islam] have understood the importance of Arabic and its significant place in Islam as well as its role in understanding God's Book [Qur'an] and the Traditions [Sunna] of his Apostle (peace be upon him: pbuh). One of their most important assaults [*muḥāwala*] was to try to weaken the bond [*ṣila*] between the Muslim and his Arabic language, weaken his commitment to stick to it and fielding strange and suspect ideas that will turn him away from the language of his religion / faith and his mission in life. These assaults / attempts lasted centuries, needed great effort and displayed relentless perseverance. There were ideas to change the grammatical rules wholly or in part. There were ideas to change the Arabic script and orthographic rules. And there were ideas to change [the composition / prosody] of Arabic poetry. These attempts and plans were part of the methods and plans that these enemies have prepared to invade the Muslim World and to destroy, among other things, its faith and human resources.
>
> [However], God Almighty has pledged to preserve the Reminder [*dhikr*] that He revealed to His Apostle and Prophet Muhammad (pbuh). This means that He has pledged to preserve His religion, His Qur'an and that of His Apostle and Prophet Muhammad (pbuh), His Arabic language which is the vessel (*wi'ā'*) of the Reminder in its totality, including its eloquence [*bayān*] and its substance [*māddatahu*] as is mentioned in the Qur'an (15:9): 'We, even We, reveal the Reminder, and We verily are its Guardian'.
>
> This [whole thing] is a trial [*ibtilā'*] from God Almighty to test His faithful believers, to find out who among them will honour the promise and the trust, and who will take the cause of His religion, the language of His Qur'an and the Traditions of His Prophet (pbuh) and who will lag behind [*yatawānā*] or weave conspiracies [*yudabbir*]. This trial will follow God's appointed ways which will come to pass, revealing His wisdom and supreme command [*qadar ghālib*].

This paratext does not specify who the enemies of Arabic and Islam are: the jacket copy talks about 'the enemies' (*al-'a'dā'*) as if they were a known category who the public can identify without help from the author. This notion of the enemy, whether insider or outsider, is a given in this kind of discourse, by virtue of being part of what is considered to be self-evident. The enemies' aim of attacking, weakening and dismantling Arabic and Islam is another given of this discourse. The public need not to be convinced of it: the idea that there are all sorts of conspiracies and conspirators, both inside and outside, is already lodged in the public's mind as a given of their ideological schema.[28] Furthermore, the enemy is conceptualised as implacable and

[28] Although the following explanation of the term in Arabic, *mu'āmara*, is meant to apply to Arab political language in the 1950s and 1960s, its core meaning is still

persistent in his efforts. This idea resonates with the public's view of how the enemy works: he does not give up easily. Ideas of changing Arabic grammar, prosody, script and orthographic rules are examples of this work, which, implicitly, cannot be considered legitimate reforms. This portion of the jacket copy may not be part of the public's common knowledge, but the public would not question its validity, because it builds on other givens in their ideological schema. If the base is regarded as self-evident, there is a tendency in ideological debates to think of what is built on this base as self-evident by association. Arabic and Islam are treated here as intertwined facets of Muslim life: an attack on one is an attack on the other, although the primary interest here is the language. Until now, the jacket copy has been concerned with the attack side of the language ideological battle.

The metaphor of protection, which will be dealt with at length below in discussing the war trope, comes in the second paragraph. The main idea here is to assure the public that God will fulfil His pledge to protect the Qur'an and, through it, He will also protect the language in which the Qur'an is revealed. Qur'an 15:9 in the jacket copy is part of the repertoire of the Arabic-speaking Muslim. The invocation of this verse is intended to let the public know that God is on the side of those who defend Arabic and

applicable today: 'Arab political climate is heavy with conspiracies and plots, for political opposition is mostly underground and secretiveness is the normal condition of political life. Thus the whispering campaign is as effective as radio broadcasts, and news is not so much reporting as reading meaning into developments and events. Just as the obvious is never taken at face value, so the hidden motive is always the object of examination and questioning. The line separating credulity from cynicism is often too thin even from the standpoint of those who are engaged in political action. The mystery permeating this atmosphere induces suspicion and mistrust; the ordinary man sees a plot behind every shift in every policy, every decision or development, whether within the army, by a foreign power, or by a political group. There is an old conspiracy, a Communist conspiracy and an imperialist conspiracy'. See Hisham Sharabi, *Nationalism and Revolution in the Arab World* (Princeton, NJ: D. Van Nostrand Company, 1966), p. 101. Commenting on conspiracy theory as a form of ideological explanation, Billig says: 'The conspiracy theory of politics . . . represents an ideological pattern especially relevant to the social psychology of explanation . . . In essence the ideology of conspiracy seeks to explain all major political events in the world in terms of an evil conspiracy, or series of conspiracies. The conspiracy theorist tells a story of hidden machinations by small groups who are plotting to subvert the natural order of the world . . . [The] conspiracy theorist offers a monomanic explanation for social events, in that all the major happenings are explained in precisely the same way: no matter what happens the conspiracy theorist sees the malign hand of hidden conspirators. In this sense conspiracy theory represents an extreme form of personal explanation in that nothing happens by chance, since all is to be explained in terms of deliberate plotting'. See Michael Billig, 'Methodology and scholarship in understanding ideological explanation', in Charles Antaki (ed.), *Analysing Everyday Explanation: A Casebook of Methods* (London: Sage Publications, 1988), pp. 201–2.

His religion, so they need not worry, because no power is greater than God Almighty's power. A modulation of this trope is then offered in the last paragraph: the public must act as part of God's design. The attack against Arabic is a trial, whose aim is to test the resolve and commitment of the believers and establish who among them will fulfil the pledge that is incumbent upon them in defending Islam and Arabic. This last idea uses the key expressions – *ibtilā'*, *yumaḥḥiṣa 'ibādihi* and *yūfi bi-l-'ahd* – that are readily reminiscent of verses in the Qur'an. The Muslim is always under trial as part of God's eternal scheme for the believers who will eventually triumph. This last idea is part of a Muslim's belief; consequently, the public, who are envisaged to be Muslim, need no convincing on this score, as what the jacket copy states must be self-evident. The second and third paragraphs are, therefore, a symbolic call to arms: they are intended to motivate task-orientation in the public sphere. Those who rise in defence of Arabic and Islam will not be on their own. They will engage in this endeavour according to a pre-set plan ordained by God, whose support they will enjoy in the knowledge that they will win their fight, in spite of all the trials and tribulations that they are bound to endure.

Like a coiled spring, the jacket copy reiterates the language ideology in the dedication and epigraph and, recursively, moves it forward on a predetermined path. It expands on the notion of attack and defence, giving examples of the former within a schema that sees the attack on language as an attack on faith and vice versa. For task orientation, the jacket copy tells members of the intended public that the attack has to be repulsed and that, for motivational effect, they will not be on their own in repulsing it. When the battle is joined, God will be with them and on their side all the way. And to ease their pain, it describes the battle as a divinely ordained trial carried out to test their resolve and prove their commitment. It must be clear from this that the jacket copy operates at heightened task-orientation pitch in a manner intended to mediate the distance between words and action with great intensity. In attempting to do this, the jacket copy trades on freely circulating items of language ideology in society to such an extent that the line separating author from public is traversed imperceptibly, calling into question the right of the author to be the sole author over the propositional substance, not words, of the content in the intellectual transaction. On the surface and legally speaking, al-Nahwi's book is published by al-Nahwi: he has copyright to it. At a deeper level, the authorship is complex: society shares in this act of authorship through its language ideology, which the jacket copy picks up, closely reflects on and circulates back into society in a recursive process, which propels the wheels of reiteration. From an Islamic perspective, this process of language ideology circulation is consistent with the rise and continued impact of Islamic-inflected politics in the Arab and Muslim worlds over the last two decades of the twentieth century and the opening decade of the twenty-first century. This context does not just encourage the reiteration of this ideology and its circulation in society, but produces dense channels for its communication through the media, the mosque and other forms and avenues of association, giving it greater currency and intensity in the social world.

Poetry and Language Ideology

Poetry is another site for the circulation of language ideology in society. This is not surprising, considering the importance of poetry in Arab cultural life since pre-Islamic times. Furthermore, poetry had a special link with grammar in the formative decades of the Arabic intellectual tradition. The early Arab grammarians used it as a fairly open corpus, from which data could be culled in developing grammatical theory.[29] In this respect, poetry was second only to the Qur'an in importance. In addition to this, poetry has been employed to comment on the role of Arabic in nation-building, intra-group conflict resolution and in task-orientation in these two endeavours. Sharkey's study of the role of poetry in Sudanese nationalism in the first half of the twentieth century is an example of this trend in Arab cultural politics. The same is true of Iraq and Palestine.[30] I can give examples from other Arab countries, but this would take us outside the current scope of this study.

However, by way of an overview, I will refer to the three major functions of poetry in the nationalist paradigm: reinforcement, legitimisation and inspiration. Reinforcement aims at using the past to cull symbols and capture moments of glory, which the poet deploys to give the nation reasons to be proud of who it is. In this regard, modern Arabic poetry continues an old tradition, wherein the poet acts as the mouthpiece and defender of his tribe or group. Poetic compositions of this kind play a motivational role in society by turning the past, which is both to be emulated and surpassed, into a springboard for future action. Legitimisation is intended to lend validity to the claims of the nation and its pedigree, so that it can move forward in an assured way. Inspiration is linked to task-orientation: it works through affect, resonance and impact. This function comes to the fore at times of

[29] See Ramzi Baalbaki, 'The historic relevance of poetry in the Arab grammatical tradition', in Ramzi Baalbaki, Salih Said Agha and Tarif Khalidi (eds), *Poetry and History: The Value of Poetry in Reconstructing Arab History* (Beirut: American University of Beirut Press, 2001), pp. 95–120; Yasir Suleiman, *The Arabic Grammatical Tradition: A Study in Ta'līl* (Edinburgh: Edinburgh University Press, 1999).

[30] See Heather J. Sharkey, *Living with Colonialism: Nationalism and Culture in the Anglo-Egyptian Sudan* (Berkeley, CA: University of California Press, 2003); Yasir Suleiman, 'The nation speaks: on the poetics of nationalist literature', in Yasir Suleiman and Ibrahim Muhawi (eds), *Literature and Nation in the Middle East* (Edinburgh: Edinburgh University Press, 2006a), pp. 208–31; Yasir Suleiman, 'Nationalist poetry, conflict and meta-linguistic discourse', in Yasir Suleiman (ed.), *Living Islamic History: Studies in Honour of Professor Carole Hillenbrand* (Edinburgh: Edinburgh University Press, 2010), pp. 252–78.

active conflict, when the nation seems to be in peril or is thought to have come under attack, either materially or symbolically, from the outside or the inside. In performing these functions, poetry can exploit the symbolic power of language as a marker of the nation.

When used in this way, language displays its two functions to full effect: that of a symbol and that of an instrument of communication. When language as an instrument comments on language as a symbol, we may refer to this kind of engagement as *meta-linguistic discourse*. This kind of discourse has a long history in Arab intellectual life, dating back to the early days of the Arabic grammatical tradition, when what were thought to be the excesses of the grammarians came under attack, as will be discussed at length below. This kind of meta-discourse has also been deployed in pedagogic grammars, which aim to teach the facts of Arabic grammar through extended poetic compositions, the best known examples of which are Ibn Malik's *Alfiyya* and Ibn Adjjurrum's (d. 723/1323) *al-Ājjurrūmiyya*.[31] Anti-Shu'ūbiyya poets used poetry meta-discursively – for example, the grammarian al-Zamakhshari (d. 538/1143), whom we encountered in Chapter 2.[32] In this section, I will deal with Hafiz Ibrahim's well-known poem on the (imagined) state of Arabic. The main focus will be on the language ideology that this poem evinces, supported by similar expressions of language ideology from other poems on the same topic.

I have chosen this poem for analysis for two reasons. First, because of the canonical nature of this poem in modern Arabic poetry, which made it a popular source of epigraphs in books on Arabic to the extent that the mere mention of two words from it can trigger the intent of the whole poem for educated Arabic speakers. This is the case in one epigraph, among others, where the two words *anā al-baḥr* ('I am the sea')[33] immediately recall this poem,[34] even if the rest of the epigraph may not seem to completely follow the language ideology of the original: *thawra 'alā al-'arabiyya al-qā'ima, wa-binā' li-'arabiyya jadīda* ('a revolution against Arabic as it is these days to build a new Arabic').[35] This act of appropriation signifies the importance of this poem. I will discuss another such act in my treatment of the war trope in Arabic language ideology later.

[31] See Michael G. Carter (ed.), *Arab Linguistics: An Introductory Classical Text with Translation and Notes* (Amsterdam and Philadelphia, PA: John Benjamins, 1981) for a translation and annotation of *al-Ājjurrūmiya* based on al-Shirbini's (d. 978/1570) commentary on this text.

[32] Bahīja Bāqir al-Ḥasanī, 'al-Zamakhsharī wa-l-shu'ūbiyya', *Majallat majma' al-lugha al-'arabiyya al-urdunnī* (1989), 37: 203–4.

[33] This title is followed by ellipses (. . .) to signal that the absent is in fact not absent at all, but ubiquitous and omnipresent through its popular circulation.

[34] al-Junaydī Kahlīfa, *Naḥwa 'arabiyya afḍal* (Beirut: Manshūrāt Dār al-Ḥayāt, n.d.), p. 5.

[35] Ibid. p. 5.

Second, the discussion is intended to underline the importance of poetry in Arab culture in discussing issues related to language in its multifarious dimensions, including language ideology, which is the main focus here. As I have argued elsewhere,[36] the excessive attention to the aesthetics of poetry in critical theory, coupled with the narrowing of disciplinary horizons in empirical terms[37] in the sociology of language or sociolinguistics and in political studies, have militated against the use of poetry as a source of information on language in society, including language ideology. While I am aware of the methodological hazards of including poetry in the empirical domain, the exclusion of poetry in studying language ideology not only deprives us of important information on this topic, but it also removes from consideration the role of poetry in circulating language ideology in society, as well as its importance in generating affect, motivation and task-orientation, which are hallmarks of all ideologies. In this respect, it would be interesting to survey the circulation of Ibrahim's poem in the education field through school curricula (formally and informally), the media, the Internet, other poetic compositions and debates on language in society as an example of the circulation of language ideology. Although this is not a task to which I can attend here, based on my scholarly and field expertise in the education sector in the Arab world, I have little doubt of the currency of this poem or at least parts of it among Arabic speakers of high school and university level.

Poetry and Language Ideology: An Example

Let me begin by first providing a translation of Ibrahim's twenty-three lined poem before discussing the language ideology that it promulgates.[38] The poem was composed and published in 1903, presaging a period – the first two decades of the twentieth century – during which discussions of language and nationalism were at their highest in Egypt. I am thinking here of the attempts to define Egyptian national identity in an Egypt-centric way, which sought to reduce the significance of the links of language and culture that Egypt had with other Arabic-speaking countries. Whether this was to be done by narrowing the gap between *fuṣḥā* Arabic and the dialect(s) or

36 See Suleiman, 'The nation speaks: on the poetics of nationalist literature'; Suleiman, 'Arabic language reforms, language ideology and the criminalisation of Sībawayhi'; Suleiman, 'Nationalist poetry, conflict and meta-linguistic discourse'; Suleiman, *Arabic, Self and Identity*.

37 See Yasir Suleiman, *The Arabic Language and National Identity: A Study in Ideology* (Washington, DC: Georgetown University Press, 2003); Suleiman, *Arabic, Self and Identity*.

38 See Shurūq Muḥammad Salmān, *Durar bahiyya fī madḥ al-'arabiyya* (United Arab Emirates: no publisher, 2007). This collection contains 28 poems about Arabic. A lot more poems have been written on Arabic in the modern period, as can be ascertained from a survey of the periodicals of the Arabic language academies.

by calling for the replacement of the former with the latter, language was a subject of debate in the political and cultural scene at the time.

The Arabic Language Laments/Bewails its Fortune among its People

1) I examined my case and so accused those who level charges against me,
I called upon my people and reckoned and wondered my fate
2) They accused me of being barren in my youth, how I wish
I was but I have not been frightened by what my enemies have been saying
3) I gave birth, but when I couldn't find for my daughters
Suitable suitors, I buried them alive
4) I was able to express God's Divine word, in form and meaning
And never felt unable to express His verses and lessons
5) So how could I be unable to describe man-made machines
And finding the right name for the right invention?
6) I am a sea in whose depths pearls are hidden
So have they [you] asked the diver about my oyster pearls?
7) Woe unto you! I am in decline and my fine attributes are getting shabby
The medication is dear and you are the source of my pain
8) Do not trust my fate to time for I fear
For you if my death is nigh
9) I see men in the West revel in glory and pride
A nation will have dignity only when their language enjoys the same
10) Men in the West have brought miracles to their people
How I wish you would just coin new words to match
11) Are you moved by a croaking voice from the West
Calling for burying me alive while still in my youth?
12) Were you to drive away [this] bird [of doom and gloom] one day, you would know
What impediments and fragmentation it hides
13) May God revive the bones of those outstanding men in the belly of the Arabian Peninsula who would be loathe to see my spears go limp
14) These bones have retained my friendship in what remains of them
And I have retained my friendship for them with a heart that is for ever in pain
15) I have vied in glory with these decomposed bones, in East and West,
Doing so with humility
16) Every day I see in the newspapers a slippery slope
Bringing me closer to my grave in haste
17) I hear writers in Egypt clamouring
And I know that those who are shouting loud are announcing my death
18) Are my people, May God forgive them, leaving me
To a language with no pedigree?
19) The pollution of the foreigners [European colonisers] runs through it
As the poison of a snake runs in the Euphrates
20) So it appears like a dress with seventy patches
Of different and diverse colours

21) To the community of writers at their full assembly
I extend my request following my complaint
22) Either give me a life that revives the dead from decomposition
And makes my remains sprout in those graves
23) Or a death from which there is no resurrection
A death the likes of which there is none.

This poem contains many of the themes that recur in Arabic language ideology. First, the idea that *fuṣḥā* Arabic has pedigree is a given of this ideology; in this respect, *fuṣḥā* Arabic is different from the dialects (*lughātin lam tattaṣil bi-ruwāti*, line 18), which, additionally, are said or believed to have been polluted by the importation of terms and turns of phrase from foreign Western languages. The injection of Western influence is described as poison (*lu'āb al-afā'ī fī masīli furāti*, line 19) that, we assume, will eventually kill the language. Second, the strongly held belief that *fuṣḥā* Arabic has the resources to deal with scientific advances is reiterated, citing as support Arabic's capacity to deal with these advances in the past and how it has been able to express the message of God's revelation (*wa-si'tu kitāba Allāhi lafẓan wa-ghāyatan*, 14). No doubt referring to the lexical domain, *fuṣḥā* Arabic is described as a sea that is full of pearls, which are waiting to be picked (*anā al-baḥru fī aḥshā'ihi al-durru kāminun*, line 6). Third, the poem links the strength of a people with the strength of their language (*wa kam 'azza aqwāmun bi-'izzi lughāti*, line 9), pointing out that this is the case in the West. The reference to the West here is intended to shame the Arabs and, at the same time, to motivate them to emulate the West in its attitudes towards its languages. Catching up with the West – as the Arabs want to do – implies copying the ways of the West in matters of language. This imperative adds to the motivation which the past glory of Arabic demands of its speakers. Fourth, the poem reiterates the belief that *fuṣḥā* Arabic is in a state of perilous decline (*arā fī kulli yawmin fī al-jarā'idi mazlaqan mina al-qabri*, line 16), as is exemplified by its poor use in the press media – this being a perennial complaint in Arabic language ideology to this day. This theme has been expanded in current language ideological discourse to include all forms of the media, including electronic media and the Internet.

The underlying theme in this poem and what, in fact, gives it its appeal and continued popularity is the attitude that it displays towards the above ideological themes: it is written as a complaint and rebuke, in which the language: (1) complains about being neglected by its own people (*fa-lā takilūnī li-l-zamān*, line 8); and (2) rebukes them for neglecting it (*fa-yā wayḥakum*, line 7). In decoding these two purposes (*aghrāḍ*), the poem reveals the morally challenging relationship between the language and its own people (*ahlihā*, as in the title, and *qawmī*, as in line 1). As a personified object, the language feels it has every right to complain and rebuke, not because of any concerns it may selfishly have about its own 'personal' fate, but because of the impact of this fate upon the people that it implicitly cares about, in spite of their less than commendable attitude and behaviour towards it. It is not surprising, therefore, that *fuṣḥā* Arabic is depicted as a mother who wants the best for her daughters: suitors of equal status (*wa lammā lam ajid li-'ar'āisī rijālan*, line 3), whose non-existence or dearth has forced her to bury those daughters alive, following the (reprehensible) practice of the Arabs in pre-Islamic times (*wa'dtu banātī*, line 3). By naming and shaming Arabic speakers, *fuṣḥā* Arabic, as a personified object, aims to impel these speakers to act before it is too late. As a speech act, the overall purpose of the poem is one of motivation and task-orientation: it lies in the perlocutionary domain. However, what makes the poem especially effective in delivering its message is that it makes Arabic speak on behalf of itself. After all, the language cannot trust its people, for the reasons that it outlines, to speak on its behalf, since they are ill-equipped to do so, both attitudinally and in terms of their faulty linguistic behaviour. Furthermore, by making *fuṣḥā* Arabic speak on its behalf in a way that exploits the symbolism of the language as a marker of identity, the poem draws attention to the instrumentality of language, highlighting, in the process, its effectiveness as an instrument in a way that decries its defective instrumentalisation among Arabic speakers. What we have here, therefore, is a multi-layered exploitation of *fuṣḥā* Arabic in the ideological domain: (1) Arabic as a personified object; (2) uses Arabic as an instrument; (3) to talk about the state of this instrument; (4) and the symbolism it carries in society; (5) as well as the defective use of this instrument by its speakers. This is an excellent example of discursive reflexivity or what I have called meta-linguistic discourse in language ideology: it contains four layers (2–5) of meta-discursivity, in addition to the initiating frame, marked as (1) above.

This poem, being one of the earliest of its kind on the topic (at least that I know of), has set a path for similar poems, which pick up some items of the language ideology that it enunciates. This is done in the titles of some of the poems that belong to this genre – for example, *Ibḥār fī a'māq al-lugha* (*Sailing in the Depth of Arabic* by 'Abd al-Rahman al-'Ashmawi)[39] and *al-'arabiyya tashkū abnā'ahā* (*Arabic Complains about its Sons and Daughters* by Walid Qassab).[40] Many of these poems parody Ibrahim's poem in ideological content. As an example, let us consider one aspect of what 'Adnan 'Ali Rida al-Nahwi says in his poems *Lughatī al-jamīla* (*My Beautiful Language*).[41] I will translate lines 15–18 from this poem, so as to illustrate this influence (the poet is speaking here):

1) I am astonished, why have my people left their language and run
   In pursuit of [a language] with low aims and the tramps [who promote it]
2) They have not adopted a good rational thought
   From the West, nor have they adopted knowledge that will grow and advance

[39] See Salmān, *Durar bahiyya fī madḥ al-'arabiyya*, pp. 22–5.
[40] Ibid. pp. 26–9.
[41] Ibid. pp. 17–19.

3) Instead they have adopted a twisted tongue
Although God has gifted them a beautiful and balanced language
4) Woe unto them! They (the dialects) have replaced clarity of expression with a stammer,
And they (the dialects) have replaced their rich eloquence with error.

These lines reiterate the point established in Ibrahim's poem – that the Arabs are 'abandoning' their language in favour of the dialects or foreign and Western languages, in spite of the fact that *fuṣḥā* Arabic, in comparison with these alternative tongues, is rich in clarity and eloquence. Moreover, the attitude that pervades these lines is one of complaint and rebuke in line with Ibrahim's poem. Instead of imitating the West in its rational thought and promotion of scientific knowledge, the Arabs are upbraided for playing havoc with their language. Some of these impulses in Arabic language ideology occur in other poems in this meta-discursive genre. In his poem *Wāqi' al-ḍādd fī al-umma* ('The State of the Language of *al-Ḍādd* in the Arab Nation'),[42] 'Allal al-Fasi[43] picks up the theme of the ability of *fuṣḥā* Arabic to express the message of God's revelation: *man ghayruhā fī lughāti al-arḍi qādiratan, 'alā adā'i kalāmi Allāhi* ('Which other language on this earth is capable of expressing God's speech', line 15). He then uses Ibrahim's 'sea metaphor' to refer to the lexical richness of the language: *wa innahā al-baḥru zakhkhārun bi-bāṭinihi, mina al-jawāhiri mā yazhū bihi al-abadu* ('It is a sea whose belly is brimming to the full, with jewels that can adorn time unto eternity', line 1.19). This same 'sea metaphor' is used by 'Abd al-'Aziz Safi al-Jil in his poem *Lughatī shamsu al-lughāt* ('My Language is the Sun to all Languages'): *lughatī ka-baḥrin minhu tazkhuru abḥuru* ('My language is a sea of seas', line 1).[44] Later in the poem, the poet refers to the lexical richness of the language: *la al-ṭibbu a'jazahā wa-laysa muhandisun illā wa-qad a'ṭathu mā yatakhayyaru* ('She [*fuṣḥā*] Arabic was not cowed by the demands made on it by medicine/medical science, and there is not an engineer to whom she did not offer a choice', line 13). Ibrahim's sea metaphor is further used by 'Abd al-Rahim Mahmud in his poem *al-Ḍādd awwal ḥā'iṭ wa-di'ām* ('The Language of *al-Ḍādd* is the First Wall and Bulwark').[45] In line 14, the poet obliquely refers to this metaphor: *al-durru fī ṭayyi al-buḥuri mukhabba'un* ('Pearls are hidden in the crevices of its [Arabic] seas', line 14).

These and other poems and references, which, for reasons of space I cannot deal with here, underscore the thesis that poetry is a rich site for culling information on Arabic language ideology in Arab culture. These references further reveal how language ideology can circulate through this

[42] For the name of the language as *al-ḍādd*, see Suleiman, *The Arabic Language and National Identity*, pp. 59–60.
[43] See Salmān, *Durar bahiyya fī madḥ al-'arabiyya*, pp. 30–2.
[44] Ibid. pp. 34–7.
[45] Ibid. pp. 40–1.

site, reiterating units of this ideology from poet to poet, both intra- and inter-generationally, across the Arab world, for enhanced dissemination. At the heart of these poetic compositions are affect, motivation and task-orientation. These and similar poems are intended to invoke the legacy of the past and point to the challenges of the present, doing so through a register of remonstration, rebuke and elegiac enunciation. These registers, embedded in well-known poetic frames, *'itāb* and *rithā'* respectively, are familiar to Arab readers and members of the public, who can activate their cultural schemata of these frames for added impact, which can lead to the intensification of meaning and attitudinal orientation on their part. This is where poetry is an especially effective and affective carrier of language ideology in Arab culture. And this is why I call for the integration of it more fully in any study of the social life of Arabic, one of the most important parts of which is Arabic language ideology.

The canonical nature of Ibrahim's poem and its circulation in the twenty-first century is evident from its presence on the Internet. A quick trawl of the Internet revealed the following titles for this poem: (1) *al-'Arabiyya tashkū abnā'ahā* ('Arabic Complains about its Sons [and Daughters]');[46] (2) *al-'Arabiyyatu tashkū ḥālahā* ('Arabic Complains about its Fate');[47] (3) *al-'Arabiyyutu tashkū al-hujrān* ('Arabic Complains of Abandonment');[48] (4) *al-'Arabiyyutu tashkū al-'arab* ('Arabic Complains about the Arabs');[49] (5) *al-'Arabiyyutu tashkū muwjjihīhā* ('Arabic Complains about Arabic Language School Inspectors');[50] (6) *al-'Arabiyyatu tashkū 'uqūq abnā'ihā* ('Arabic Complains about its Sons [and Daughters]' Recalcitrance [towards their Mother]');[51] (7) *al-'Arabiyyutu tashkū ahlahā fa-man min sāmi'*? ('Arabic Complains about its People: Will They Listen?');[52] (8) *al-lughatu al-'arabiyyatu tudāfi' 'an nafsihā* ('The Arabic Language Defends itself');[53] (9) *al-Lughatu al-'arabiyyatu tataḥaddath 'an nafsihā wa tashkū li-ḥālihā* ('The Arabic Language talks about itself and Complains about its Fate');[54] (10) *al-Lughatu al-'arabiyyatu tashkū al-jafā'* ('The Arabic Language Complains of being

46 See http://www.khayma.com/salehzayadneh/poets/hafez/hafez1.htm (accessed 26 January 2012).
47 See http://ejabat.google.com/ejabat/thread?tid=1d703b25815ee231 (accessed 26 January 2012).
48 See http://ar-ar.facebook.com/video/video.php?v=1732340966176 (accessed 26 January 2012).
49 See http://stibda3.123.st/t692-topic (accessed 26 January 2012).
50 See http://pulpit.alwatanvoice.com/content/print/133295.html (accessed 26 January 2012).
51 See http://www.aleqt.com/2010/03/29/article_370837.html (accessed 26 January 2012).
52 See http://tolab.justgoo.com/t2529-topic (accessed 26 January 2012).
53 See http://www.lq8.org/vb/showthread.php?t=1622 (accessed 26 January 2012).
54 See http://www.monms.com/vb/t27181.html (accessed 26 January 2012).

Shunned/Alienated');[55] (11) *al-Lughatu al-'arabiyyatu tashkū jafā'a abnā'ihā* ('The Arabic Language Complains about the Antipathy of/being Shunned by its Sons [and Daughters]');[56] (12) *al-Lughatu al-'arabiyyatu tukhāṭibukum* ('The Arabic Language is Addressing You');[57] and *al-Lughatu al-'arabiyyatu tantaḥib kull yawm bi-sababikum* ('The Arabic Language Wails Every Day Because of You').[58]

The fact that different people feel that they can suggest different titles for Ibrahim's poem is indicative of its continued resonance into the present day. Some of the titles direct the complaint that Arabic makes at its sons and daughters or at the Arabs as a whole. By referring to sons and daughters or children (the word *abnā'ahā* occurs three times above), the titles underline the role of Arabic as a 'mother language or tongue', which expression is no longer just a stock term of the kind that we find in modern linguistics, but one of live, metaphorical flesh and blood. This conceptualisation strikes a deep moral chord in Arab and Islamic cultures, because of the revered position of maternity (and paternity) in these cultures. Title six brings this connection to the surface through the term *'uqūq* (disobedience), which invariably triggers a morally loaded connection with *wālidayn* (parents) in Arabic in a way that reflects very badly on the children.[59] In this context, the children are accused of antipathy in their treatment of their mother (the word *jafā'* occurs in two titles): this is a morally serious charge. In one title, Arabic complains about the Arabic language school inspectors, presumably because they have failed to protect and promote the language in the educational sector. In making this complaint, the title propels the poem right into heated, ideologically impregnated debates about the poor standards of Arabic in schools, which is invariably attributed to the dominance of the colloquials and the lure of foreign languages. In one title (title 12), the poem addresses the Arab readers pointedly (*tukhāṭibukum*) in a manner that puts them directly in the firing line as the guilty party.[60] More flesh is put on this interpretation in title 13: Arabic bewails her fate every day, because of what you, its Arab readers, have done

55 See http://www.vb.herealmukalla.com/vb/showthread.php?t=16114 (accessed 26 January 2012).

56 See http://www.tech4c.com/vb/threads/23499 (accessed 26 January 2012).

57 See http://www.lahdah.org/vb/t4351.html (accessed 26 January 2012).

58 See http://www.alsaha.com/sahat/3/topics/168352 (accessed 26 January 2012).

59 The term *'uqūq* reminds the Arabic reader of Qur'an 17:23–4, which is ever-present when reflecting on the proper relationship between parents and children. Addressing the children, these verses read as follows in translation: '(23) Your Lord has decreed that you worship none except Him, and (that you show) kindness to parents. If one of them or both of them attain old age with you, say not "Fie" to them nor repulse them, but speak to them a gracious word. (24) And Lower to them the wing of submission through mercy, and say: My Lord! Have mercy on them both as they did care for me when I was little'.

60 Some of these titles are found on websites with pedagogic intent.

to it. This is a direct accusation, which, when made by a mother, has great moral force, regardless of whether it is justified or not.

As baptismal acts of designation, the new titles are, in effect, acts of appropriation, which suggest that Ibrahim's poem continues, more than 100 years after its initial publication, to speak to different audiences through a network of overlapping interpretations in the service of one overarching purpose: that of task-orientation, which is an integral part of any language ideology. By so doing, these baptismal acts of appropriation enhance the circulation of the poem and the Arabic language ideology that it carries by exploiting the reach of new media to new generations in an expanding circle of motherhood. The titles above are intended to entice, in order to deliver their message, which they do through emotional appeals, acting to induce in the public and readers feelings of shame and guilt. These feelings are cast in a moral framework, which is dominated by deep-rooted cultural and religious impulses that need little prompting to be activated and brought to bear on the situations to which they relate. Here, Arabic language ideology is not presented in a detached or dry manner as a theme in an argument, but as a 'flesh and blood' matter, in which the mother-child relationship carries morally sanctioned obligations from the latter towards the former. Language ideology is perhaps most effective when it is deployed in the court of emotional appeal, as is clearly the case here.

Tropes of Arabic Language Ideology: The Crisis Trope

The above exploration of Arabic language ideology through paratexts and poetry highlights some of the tropes in which this ideology is encoded. The tropes of neglect, crisis, attack and defence are paramount narrative strands in this language ideology, but they are not the only ones, as I will explain below. The idea of individual responsibility is embedded in this ideology: Arabs as individuals have a direct responsibility to defend the language and breathe new life into it through committed linguistic behaviour. In the remaining part of this chapter, I will deal with some of the major tropes of Arabic language ideology. As understood here, a language ideology trope is a figurative use of an expression that has currency in talk about a given language – in this case, Arabic. Tropes act as headings under which ideas and metaphors about language ideology coalesce. Their instrumental value, therefore, is one of designation and taxonomy. Serving in this capacity, language ideology tropes are non-discrete entities: they overlap with each other to form a network that helps map a society's perspective on its language.

Tropes of language ideology may have cross-cultural currency as frames of classification, but they do not necessarily have to share the same content. And in spite of the differences that these tropes may exhibit in different societies, they are most probably driven by a variety of factors, including language anxiety and task-orientation, as impulses of wider symptoms and projects in society. Celebratory tropes abound in all of the language ideologies that I know of, occurring under such headlines as beauty, excellence, richness, logicality and musicality, which, in the literature, are called language myths.[61] I will not deal with celebratory (of the in-group) or deprecatory (of the out-group) tropes here. Instead, I will focus on a small set of in-group tropes in Arabic language ideology that respond to the idea of the 'fray' in the title of this book. The first of these tropes is that of 'crisis'.

The crisis trope occurs in the titles of books dealing with different aspects of the Arabic language situation in the modern world. In some cases, this trope is marked directly by the Arabic word *'azma'*, which means 'crisis' or 'emergency'. Cognate words listed in Hans Wehr's *A Dictionary of Modern Arabic* (1980) are *'azama'* (to become critical, come to a head) and *'ma'zūm'* (victim of a crisis). Hans Wehr does not list the word *azma* in its medical sense to refer to 'asthma', although this meaning is important in understanding this language ideology trope: the constriction in the linguistic air pipes of the language results in the loss of the oxygen flow that it needs to live and prosper, making it less fit for purpose. Examples of book titles where the crisis trope is overtly marked are: *Azmat al-muṣṭalaḥ al-'arabī fī al-qarn al-tāsi''ashar* (*The Crisis of Arabic Terminology in the Nineteenth Century*);[62] *Azmat al-ta'rīb* (*The Crisis of Arabisation/Arabicisation*);[63] *Azmat al-lugha al-'arabiyya fī al-maghrib bayna ikhtilālāt al-ta'addudiyya wa-ta'aththurāt al-tarjama* (*The Crisis of the Arabic Language in Morocco between the Disorder of Plurilingualism and the Pitfalls of 'Translation'*);[64] and *al-Tārīkh al-fikrī li-azmat al-lugha al-'arabiyya* (*The Intellectual History of the Crisis of the Arabic Language*).[65] The same term occurs in c. 1550 items on the Arabic language that I found on al-Jazeera's website, some as inter-titles in transcripts of news reports.[66] The same trope is deployed in the press media, too, both in common parlance on the language and in highbrow publications aimed at the non-specialists.[67] A

61 See Laurie Bauer and Peter Trudgill (eds), *Language Myths* (London: Routledge, 1998); Joshua Fishman, *Language and Nationalism: Two Integrative Essays* (Rowley, MA: Newbury House Publishers, 1972).

62 Muḥammad Sawwā'ī, *Azmat al-muṣṭalaḥ al-'arabī fī al-qarn al-tāsi' 'ashar: muqaddima tārīkhiyya 'āmma* (Damascus: al-Ma'had al-Faransī li-l-Dirāsāt al-'Arabiyya bi-Dimashq, 1999).

63 Muḥammad Fawzī al-Mināwī, *Azmat al-ta'rīb* (Cairo: Markiz al-Ahrām li-l-Tarjama wa-l-Nashr, 2003).

64 'Abd al-Qādir al-Fihrī al-Fāsī, *Azmat al-lugha al-'arabiyya fī al-maghrib: bayna ikhtilālāt al-ta'addudiyya wa-ta'aththurāt 'al-tarjama* (Rabat: Manshūrāt Zāwiya, 2005).

65 Ṣādiq Muḥammad Nu'aymī, *al-Tārīkh al-fikrī li-azmat al-lugha al-'arabiyya* (Rabat: Ifrīqyā al-Sharq, 2008).

66 The search was made on 30 January 2012.

67 An example of the use of the crisis trope in highbrow publications is Aḥmad Mukhtār 'Umar, 'Azmat al-lugha al-'arabiyya wa-l-ḥāja ilā ḥulūl ghayr taqlīdiyya', in Amīn Maḥmūd al-'Ālim (ed.), *Qaḍāyā fikriyya: lughtatunā al-'arabiyya fī ma'rakat al-ḥaḍāra (Vols 17 and 18)* (Cairo: Qaḍāyā Fikriyya li-l-Nashr wa-l-Tawzī', 1997), pp. 65–80. This appeared in a special edition of *Qaḍāyā fikriyya* entitled *lughatunā*

content analysis of a selected corpus of writings on Arabic would be needed to establish the frequency and currency of this trope, but I will not undertake this here for reasons of space.

In some cases, the crisis trope is obliquely invoked. An example of this is *Inqādh al-lugha al-'arabiyya, inqādh al-huwiyya: taṭwīr al-lugha al-'arabiyya* (*Rescuing the Arabic Language, Rescuing [Arab] Identity: Developing the Arabic Language*),[68] the implication here being that Arabic is in crisis, from which it needs to be rescued. This inference is supported by the mention of the term *azma* twice in the jacket copy of this book. This copy offers us a glimpse of what the crisis trope consists of; because of this, I will translate it below, before proceeding to discuss aspects of it:

> Arab identity in our time is experiencing a devastating crisis (*azma ṭāḥina*) that is being made even more critical by its enemies, with witting or unwitting support from some of its children. Should this crisis (*azma*) be left to fester, it will lead to disfiguring the nation's past, cast doubt on its worth in the present and spread despair about its future in ways that will lead to dismantling its civilizational structure.
>
> Arabic is an important pickax in the hand of those who wish to destroy this identity. By the same token, it is an effective instrument in the hand of those who want to preserve this identity. Has not the revival of the Hebrew language helped her children to gather together, end their Diaspora and build their state? Has not careful scientific planning helped the francophone movement to preserve the influence of French culture in the world even after the dissolution of the French Empire? Is it possible for knowledge to take root in a nation's soil except through its national language? Is Arabic a frozen language that can defy all means to reform the way it is taught, keeping it unable to meet the needs of modern times?
>
> To what extent will the dangerous path we are embarked on lead in the direction of Westernisation and estrangement than that of Arabisation?

According to this jacket copy, a crisis of the Arabic language is a crisis of Arab identity, as the title page also makes clear (see Figure 3.8). The copy alludes to the accusation or view that Arabic is a frozen or fossilised language that cannot be rescued by advances in pedagogy. Because of this, Arabic is said to be unfit to handle the communicative demands of modernity. These views make the language an instrument of destruction (*hadm*), rather than one of construction (*binā'*) in civilisational terms. They are also said to lead the Arab nation away from the path of Arabisation, by creating new terminologies, to that of Westernisation, by adopting foreign languages and foreign terms. This language-cum-identity crisis in Arab societies is said to be nurtured by external enemies and aided and abetted by members of the Arab nation, who

al-'arabiyya fi ma'rakat al-ḥaḍāra, edited by the Egyptian intellectual Maḥmūd Amīin al-'Ālim.

68 Darwīsh, *Inqāẓ al-lugha, inqāẓ al-huwiyya: taṭwīr al-lugha al-'arabiyya.*

do so wittingly or unwittingly. This situation is said to differ from that pertaining in Hebrew, wherein the language was revived and used as a means of gathering the Jews of the diaspora as a first step towards establishing their state. It is also different from the situation of the French language, which, through careful planning, has retained its influence in the world, in spite of the dissolution of the French Empire, which promoted it on the world stage during the colonial period. These two comparisons are intended to rub salt into the Arabs' linguistic wounds. The mere mention of these examples is intended to say to the Arabs the following: Look at what your enemies have done on behalf of and through their languages and learn from them. Only by amending your ways and emulating their example will you be able to avoid the fate that awaits your language and, willy-nilly, your civilisation as a nation. Let it be known that scientific progress cannot be secured if it does not use the indigenous language as its medium.

As a paratext, the jacket copy operates in the court of emotional appeal. One expects the text of the book to go beyond this appeal and to do the intellectual legwork of providing a precise diagnosis of the crisis facing Arabic – this, the text does not do. Similarly, the text does not present a description of the cure for rescuing Arabic from its crisis. What we have here, therefore, is no more than a reiterative discursive act that circulates and keeps alive aspects of the dominant language ideology in Arab society. There is no innovation here, but there is purpose: the public need to be constantly reminded of this ideology to ensure that it maintains its position in the public sphere, wherein it has become an article of faith, socially speaking. This is effectively done, paratextually, through tropes that resonate with matrix ideologies in society by exploiting the feelings of anxiety and shame and the moral hazards of complicity or negligence. Behind all of this lies the ever-present desire to motivate and task-orient: Arabic speakers need to stand up, linguistically, and be counted.

This attention to task-orientation in Arabic language ideology characterises the preface which the famous Egyptian scholar Shawqi Dyaf[69] wrote for al-Minawi's book: *Azmat al-ta'rīb* (*The Crisis of Arabisation*).[70] This is what Dayf says about the book:

> [This book] is addressed to the readers as a fully-fledged result (*thamara nāḍija*, literally 'ripe fruit') of the author's experience [in the medical field] . . . by which he wishes to awaken their minds and strengthen their resolution (*yashḥadh al-himam*) so that the sons and daughters of Arabic will spring forth to promote their language, treat her against the weakness that has struck her, and offer her the right medication against the diseases which have afflicted her for no fault of

[69] Ḍayf published widely on Arabic language and literature. He also served as the President of the Arab Language Academy in Egypt.

[70] Muḥammad Fawzī al-Mināwī, *Azmat al-ta'rīb* (Cairo: Markiz al-Ahrām li-l-Tarjama wa-l-Nashr, 2003).

> her own, but because her people have not given her the respect it deserves nor offered her the attention and care it is worthy of.[71]

Task-orientation is intended to be made effective here, because Arabic is treated as a living mother who suffers from ill health and the neglect of her children, putting her health and life at great risk. The book is therefore both an appeal to action and a specification of the medicine to be prescribed. Task-orientation, in this context, is presented as a matter of life and death of a mother who is guilty of nothing, but is paying the price of her children's actions in a reversal of the Biblical proverb, wherein the linguistic sins of the children are visited upon their mother. This culturally and religiously inscribed appeal of language ideology is couched in an idiom of emotions, duties and responsibilities to make it effective.

Related to the crisis trope is the metaphor of suicide, which is pressed into service in Arabic language ideology to highlight the depth of the crisis facing Arabic. I would like to cite two examples of this metaphor here. The first occurs in the title of al-Misaddi's book *al-'Arab wa-l-intiḥār al-lughawī* (*The Arabs and Linguistic Suicide*).[72] On the bibliographic page, the subject of the book is given as *maṣīr al-'arabiyya* (*The Fate of Arabic*), which justifies linking it to the crisis trope. The jacket copy continues this theme, with characteristic attention directed to task-orientation:

> In this book the author activates all danger buttons (*yaduqq kull nawāqīs al-khaṭar*) to alert [us] to the fate/perilous state of the Arabic language. This is a cry of despair and a late appeal (*ṣayḥat hala' wa-istinfār*) to decision makers to come to the aid of the language of *ḍādd* [Arabic] before it joins other languages that are on their way to extinction (*inqirāḍ*).

This sense of panic about the language is obliquely encoded in the second book *hal tantaḥir al-lugha al-'arabiyya* (*Will the Arabic Language Commit Suicide?*) by al-Naqqash.[73] This is how al-Naqqash frames this problem:

> This wave (*mawja*) of running away from Arabic is a kind of linguistic suicide (*intiḥār lughawī*). It is in fact our people who are executing Arabic with their own hands. And no one sheds a tear! Many in fact are embarrassed by the language and have no confidence in it ... This is the case of linguistic frustration (*iḥbāṭ lughawī*) we live now ... So how can we help revive Arabic and protect it against suicide and death (*mufāraqat al-ḥayā*)?[74]

71 Ibid. p. 15.

72 'Abd al-Salām al-Misaddī, *al-'Arab wa-l-intiḥār al-lughawī* (Beirut: Dār al-Kitāb al-Jadīd al-Muttaḥida, 2011).

73 Rajā' al-Naqqāsh, *hal tantaḥir al-lugha al-'arabiyya?* (Cairo: Nahḍat Miṣr, 2009).

74 Ibid. pp. 27–8.

Again, both writers have task-orientation firmly fixed in their gaze. Al-Misaddi is, in fact, open about this, as his reference to decision-makers (*aṣḥāb al-qarār*) in the jacket copy makes clear.

However, task orientation does not have to be couched in the language of anxiety, shame, negligence and complicity, although this language of guilt is, more often than not, the norm in Arabic language ideology. A good example of this exception is Sawwa'i's book (see Figure 3.9): *Azmat al-muṣṭalaḥ al-'arabī fī al-qarn al-tāsi' 'ashar: muqaddima tārīkhiyya* (*The Crisis of Arabic Terminology in the Nineteenth Century: A Historical Introduction*).[75] Sawwa'i returns to a critical moment in the modern history of the Arabic language: the encounter between the Arab world, represented by Egypt, and Europe in the nineteenth century. Here he describes how, at this juncture, Arabic was found wanting in the lexical sphere, lacking many of the terms that are needed to transfer modern scientific concepts from the European languages into Arabic culture. In addition to the term *azma* (crisis) in describing this situation, Sawwa'i uses, in the preface (*tawṭi'a*),[76] the expressions *ḥiddat al-mu'ānā al-lughawiyya* (intense linguistic suffering),[77] *fatra 'aṣība* (critical period)[78] and *tawattur* (nervous tension) in a way which casts the crisis trope in a medical horizon of meaning. However, instead of invoking the feelings of shame and complicity in the public or readers in dealing with this trope, Sawwa'i highlights the success of the translation movement in Egypt in the nineteenth century in plugging lexical gaps in Arabic and uses this as positive motivation and task-orientation, building in this respect on a similar success in the classical period of Islam, when Greek knowledge and science were translated into Arabic. In other words, instead of self-flagellation as a force in Arabic language ideology, Sawwa'i excavates the past for its successes, rather than its failures, to encourage the Arabs to continue on its positive path.

Let me consider another publication in whose title the crisis trope is overtly marked: *al-Tārīkh al-fikrī li-azmat al-lugh al-'arabiyya* (see Figure 3.10).[79] The allure factor in this title resides in the promise of providing an intellectual history of the crisis trope in Arabic language ideology. The book does not do this, exemplifying, in this respect, the second part of the following statement from Genette concerning titles: 'a book more tempting than its title is better than a title more tempting than its book'.[80] However, the fact that the crisis trope is projected to have an intellectual history in this title suggests that the problems facing Arabic are believed to be deep-rooted in Arab culture. The same point about falling short of promise applies to the jacket

[75] Sawwā'ī, *Azmat al-muṣṭalaḥ al-'arabī fī al-qarn al-tāsi' 'ashar: muqaddima tārīkhiyya 'āmma*.
[76] Ibid. pp. 13–17.
[77] Ibid. p. 14.
[78] Ibid. p. 14.
[79] Nu'aymī, *al-Tārīkh al-fikrī li-azmat al-lugha al-'arabiyya*.
[80] Genette, *Paratexts: Thresholds of Interpretation*, p. 94.

copy, as well as the book as a whole. However, in addition to serving the function of reiteration and circulation, this book adds two interesting points to the content of the crisis trope. The first concerns the assumed sacredness of Arabic, signalled in the inter-title *hal al-lugha al-'arabiyya muqaddasa*? (*Is the Arabic Language Sacred?*), which is said to lead to a societal attitude that resists linguistic change and development on false doctrinal grounds: 'The danger in linking language with the scared may in fact make it (the language) a frozen being that does not change or develop'.[81] In addition, this linkage casts Arabic in a religious light, when, in fact, it is more important to recognise its role in marking the identity of the Arab nation. This point is captured in the inter-title *al-lugha [al-'arabiyya] hiya bu'd qawmī wa-ḥayātī wa-laysat bu'dan dīniyyan* (*Arabic is a Dimension of the Nation and Everyday Life rather than a Religious Dimension*).[82] The other point concerns the devastating effect that the nation-state (*al-dawla al-quṭriyya*)[83] has had on the unity of the Arabic language in the Arabic-speaking world. Instead of language planning being uniformly applied to all Arabic-speaking countries, this planning is done on a country-by-country basis, forgetting, in the process, the common linguistic passport that Arabic provides. Al-Minawi points to another component of the crisis trope: the lack of commitment to the Arabisation/Arabicisation of science teaching at the pan-Arab level. This is a political problem and not a problem as to whether Arabic can serve as the language of instruction in the sciences. It is also characterised as a psychological problem (*qaḍiyya nafsiyya*)[84] or a problem of self-confidence in Arab society. Jubran considers this lack of confidence and the feeling of inferiority towards Western languages and culture to be major factors in the predicament facing the Arabic language.[85]

Al-Fihri (see Figure 3.11) links the crisis of Arabic in Morocco to three fields of activity.[86] In the educational field, students suffer from poor language standards, diglossia and bilingualism, an over-complex *fuṣḥā* Arabic, lack of well-trained teachers and poor curricula and language materials in the schools. In public life, Arabic suffers from exclusion from certain fields of communication in society, due to the unfair advantage of foreign languages in terms of employment, owing to their prestige and the lack of political will to give Arabic greater currency in the media and in government administration. At the institutional level, Arabic lacks the dedicated

81 Nu'aymī, *al-Tārīkh al-fikrī li-azmat al-lugha al-'arabiyya*, p. 57.

82 Ibid. p. 71.

83 Ibid. p. 79.

84 Muḥammad Fawzī al-Mināwī, *Azmat al-ta'rīb* (Cairo: Markiz al-Ahrām li-l-Tarjama wa-l-Nashr, 2003), p. 30.

85 Sulaymān Jubrān, *'Alā hāmish al-tajdīd wa-l-taqyīd fi al-lugha al-'arabiyya al-mu'āṣira* (Haifa: Majma' al-Lugha al-'Arabiyya, 2009), p. 31.

86 al-Fāsī al-Fihrī, *Azmat al-lugha al-'arabiyya fi al-maghrib: bayna ikhtilālāt al-ta'addudiyya wa-ta'aththurāt 'al-tarjama*.

support from specialised institutions, which could effectively promote it in official domains, in addition to the absence of a legal framework that can give expression to the primacy of Arabic in public life. Al-Fihri ascribes this to the non-existence of language research centres and the lack of serious language-planning policies.

In comparison to the above applications of the crisis trope, al-Fihri seems to be least ideological: the issues that he raises have been the subject of a sizeable body of robust research in the literature. However, ideology comes into play through the use of the term crisis to designate these concerns. Why not call these concerns language-planning problems?[87] At what point does a language problem become a crisis? Are we dealing with a linguistic crisis or some other crisis in the public sphere that is camouflaged as a linguistic crisis? In other words, is the linguistic crisis of Arabic in Morocco a proxy for other crises in Moroccan society and political life? Al-Fihri does not raise these issues, not because he cannot deal with them (he is a leading linguist, after all), but because of the social 'naturalness' that the crisis trope has acquired in society and the hold it has in the discourse on Arabic language ideology. Because of this, it is, in fact, unlikely that the public or readers of al-Fihri's title and text, respectively, would question the use of the crisis trope in this book.

Tropes of Arabic Language Ideology: The Fossilisation Trope

The fossilisation trope is inscribed in language ideology in descriptions of Arabic, such as '*jāmida*' (frozen, ossified), '*mu'aqadda*' (complex) and therefore difficult (*ṣa'ba*) to learn, *badawiyya* (Bedouin)[88] and by the participle *taqyīd* (restriction), as opposed to *tajdīd* (renewal) in, for example, the title of Jubran's book *'Alā hāmish al-tajdīd wa-l-taqyīd fī al-lugha al-'arabiyya al-mu'āṣira* (*On the Margins of Restriction and Renewal in Contemporary Arabic*). A search of the Aljazeera Arabic website (accessed 1 February 2012) has unearthed 92 occurrences of the term *jāmida* (fossilised) in items connected with the Arabic language. Unlike the crisis trope, the fossilisation trope is rarely marked in book titles. This is not surprising, considering the fact that this trope represents a criticism of the dominant Arabic language ideology, in which the virtues of the language, both instrumentally and symbolically, are extolled in traditions of beauty, logicality, lexical richness and divine

[87] See, for example, the title of Frayḥa's book: *Fī al-lugha al-'arabiyya wa-ba'ḍ mushkilātihā* (*The Arabic Language: Some Problems*) (Beirut: Dār al-Nahār, 1980). Also, see the title of al-Barāzī's book: *Mushkilāt al-lugha al-'arabiyya al-mu'āṣira* (*Problems of Modern/Contemporary Arabic*) (Amman: Maktabat al-Risāla, 1989).

[88] The term *badawiyya* implies that *fuṣḥā* Arabic is still rooted in a backward desert culture that makes it unfit for modernity, and, hence, fossilised. See Ibrāhīm Anis, 'hal al-lugha al-'arabiyya badawiyya?', *Majallat Majma' al-Lugha al-'Arabiyya* (1969), 24: 172–80, for a discussion of this concept.

election through its association with the Qur'anic Revelation. The notion of divine election is captured with great swagger in the following line of poetry, in which Arabic is declared the dame of all languages, well ahead of Latin in prestige: 'If the languages of the earth have not a commanding Dame [i.e. Arabic], God would have revealed a Qur'an to the Romans / Latin Speakers' (*law lam takun li-lughāti al-arḍi sayyidatan/la-anzala Allahu fi al-lātina qur'ānan*).[89] This is a compliment to Latin and the Romans, but one with a cultural sting: neither the language nor the people can match Arabic or the Arabs in excellence.

One target at the receiving end of the fossilisation trope are the grammarians of old, who were the butt of mocking poetic compositions. In a poem dating back to the ninth century, grammarians are mocked for their abstruse rules – for example, those dealing with the subjunctive. Van Gelder mentions one poem on the topic, in which the poet says: 'I have thought about grammar until I was bored / I have wearied my body with it and my soul'.[90] Referring to *qiyās* (grammatical analogy) as a method of the grammarians, another poet writes: 'They are a pain these would-be Arabs and that thing of theirs / They have invented, called 'Grammatical Analogy!'[91] The ethnic overtone in this poem is very clear: it describes the grammarians as 'would-be Arabs' in contrast to the real Arabs, who we take here to be the Bedouins. Contrasting his innate knowledge of the rules of Arabic with those artificially constructed by the grammarians, the same poet says: 'How different are those who must make efforts when they speak / From those who, by their nature stamped, speak perfect Arabic!'[92] A ninth century poet attacked the artificiality of Arabic grammar, linking it indirectly to *shu'ūbiyya* – which I discussed in detail in Chapter 2 – as the reference to the Nabataeans reveals:

1. In the past the old Bedouin language was used
   As our standard to argue in grammar,
2. Until people arrived whose standard is now
   From the slang of old men in Quṭrubul.
3. And yet others have come, whose standards derive
   From the tongue of the vile Nabataeans.
4. Thus they are all at work in destroying the ways
   That the truth may be found, without tiring.[93]

[89] Salmān, *Durar bahiyya fi madḥ al-'arabiyya*, p. 116.
[90] Geert Jan van Gelder, 'Against the Arabic grammarians: some poems', in Bilal Orfali (ed.), *In the Shadow of Arabic: The Centrality of Language to Arabic Culture* (Studies Presented to Ramzi Baalbaki on the Occasion of his Sixtieth Birthday) (Leiden and Boston, MA: Brill, 2011), p. 250.
[91] Ibid. p. 254.
[92] Ibid. p. 254.
[93] Ibid. p. 255.

A tenth century poet continues this attack on the grammarians:

1. Grammar I'll leave to those who practice it;
   I'll turn my mind to hunting.
2. Grammarians have minds that bear the stamp
   Of scheming and cunning.[94]

The artificiality of Arabic grammar is an important strand in the fossilisation trope. Artificiality is projected not as a property of the language in the first centuries of Islam, but of the work of the grammarians. With time, this artificiality transmuted into a description of the language itself and was received in this light in post-classical conceptualisations of Arabic. Artificiality in a living organism (*kā'in ḥayy*), as Arabic is often conceptualised in language ideology, leads to fossilisation. One of the most canonical expressions of the fossilisation trope in the modern period is a piece by the American Lebanese writer Gibran Khalil Gibran called *lakum lughatukum wa lī lughatī* ('You have your language. And I have mine'). In view of the iconic status of this composition in modern Arab culture – witness the fact that it is frequently used as a source of epigraphs in books on Arabic language ideology – I will translate it below to give the reader a flavour of this trope:

1. To you your language, and to me my language.
2. You have what you want of Arabic. I will have what fits my thoughts and feelings.
3. You have its words and their linear arrangements. I will have what the words signal but do not touch, and what linear arrangement aims at but does not reach.
4. You will have in her frozen, embalmed and fossilised corpses which you consider the be all and end all. I will have from her bodies which are worthless in themselves: bodies whose value lies in the souls in which it resides.
5. You have in her an assigned place of pilgrimage which you seek with unswerving [intent]. I have in her a changing means [of expression] that does not satisfy me until it transmits what is hiding in my heart to other hearts and what is swirling in my conscience/mind to other minds.
6. You have in her prescriptive/obligatory and rigid rules. I have in her tunes that chime with the tunes of the mind, the tones of desire and their impact on the senses.
7. You have in her dictionaries, lexica and long treatises. I have in her what the ear sifts and the memory preserves of what people say, exchange and feel at home in good times and bad.
8. You have in her what Sibawayhi, Abu al-Aswad and Ibn 'Aqil brought,[95] and those who came before them and after them, a boring lot they all are.

94 Ibid. p. 256.

95 These are the names of well-known Arab grammarians. Sibawayhi (d. 180/796) is the author of the foundational treatise on Arabic grammar *al-Kitāb*; Abu al-Aswad

I have in her what the mother says to her baby, what the lover says to his companion and what the ascetic says in the silence of the night.

9. You have in her the eloquent/lofty (*faṣīḥ*) not the feeble/lowly (*rakīk*), the refined (*balīgh*) not the vulgar (*mubtadhal*). I have in her what the wild person mutters because it is all eloquent, and what the person in pain chokes on because it is all profound and what a trapped person lisps because all of it is eloquent and profound.
10. You have in her ornamentation (*tarṣī'*), adornment (*tanzīl*) and embellishment (*mubtadhal*) and all the acrobatics of fabrication. I have in her words when uttered transform the hearer beyond speech and, when written, create rhetorical expanses for the reader that the ether cannot bound.
11. You can seize on the tattered portions of your language dress. I will tear to pieces all the old and worn-out garments, casting on both sides of the road all that impedes my progress to the top of the mountain.
12. You can keep her severed and diseased parts, preserving them in your mental museums. I will burn every dead part and every paralysed joint.
13. You have your language, a disabled hag. I have my language, a young woman immersed in the sea of her youthful dreams.
14. What will happen to your language and all that you have invested in it when the curtain is raised on this old hag? And what will happen when it is raised by my young woman?
15. I say: your language will turn into nothing.
16. I say: a lamp that is running out of oil will not stay alight for a long time.
17. I say: life does not go back.
18. I say: the wood of a coffin does not produce roses or fruit.
19. I say to you what you reckon as eloquence is no more than sterile adornment and ossified stupidity.
20. I say to you: poetry and prose are feelings and thoughts. Anything else is feeble yarn and broken strings.

Gibran's composition offers a satirical characterisation of the fossilisation trope to mock and hurt. It is a scathing attack on the traditionalists, who would rather have a pure form of Arabic, even though it is a corpse, than an evolving form of the language, which can keep pace with modern life. Gibran ridicules the traditionalists, calling their Arabic a disabled old hag who peddles fossilised modes of expression. In comparison, the Arabic that he champions is a young woman that is full of life, with turns of expression to match. Gibran's composition derives its power from its intertextuality with Chapter 109 in the Qur'an. In Arabic, this chapter is called *al-Kāfirūn* ('The Disbelievers'), within which the last verse is structured around the oppositional formula or dichotomy: *'la-kum dīnukum wa li-ya dīn'* ('To you

(d. 69/688) is credited with carrying out the first orthographic reform of the Arabic script in Islam; and Ibn 'Aqil (d. 769/1367) is best known for his commentary on the *Alfiyya* of Ibn Malik.

your religion, and to me my religion'). The syntactic frame underlying this verse serves as a template for Gibran's composition on the fossilisation trope, effectively giving it great mnemonic power. This, I believe, is what gives this piece its salience in Arabic language ideology.

By invoking the Qur'an through intertextuality, Gibran wishes to declare that the traditionalists are linguistic disbelievers, who are opposing a new form of Arabic, much in the same way that Muhammad's opponents opposed his new religion. In spite of this opposition, the new form of Arabic, he proclaims, will triumph over the old, fossilised form of the language in the same way that Islam triumphed over the Arabs' pagan idols. This is a bold comparison to make, considering the fact that Gibran was Christian. However, by appropriating this frame of argumentation, Gibran gives the Qur'anic formula a cultural interpretation that moves away from Islam, but without severing its connections with it. Here, Gibran, author of the well-known book *The Prophet*, acts as though his kind of Arabic has divine support and that he, in heralding its arrival, is an Apostle or Prophet of a new dawn, in which the old linguistic fossil will die, to be replaced by a more vibrant form of the language. The references to paralysis, coffins, tatters and museums of the brain as metaphors of the fossilisation trope in the above composition are intended to make this point.

The reference to Sibawayhi in Gibran's composition is reiterated in the titles of two books that deal with the fossilisation trope – the first is Zakariya Uzun's *Jināyat Sībawayhi: al-rafḍ al-tāmm li-mā fī al-naḥw min awhām* (*Sibawyhi's Crime: A Complete Rejection of the Delusions of Grammar*);[96] the second is Sharif al-Shubashi's *Li-taḥyā al-lugha al-'arabiyya: yasquṭ Sībawyhi* (*Long Live Arabic!: Down with Sibawayhi!*).[97] These two titles (see Figures 3.12 and 3.13, respectively) raise the pitch of the attack on Sibawayhi within the fossilisation trope.[98] Whereas Gibran says to the traditionalists, with a mocking tone of voice, 'you can have Sibawyhi' ('I don't want him, so good riddance'), Uzun and al-Shubashi go beyond this statement, adopting an openly condemnatory attitude towards the grammarian. In this respect, Uzun and al-Shubashi break a major taboo of the Arab cultural tradition, in which Sibawyhi is accorded the status of a pioneer, complete with an unassailable legacy. Criticising Sibawayhi is one thing, but openly condemning him is completely different: for the language defenders and guardians and others, this would be a step too far. This is the case because – in all three

[96] Zakariyyā Ūzūn, *Jināyat Sībawayhi: al-rafḍ al-tāmm li-mā fī al-naḥw min awhām* (Beirut: Riyād al-Rayyis li-l-Kutub wa-l-Nashr, 2002).

[97] See Sharīf al-Shūbāshī, *Li-taḥyā al-lugha al-'arabiyya: yasquṭ Sībawayhi* (Cairo: Madbūlī al-Ṣaghīr, [3rd printing] 2004). For an earlier discussion of these two books, see Suleiman, 'Arabic language reforms, language ideology and the criminalisation of Sībawayhi'.

[98] For an introduction to Sibawyhi and his grammatical legacy, see Michael G. Carter, *Sibawayhi* (London: I. B. Tauris, 2004).

examples – Sibawyhi is deployed as a symbolic motif, which iconically stands for the whole of the Arabic grammatical tradition.

Let us now consider the fossilisation trope in Uzun's book, as presented in three of its paratexts: title, jacket copy and dedication. The title is intended to both allure and generate a reaction from the public and potential would-be readers. The term 'crime' (*jināya*) in the title sends an electric shock through the sinews of members of the public who are aware of the unsurpassable contribution that Sibawayhi made to Arabic grammar. Describing this achievement as a crime and naming Sibawayhi as its perpetrator is a step too far, as I have already stated above. The use of the colour red in the main title underscores the gravity of the crime: visually, the title is dripping with blood. The title further invites us to speculate on who the victims may be, and there is no doubt that the main target in this context – in addition to the Arab people as a whole (*al-sha'b al-'arabī*), as the jacket copy makes clear – is the educational establishment which, wittingly or unwittingly, victimises Arabic language students by exposing them to fossilised, complex and difficult grammatical rules. This interpretation is supported by the text of the book. Moving to the subtitle – it directs the public to reject Arabic grammar lock, stock and barrel, because of the delusions it contains: Sibawayhi's delusions and those of his elk who helped to promote and perpetuate them to the present day. The use of the term delusions (*awhām*) brands Sibawayhi and the grammarians as misguided or, under a stronger interpretation, as suffering from some form of psychic disorder that refuses to let go.

The jacket copy (see Figure 3.14) specifies some of the content of the crime and the delusions that the subtitle refers to in a manner that sheds light on the crisis trope:

> This book sets out to show in a simple, critical and brief/condensed manner that the rules of Arabic grammar are a form without content; that learning these rules is a waste of time and a dissipation of mental energy; and that these rules are confused givens (*mu'ṭayāt*) full of delusions and padding. Because of these reasons, the majority of the Arab people (*sha'b*) have not learnt them and will not learn them for use in their daily-lives, whether for practical or scientific purposes. The Arab nation (*umma*) will not develop intellectually or achieve precision [in what it says and does], which are a hallmark of the [modern] age, without considering its position on many issues pertaining to Arabic, top of which being the dominant/domineering rules of grammar.

The subtext behind this far-reaching condemnation of Arabic grammar is its fossilisation as a construct that no longer responds to the modern condition of the Arabs. As a fossilised, complex and difficult construct, grammar is an obstacle to progress and renewal in Arab life. This analysis implies that the Arabs will not advance until they take the grammar bull by the horns, tame it and make it suitable for a different pedagogic and social aesthetic. A similar point was made more than a millennium ago by Jahiz, who warned against the complexity of grammar in pedagogy in his advice to schoolmasters; this advice clearly reveals the perennial nature of the problem. Owing to the canonicity of this advice in discussions of pedagogic grammar, I will give it below in full:

> As regards grammar, do not encumber your pupil's mind with more than is necessary to save him from serious solecisms and preserve him from the ignorance of the mob when it comes to drafting a letter, reciting verses or giving a description of something. Anything more may prevent him acquiring more appropriate skills and make him neglect more valuable accomplishments, such as knowledge of current proverbs, accepted traditions and praiseworthy poems. Only a man with no ambition to learn about important matters, to give serious thought to taxing problems such as the interests of the country and humanity, or to understand the pillars and the pole about which the earth's millstone revolves (or one with no resources or means of livelihood) would wish to make an exhaustive study of grammar or go beyond the stage of a reasonable knowledge of it. Fine points of grammar are the last sort of problem likely to arise in polite society, and there is no need to bother with them.[99]

Uzun continues the fight against grammar in the dedication (see Figure 3.15). Addressing the public and his putative readers, he encodes his message in motivational language, which is no doubt intended for task-orientation:

> To those who respect and appreciate reason; to those who apply reason in evaluating transmitted knowledge; to those who light the candle of creativity to dispel the darkness of blind imitation and uncritical adherence to received knowledge; to those who light the candle of [free] thinking to dispel the darkness of [blind] analogy and adherence to the [inherited] lore of the forefathers; to those who love all people regardless of their race, religion or creed; to all and everyone of these I dedicate my first book.

This is an impassioned appeal to the public and putative readers to take up the fight on behalf of a new form of Arabic, against the grammarians and their fossilised rules, which, transitively, have led to the fossilisation of *fuṣḥā* Arabic. The trope of fossilisation is, in fact, mentioned in the preface, when the author says:

> As for our rule-ridden Arabic (*al-'arabiyya al-muqa'adda*, in a metathetical play on the word *mu'aqadda* which denotes complex), it has remained fossilised (*jāmida*). In fact, it has retreated internationally to the extent that its people no longer pay attention to it.

[99] Charles Pellat, *The Life and Works of Jāḥiẓ: Translations of Selected Texts*, trans. D. M. Hawke (London: Routledge & Kegan Paul, 1969), p. 113.

Uzun ascribes this fate to grammar and to the derivational system of the language, which makes it difficult to coin new words. The references to reason and light in the dedication work through exclusion: they exclude the grammarians, who reject reason and prefer to live in the dark.

Let us now turn to al-Shubashi's book. In discussing the temptation function of titles above, I have referred to the title of this book as a good example of this function in the field of Arabic language ideology. The title consists of two parts separated by a colon: (1) *li-taḥyā al-'arabiyya* (*Long Live Arabic!*); and (2) *yasquṭ Sībawayhi* (*Down with Sibawayhi!*). In normal practice, the first part would be the title and the second part would act as subtitle, but the size of the font of the second part and the bolder colours chosen to render it give it greater visibility in comparison to the first part in a way that inverts this relationship. This is true of the two different editions that I have used for this research (the first and third editions), which exhibit some design differences, but not in this particular portion of the front cover (see Figures 3.13 and 3.16). The public and most of putative readers would, we can assume, be supportive of the first part. This, however, is more than cancelled out by the second part, because, as I have explained above, it touches in a very negative way on a revered figure of the Arabic grammatical tradition. For the public and putative readers, al-Shubashi's title gives with one hand and takes away with another. The first part lulls the public and readers into a false sense of cultural security by appealing to their language ideology, which receives positive affirmation here, before it denudes them of a sense of security in one fell swoop through the second part. The formal balance of the title between its two parts therefore gives way to a feeling of bias in favour of the second. There is no doubt that al-Shubashi wants Arabic to live and prosper, as he, in fact, tells us repeatedly within the text of the book, but he seems to premise this on the downfall and demise of Sibawayhi and what he iconically stands for in Arab culture. If al-Shubashi wanted to allure and shock at one and the same time, he could not have chosen a better title, as the furore the book caused in the media after its publication revealed.[100] The fact that the subtitle is reminiscent of political slogans that the Arabs employed during the colonial and postcolonial period, aimed at calling for the downfall of imperialism, Zionism or corrupt Arab rulers, undoubtedly added to the angst that the public and its readers felt towards the book and its author. It is, in fact, this same formula or a variation on it using the root *s-q-ṭ* (to fall) that demonstrators deployed in the Arab Spring uprisings to call for the downfall of their corrupt rulers: *al-sha'b yurīd isqāt al-niẓām* ('The people want to bring the regime down'), which reverberated through the streets of Tunisia, Egypt, Libya, Yemen and Syria. If

[100] See Yasir Suleiman, 'Arabic language reforms, language ideology and the criminalisation of Sībawayhi', in Edzard Lutz and Janet Watson (eds), *Grammar as a Window onto Arabic Humanism: A Collection of Articles in Honour of Michael G. Carter* (Wiesbaden: Harrassowitz Verlag, 2006b), pp. 66–83 for the debate that the book generated in the media.

there was ever a need to talk about how grammar can be deployed in cultural politics, al-Shubashi's title is one good example of this.

Reflecting on the furore that his book caused in Egypt in the preface to the third edition, al-Shubashi says that he did not expect, when he took his manuscript to the publisher in April 2004, to be carrying a ticking timebomb in his arms (*lam akun atakhayyal annanī aḥmil bayna yadayy qunbula mawqūta*).[101] In a comment on the reception of the book in *al-Wafd* newspaper, Usama Anwar 'Ukasha continues with this war imagery, describing the reaction to the book in similar terms:

> Sharif al-Shubashi has stormed a minefield (*ḥaql al-ghām*) . . . which in the past exploded underneath anyone who tried to come close to the taboos of the Arabic language (*tābūhāt al-lugha al-'arabiyya*) with the intention of liberating it from its [state of] fossilisation (*jumūdihā*), reviving it (*iḥyā'ihā*) and pumping the life (*mā'ihā*, 'water' in the original) of development in its being (*awṣāliha* 'joints and limbs' in the original) which have gone dry (*tayabbasat*) under the influence of ancient grammars (*qawā'id al-zaman al-ghābir al-ba'īd*) that grammarians such as Sibawayhi established.[102]

'Ukasha further describes al-Shubashi's book as a penetrating and busting explosive (*qadhīfa nāfidha*), as an opening salvo in a debate that must take place, without any fear (*dūna khawf aw jaza'*) concerning the state and future of Arabic. Commenting on the temptation function of the title of his book, effectively drawing a distinction between the public and its readers, al-Shubashi stated: 'I was astounded to know that the vast majority of those who responded to the book had not in fact read it. Their comments revealed the truth of the proverb that "a book is read from its title (lit.)"'. If anything, this is a perfect example of the point made earlier – that the public have greater power and potency in circulating a book than its readers.

But what is it that al-Shubashi wanted to counter in Arabic language ideology through his book? The answer is the fossilisation of the language which traditional and classical Arabic grammar has visited upon it, leading one scholar to call for rescuing Arabic from the grammarians (*inqāẓ al-lugha min aydī al-nuḥā*).[103] References to Arabic as a dead language (*lugha mayyita*)[104] characterised by extreme fossilisation (*jumūd wa-taḥajjur*),[105] linguistic backwardness (*takhalluf lughawī*)[106] and linguistic poverty (*faqr*

[101] al-Shūbāshī, *Li-taḥyā al-lugha al-'arabiyya: yasquṭ Sībawayhi*, p. 5. The book went into three printings in the first year of its publication (2004). This indicates the high demand for the book among the public and readers.

[102] Ibid. p. 238.

[103] Aḥmad Darwīsh, 'Inqāẓ al-lugha min aydī al-nuḥā', in Maḥmūd Amīn al-'Ālim (ed.), *Qaḍāyā fikriyya: lughatunā fi ma'rakat al-ḥaḍāra* (1997), 17–18: 81–91.

[104] Sharīf al-Shūbāshī, *Li-taḥyā al-lugha al-'arabiyya: yasquṭ Sībawayhi* (Cairo: Madbūlī al-Ṣaghīr, [3rd printing] 2004), p. 8.

[105] Ibid. p. 14.

[106] Ibid. p. 22.

lughawī)[107] – these are all metaphors of the fossilisation trope. The fossilisation trope is further deployed in the following conclusion concerning Arabic in the modern period:

> To sum up, Arabic is the only language on the face of the earth whose grammar, in its morphological and syntactic components, has not developed for the past one thousand and five hundred years. It is also the only language in the world whose speakers insist on mummifying it (*taḥnītihā*) under the pretext of keeping it 'pure'.[108]

The remedy, according to al-Shubashi, is: 'mounting an urgent modernising intifada/uprising . . . to ensure that the language does not face the dangers of [linguistic] introversion (*taqawqu'*) or maybe extinction (*ikhtifā'*)'.[109] Here we have further terms with which to describe the fossilisation trope: *taḥjjur* (petrification), *taḥnīṭ* (mummification), *taqawqu'* (becoming shell-like) and *ikhtifā'* (extinction).

Al-Shubashi fights a battle against the fossilisation of the language using some of the terms and metaphors I have mentioned above, as well as others that exploit the language of war, as will be discussed in the next section. He reserves his most trenchant criticisms for religious scholars and traditional grammarians, whom he accuses of wrongly ascribing 'sacredness' to Arabic, which it does not possess. In effect, al-Shubashi seems to believe that linking Arabic to Islam through a spurious principle of sacredness is another culturally embedded reason behind its fossilisation. He expresses this as follows:

> Those who call for the mummification of [Arabic] . . . do in effect wish death on it, because mummification/embalming is for the dead only and not for those who are alive. And those who refuse to develop the language reject the idea that it is a living being, packaging it with the halo of religion in a way that renders it in their eyes as a language unlike other languages, a language *sui generis*.[110]

The epigraph in al-Shubashi's book makes this point clearly: 'Language does not belong to the religious scholars . . . It is owned by all those who speak it regardless of nation or generation'. In addition to making the point about the separation of religion and language, this epigraph, being a quotation from Taha Husayn's famous book *Mustaqbal al-thaqāfa fī miṣr* (*The Future of Culture in Egypt*, first published in 1938),[111] is intended to give al-Shubashi's book pedigree. One may go even further and suggest that knowing what the traditionalists think of Husayn's controversial book, al-Shubashi may,

107 Ibid. p. 22.
108 Ibid. p. 63.
109 Ibid. p. 60.
110 Ibid. p. 80.
111 For a discussion of this book, see Suleiman, *The Arabic Language and National Identity*, pp. 190–7.

in fact, have wanted to raise a red rag to what he knew would be an angry bull. If this is the case, al-Shubashi must have intended to stoke the fires of linguistic controversy, as Husayn's book had done before it. This al-Shubashi achieved, in spite of his protestations of innocence in the media. As a broker of Arabic language ideology, al-Shubashi is second to none.

The fossilisation trope seems to be directed more at Arabic grammar than the Arabic language. This raises an important question concerning the extent to which ideological claims about overt grammar – the grammar of the grammarians, rather than covert grammar, the grammar of the language – can be transferred to the language. This is a question of epistemology and attitude: epistemology in academic discourse and attitude in language ideology. In brief, if, epistemologically speaking, overt grammar is thought to capture what are believed to be the inherent features of the language, then the ideological claims made about this grammar can legitimately be transferred to the language. I have argued elsewhere[112] that Arabic grammatical theory adheres to an essentialist or naïve realist epistemology, which implies that overt Arabic grammar is thought by the grammarians to capture the covert grammar of the language and, therefore, that this overt grammar is a true description of its covert counterpart. Versteegh captures this point well when he writes: 'behind the linguistic rules [of the Arabic language] there is a hidden truth [which reflects] God's hand in the creation of [that] language. It is the task of the grammarian to *reveal* [emphasis added] these hidden truths'.[113] Grammar-making, in this sense, is not an act of construction or discovery, but, to coin a term, one of uncovery. This epistemology is deep-rooted in the Arabic grammatical tradition. Al-Khalil (d. 171/787) is reputed to have issued a challenge to Arabic grammarians to produce an account of the language that is truer than his. He expresses this as a challenge (*i'jāz*), a kind of grammatical inimitability, which he encodes in the expression *'fa-lya'ti bihā'* ('let him come forth with it'), referring to linguistic causes (*'illa*s) as descriptive and explanatory facets of Arabic grammatical theory.[114] The Arabic expression above reminds us of the challenge that God poses in Qur'an 52:34, in which is found the expression *'fal ya'tū bi-ḥadīthin mithlih in kānū ṣādiqīn'* ('let them produce a speech the like of it if they are truthful')

[112] See Yasir Suleiman, 'The methodological rules of Arabic grammar', in Kinga Dévényi and Támash Iványi (eds), *Proceedings of the Collouium on Arabic Grammar/ The Arabist: Budapest Studies in Arabic* (Budapest: Etövös Loránd University and Csoma De Körös Society, 1991), pp. 351–64; Yasir Suleiman, *The Arabic Grammatical Tradition: A Study in Ta'līl* (Edinburgh: Edinburgh University Press, 1999); Suleiman, 'The nation speaks: on the poetics of nationalist literature'; Suleiman, 'Arabic language reforms, language ideology and the criminalisation of Sībawayhi'; Suleiman, *Arabic, Self and Identity*.

[113] Kees Versteegh, *The Explanation of Linguistic Causes: Az-Zajjājī's Theory of Grammar* (Amsterdam and Philadelphia, PA: John Benjamins, 1995), p. 21.

[114] See Versteegh, *The Explanation of Linguistic Causes: Az-Zajjājī's Theory of Grammar*, p. 89, for a full translation of what al-Kahlil says in this context.

– the implication being that they will not be able to do so. And so it also will be in the case of al-Khalil's challenge.

The circulation of overt grammar through education down the ages, its link with the Qur'an and the Arabic intellectual tradition and the authority bestowed upon it because of its antiquity create an ideological schema that is receptive to this naïve realist or essentialist epistemology to the extent that ideology and epistemology imperceptibly merge with each other in the public imaginary and academic discourse. Under this interpretation, the claim that Arabic grammar is fossilised, effectively encoded in a variety of expressions in Arabic, becomes a claim about the language itself: if Arabic grammar is fossilised, then the Arabic language must be fossilised. This conflation of overt grammar with language explains the ideological vehemence with which rebuttals of the fossilisation trope are expressed. Furthermore, it explains why the brokers of the fossilisation trope are unable to make their claim stick, to dislodge the authority of overt grammar from the public imaginary or to challenge its commanding position in academic discourse. When language and overt grammar become two sides of the same coin, any claim about the latter will be automatically translated as a claim about the former, in spite of the fact that overt grammar is no more than a constructed and, in some sense, hocus-pocus account of the language.

Tropes of Arabic Language Ideology: The War Trope

The war trope is encoded in a variety of expressions in ideological talk about the Arabic language. The term *ḥarb* (war) encodes it directly, as in al-Kattani's book title *Thamānūn 'āman min al-ḥarb al-frankūfūniyya ḍidd al-islām wa-l-lugha al-'arabiyya* (*The Francophone War on Islam and the Arabic Language: Eighty Years [and Beyond]*).[115] This term (*ḥarb* / war) is used in a more emotive way on the Aljazeera website in a transcript of a programme broadcast on 29 April 2001: *al-ḥarab al-ṣalībiyya 'alā al-'arabiyya juz' min ḥamlatihā 'alā al-islām* (*The Crusading War against Arabic is Part of its Campaign against Islam*).[116] Calling the war on Arabic a crusade has the effect of embedding the war trope in an inimical and emblematic historical encounter between Islam and the Christian West for enhanced task-orientation. Another term that encodes the war trope directly is *ma'raka* (battle), as in al-'Alim's edited volume *Lughatunā al-'arabiyya fī ma'rakat al-ḥaḍāra* (*Our Arabic Language in the Battle of Civilisation*).[117] Derivatives of the term *yuwājih* (to confront) encode this trope, but at a lower degree of intensity in terms of task-orientation: on a peril scale,

115 Idrīs al-Kattānī, *Thamānūna 'āman mina al-ḥarb al-frakūfūniyya ḍidd al-islām wa-l-lugha al-'arabiyya* (Rabat: Manshūrāt Nādī al-Fikr al-Islāmī, 2000).

116 See http://www.aljazeera.net/channel/archive/archive?ArchiveId=91425 (accessed 4 February 2012).

117 Maḥmūd Amīn al-'Ālim (ed.), *Qaḍāyā fikriyya: lughtatunā al-'arabiyya fī ma'rakat al-ḥaḍāra (Vols 17 and 18)* (Cairo: Qaḍāyā Fikriyya li-l-Nashr wa-l-Tawzī', 1997).

'confrontation' is less dangerous than 'battle', and this, in turn, is less dangerous than 'war'. Examples of the war trope in its confrontation guise are al-Ashtar's book title *al-'arabiyya fi muwājahat al-makhāṭir* (*Arabic: Confronting Perils/Threats*)[118] and 'Abd al-Rahman's title *al-'Arabiyya tuwājih al-taḥaddiyāt* (*Arabic Confronts/Faces Challenges*).[119] Of the two cognates *muwājahat* and *tuwājih*, the former carries a stronger meaning. This is strengthened through collocation with *makhāṭir* (dangers) in the first title, which has a stronger meaning on the peril scale than *taḥaddiyāt* (challenges) in the second title. The war trope may also be encoded by the term *zaḥf* (march), as in 'Attar's book title *al-Zaḥf 'alā lughat al-qur'ān* (*Marching against the Language of the Qur'an*).[120] The term *zaḥf* implies that a war is impending, but that the battle has not yet been joined. As with al-Kattani's and Aljazeera's titles above, this title links the war on Arabic with the war on Islam. In a more oblique manner, the war trope may be expressed through a defence metaphor, as in the title of Jamali's book *Difā'an 'an al-'arabiyya* (*In Defence of Arabic*).[121] The emphasis here is on defending Arabic against the war, battle, confrontation or march that is being perpetrated against it, rather than being one of initiating a war without provocation. The title also implies that the text is part of this defence of the language.

The first point to consider in the war trope is the identity of the enemy. There is, of course, the external enemy: the colonialists who were able to impose a language policy that instrumentally discriminated against Arabic, as the French similarly achieved in North Africa during the colonial period. This is not a matter of ideology or invention, it is one of fact. British language policy in the Arabic-speaking world was less coercive. It recognised the local language, but did not raise it to the same status as the colonial language in certain sectors of the administration. Symbolically, Arabic came under attack in terms of comparative prestige with the colonial languages. Narratives of the war trope consider the reduction in the symbolic capital of the language to be an outcome of colonialism and its continued hegemony in the Arabic-speaking world through imperialism in its political, economic and cultural guises. Globalisation, *'awlama*, is treated as the most recent phase in this imperialist encounter.[122] As soft power, globalisation is less

[118] 'Abd al-Karīm al-Ashtar, *al-'Arabiyya fi muwājahat al-makhāṭir* (Beirut: al-Maktab al-Islāmī, 2006). The title page carries the word Arabic in disconnected letters in red surrounded with arrows that are aimed at it from three directions.

[119] Ṭālib 'Abd al-Raḥmān, *al-'Arabiyya tuwājih al-taḥaddiyāt* (Qatar: Wazārat al-Awqāf, 2006).

[120] Aḥmad 'Abd al-Ghafūr 'Aṭṭār, *al-Zaḥf 'alā lughat al-qur'ān* (Beirut: no publisher, 1966).

[121] Fāḍil al-Jamālī, *Difā'an 'an al-'Arabiyya* (Tunis: Mu'assassāt 'Abd al-Karīm Bin 'Abdallaa, 1996).

[122] Gunvor Mejdell, 'What is happening to *lughatunā al-jamīla*? Recent media representations and social practice in Egypt', *Journal of Arabic and Islamic Studies* (2008), 8: 112–13. Basing herself on a survey of press media materials in Egypt

intrusive, but more effective, because it works from the inside, rather than the outside.[123]

The internal enemy is depicted as acting, wittingly or unwittingly, as an agent or extension of the external enemy. In the imperialist paradigm and under the banner of globalisation, the internal enemy acts as the channel through which the soft power of the external enemy infiltrates society and attacks its linguistic fibre (*nasīj lughawī*). In this respect, the external enemy does not use weapons or violence, but employs devious methods (*asālīb mākira*).[124] The reference to deviousness occurs in other discussions of the war trope – for example, the guest preface in 'Abd al-Rahman's book mentions *makr al-'a'dā' wa-l-khuṣūm* ('the deviousness of enemies and adversaries').[125] The author of the first preface, 'Umar 'Ubayd Hasna, uses an incredible array of terms and expressions with which to narrate the war trope. I will list some of these terms here to show the lexical diversity in this narration: *tadmīr*

during the years 1997–8, 2001–2 and 2006–7, Mejdell describes the threat posed by globalisation as follows: 'The external threat is perceived as coming from the pressures of globalisation ... imposing Western political, economic and cultural hegemony. The notion of conflict ... is couched in strongly marked evaluative terms (rape, evil forces, etc.). "Our beautiful language is being raped in commercials, on shop facades, in the streets in schools and universities," complains the Egyptian opposition paper, *Al-Sha'b* [quoted in *Al-Ahram Weekly* on 21 October 1999], and likens the present situation to the darkest days of British occupation. The centrality of [*fuṣḥā* Arabic] for the construction of national identity is repeatedly evoked, e.g. "We must cling to al-'Arabiyya to safeguard our identity in the face of the pressure of globalisation" reads a typical headline in *Al-Ahram* (27 June 1997). To the writer Muhammad Jalal, interviewed in *Sawt al-Azhar* (21 July 2006), [*fuṣḥā* Arabic] is "the daughter of the people ... whose position will be strong or weak depending on her family ... In times of hardship we cannot expect too much of her". Nowadays, however, there is a genuine awakening in the Arab world, claims Jalal, which is "ready to stand against the evil forces which do not wish ... the Arab nation [well], and want it to be more fractured than it is". But the Arab people have learnt to fight for their values, he says, and the real value of the nation is the Arabic language, which will remain strong, because it is the language of the Qur'an, which protects its honour (*sharaf*). There must be a common awareness that the honour of this nation *is* the Arabic language, and that the nation must stand united to protect the honour of this Arabic language/daughter'.

123 See Aḥmad bin Muḥammad al-Dubayb, *al-Lugha al-'arabiyya fī 'aṣr al-'awlama* (Riyadh: Maktabat al-'Ubaykān, 2001) for a discussion of Arabic and globalisation. This discussion, which reads globalisation as a form of cultural invasion, is not untypical in Arabic language ideology. See Suleiman, *Arabic, Self and Identity* for an extensive discussion of the topic.

124 al-Kattānī, *Thamānūn 'āman mina al-ḥarb al-frakūfūniyya ḍidd al-islām wa-l-lugha al-'arabiyya*, p. 7.

125 'Abd al-Raḥmān, *al-'Arabiyya tuwājih al-taḥaddiyāt*, p. 17.

al-lugha wa muḥāṣaratuhā ('laying siege to the language and destroying it'),[126] *ma'ārik* ('battles'),[127] *hajma* ('attack'),[128] *muwājahāt* ('confrontations'),[129] *ithārat al-shubuhāt* ('raising suspicions / doubts'),[130] *khuṣūm al-lugha* ('adversaries of the language'),[131] *iqitlā' al-'arabiyya* ('uprooting the Arabic language'),[132] *silāh qadīm jadīd min al-'udwān 'alā al-'arabiyya* ('an old-new weapon in the attack on Arabic'),[133] *asliḥa fāsida wa-mashbūha* ('corrupt and suspect weapons').[134] In the second preface, the author adds the following expressions: *inna al-'arabiyya ṣārat maydānan yatadarrab bi-l-hujūmi 'alyh kull man amsaka bi-l-qalam* ('Arabic has become a battlefield for anyone who wants to try his luck using his pen');[135] *ightiyāl al-'arabiyya wa-wa'duhā* ('assassinating Arabic or burying it alive'). The author of the first preface accuses the internal enemies of the language of cultural treason (*'amāla thaqāfiyya*), effectively telling them that the attack on Arabic will lead directly to:

> disabling the vitality of the nation, extinguishing its spirit, freezing its ability to act, cutting it off its roots, diverting it away from its heritage, putting it in the service of the Other, and destroying any sense of hope it may have if not its ability to think.[136]

This is how serious the attack on Arabic is in the eyes of this writer. On the defence side, the first preface employs such terms as *ḥuṣūn* [*al-lugha*] *qawiyya ṣāmida* ('The language forts are strong and able to resist'),[137] *ḥirāsāt al-lugha* ('linguistic lines of defence')[138] in references to Arabic lexica, *ḥimāyat al-lugha* ('defence of the language')[139] and *mawqif difā'ī* ('a defensive posture').[140]

Al-Jamali calls the enemies of Arabic *ghuzā* (invaders), and he seems to think that the internal enemies of the language are more dangerous than its external ones, judging by the fact that he devotes most of his attention to the former category in his book *Difā'an 'an al-'arabiyya* (*In Defence of Arabic*). He defines the invaders of Arabic as: 'those who seek to demolish it completely or those who treat it as sterile or unfit for modern life'.[141] He then adds that:

[126] Ibid. p. 14.
[127] Ibid. p. 14.
[128] Ibid. p. 14.
[129] Ibid. p. 17.
[130] Ibid. p. 17.
[131] Ibid. p. 18.
[132] Ibid. p. 22.
[133] Ibid. p. 23.
[134] Ibid. p. 24.
[135] Ibid. p. 25.
[136] Ibid. p. 14.
[137] Ibid. p. 14.
[138] Ibid. p. 16.
[139] Ibid. p. 17.
[140] Ibid. p. 17.
[141] al-Jamālī, *Difā'an 'an al-'Arabiyya*, p. 32.

'there are different kinds of invader, most of them are not outside/external invaders, but invaders from within: sons and daughters of Arabic who, however, drink from a foreign cup'. There is no doubt that some would consider Uzun and al-Shubashi part of this inside contingent, precisely as Salama Musa, Taha Husayn and Luwis 'Awad were treated as fifth columnists by the defenders of Arabic language ideology in the twentieth century.[142] Whether al-Jamali would have treated Uzun and al-Shubashi in this manner is an open question. My guess is that he might not have done so on the purely ideational level, but that he would have done so on the attitudinal front, because of the vehemence of the attacks mounted against the grammarians by these two writers, as their titles indicate.

Al-Jamali points out that the invasion of Arabic operates in a variety of ways: (1) through the calls to give the dialects a more prominent place in Arab cultural life and the replacement of the Arabic script by the Latin script; (2) by insiders who prefer to use foreign languages to Arabic, either because they were educated in foreign schools or because they believe that these foreign languages are more prestigious than Arabic; and (3) by mixing Arabic with foreign languages, as though Arabic was not able to provide the lexical resources the speakers need to express themselves. Mahmud[143] calls language mixing *ḥawal lughawī* (linguistic squinting) and considers it a phenomenon of deviation (*inḥirāf*) from the right path and an expression of decay (*inḥiṭāṭ*) in linguistic behaviour. The last two phenomena are related to globalisation and, to a lesser extent, modernity in Arabic language ideology. Globalisation is a recent factor in ideological narrations of the war trope in Arab society. I have dealt with this at some length in my book *Arabic, Self and Identity: A Study in Conflict and Displacement*.[144] The main point in this discussion is the linking of globalisation with anxiety and trauma. Qassab considers modernity to be responsible for aspects of the war against Arabic. One such aspect is championing the dialects in literature in the name of realism by recording what people say in their mother tongues. Another aspect is the total disregard for the rules of grammar (*tadmīr al-qawā'id*),[145] which has spawned a nonchalant attitude towards Arabic (*al-istihāna fī al-lugha* or *imā'at mafhūm al-lugha*).[146] Qassab calls this aspect of the war trope a crime

[142] Suleiman, *The Arabic Language and National Identity*, pp. 180–204.

[143] Sa'd Ḥāfiẓ Maḥmūd, 'al-Ḥawal al-lughawī: ta'ammulāt fī ẓāhirat inḥirāf wa-inḥiṭāṭ al-lugha', in Maḥmūd Amīn al-'Ālim (ed.), *Qaḍāyā fikriyya: lughatunā fī ma'rakat al-ḥaḍāra (Vols 17–18)* (Cairo: Qaḍāyā Fikriyya li-l-Nashr wa-l-Tawzī', 1997), pp. 131–4.

[144] Suleiman, *Arabic, Self and Identity*, pp. 124–41.

[145] Walīd Ibrāhīm Qaṣṣāb, 'Jināyat al-ḥadātha al-mu'āṣira 'alā al-lugha al-'arabiyya', *Majallat Kulliyat al-Dirāsāt al-Islāmiyya wa-l-'Arabiyya (United Arab Emirates)* (1994), 9: 201–22.

[146] Ibid. pp. 205, 203 (respectively).

(*jināya*) against Arabic – this being the same term that Uzun uses to refer to Sibawayhi.

Let us now consider the epigraphs in some of the publications above, in order to gain further insight into the war trope in their language ideologies. Al-Jamali uses eight lines of Hafiz Ibrahim's poem as an epigraph. This reflects the iconic place of this poem in Arabic language ideology, as has been explained above at length. Its use here implies that Arabic is in dire straits and that it needs defenders (*ḥumātuhā*)[147] to ensure that it is protected against all kinds of attack. Al-Jamali defines the defenders of Arabic as: 'those who protect Arabic jealously and therefore use it in their daily lives and work to enhance its status and to spread it among the people'.[148] Al-Jamali recognises three categories of defender. The first category consists of a group of stern (*mutazammitūn*)[149] grammarians and writers who are unwilling to compromise (*mutaṣallibūn fī ārā'ihim*),[150] hold fast to traditional grammar and disallow any movement (*zaḥzaḥa*)[151] or change in the language. Of the writers dealt with in this chapter, al-Nahwi comes closest to being a member of this category. Although al-Jamali has little sympathy with this group of language defenders, he still thinks that they perform a useful function – that of 'an alert watchman/guard' (*al-khafīr al-yaqiẓ*),[152] who issues the first warnings of danger. The second category includes those who adopt a more relaxed attitude towards Arabic grammar (*muyassirūn*),[153] allowing Arabic grammar to be simplified. The Lebanese Anis Frayha, whom I mentioned in passing above, and al-Fihri would be assigned to this group. The third category would include intellectuals and other members in society who give life to Arabic by using it for different purposes in society.

'Abd al-Rahman[154] uses as his epigraph three verses from the Qur'an that implicitly refer to God's Revelation being in Arabic (Qur'an 26:193–5): 'With it [Revelation, Qur'an] came down the Spirit of Faith and Truth to your heart and mind so you [Prophet Muhammad] may admonish, in the perspicuous Arabic tongue'. In addition to this implicit reference to Arabic, the second verse considers the Prophet as one who warns his people against deviation from the right path, doing so in perspicuous Arabic. As an act of appropriation, the epigraph now additionally means that 'Abd al-Rahman's book is a warning in plain and simple Arabic against the enemies of the language and that, at the same time, it is a reminder to the public and putative readers that

147 al-Jamālī, *Difā'an 'an al-'Arabiyya*, p. 13.
148 Ibid. p. 29.
149 Ibid. p. 29.
150 Ibid. p. 29.
151 Ibid. p. 29.
152 Ibid. p. 29.
153 Ibid. p. 30.
154 Ṭālib 'Abd al-Raḥmān, *al-'Arabiyya tuwājih al-taḥaddiyāt* (Qatar: Wazārat al-Awqāf, 2006).

it is their duty to fight these enemies using plain and simple Arabic. This motivational message is in line with task-orientation in Arabic language ideology, as in all language ideologies.

Let us now consider two dedications in books employing the war trope in Arabic language ideology. The first is Farrukh's book *al-Qawymiyya al-fuṣḥā* (*Eloquent/Pure Arab National Identity*).[155] I dealt with this book above and also previously in Chapter 2, where I referred to its title as a portmanteau. The dedication in this book is an excellent example of the war trope in language ideology:

> To the garrisoned troops (*murābiṭūn*, 3:200) who know they are members of the home front! To the first generation of holy warriors (*mujāhidūn*, 95:4) who stood together shoulder to shoulder (*marṣūṣ*, 4:61)! To those who carried the burning flame of pure Arabism and pure Arabic to the four corners of the universe in storm-swept conditions! . . . To those who stood their ground in the heat of the battle! To those who put the confidence back in the hearts of the Arabs after their eyes had become distracted and their hearts had risen up to their throats (*zāghat al-abṣār wa-balaghat al-qulūb al-ḥanājir*, 10:33)! To all of these I dedicate this book in admiration of the past glories, appreciation of the present effort, and because of confidence in the future.[156]

There is no mistaking the omnipresence of the war trope in this dedication. The language and, therefore, nation-defenders are described as garrisoned troops, holy warriors, committed visionaries and steadfast soldiers, who put confidence back into Arab life during a perilous period (colonialist period) in modern Arab history. This group is not named. In this respect, it is an open category and not a closed set – a fact that makes it available for self-inclusion, as well as self-exclusion, on the part of the public or the putative reader. However, considering the rousing nature of this dedication and its strong Qur'anic references given in the brackets above, it is a safe bet to say that self-inclusion would offer a greater pull to the public and putative readers than self-exclusion. This is important in motivation and task-orientation, which are of principal importance in language ideology, as it seeks to build on the past to shape the present and future. The fact that we are not told when the defenders stood their ground and what battle they were fighting heightens the drama painted in the dedication and gives us, as members of the public or readers, the space to interpret the dedication in a way that resonates with our ideologies of our language and our nation. Put differently, the openness or vagueness of the dedication works to its advantage: it gives us some right of authorship over it through the act of interpretation. And by appropriating the dedication and making it ours, we are, to some extent, more likely to commit ourselves to it. It is in this way that the author enlists us – in a

155 'Umar Farrūkh, *al-Qawmiyya al-fuṣḥā* (Beirut: Dār al-'Ilm li-l-Malāyīn, 1961).
156 Ibid. pp. 5–6.

near-literal sense of the term – as combatants in his ideological cause. The war trope is an excellent vehicle for achieving this.

A similar dedication is offered by ʻAttar:

> To the protectors of *fuṣḥā* Arabic who strive for Allah with the endeavour which is His right (*al-ladhīna yujāhidūna fi Allāhi ḥqqa jihādih*, 22:78) by promoting/adhering to the language of the Qur'an, its literatures and sciences; to those who defend [Arabic] and fight the peddlers of the doctrines of destruction and sabotage by which they aim to demolish the Qur'an, destroy the [Prophet's *ḥadīth*, erase Islam and dismantle Arabic by dismantling its grammar, literatures, sciences and arts as well as by supporting the colloquials, giving them aid and succour to help them triumph over the *fuṣḥā*.[157]

The same comments, concerning the openness of the protectors as a group and the effect of this on interpretation and task-orientation, apply here. The term *anṣār* (supporters) reminds us of the Medinan Muslims, who came to the aid of the Prophet when he and his original band of followers came under attack from his own people in his hometown, Mecca, at the start of his mission. The use of this term puts those who support Arabic symbolically in the same category as the Medinan supporters of the Prophet. By implication, this makes those who oppose Arabic similar to the Meccans who opposed Muhammad and rejected his mission at the start of his Prophethood. Therefore, there is no doubt that the moral scales are weighted in favour of the defenders of the language, who cannot but stand up to the religious and cultural saboteurs in their midst. The trope of war, displayed through culturally translucent references to attack and defence, dominates this dedication and offers an organising principle around which it can be structured and deployed to best effect.[158]

In discussing the above tropes of Arabic language ideology, I am aware that they mesh with each other, making their separation here somewhat artificial. Fossilisation fades into crisis, and the two fade into war and vice versa. What matters for us here is to emphasise the connectedness among these tropes and to treat this connectedness as a case of mutual reinforcement in the structure of language ideology. One trope recalls the others, ensuring, through the process of mutual recall, greater circulation for the whole ideological edifice in society, than for each separately. I should also add that the list of tropes I have given here is not exhaustive. Other tropes may be identified. My aim here, however, is to draw attention to the fact that language ideology is amenable to some systematisation, but only if systematisation is not treated as a straightjacket, hence my preference for the term 'amalgam' to 'system' in the working definition of ideology that I have adopted in this

[157] See ʻAbd al-Ghafūr ʻAṭṭār, *al-Zaḥf ʻalā lughat al-qur'ān*.

[158] The war trope is used in poetry; however, I will not deal with this here, simply due to lack of space.

book. Finally, at no point in the above discussion have I tried to question the veracity of the ideological tropes I have identified. Whether Arabic is in crisis, fossilised or in a state of war is of no material concern to us here. What is of concern to us is the existence of these tropes, their occurrence and circulation in society, the terms and metaphors in which they are encoded, some of the sites in which they are enunciated and the objectives they are intended to serve.

Conclusion

The above discussion reveals that language ideology is a productive site for getting at the amalgam of ideas that relate language to faith, morality, politics and culture in the widest sense in society. Therefore, it is inconceivable that we could construct a picture of the role of language in the social world, without delving into language ideology. For most people, language ideology remains invisible, as if it were a category of nature. This is the case for standard language ideologies, including *fuṣḥā* Arabic. I have tried to show elsewhere[159] that the consecration of *fuṣḥā* Arabic as a standard language has been subject to ideological fashioning or manipulation at the deepest level and that this ideology was driven, among other things, by issues of faith and group worth. The latter set of issues is spun around a host of traditions (I now prefer this term to 'myths', in spite of the fact that this term has greater currency in the literature) whose origin is unknown, but whose status in society as narrative templates of excellence and election is almost unquestionable. In this chapter, I have tried to stay away from this celebratory ideological terrain or its deprecatory counterpart, which pits one language against others in the stakes for excellence and election. Instead, I have tried to abstract three tropes of Arabic language ideology from a wide and varied set of readings, treat these tropes as headings, identify some of the terms and metaphors in which they are encoded, consider two major sites for ideological performance in which these metaphors are displayed, discuss the strategies of 'persuasion' that these tropes deploy and highlight the attention they pay to motivation and task-orientation. My ulterior motive behind all of this is to show how the quotidian is full of meaning and that it is only by looking at it afresh, as if to make the familiar unfamiliar, that we can extract the meanings it carries.

Let me consider the issue of sites first. I have concentrated on paratexts and poetry for a variety of reasons, although language ideology can be found in different (and perhaps more obvious) locations within society. Paratexts are generally ignored in the study of language ideology in Arabic and other languages. The importance of paratexts, however, relates to the fact that they show the far reach of language ideology in society. By distinguishing between the public and readers, I have been able to show that one does not

[159] See Suleiman, 'Ideology, grammar-making and the standardisation of Arabic'.

have to read a book from cover to cover or even to read significant portions of it to become a language ideology broker who participates in its dissemination in society. The old adage that one can read a book from its cover is not devoid of truth in this case. Titles, dedications, epigraphs, prefaces and jacket copies are major carriers of language ideology, doing so either telegraphically or with a great economy of words. In processing the content of these locations of ideology, the reader often brings elements of this same ideology to bear on them. In other words, these thresholds in a text act as a point of contact between overt and covert language ideology, where the public invoke and apply their covert ideological frames of reference to interpret what are largely overt ideological pronouncements, which, more often than not, have little intellectual depth. The fact that there may be little cognitive distance between the overt and the covert here may be considered by hard-headed scholars as a sign that the intellectual transaction on both sides, if it could be described in this way, is a sterile exercise in repetition or affirmation. I have tried to counter this by distinguishing between repetition and reiteration. Although repetition and reiteration are formally the same in propositional terms, reiteration works as a recursive *performance* with the aim of affirming the dominant language ideology in society in each repetitive telling or giving it a different colouring to fit the socio-political context of the time. Reiteration is purpose- or objective-oriented, unlike repetition, which, in terms of gaze, is content-bound. And since language ideology tries to work through the illocutionary and task-orientation dimensions of discourse, reiteration is angled towards attitudinal motivation and task-orientation. In this respect, every reiterative telling of a particular aspect of a language ideology is an attempt at influence and action. Telling the public and readers that Arabic is in crisis or that a war is being waged against it is intended to activate an attitudinal consciousness or to ensure that this consciousness receives a cognitive charge that can make it ready to spring into action in defence of the language and its web of symbolisms in society. Reiteration is also a form of circulation, of renewing the life of an ideological trope in society.

This chapter also reveals that poetry is another productive site of language ideology in Arab culture. Through its culturally sanctioned position, poetry is an excellent carrier of Arabic language ideology: its aesthetic power can give life to aspects of covert language ideology in a way that gives them freshness, as if they were crafted anew. Ibrahim's poem has continued to resonate with Arab readers for more than 100 years since its publication in 1903, not just because it encapsulates aspects of their language ideology, but also because: (1) it does so in cadences and word choices that hit a raw nerve in every act of audible or inaudible recitation, making these acts more than ordinary reiterations, as the 13 titles from the Internet given above reveal; and (2) because of this, the poem has proved to be an excellent vehicle for circulating aspects of Arabic language ideology by serving as an epigraph, in whole or part, or as an inspiration for other poetic compositions that carry this ideology from generation to generation, as has been shown above. This is also true of Gibran's prose composition. Both literary pieces have achieved canonical status in Arab culture and in articulating aspects of Arab language ideology. They may, in many respects, be considered mascots of Arabic language ideology. Because of this, poetry and prose must be given the recognition that they deserve, in disciplinary terms, as sites for investigating language ideology and its circulation in society.

What armoury does language ideology employ in delivering its message? We have seen a variety of weapons above. One is invoking the sacred to lend support to a particular aspect of language ideology. By using a limited set of verses from the Qur'an in epigraphs, prefaces and jacket copies, a reiteration of language ideology can invoke the full weight of faith to deliver its charge. Most of the verses in such epigraphs refer to the triadic link among Revelation, Prophethood and language in a manner that reduces the distance among them and makes the invocation of one trigger the others. An attack on language, therefore, becomes an attack on faith and vice versa. Moreover, the fact that this triad is often invoked in discussions of inimitability and *shu'ūbiyya* means that language ideology is directly linked with the past, which meanings can, as a result, be carried forward into the present. For the elites, the war trope trades on this past when these verses from the Qur'an are employed.

Another weapon in the armoury of Arabic language ideology is the personification of Arabic, which runs through all three tropes. We have seen how Arabic is depicted as a mother in some compositions. This is a powerful metaphor in Arabic language ideology. First, it enables this ideology to align itself with faith, again by exploiting the theological imperatives that are associated with motherhood, more, in fact, than fatherhood, in Islam. Neglecting Arabic is therefore projected as tantamount to neglecting one's mother, complete with all the religious consequences that this carries. Second, failing to come to the rescue of Arabic as an objectified mother at its (or her) hour of need is considered an abdication of responsibility in a moral economy in which a person's social worth depends on discharging this responsibility. Socially speaking, this is symbolic suicide. Here the imperatives of faith and the society's code of honour coalesce to produce a powerful drive for action. This is a particularly powerful message in motivation and task-orientation. Third, by depicting the language as a human being, the mother metaphor anthropomorphises the ideological tropes we have discussed above, removing them from the domain of the abstract and bringing them into the realm of symbolic flesh and blood. Linguistic pain and suffering are no longer part of a different ontology: they metamorphosise and start to belong to us as creatures of flesh and blood. In fact, the symbolic acquires materiality, which, when considered in conjunction with the preceding two points, generates not just sympathy, but empathy, which is one of the most potent forces in task-orientation. Fourth, having become a mother to its speakers, the language can now apply all the instruments of attitudinal pressure at its disposal. It acquires the right to complain, rebuke, point out the failings of her children, take them to task, name them and shame them and, above all, induce feelings of guilt in them. Arabic is a loving and caring mother, as mothers are supposed to be, but she expects love and care in return.

Another important weapon in Arabic language ideology is the invocation of the past in its full glory. Here, Arabic has a lot to be proud about. It is the language of one of the world's greatest religions – in fact, the world's greatest religion in the eyes of its believers. It is the language of a great culture, which dominated the world stage for centuries. And it was also the language of an imperial administration that dominated large swathes of the world where great civilisations before Islam had flourished and held sway. If this past is anything to go by, Arabic is clearly able to handle the instrumental demands imposed upon it, including the challenges of modernity in our age. Any failing in this respect is not a failing of the language, but of the people who use it. This is a double-edged message. While on the one hand, it issues a message of hope and confidence to the Arabs, it does so, on the other hand, against a background of lack and failings. And while it says to the Arabs that, based on their past, they can rise to the challenge of modernity, it tells them, at the same time, that there is something wrong with them and that is why they are not able to. As in all nationalisms, the past comes with its successes and failures and its glories and pains in language ideology. It can therefore be energising or debilitating, with little or no certainty about the direction in which it may develop.

Finally, language ideology cannot do its job without enemies. All three tropes above, but especially the war trope, are constructed around the notion of the enemy. As has been mentioned, the enemy can be an outsider or an insider. External enemies work through careful planning to serve their own interests. Weakening Arabic and shaking the confidence of its people in it are two ways of weakening the Arabs and Islam. Internal enemies are considered more dangerous, because they work from the inside as a fifth column. Some work wittingly for objectives that are inimical to Arabic and the Arabs and/or Islam and Muslims. Enemies of this kind may ally themselves with external enemies. Some internal enemies fall into this category unwittingly. They fall prey to the subterranean workings of the external enemies' soft power, smuggled into the midst of Arabic speakers on the back of a seemingly neutral modernity or through globalisation.

I have referred above to the use of language as proxy for other issues of concern in society. The idea that Arabic is in crisis, that it is in a state of fossilisation or that it is the target of wars and conspiracies may, in fact, be an extra-linguistic statement about a host of concerns in the political, economic or social spheres. Language ideology, in this case, plays a mediating role in society by serving as a backdoor channel, enabling other issues to be aired. A close reading of al-Shubashi's book would reveal that although traditional grammar and Sibawayhi were his most immediate targets of attack, his main battle, in fact, was with the religious scholars, who come in for scathing criticism in his book, because of their conservatism. Al-Shubashi uses the (suspect) notion of the sacredness of Arabic as a conduit for accusing the religious scholars of appropriating linguistic powers that are not theirs, in spite of the fact that they are ill-equipped to exercise those powers to benefit progress and enlightenment in society. There is nothing new in the appropriation of language as proxy. This practice has a long past and cross-cultural currency. To illustrate the latter, I will quote from a book on English language anxiety:

> When English speakers have lamented the condition and goals of schools, they have cited the state of language usage as both cause and consequence of this usage. When they have worried over the integrity and diversity of society, they have argued for and against the persistence of non-English languages [for example in the United States, Australia or New Zealand]. And when they have identified signs of a literal or figurative apocalypse, they have pointed to language and how it, in turn, points to social and moral issues beyond itself.[160]

Linked to the notion of the enemy in Arabic language ideology is a deep sense of language anxiety. The tropes of crisis, fossilisation and especially war are inseparable from this anxiety, which, in turn, points to other anxieties of a political and social nature in society.[161] I have referred to language ideology as part of a larger ideological matrix, which sees the Arabs as the target of outside conspiracies that are aided and abetted by Arabs on the inside. Arab political and social life is seen to be both in crisis and in a state of fossilisation. Islam and Muslims are seen to be under attack, externally and internally. The above ideological language tropes may therefore be read as tropes of a more overarching ideological configuration, in which the same forces of threat and decay are at work in different aspects of the social world. This fact points to a confluence of ideologies that aids the promulgation, circulation and naturalisation of language ideology beyond its restricted sphere. When language ideology is in step with a host of other ideological formations in society, language ideology does not need to work hard to be accepted as valid in perceptual terms. This confluence leads to a lowering of the bar on evidence, proof and, therefore, acceptability, in spite of the fact that these criteria are incidental to the workings of ideology; hence the use of the term 'perceptual' in the preceding sentence.

Language ideology provides an excellent arena for linking Arabic with cultural politics. This book is based on the idea that culture is political (with a small 'p') in a way that is not always operationalised or applied in political science. The same sense of exclusion is true of descriptive and structural linguists, who consider anything that lies outside language systemology not

160 Tim William Machan, *Language Anxiety: Conflict and Change in the History of English* (Oxford: Oxford University Press, 2009), p. 3.

161 See Suleiman, *Arabic, Self and Identity*, for a discussion of language anxiety.

to be 'linguistic' in their strict interpretation of the term.[162] This is particularly true of modern studies of the Arabic language. Yet the above discussion shows how by linking language to faith, identity and anxiety, we can, in fact, tap a rich canvas of political impulses and meanings in society. The idea that Arabic is under attack is an integral part of a political imagining in the Arab political sphere that conceptualises modern Arab history against the background of colonialism and the postcolonialist encounter in the fields of politics and economics. This imagining is built around the double jeopardy of external attack and internal collaboration, regardless of whether or not there is an empirical basis for this imagining. Conspiracy theories are linked directly to this imagining, which, as we have seen, applies to language ideology with full force. The tropes of language ideology that I have identified help to illuminate this imagining.

Furthermore, language ideology also reveals that cultural politics tracks larger political issues in society. As I have shown in my book *The Arabic Language and National Identity: A Study in Ideology*, most of the ideological talk about Arabic in the latter half of the nineteenth century and the first seven decades of the twentieth was imbued with a secularist spirit, which reflected the pan- and territorial nationalisms that dominated the scene during this period. The rise of Islamic-inflected politics since the 1970s had a direct impact on the direction of Arabic language ideology, as the works that I have discussed in this chapter amply suggest. It is, of course, not possible to separate the two trends from each other, yet the preponderance of works from one or the other trend at different periods in the modern history of the Arabic-speaking peoples does suggest that language can offer, through its associated ideology, a barometer for tracking larger politics in society. It is this intertwining of language with culture and politics that makes language ideology an area of study that is full of interdisciplinary promise.

162 See Robin Tolmach Lakoff, *The Language War* (Berkeley, CA: The University of California Press, 2000), p. 2. Lakoff says linguists of this kind: 'tend to be interested in discovering the abstract properties of languages, the grammatical rules that make them up, and the structures that make them different from one another, yet basically similar'.

Figure 3.1 *Why Arabic?* front cover (al-Naḥwī)

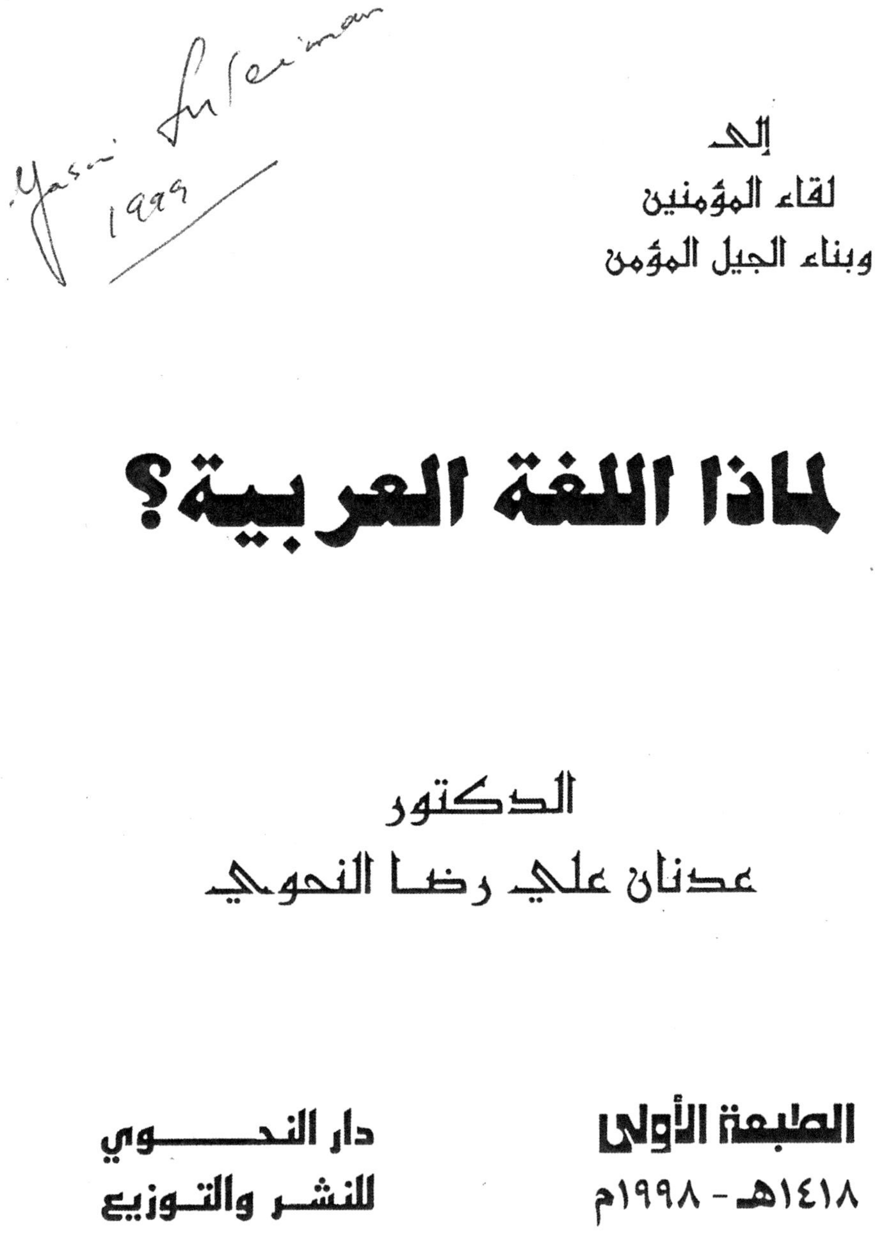
Yasir Suleiman
1999

إلى
لقاء المؤمنين
وبناء الجيل المؤمن

لماذا اللغة العربية؟

الدكتور
عدنان علي رضا النحوي

الطبعة الأولى
١٤١٨هـ - ١٩٩٨م

دار النحوي
للنشر والتوزيع

Figure 3.2 *Why Arabic?* inside cover (al-Naḥwī)

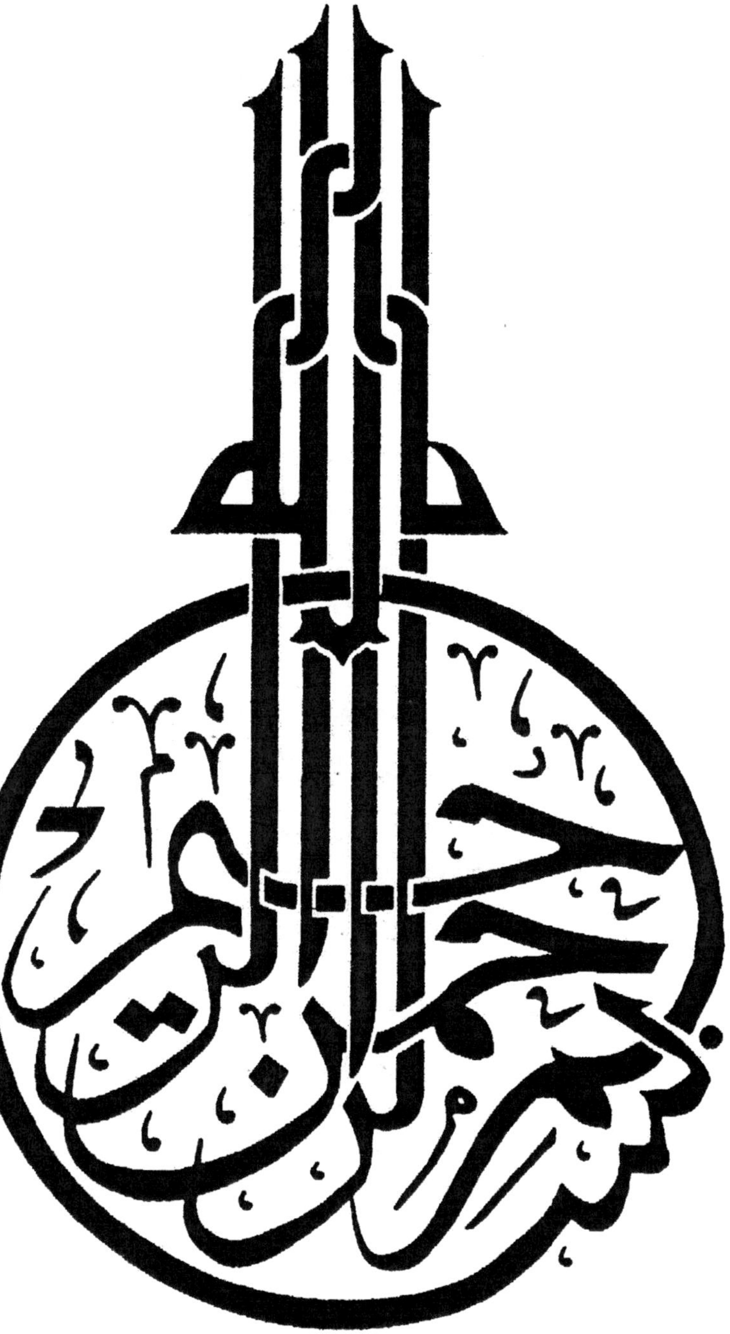

Figure 3.3 'In the Name of God the Compassionate, the Merciful' (al-Naḥwī)

جميع الحقوق محفوظة للمؤلف

الطبعة الأولى

١٤١٨هـ - ١٩٩٨م

دار النحوي للنشر والتوزيع

دار النحوي للنشر والتوزيع

تلفون وفاكس : ٤٩٣٤٨٤٢

ص.ب : ١٨٩١ الرياض : ١١٤٤١

المملكة العربية السعودية

Figure 3.4 Publisher's logo: name and crescent (al-Naḥwī)

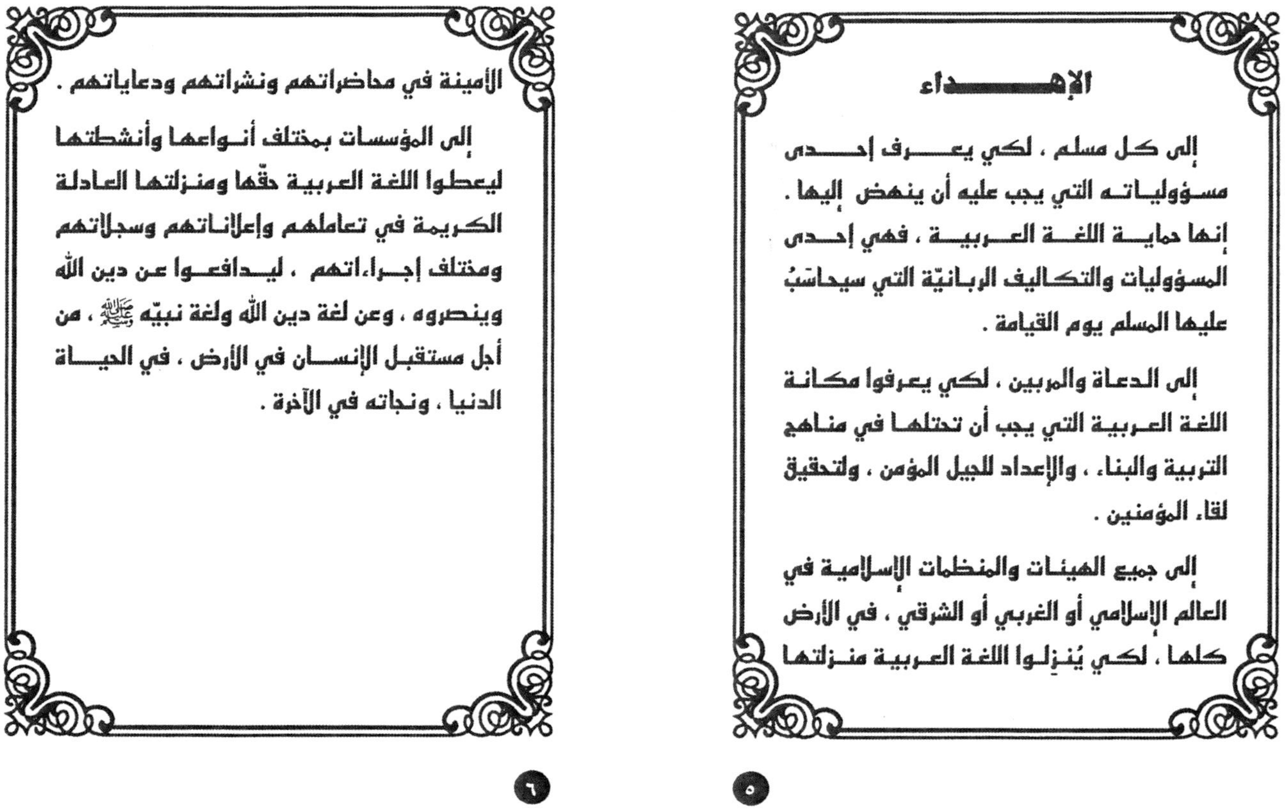

الإهـــــــداء

إلى كل مسلم ، لكي يعـــرف إحـــدى مسؤوليـاتـه التي يجب عليه أن ينهض إليها . إنها حمايــة اللغــة العــربيــة ، فهي إحــدى المسؤوليات والتكـاليف الربـانيّة التي سيحاسَبُ عليها المسلم يوم القيامة .

إلى الدعـاة والمربين ، لكي يعرفوا مكـانـة اللغـة العـربيـة التي يجب أن تحتلهـا في منـاهج التربية والبنـاء ، والإعداد للجيل المؤمن ، ولتحقيق لقاء المؤمنين .

إلى جميع الهيئـات والمنظمات الإسلاميـة في العالم الإسلامي أو الغربي أو الشرقي ، في الأرض كلهـا ، لكـي يُنـزِلـوا اللغـة العـربيـة منـزلتهـا

٥

الأمينة في محاضراتهم ونشراتهم ودعاياتهم .

إلى المؤسسات بمختلف أنـواعها وأنشطتها ليعطوا اللغة العربيـة حقّها ومنـزلتها العـادلة الكـريمة في تعاملهـم وإعلانـاتهم وسجلاتهم ومختلف إجـراءاتهم ، ليـدافعـوا عن دين الله وينصروه ، وعن لغة دين الله ولغة نبيّه ﷺ ، من أجل مستقبـل الإنســان في الأرض ، في الحيـــاة الدنيا ، ونجاته في الآخرة .

٦

Figure 3.5 Dedication (al-Naḥwī)

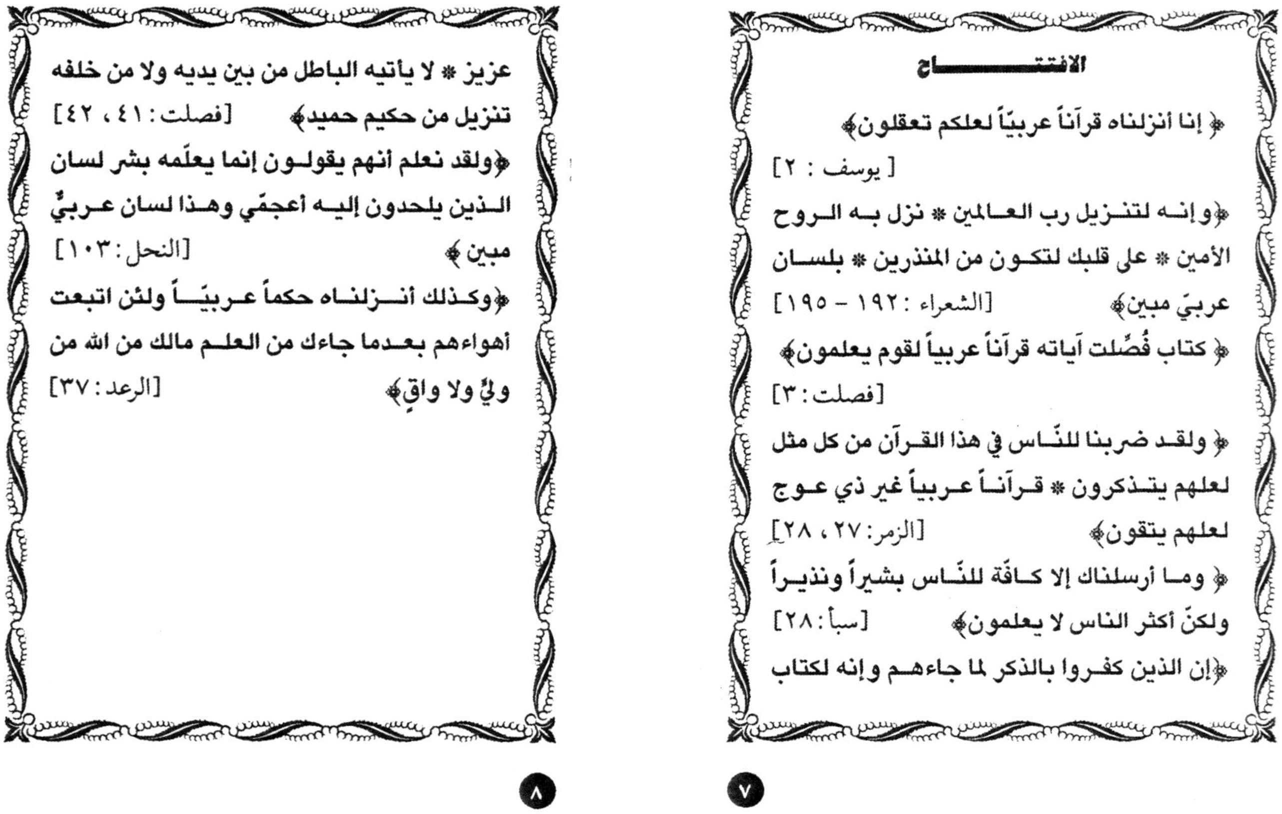

الافتتـــــــاح

﴿ إنا أنزلناه قرآناً عربيّاً لعلكم تعقلون﴾

[يوسف : ٢]

﴿وإنـه لتنـزيل رب العـالمين * نزل بـه الـروح الأمين * على قلبك لتكـون من المنذرين * بلسـان عربيّ مبين﴾ [الشعراء : ١٩٢ - ١٩٥]

﴿ كتاب فُصِّلت آياته قرآناً عربياً لقوم يعلمون﴾

[فصلت : ٣]

﴿ ولقـد ضربنا للنّـاس في هذا القـرآن من كل مثل لعلهم يتـذكرون * قـرآنـاً عـربياً غير ذي عـوج لعلهم يتقون﴾ [الزمر: ٢٧ ، ٢٨]

﴿ ومـا أرسلناك إلا كـافّة للنّـاس بشيراً ونذيـراً ولكنّ أكثر الناس لا يعلمون﴾ [سبأ: ٢٨]

﴿إن الذين كفـروا بالذكر لما جاءهـم وإنه لكتاب

٧

عزيز * لا يأتيه الباطل من بين يديه ولا من خلفه تنزيل من حكيم حميد﴾ [فصلت : ٤١ ، ٤٢]

﴿ولقد نعلم أنهم يقولـون إنما يعلّمه بشر لسان الـذين يلحدون إليـه أعجمّي وهـذا لسان عـربيٌّ مبين﴾ [النحل: ١٠٣]

﴿وكـذلك أنـزلنـاه حكماً عـربيّـاً ولئن اتبعت أهواءهم بعـدما جاءك من العلـم مالك من الله من وليٍّ ولا واقٍ﴾ [الرعد: ٣٧]

٨

Figure 3.6 Epigraph (al-Naḥwī)

مع هذا الكتاب

لقد أدرك الأعداء أهمية اللغة العربية وخطورة منزلتها في الإسلام وفي فهم كتاب الله وسنة رسوله ﷺ . فكان من أهم محاولاتهم إضعاف صلة المسلم بلغته العربية ، وإضعاف شعوره بضرورة التمسك بها ، وطرح أفكار غريبة مريبة تصرف المسلم عن لغة دينه ورسالته في الحياة ، واستمرت هذه المحاولات قروناً واستغرقت جهوداً كثيرة ، ومتابعة متواصلة دون ملل . فطُرِحَتْ أفكار لتغيير قواعد اللغة العربية أو بعضها ، وأفكار لتغيير أحرفها وكتابتها ، وأفكار لتغيير الشعر العربي . وكانت هذه المحاولات والأفكار التي تُطْرَح مرتبطة بسائر المناهج والتخطيط الذي يضعونه لغزو العالم الإسلامي ،وتدمير طاقاته الإيمانية والبشرية وغيرها .

ولقد تعهد الله سبحانه وتعالى بحفظ الذكر الذي أنزله على رسوله ونبيه محمد ﷺ . وهذا يعني أنه تعهدَّ بحفظ دينه وقرآنه وسنة نبيه محمدٍ ﷺ واللغة العربية التي هي وعاء الذكر كله وبيانه ومادته :

﴿ إنا نحن نزلنا الذكر وإنا له لحافظون ﴾. [الحجر : ٩]

ولكنه ابتلاء من الله سبحانه وتعالى ليمحّص عباده المؤمنين ، وليرى من يوفي بالعهد والأمانة ، ومن ينهض للغة دينه وقرآنه وسنة نبيه ﷺ ، ومن يتوانى أو يدبر . ويمضي الابتلاء على سنن لله ماضية ، وحكمة بالغة وقدر غالب .

مطابع دار طيبة ـ الرياض ـ ت : ٤٢٨٣٨٤٠
ردمك ٩٩٦٠-٦٨٧-٤١-٤

Figure 3.7 Jacket copy (al-Naḥwī)

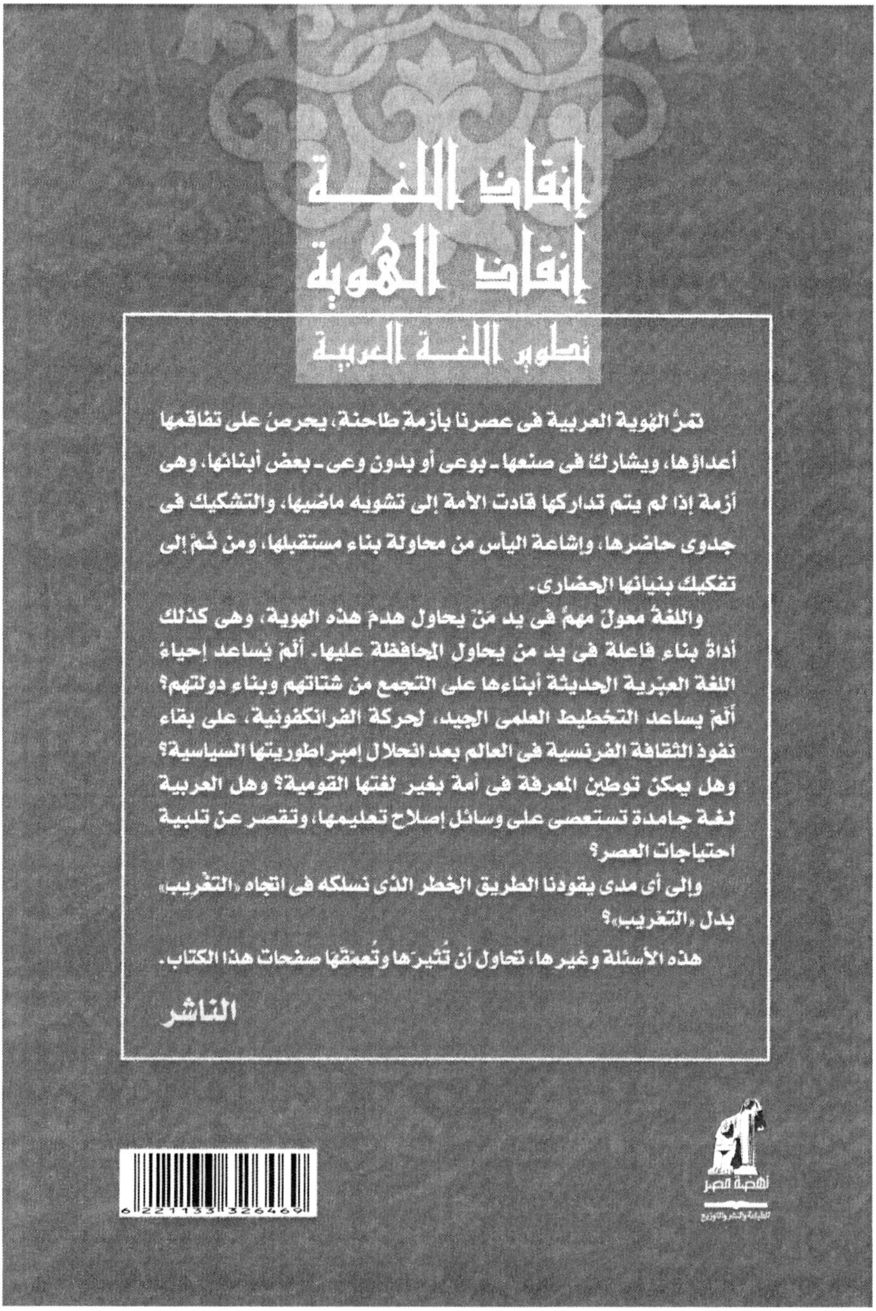

Figure 3.8 *Rescuing Arabic, Rescuing Arab Identity* (Darwīsh)

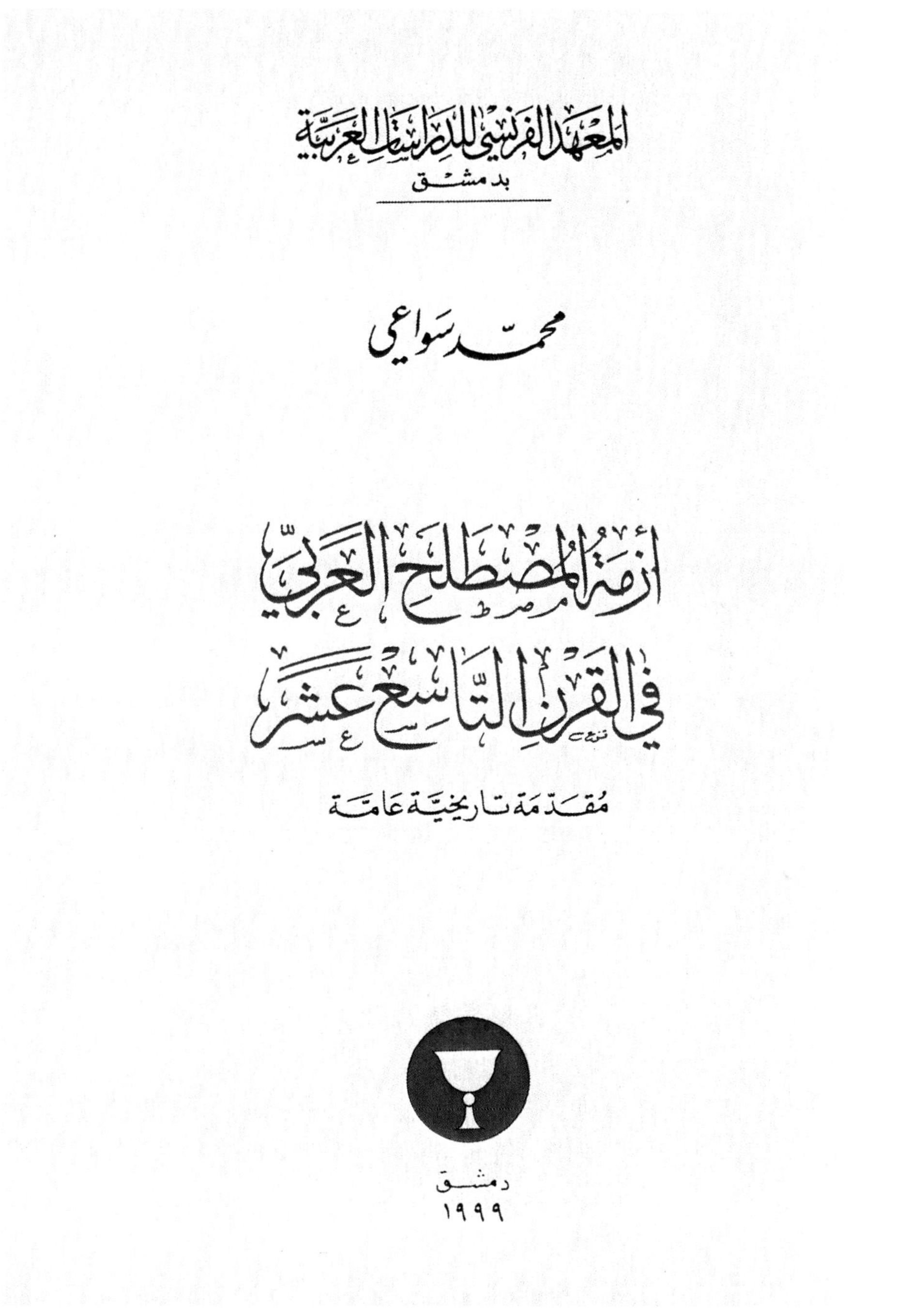
المعهد الفرنسي للدراسات العربية
بدمشق

محمد سواعي

أزمة المصطلح العربي
في القرن التاسع عشر

مقدمة تاريخية عامة

دمشق
١٩٩٩

Figure 3.9 *The Crisis of Arabic Terminology in the Nineteenth Century* (Sawwā'ī)

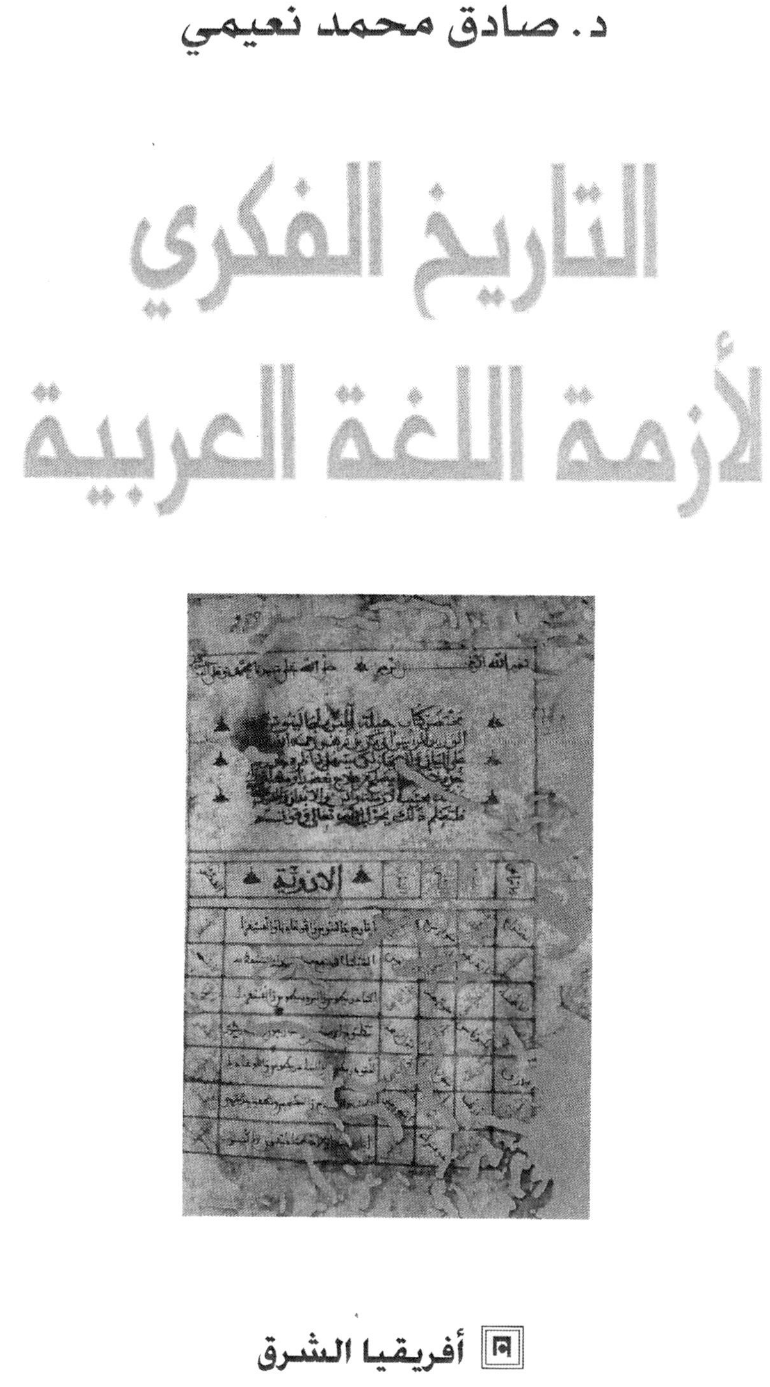

Figure 3.10 *The Intellectual History of the Crisis of Arabic* (al-Nu‘aymī)

Figure 3.11 *The Crisis of the Arabic Language in Morocco* (al-Fihrī)

Figure 3.12 *Sibawayhi's Crime* (Ūzūn)

Figure 3.13 *Long Live Arabic!* (al-Shūbāshī), first edition

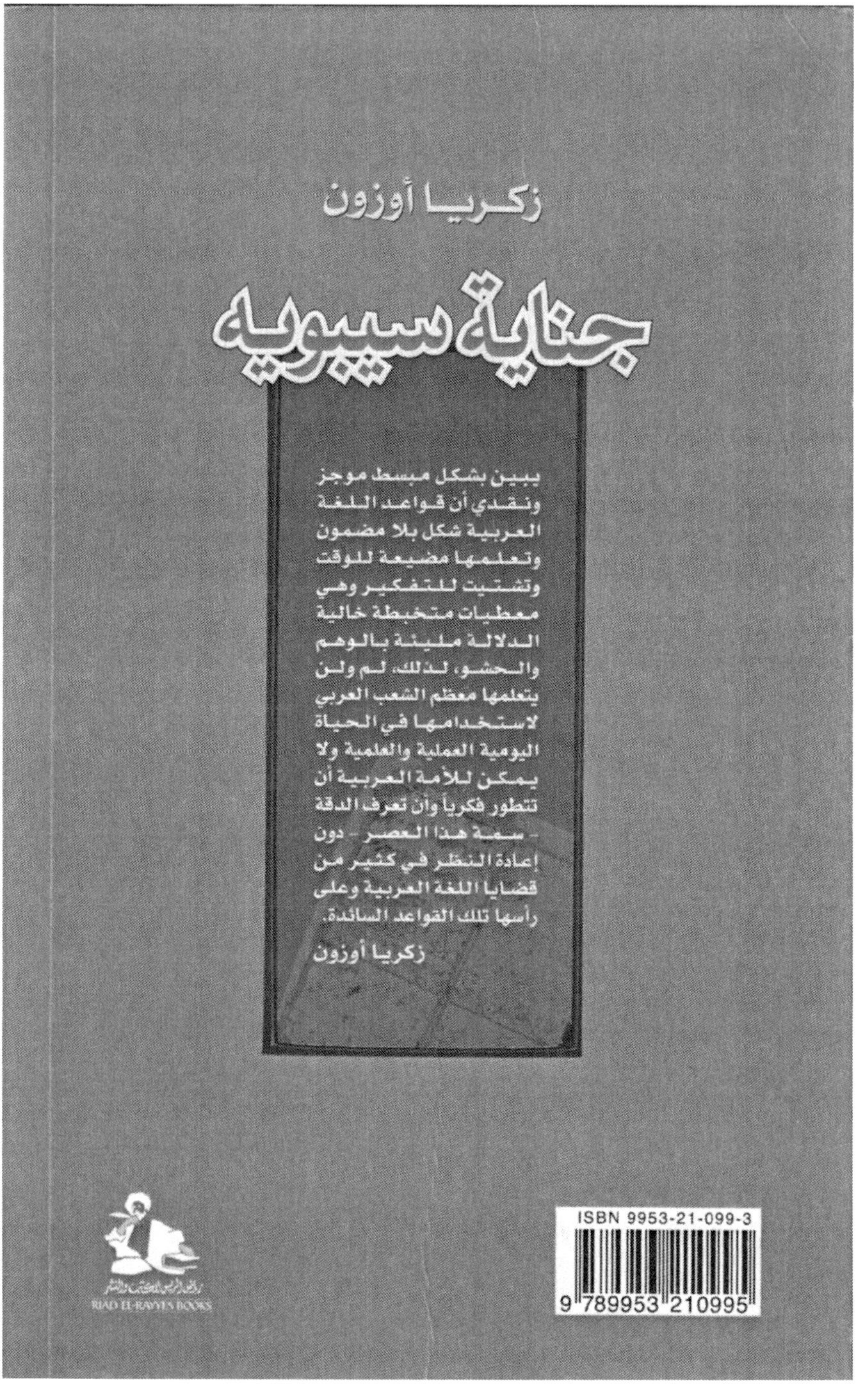

Figure 3.14 Jacket Copy (Ūzūn)

الإهداء

إلى كل من يحترم العقل ويقدره...
إلى كل من يحتكم إلى العقل في الحكم على النقل...
إلى كل من أضاء شمعة الإبداع في ظلام التقليد الأعمى والتبعية...
إلى كل من أضاء شمعة الفكر في ظلام القياس والآبائية...
إلى كل من أحب الناس على اختلاف أجناسهم وأديانهم ومعتقداتهم...

إلى هؤلاء أهدي باكورة أعمالي

Figure 3.15 Dedication (Ūzūn)

Figure 3.16 *Long Live Arabic!* (al-Shūbāshī), third edition

CHAPTER

4

HYBRIDITY, LANGUAGE IDEOLOGY AND CULTURAL POLITICS

This chapter pursues the twin themes of language ideology and cultural politics by considering issues of textual identity and language choice in hybrid texts. As understood here, hybrid texts (prose fiction) are texts written by authors of Arab origin – descent or heritage – not in Arabic, but in another language, such as French, English or Hebrew, among Palestinians in Israel. These texts are assigned to different cultural locations, which may be defined by the dominant language of the text, the background of the author or in a third space or twilight zone between these two worlds. One of the main arguments of this chapter revolves around the dialogic nature of these texts in the linguistic sphere, in the sense that the overt/present language of the text always recalls its covert/absent language. The interplay between languages, their ideologies and cultural politics is enacted through this dialogism. Language symbolism and language as proxy are used as the main tools for investigating the above issues. This chapter reveals that hybrid texts are another rich site for exploring language in the social world and never more so than when conflict, whether in reality or as memory, is simmering in the background.

Introduction: A Question of Identity

> *A French writer is a person writing in French. A foreign writer is a person writing in Foreign. A Dutch writer is a person writing in Dutch . . . I refer those who claim that I write in an Arabic kind of Dutch to the movement of the 'Tachtigers'* ('the people of the eighties,' a Dutch literary movement in the 1880s known for its baroque use of language). *I am clearly part of the Dutch linguistic tradition . . . I am so fed up with all the nagging about identities.*[1]

[1] Hafid Bouazza, cited in Marlous Willemsen, 'Dutch authors from the Arab world: a relief to the multilingual society', *Alif: Journal of Contemporary Poetics* (2000), 20: 81 [emphasis added].

The above quotation raises the important question of the identity of 'hybrid' literary texts.[2] Hafid Bouazza is a Dutch fiction writer of Moroccan descent. What makes his fiction writing 'hybrid', it seems, is the uncomfortable fit between his 'descent', rather than his citizenship, and the language in which he chooses to write. This lack of fit occurs because of an essentialist understanding of identity that links Moroccan descent to one or more of the indigenous languages of Morocco: Arabic, Berber or both. Thus, when a writer of this descent writes in a 'non-indigenous' language, even though this may be the primary language of his country of citizenship and his only medium of literary expression (Dutch, in this case), he or she is (or at least may be) assigned to the margins of this language, with all the identity implications that this entails for the subsequent literary production, in terms of categorisation, reception and circulation. This is true of writers of Moroccan, Algerian, Tunisian, Lebanese or Egyptian descent (among others) writing in French, regardless of whether they are French citizens or not. It is also true of Arab writers writing in English or German and of Palestinian writers in Israel writing in Hebrew. Hybridity, in all of these cases, is a matter of hyphenation, of being both inside and outside in varying degrees in terms of identity. This applies to both sides of the hyphen, although the direction of deviation is generally considered to be from the language of the text as the primary locus of classification to the language of descent, rather than vice versa. The

[2] Different labels are used to designate this literature, including transnational, translingual, postcolonial and minor literatures. At the heart of the debate about hybridity is: 'the ability of one language to express ideas specific to another culture'. See Anne Armitage, 'The debate over literary writing in a foreign language: an overview of Francophonie in the Magreb', *Alif: Journal of Contemporary Poetics* (2000), 20: 52. Armitage cites the well-known Moroccan novelist and critic Mohamed Berrada, who raises a similar point (Ibid. p. 52): 'Can the [Moroccan] writer using the French language really produce a universal work, investing it with all the richness of the Moroccan imagination?' The classic text on 'minor literature' is Deleuze and Guattari, who define it as the: 'literature which a minority constructs within a major language'. See Gilles Deleuze and Félix Guattari, *Kafka: Toward a Minor Literature*, trans. Dana Polan (Minneapolis and London: University of Minnesota Press, 1986), p. 16. This literature is said to exhibit three characteristics: deterritorialisation and reterritorialisation of the majority language, the politicisation of subject matter and its collectivisation. Hebrew literature by Palestinians in Israel may be considered minor literature, although I would prefer to replace deterritorialisation and reterritorialisation by de-ethnicisation and re-ethincisation, respectively, in this case. Hever and Gensler (1987) and, less so, Brenner (2001) do not fully accept this classification in the way that it may apply to Anton Shammas' *Arabesques* – the best known Hebrew novel by a Palestinian writer in Israel. See Hanan Hever and Orlin D. Gensler, 'Hebrew in Israeli Arab hand: six miniatures on Anton Shammas's *Arabesques*', *Cultural Critique* (1987), 7: 47–76; Rachel Feldhay Brenner, 'The search for identity in Israeli Arab fiction: Atallah Mansour, Emile Habiby and Anton Shammas', *Israeli Studies* (2001), 6: 91–112.

onus is always on those who wish to override the language of a hybrid text to offer alternative ways of deciding its identity.

But hyphenation goes much deeper here: it assumes the existence of a *dialogic* tension between an *absent* or covert language of descent, be it Arabic or Berber, and the *present* or overt language of the text, be it Dutch, English, French, German or Hebrew, as in the above examples. In fact, the tension is not between two languages that may or may not be mixed with each other textually, but, more importantly, between their ideologies, which is one of the main topics of concern in this chapter, as will become clear later. This tension between the *covert*, which exists through assumption and not manifestation, and the *overt*, as tangible manifestation of the text, signals the strong link in the public imagination between language and 'original' ethnicity or nationality on the one hand and the relatively weak link language contracts with citizenship when descent is invoked as a criterion of identity on the other. We may characterise this difference in the language-identity link as belonging to the realm of the *perennial* in the former case and that of the *constructed*, with all its implications of fabrication and invention, in the latter. But there is another side to the tension alluded to above: it is based on a conflation of writer with text, treating the latter as an inalienable extension of the former, as though a text cannot stand on its own two feet in deciding on its national identity.

The preoccupation with fixing the identity of literary texts, especially those that are considered hybrid, underlines Bouazza's exasperation in the excerpt above: 'I am so fed up with all the nagging about identities'. But this 'nagging' requires some deconstruction, because of its persistent presence, as the term 'nagging' implies. Why is the 'nagging' persistent? And who does the 'nagging'? Let us deal with the first question by suggesting that the nagging both exists and persists because the issue of identity is considered to be important in thinking about literary texts and in life more generally. In the academy and the market of cultural products, literary texts are, among other things, organised along national lines for pragmatic and other reasons that are pretty obvious. It would seem at first sight that the language of a text ought to be the primary criterion for deciding the identity of that text. This, indeed, is what Bouazza argues in the above excerpt when he says: 'A French writer is a person writing in French . . . A Dutch writer is a person writing in Dutch', interjecting the statement: 'A foreign writer is a person writing in Foreign' between these two statements to show his exasperation and reveal the absurdity of dissociating the identity of a text from the language in which it is written. If 'Foreign' were to be a language, then a person writing in it would be Foreign (by nationality). However, I am not sure if '*f*' in the first occurrence of 'foreign' in the original of the above quotation is intended to be in lower, rather than upper, case. If it is a lower case '*f*', it may be possible to interpret Bouazza's statement as saying that because the writer of hybrid literature is perceived to be of foreign descent, then he must be judged to write in a language called 'Foreign', hence the absurdity. Either way, the idea that the identity of a text is inseparable from the language in which it is written, whether real (French or Dutch) or imagined (Foreign), is a strong argument for Bouazza, who uses it as a way of countering his other-imposed marginality within the Dutch literary tradition.

I have related the fixation with the identity of hybrid texts above to an essentialist understanding of identity – 'the nostalgic fantasy of a return to oneness',[3] to apply an expression used by Woodhul – that is all too well-known in the literature.[4] This fixation may be further read as a sign of anxiety and an attempt to protect the border or frontier that language, as an instrument of literary and social production, is supposed to set up between people of different ethnicities, nationalities or cultures. Citizenship as a common category does not seem, as in Bouazza's case, to be able to override the differentiations that ethnicities and nationalities, with all of their linguistic consequences, are made to entail. Hybrid texts, by virtue of being considered inbetween texts, may therefore be conceptualised as transgressive texts that compromise the integrity of this border or frontier as a mechanism of separation. They are, in this regard, unlike translations, whose movement from one side of a linguistic border to the other is highly regulated as a transfer between languages or language areas. The 'nagging' that Bouazza talks about is nothing but an expression of this essentialist understanding of identity, with all the anxieties of border transgression or crossings that are associated with it.

This 'nagging' may originate from either side of the linguistic border/frontier, but, in this case, it seems to be related to the Dutch literary establishment. The above quotation pertains to the view that Bouazza's innovative use of Dutch and some of the creative liberties he takes with it are due to an Arabic (or other) substratum that acts through his narrative, rather than as a free choice motivated by stylistic and other considerations.[5] In standard

3 Winifred Woodhul, *Transfigurations of the Maghreb: Feminism, Decolonisation and Literatures* (Minneapolis and London: University of Minnesota Press, 1993), p. 176.

4 Mortimer confirms this 'obsession' with identity in Francophone Maghrebian texts, as we shall see below: 'The theme that still dominates Francophone Maghrebian literature is the identity quest'. See Mildred Mortimer, 'Introduction', in Mildred Mortimer (ed.), *Maghrebian Mosaic: A Literature in Transition* (Boulder and London: Lynne Rienner Publishers, 2001), p. 5. For an essentialist view of Francophone North African literature, see Georges J. Joyaux, 'Driss Chräibi, Mohammed Dib, Kateb Yacine, and Indigenous North African Literature', in Issa J. Boullata (ed.), *Critical Perspectives on Modern Arabic Literature 1945–1980* (Washington, DC: Three Continents Press, 1980), pp. 117–27.

5 Marlous Willemsen, 'Dutch authors from the Arab world: a relief to the multilingual society', p. 77. Willemsen explains some of Bouazza's linguistic innovations as follows: '[Bouazza's] use of words, although sometimes far-fetched and clichéd, is generally impressively creative and wide-ranging. He constructs convincing and funny new words whose meanings are immediately grasped in the context, despite the fact that the reader will surely never have read them as such before'.

postcolonial theory, such influence is treated as subversion of the language of the text to gain authorial voice, or to appropriate the language and use it as an instrument of resistance to the continued influence or legacy of the erstwhile colonial power, or against the structures of domination in multicultural societies in which migration may be an issue of concern in society.[6] I will challenge and seek to modify this standard interpretation below. What matters to us here, however, is the fact that Bouazza is aware of this standard interpretation in postcolonial theory, which he seems to reject in favour of positioning his creative use of Dutch in relation to a Dutch literary tradition that goes back 200 years. Bouazza seems, here, to be arguing against Dutch critics, who ascribed his linguistic innovations to a non-Dutch source, rather than placing them in the full stream of Dutch literature. By making this argument, Bouazza is resisting the attempt to marginalise himself in the Dutch literary scene by imputing a foreign language quality to his style – with all the ideological stereotyping that this carries – which, one assumes, is attributed to him because of his Moroccan descent. Here, issues of style, as micro-level language choices, become issues of identity by projecting the ethnic identity of the author onto the hybrid text. As islands in a linguistic ocean, non-standard stylistic choices in hybrid texts are liable to be treated as indexes of identity in a prior ethnicity or nationality.

Let us consider the issue of the identity of hybrid texts written by authors of Arab descent or Arabic cultural heritage against a broader canvas. The best-known example of this kind of writing is North African Francophone[7] literature, but this is not the only one. We may also point here to Anglophone literature by writers of Arab descent, although this literature has not

[6] For the notion of subversion, see Bill Ashcroft, Gareth Griffiths and Helen Tiffin, *The Empire Writes Back: Theory and Practice in Postcolonial Literatures*, 2nd edn (London and New York, NY: Routledge, 2002); Ismail Talib, *The Language of Postcolonial Literatures: An Introduction* (London and New York, NY: Routledge, 2002).

[7] See Dennis Ager, *'Francophonie' in the 1990s: Problems and Opportunities* (Cleveland, OH: Multilingual Matters, 1996), foreword. Francophonie is defined in three ways: 'by the use of the French language; by membership of a formal, organised community of nations; or by the acceptance and promotion of a set of values and beliefs'. Ager identifies three groups of countries in Francophonie (Ibid. p. 6): 'France itself, parts of Belgium, Switzerland, Luxembourg and Italy – form "frontier Francophonie", situated in Europe and bordering France itself. Countries and regions where French is the result of emigration and settlement – Quebec, Haiti, Mauritius and other areas settled principally before the eighteenth century – form a second group . . . Where French is the result of the massive colonial expansion, mainly in the late nineteenth and early twentieth centuries, now independent countries, many of them in Africa, form a third group. For these, French, in general, has not become the normal language of all the population, and retains elitist connotations: it is an official, governmental [or] educational language'. In this chapter, the term 'Francophone literature' refers to works emanating from the Arabic-speaking countries in the third group.

achieved the same canonical status in discussions of literary hybridity or postcoloniality in the Arabic-speaking world, for reasons that will become clear below. And still less known is (what might be called) Hebrewphone literature by a small number of Palestinian writers in Israel.[8] As in the above

[8] This literature is little known outside Israel, including in the Arab world, where it is also little understood, not just because it is in Hebrew, which language is not widely known among Arabs, but, additionally, because of the shadow that the Arab-Israeli conflict casts on the Arab literary scene. See Mahmoud Kayyal, 'Arabs dancing in a new light of *Arabesques*': minor Hebrew works of Palestinian authors in the eyes of critics', *Middle Eastern Literatures* (2008), 11: 31–51. The best-known Arab writers of Hebrew fiction in Israel are Anton Shammas and Sayed Kashua. In interviews that I conducted with Palestinian and Jewish writers and critics in Israel (September 2011 and June 2012, respectively) opinions differed as to whether these two writers are Hebrew writers or (Palestinian or Arab writers) writing in Hebrew. For example, on the Jewish side, Meir Shalev (Personal Interview, 19 June 2012, Alonei-Abba) and Gayil Haraven (Personal Interview, 16 June 2012, West Jerusalem) considered Shammas to be a Hebrew writer, but they were contradicted by A. B. Yehoshua, one of Israel's foremost writers, who considered Shammas to be a Palestinian writer writing in Hebrew (Personal Interview, 17 June 2012, Haifa). Similar divisions existed among Palestinian writers. Naim Araidi (Personal Interview, 23 September 2011, Al-Maghar) considered Shammas one of the finest Hebrew writers, whereas Oudeh Bisharat (Personal Interview, 22 September 2011, Nazareth) considered him to be a Palestinian writer writing in Hebrew. Sayed Kashua was more problematic to classify. He tends to generate a lot of conflicting feelings among Palestinians, because of his satirical style that pokes fun at Palestinians (washing their dirty linen in public) and, they believe, less so towards Jews. On the Jewish side, Almog Behar (Personal Interview, 20 June 2012, West Jerusalem), Galit Dahan-Karlibach (Personal Interview, 20 June 2012, West Jerusalem), Gayil Haraven (Personal Interview, 16 June 2012, West Jerusalem) and Dror Mishani (Personal Interview, 17 June 2012, Tel Aviv) considered Kashua a Hebrew writer, but there was also a great deal of ambivalence towards his writings (for different reasons), among others, which made them reluctant to classify him as a Hebrew writer – for example, Hanan Hever (Personal Interview, 18 June 2012, Tel Aviv), Meir Shalev (Personal Interview, 19 June 2012, Alonei-Abba) and Yehouda Shenhav (Personal Interview, 18 June 2012, Tel Aviv). On the Palestinian side, Naim Araidi (Personal Interview, 23 September 2011, Al-Maghar) considered Kashua to be an Arab writer who writes in Hebrew, rather than a Hebrew writer. When I pressed Al-Araidi on this point, he said that, unlike Shammas – whose *Arabesques* is in the tradition of canonical Hebrew writings in terms of style, aesthetic sensibility and linguistic virtuosity – Sayed Kashua does not display these characteristics to the same extent. This rationale was questioned by Ala Hlehel (Personal Interview, 25 September 2012, Acre) and Dror Mishani (Personal Interview, 17 June 2102, Tel Aviv). Mishani made the interesting point that Sayed Kashua's satirical stance is very much in the style of diasporic Jewish writers, who, like Kashua, poked fun at their own community and the 'Other' outside it. Gayil Haraven and Galit Dahan-Karlibach saw no difference between Sayed Kashua's style and use of Hebrew and the young generation of Jewish writers writing in Israel today. What makes

discussion of the excerpt from Bouazza, the language-identity link will be my primary concern, whether it is asserted or denied. For the most part, the following discussion will operate on the macro-level, rather than at the level of micro-analysis, by considering specific examples of language use. Most of the discussion will relate to the symbolic role of language – a major theme in this book – rather than its instrumental function.

One of the best metaphors for approaching Arabic discussions of this topic is provided by the Egyptian writer Edwar al-Khrarrat[9] under the *qalb* (heart) versus *qālib* (form) formula, whereby the former refers to the content of a hybrid text and the latter to its language.[10] Acting as a dichotomy for practical reasons – although the relatedness of the two terms in this dichotomy is

Kashua different for them is his subject matter, in which the Palestinians in Israel figure prominently. These differences of opinion reveal the problematic nature of classifying literary texts – a point that Gayil Haraven made several times when I interviewed her. To add to this complexity, we may refer to a view expressed by Naim Araidi, according to which Arabic literature in Israel is Israeli, not Palestinian, literature. Ramras-Rauch explains this as follows: 'Araidi argues that the Arabic literature produced in Israel cannot be considered "Palestinian" because it was not created in a Palestinian state and was not influenced by the tradition of Palestinian literature of pre-1948 era, when Palestine did exist. Only after 1967 was there a surge in the quantity of Arabic literature written in Israel. But Araidi takes note of the fact that many of the writers in question were educated in the state of Israel; their formative reading was in Hebrew literature and world literature translated into Hebrew – thereby giving to Arabic literature written in Israel its "Israeli" character'. See Gila Ramras-Rauch, *The Arab in Israeli Literature* (Bloomington and Indianapolis, IN: Indiana University Press, 1989), p. 194. It is clear that Araidi considers enclosure or membership in a state and its cultural consequences to be a defining principle of literary classification.

9 See Edwār al-Kharrāṭ, 'Miṣriyyūn qalban . . . frankūfūniyyūn qāliban: shahāda shakhṣiyya', *Alif: Journal of Contemporary Poetics* (2000), 20: 8–24 (Arabic section); Edwār al-Kharrāṭ, 'Fī al-baḥth 'an huwyyat al-adab al-frankūfūnī', *Al-'Arabī* (2001), 515: 76–9.

10 This formula is reminiscent of Chinua Achebe's (1994: 428) formulation of the parameters for defining African literature. See Chinua Achebe, 'The African writer and the English language', in Patrick Williams and Laura Chrisman (eds), *Colonial Discourse and Postcolonial Theory: A Reader* (New York, NY: Columbia University Press, 1994), p. 428. Reflecting on the deliberations of 'A conference of African writers of English expression' held in Makerere, Kenya, in 1952, Achebe offers the following observation: 'Was [African literature] literature produced *in* Africa or *about* Africa? Could African literature be on any subject, or must it have an African theme? Should it embrace the whole continent south of the Sahara, or just *Black* Africa? And then the question of language. Should it be in indigenous African languages or should it include Arabic, English, French, Portuguese, Africans, et cetera?' Achebe then says that: 'the conference produced a tentative definition of African literature as follows: "Creative writing in which an African setting is authentically handled or to which experiences originating in Africa are integral"'. This definition corresponds to the *qalb* view, as we shall see below.

captured in their common root *q-l-b* – this metaphor declares language to be: (1) the only criterion of identity under its *qālib* end; and (2) as lacking definitional power under its *qalb* end. If we apply the *qālib* criterion, then we would have to treat all hybrid texts as belonging to the literary traditions of the languages in which they are written.[11] This would make *In the Eye of the Sun* by Ahdaf Soueif (of Egyptian origin) an English novel and *Arabesques* by the Palestinian writer Anton Shammas a Hebrew novel. The same would be true of the fictional writing of the Algerian writer Malek Haddad. Kharrat treats his novels in French as French novels, because of their linguistic medium, justifying this by referring to Haddad's famous statement that French was his exile.[12] According to this argument, Haddad may have a linguistic home outside his language of exile, but what defines his literature is precisely the language of the exile in which he intellectually resides, not the language of home to which he (ethnically) belongs or emotionally yearns. Citing the use of Arabic terms in Haddad's novels as evidence of the Arabness of these novels is, according to Kharrat, not a convincing argument. On the one hand, the quantity and literary impact of these terms is not strong enough to rupture their French linguistic edifice, causing us to evaluate these novels as Arabic works; on the other hand, Arabic terms in these works – especially idiomatic and fossilised expressions or culturally loaded words and phrases – acquire additional meanings, mainly due to the semantic value of being foreign or exotic – a fact that makes them different from their purely Arab counterparts.

If, however, we apply the *qalb* criterion, coupling it with the criterion of descent (as this is usually the case), we would be obliged to treat Ahdaf Soueif's novel as an Egyptian Arab novel and Anton Shammas' as a Palestinian Arab novel. Both novels deal with cross-cultural or political encounters full of strong 'indigenous' flavour permeating the narrative. According to the *qalb* criterion, one would be justified in describing these two novels as Arab novels, which were written in foreign languages – English and Hebrew, respectively – rather than as fully-fledged English and Hebrew novels. This kind of position seems to be encoded in the title of Mahmud Qasim's book *al-Adab al-'arabī al-maktūb bi-l-faransiyya* (*Arab Literature in the*

[11] The *qalb* versus *qālib* argument is a variation on the following way of thinking about Francophone texts: 'To define a literature as "francophone" is to draw attention to its language. In many cases the term is used in conjunction with national appellations, such as "Francophone Cameroonian" . . . To describe it in this way draws attention not only to the constituent texts *national* status, but also to the lack of consonance between language and national identity'. See Belinda Jack, *Francophone Literatures: An Introductory Survey* (New York and Oxford: Oxford University Press, 1996), p. 15.

[12] See Richard Serrano, 'Translation and the interlingual text in the novels of Rachid Boudjedra', in Mildred Mortimer (ed.), *Maghrebian Mosaic: A Literature in Transition* (Boulder and London: Lynne Rienner Publishers, 2001), p. 21.

French Language).[13] Qasim argues that the language of a literary text does not define its national identity, but that authorial voice, setting, characters and the worldview of the text concerned together play the determining role.[14] The fact that most hybrid texts, as I have said above, include local narratives, characters, voices, settings, linguistic innovations, material in Arabic script, names (personal, fauna, flora and items of material culture, such as food),[15] obscene vocabulary and also idiomatic or fossilised expressions from the indigenous language warrants, in Qasim's view, treating them as Arab works in foreign languages. Qasim's argument is based on a double erasure of language as a criterion of identity. It erases both the language of the text (what is present) and the Arabic language (what is absent) as criteria of definition, hence my rendering of the term *al-'arabī* in the title of Qasim's book as 'Arab', not 'Arabic', to distance it from language – the Arabic language. In a method reminiscent of the Dutch critics in the case of Bouazza, Qasim applies the criteria of ethnicity, nationality or descent to decide the identity of hybrid texts. The 'naggers', to use Bouazza's term, come from both sides of the linguistic border / frontier, and they think of identity in equally essentialist terms.

Let us develop this argument further. In his discussion of hybrid texts, the Lebanese writer Ghalib Ghanim provides a variation on the *qalb* argument. The title of his book *Shi'r al-lubnānyyīn bi-l-lugha al-faransiyya* (*The Poetry of the Lebanese in the French Language*) shifts the attention from texts to writers in a subtle way. Ghanim avoids the expression *al-shi'r al-lubnānī* (Lebanese poetry), so as to eschew the ascription of a particular nationality to this poetry in French, but he hardly succeeds in this. The connection between nationality and identity may not be highly marked in this title, but it is still encoded by virtue of the fact that what belongs to the Lebanese as individuals, whether at home or in the diaspora, is Lebanese by nationality / ethnicity under a Lebanese political formula of 'once a Lebanese, always a Lebanese'. This ambiguity is resolved in a later essay on the topic with the title: *al-adab al-lubnānī bi-l-lugha al-faransiyya 'alā imtidād al-qarn al-'ishrīn*, ('Lebanese literature in the French language in / throughout the twentieth century', 2001), in which the term 'Lebanese' is used to denote nationality, rather than

13 See Maḥmūd Qāsim, *al-Adab al-'arabī al-maktūb bi-l-faransiyya* (Cairo: al-Hay'a al-Miṣriyya al-'Āmma li-l-Kitāb, 1996).

14 Qāsim (2000) holds a similar opinion in his analysis of what may be called hybrid cinema, to which he refers to as Arab cinema in the French language. See Maḥmūd Qāsim, 'al-Sinimā al-'arabiyya al-nāṭiqa bi-l-faransiyya: ḥālat Mahdī Sharaf', *Alif: Journal of Contemporary Poetics* (2000), 20: 117–32.

15 Farida Abu-Haidar mentions the use of personal names in the titles and narratives of Francophone (North African works): '[Personal] names invariably give characters in Francophone works a Maghrebian [North African] identity, and some writers tend to choose them carefully to convey certain meanings'. See Farida Abu-Haidar, 'Inscribing a Maghrebian identity in French', in Mildred Mortimer (ed.), *Maghrebian Mosaic: A Literature in Transition* (Boulder and London: Lynne Rienner Publishers, 2001), p. 22.

deploying it as a description of individuals. In the aforementioned article, Ghanim makes the argument that, since Lebanon is a multilingual country, it follows that its literature will be expressed in a multiplicity of languages 'indigenous' to it, French being one of them.

By making this argument, Ghanim effectively places literature in French, in classificatory terms, on par with literature written by Lebanese in Arabic, in its different forms, or in English or any other language that is part of the multilingual landscape of Lebanon. A multilingual country will, perforce, have a corpus of literature that is multilingual – a fact that denies the hybridity of any of its literatures, regardless of the language in which they are encoded, inscribed or 'lettered', to use a more accurate term. It is not hard to notice, however, that this argument decentres Lebanese literature in Arabic, at least in classificatory terms, in spite of its being the major expression of the Lebanese in the literary field. By doing this, Ghanim effectively decouples the exclusive link between Arabic and identity in the Lebanese political and literary spheres and its use in Arab nationalist discourse as an index of a restrictive or exclusive national definition centred on the language. Lebanese literature in Arabic does not make this literature, or the country to which it belongs, Arab. This is an interesting argument: it is tantamount to espousing and promoting a particular brand of state nationalism and rejecting, at the same time, the notion of an Arab nationalism in the cultural sphere, lest, we assume, it transmutes itself into a political form of Arab nationalism. Therefore, Ghanim's titles provide excellent examples of how culture is read politically or how to do politics through culture, to argue about the identity of texts and countries against other readings that may be applied to them for competing political definitions. Although the discussion here is, in the first instance, concerned with literature as a cultural product, political currents run underneath in a way that shows the power of literature and culture as proxies in the political arena. This is equally true of Qasim's treatment of the hybrid literature of writers of Arab(ic) descent or heritage as Arab literature. Here, again, culture and politics mix, with language mediating the relationship between them in ideologically impregnated ways.

Let us now consider the question of hybridity from a different angle – that of translation. Personal reflections and critical studies of hybrid literature invoke translation as an interpretive concept in one way or another.[16] Anton Shammas said about *Arabesques*, which was published in 1988: 'Sometimes

[16] This point is made by the Palestinian writer Soraya Antonius in reflections on her writing in English: 'Perhaps one is only nourished by one's own language, even when using another to write in, because one understands the land and the living experiences that informed it . . . In this sense those who write in a foreign language are really translators of their own essence'. See Soraya Antonius, 'The day of outside education', *Alif: Journal of Contemporary Poetics* (2000), 20: 267. Here 'essence' is a kind of subterranean text revealing the metaphorical nature of the translation motif in discussing hybridity.

I *feel* that this book is written in Arabic in Hebrew letters'.[17] This statement does not say that *Arabesques* is a translated book, but that it feels like a translated book. This suggests that translation is used here as some kind of metaphor, rather than as a technical term, to express the hybridity of the novel. Amin Malak describes Ahdaf Soueif's works in a similar manner: 'The reader *feels* that the English text is actually a translation whose original, once existing in the author's mind, is now non-existent'.[18] Witness the reference to 'feeling' in this statement, too. Hilary Kilpatrick makes more or less the same point in her discussion of Ahdaf Soueif's *Aysha*, giving the following excerpts to illustrate her view (the following extracts feel like direct translations from Egyptian Arabic or have, or are believed to have, a strong Arabic flavour):

> Excuse me, excuse me, mother, could you move a little sister? Just a tiny bit. That's it. Thank you . . . We want to get through, pretty one.
>
> There is nothing wrong with you, child, and a thousand men would desire you. But these things are in the hand of God.
>
> Nobody is good enough for her. No body fills her eye.[19]

The celebrated Egyptian novelist and critic Radwa 'Ashur refers to the use of translation in Ahdaf Soueif's *In the Eye of the Sun* in a way that highlights the hybridity of her work:

> Ahdaf Soueif embossed/inlaid (*ṭa'ammat*) her language with many popular expressions from [Egyptian] daily life, verses from the Qur'an, Prophetic *hadīths*, popular sayings, proverbs, songs and images. [She also] used translation in abundance and without hesitation in rendering the dialogue among Egyptian characters in many parts of the novel. [As a result] the true spirit of Egyptian Arabic comes through, [conveying] its lexicon, images/style, syntax, rhythms and comical and satirical feel.[20]

17 See Rachel Feldhay Brenner, 'In search of identity: the Israeli Arab artist in Anton Shammas's *Arabesques*', *Modern Language Association* (*MLA*) (1993), 108: 431 [emphasis added]. In another reflection, Anton Shammas seems to argue against this: 'I don't think writers engage in cultural translation as an intentional act of choice, as they write. Rather, their readers are those who choose to see in their writing that trait of cultural translation'. See Anton Shammas, 'The drowned library: reflections on found, lost and translated books and languages', in Isaebelle de Courtivron (ed.), *Lives in Translation: Bilingual Writers on Identity and Creativity* (New York, NY: Palgrave Macmillan, 2003), p. 124. The matter here hinges on the extent to which the 'intentional' act of cultural translation precludes the possibility of its occurring unintentionally or subconsciously.

18 Amin Malak, 'Arab-Muslim feminism and the narrative of hybridity: the fiction of Ahdaf Soueif', *Alif: Journal of Contemporary Poetics* (2000), 20: 161 [emphasis added].

19 Hilary Kilpatrick, 'Arab fiction in English: a case of dual nationality', *New Comparisons* (1992), 13: 51.

20 Cited in Sāmya Miḥriz, 'Khāriṭat al-kitāba: ḥiwār ma' Ahdāf Suwayf', *Alif: Journal of Contemporary Poetics* (2000), 20: 169 [inserts added].

The use of translation is inevitable in hybrid texts, because of their strong cross-cultural character and the imperatives of authenticity in characterisation.[21] Radwa 'Ashur uses the term translation in a way that echoes its technical sense, but without relinquishing the idea of it being a metaphor. Transferring the cultural tropes of one culture into another is not an easy task: it remains a matter of approximation at best. Writers resolve this by providing glosses or textual clues to help the reader understand the text in a way that cannot but draw attention to these foreign or indigenous elements. In some cases, they may decide not to do so, in order to create a sense of distance between the text and its reader or to remind the readers that the text is not fully monolingual.[22] This is what is meant by subversion and deterritorialisation in postcolonial theory, which the Tunisian Francophone writer Abdelwahab Meddeb expresses with characteristic flourish:

> Writing in French surrenders us to the other, but we will defend ourselves with arabesque, subversion, labyrinthine constructions, the incessant decentring of

[21] This sense of what may be called implicit or covert translation is characteristic of some autobiographies. Edward Said comments on this in the introduction to his autobiography *Out of Place*: 'More interesting for me as author was the sense I had of trying always to translate experiences that I had not only in a remote environment but also in a different language . . . The basic split in my life was the one between Arabic, my native language, and English, the language of my education and subsequent expression as a scholar and teacher, and so trying to produce a narrative of one in the language of the other [in *Out of Place*] has been a complicated task'. See Edward Said, *Out of Place: A Memoir* (New York, NY: Alfred A. Knopf, 1999), pp. xiii–xiv.

[22] Farida Abu-Haidar considers this in the context of North African/Maghrebian Francophone writers as a strategy for inscribing these works with a Maghrebian identity: 'Most Francophone writers . . . seem to breathe a new life into standard French by honing it and shaping it to approximate their own mother tongue varieties. In their efforts to give their writing a distinctly Maghrebian identity, writers resort to using Arabic or Berber words and expressions or change the word order of a sentence to resemble Arabic syntax. This practice seems to have begun by some of the first Francophone writers and has continued until the present. In a number of works by Beur writers born in France, it is not unusual to come across Arabic or Berber terms and expressions, even whole sentences in the mother tongue'. See Abu-Haidar, 'Inscribing a Maghrebian identity in French', p. 14. However, the number of such words is by no means large. Hargreaves refers to a study in the 1980s by Jamila Boulal of ten Beur novels, in which she identifies 138 Arabic or Berber words only. See Alex G. Hargreaves, 'Writers of Maghrebian immigrant origin in France: French, Francophone, Maghrebian or Beur?', in Laila Ibnifassi and Nicki Hitchcott (eds), *African Francophone Writing: A Critical Introduction* (Oxford and Washington, DC: Berg, 1996), p. 38. Hargreaves (Ibid. p. 38) glosses this finding by saying that: 'the terms included here or there are no more than linguistic spice added to the main ingredients'.

> the sentence and of language so that the other will lose the way just as in the narrow streets of the *casbah*.[23]

Hybrid literature may also reflect upon the hazards of lexical translation, because of the complexity of cultural tropes and their interconnectedness in the cultural lexica of their own societies. A brilliant example of this is to be found in Ahdaf Soueif's *In the Eye of the Sun*, when Asya, the Egyptian protagonist, explains to Gerald the difficulty of translating some Arabic words to English. She illustrates this with the first two lines of a poem in Egyptian Arabic by the celebrated poet Ahmad Fouad Nagm, which the blind singer Shaykh Imam made famous: *sharraft yā Nixon bābā; Yā btā' il-Watergate*. Asya tells Gerald:

> Well, . . . as I said, he says, 'you've honoured us, Nixon Baba' – 'Baba' means 'father' but it's used, as it is used here, as a title of mock respect – as in 'Ali Baba', for example that's derived from Muslim Indian use of Arabic – but the thing is you could also address a child as 'Baba' as an endearment – a sort of inversion: like calling him Big Chief because he's so little – and so when it's used aggressively – say in argument between two men – it carries diminutivising, belittling signification. So here it holds all these meanings. Anyway, 'you've honoured us, Nixon Baba' – 'you've honoured us' is, by the way, the traditional greeting with which you meet someone coming into your home – it's almost like 'come on in' in this country [England]. So it functions merely as a greeting and he uses it in that way but of course he activates – ironically – the meaning of having actually 'honoured' us. 'You've honoured us Nixon Baba / o you of Watergate' I suppose would be the closest translation – but the structure 'bita' el-whatever' (el-is just the definite article coming before a noun') posits a close but not necessarily defined relationship between the first noun (the person being described) and the second noun. So 'bita' el-vegetables' would be someone who sold vegetables, while 'bita' el-women' would be someone who pursued women. So Nixon is 'bita' el-Watergate' which suggests him selling the idea of Watergate to someone – selling his version of Watergate to the public – and pursuing a Watergate policy, but all in a non-pompous, street vernacular, jokingly abusive kind of way. The use of 'el-' to further specify Watergate – a noun which needs no further defining – is necessary for the rhythm and adds comic effect.[24]

This excerpt illustrates the rhizomatic nature of cultural tropes, as we have seen in Chapter 3, and the impossibility of transferring their meanings through lexical translation from one language to another in hybrid texts

[23] See Samia Mehrez, 'The subversive poetics of radical bilingualism: postcolonial francophone North African literature', in Dominick La Capra (ed.), *The Bounds of Race: Perspectives on Hegemony and Resistance* (Ithaca and London: Cornell University Press: 1991), p. 269.

[24] See Ahdaf Soueif, *In the Eye of the Sun* (London: Bloomsbury, 1994), pp. 496–7.

without incurring a massive loss in signification. The value of the translation metaphor, however, resides in its ability to draw our attention to the dialogic existence of languages and language ideologies side-by-side in hybrid texts in the two modes of overtness and covertness (mentioned above). The language of the text and its associated ideology are overtly marked in the text concerned. They are foregrounded. The indigenous language of descent and its associated ideology is covertly inscribed. It is part of the background. A hybrid text, in this sense, is a dialogic palimpsest: it consists of a number of intertwined layers, with some closer to the surface than others.[25] Assia Djebar must have had this point in mind when she described her fellow Francophone Algerian writer Katib Yacine as being: 'between two languages, his written French *running alongside* his Arabic mother tongue'.[26] Again, reflecting on the language of Francophone Algerian women writers – for example, Marie-Louise Amrouche and Djamila Debèche – Assia Djebar further invokes the translation metaphor: 'I could say "stories translated from . . ." but from which language? From [*fuṣḥā*] Arabic? From vernacular Arabic, or from a feminine Arabic; this is almost to speak of a subterranean Arabic'.[27] However, the translation metaphor grants chronological and constitutive primacy to what is absent and in the background as *source* material over what is present and in the foreground as *target* material. Those who invoke the language of hybrid texts, the *qālib,* as their criterion of identity reject this primacy and, consequently, judge the translation metaphor to be unhelpful. Those who give primacy to *qalb* as the criterion of definition favour this metaphor. Communication by metaphor is not surprising here, not just because of the suggestiveness of metaphors, but also because of the complexity and inchoateness of the ideas that they set out to express.

Although generally conceived in an essentialist manner, the ascription of identity to hybrid texts is subject to some fluctuation: it oscillates between *qalb, qālib* and descent, depending on contextual factors. Abdullah Rukaybi, an Algerian critic, provides a good example of this fluctuation, ignoring the language factor, the *qālib,* in one case and re-instituting it in another. He tells us that in the 1960s he considered the literary output of Algerian writers in French to belong to Algerian literature, using the *qalb* end of the *qalb* versus *qālib* formula to justify this classification. The literature of this period was conceived (in most cases) and received among Algerians as a contribution to

[25] Applying this notion to the works of Ahdaf Soueif, Malak describes the 'palimpsesting process' as indicating: 'at once erasure, reconstitution and reorientation, thus straddling cultures, interfacing texts and (re)defining enunciation to fit the requisites of the re-inscribed version [of the native story] in English'. See Malak, 'Arab-Muslim feminism and the narrative of hybridity', p. 161.

[26] See Abu-Haidar, 'Inscribing a Maghrebian identity in French', p. 14 [emphasis added].

[27] Cited in Armitage, 'The debate over literary writing in a foreign language', p. 55.

the national struggle against French colonialism and its legacy in Algeria. The use of French was therefore a strategic and historically conditioned choice, because it took the fight to the French colonialists directly – something which writing in Arabic would not have been able to do. In addition, most of the early writers were not proficient in Arabic, because of the colonial policies that favoured French over Arabic, in what the Moroccan Francophone poet and novelist Taher Ben Jelloun calls an act of 'colonial violence'.[28] Their use of French was therefore one of necessity, not choice, and some, in fact, had expressed regret for not being able to write in Arabic. Later writers (particularly those writing in the 1990s) could not complain about a lack of knowledge of Arabic, according to Rukaybi. Their use of French in writing was one of choice, not necessity. By using French, these writers create cognitive dissonance by turning what was thought to be temporary (*al-mu'aqqat*) into something permanent (*al-ladhī yadūm*) for ideological reasons, which trade on the stereotypes of the 'modernity' of French and the 'backwardness' of Arabic, or for wanting to replace Algeria's Arab locus of identity with a Mediterranean one that continues to link the country to the former colonial power. For these reasons, Rukaybi argues that these later works are not part of Algerian literature, rejecting the *qalb* criterion in favour of its *qālib* counterpart as a principle of classification that assigns them to French or Francophone literature.

The case of George Shehadé – a French poet and playwright of Lebanese origin – exemplifies the mutations in identity ascription that we have highlighted above.[29] In the 1950s, Shehadé was considered a French writer without foreign inflection, not just because of his native-like use of French, but also because the content of his literary output was not rooted in a Lebanese setting. In other words, Shehadé satisfied the *qalb* and *qālib* criteria for being considered a French writer on par with other canonical French writers, the identity of whose works as indubitably and fully-fledged French was not in question. However, the emergence of postcolonial theory led to a reconsideration of this identity classification, resulting in treating Shehadé as a Francophone writer and officially consecrating this new status by making him the first recipient of the Prize of the Francophone States in 1986. This reclassification pushed Shehadé from the centre of French literature to its margins. Furthermore, this reclassification led to a re-evaluation of Shehadé's inventive use of French, treating it as an attempt at subverting French by inflecting it towards, one assumes, his language of descent, rather than as something that belongs to the French literary tradition in a manner that reflects the complaint made by Bouazza above. While, in Rukaybi's case, the change in identity interpretation or ascription is avowedly political and ideological, in Shehadé's case, it is tied to a change in literary sensibility,

[28] See Serrano, 'Translation and the interlingual text in the novels of Rachid Boudjedra', p. 28: 'Writing in French is not a choice: it is the result of colonial violence'.

[29] See Walīd al-Khashshāb, 'al-Iflāt min mu'assasat al-huwiyya wa-l-thaqāfa: George Shehadé musāfiran', *Alif: Journal of Contemporary Poetics* (2000), 20: 54–76.

which, nevertheless, cannot be divorced from political and ideological considerations. To this, we may add that while the shift in Rukaybi's classification is from *qalb* to *qālib*, in Shehadé's case, the *qalb* and *qālib* criteria are jettisoned in favour of descent as an index of outside ethnicity, which, in metropolitan France, seems to act selectively. The discrepancy in dealing with Taher Ben Jelloun and Samuel Beckett exemplifies this point:

> When [Taher Ben Jelloun] won the Prix Goncourt in 1987, several bookstores in Paris moved his novels from their 'Mahgrebi' [North African] or 'foreign' literature shelves to those labelled 'French' literature, but he is still classified in the 'Maghrebi' sections of most libraries and book shops. Is Ben Jelloun a 'French' or a 'Francophone' writer? If he is classed as Francophone because of his foreign origins [descent], why is the same label not also applied to writers such as Samuel Beckett, who, like Ben Jelloun, lived in a foreign land before settling in the country of his adoptive language, yet is commonly classified by librarians and booksellers as part of French literature? . . . Andrë Makine was born in Russia and had lived in France for only eight years before winning the 1995 Prix Goncourt for his novel *Le testament français*. That and his previous novels are shelved as a matter of course with 'French' literature. Ben Jelloun, a Goncourt winner eight years previously, is still generally categorised as 'Maghrebi', yet I have never seen Makine classified as Russian.[30]

This differential classification of literary identity on the basis of selective descent, rather than language, is applied to second-generation North African writers in France, referred to as Beurs. Hargreaves notes that the works of some of these writers feature in Francophone anthologies and that, when taught in French universities, they are treated: 'as part of Francophone or Comparative literature, not within French Departments'.[31] The use of anthologies to determine the identities of texts and writers reflects a stance that is sometimes more political than literary or linguistic in nature. Anthologies reflect the dominant identity narratives in society, including those of the literary establishment.[32] Thus, the inclusion of Shehadé, Ben Jelloun and

[30] Alec G. Hargreaves, 'Francophonie and globalisation: France at the crossroads', in Kamal Salhi (ed.), *Francophone Voices* (Exeter: Elm Bank Publications, 1999), p. 51.

[31] See Hargreaves, 'Francophonie and globalisation: France at the crossroads', p. 52. This problem of classification is replicated in the way that these books are marketed in French bookshops; see Hargreaves, 'Writers of Maghrebian immigrant origin in France: French, Francophone, Maghrebian or Beur?', p. 33, who also provides interesting comparisons, in terms of ethnographic positionality, between the gaze of Francophone North African writers in the traditional sense of the term and those of Beur writers, although a French metropolitan target readership is uppermost in their minds.

[32] Anthologies, encyclopaedias and bibliographic dictionaries can offer further clues about issues of identity. Salma Khadra Jayyusi's (1992) *An Anthology of Modern Palestinian Literature* lists six Palestinian writers writing in English. See Jayyusi,

Beur writers in Francophone literature must be justified by reference to their being part of the colonial legacy, in terms of descent or ethnicity – a factor that excludes assigning Samuel Beckett (of Irish origin) and Andrë Makine (of Russian origin) to this category of definition.

Zygmunt Bauman tells us that the: '*idea of "identity" was born out of the crisis of belonging*'.[33] Its link to anxiety (which I have alluded to above) is therefore understandable. The more intense the crisis of belonging, the greater the interest in identity and the more pronounced the anxiety that surrounds it. Bauman further adds that a: 'battlefield is identity's natural home. Identity comes to life only in the tumult of battle; it falls asleep and silent the moment the noise of the battle dies down'.[34] The intense interest in the identity of hybrid literary works suggests that battles of different sorts are being fought on behalf of the nation. The interest in the identity of Francophone literature in the Arabic-speaking world is conducted against the backgrounds of colonialism, decolonisation and nation-building in North Africa. In fact, this interest is more pronounced in Algeria, which fought a long and bloody war for its independence from France, than it is in Morocco and even less so than it is in Tunisia.[35] Language is at the heart of this battle, because of its ideological loadings. The situation is similar for Palestinian writers writing in Hebrew

Salma Khadra (ed.), *An Anthology of Modern Palestinian Literature* (New York, NY: University of Columbia Press, 1992). Meisami and Starkey's (1998) *Encyclopaedia of Arabic Literature* does not provide entries for any of these six writers, but lists others, for example, the Algerian Katib Yacine, although they accept the 'principal of "Arabic literature" as literature written in Arabic' (p. xi). See Julie Scott Meisami and Paul Starkey (eds), *Encyclopaedia of Arabic Literature* (London and New York, NY: Routledge, 1998), p. xi. In their bibliographic dictionary, *Tarājim wa-āthār fi al-adab al-'arabī fi isrā'īl*, Moreh and 'Abbasi (1987) take language as a criterion of classification, thus listing Jewish writers, mainly from Iraq, writing in Arabic alongside Arab Palestinian ones. However, the term '*arabī*' in this title refers to language, not ethnicity, although some of these writers – for example, Sami Michael – would identify as Arab Jews (Personal Interview, Haifa, 20 June 2012). This is also true of Almog Behar – a second generation Iraqi Jew in Israel, whose poem 'My Arabic is Mute' is an expression of this identity (Personal Interview, West Jerusalem, 20 June 2012). This poem is appended at the end of this chapter.

33 Zygmut Bauman, *Identity* (Cambridge: Polity, 2004), p. 20 [emphasis in the original].

34 Ibid. p. 77.

35 Armitage ('The debate over literary writing in a foreign language', p. 52) sums up the difference between Tunisia and the other countries of the Maghreb, with respect to colonial language policy as follows: 'The use of Arabic was never interrupted by a French acculturation programme, as it was in Algeria and to a lesser extent in Morocco, but rather was used alongside French in the newly introduced French schools. After independence in 1956, the state made a conscious decision to introduce a bilingual policy in schools. Because of this, choice of language has not been seen as such a thorny and emotive issue as it is elsewhere in the Marghreb'. This is different from Algeria, which promoted a vigorous, some would say 'aggressive', Arabisation programme after independence in 1962.

in Israel, in spite of the fact that this is a more recent and less pronounced phenomenon, at least in the quantity of works produced.[36] In comparison, the question of identity may be less salient for Anglophone works, because of the ideologically less pronounced meanings of English in comparison to French or Hebrew in terms of nation-building. Even for India, which lived under British rule for a long time, English is: 'less and less signified as a colonial remnant and more as a contemporary global attribute',[37] making Indian literature in English less postcolonial and more transnational[38] – a position French has not yet fully achieved. The less assimilationist policies of Great Britain towards its colonies and the rise of English as the international *lingua franca* in recent decades have altered assessments of it as a colonial language in the Arab imaginary in comparison to French.

Language is located at the heart of this debate about identity, most directly through the *qālib* criterion. Classifying a hybrid text according to its language makes sense, not least because of the role language plays, both symbolically and instrumentally, in marking identities. Language moulds content. In fact, it is impossible to imagine content without language in any literary work, whether of the hybrid kind or not. In theory, there should therefore be no problem aligning identity with language in classifying literary works. A novel in French is a French novel. However, this rule is breached in classifications of hybrid texts in two ways – one centrifugal and the other centripetal. The recognition of a category of Francophone works is an expression of the centrifugal forces at work in society and the literary establishment in metropolitan culture: it effectively brands works in French by writers with descent in the Arabic-speaking world (among others) as less French than those of French canonical writers, hence their hybridity at the ideological or sociological level. This is tantamount to saying that language on its own is not enough as a marker of identity, in spite of the fact that French national identity is linked to French as one of its primary markers.

The centripetal forces operate on the other side of the language divide. Again, descent is invoked here to argue the opposite point: the fact that a North African writer writing in French does not become a French writer; he remains North African (Algerian, Moroccan or Tunisian) by virtue of the

[36] See Mahmūd Darwīsh, who describes this phenomenon as the choice of a small minority of Palestinians in Israel (*aqaliyya maḥdūda*) who write in Hebrew as a 'kind of fashion' (*mā yushbih al-mūḍa*) 'out of a desire to integrate culturally in Israeli society' (*al-indimāj al-thaqāfī fī al-mujtama' al-isrā'īlī*) or as a 'kind of resistance against Israelis through their very language' (*naw' min al-muqāwama ḍidd al-isrā'īliyyīn fī lughatihimnafsihā*). See: http://www.alquds.com/news/article/view/id/39002 (accessed 26 August 2012).

[37] Rashmi Sadana, 'A suitable text for a vegetarian audience: questions of authenticity and the politics of translation', *Public Culture* (2007), 19: 315.

[38] See Rashmi Sadana, 'Two tales of a city: the place of English and the limits of postcolonial critique', *Interventions* (2009), 11: 1–15.

content of his work, in terms of setting, themes, characters and worldview. This *qalb*-based argument cannot, however, afford to ignore language completely as the primary marker of identity. The reference to the practice of subversion, appropriation and deterritorialisation, whether or not intended by the writer, rehabilitate the *qālib* argument through the backdoor by making aspects of this practice definitional of the identity of a hybrid work. We may express this in a different way by reference to the palimpsest metaphor used above: the less visible strand in the palimpsest under the *qalb* approach is given salience, so as to highlight the impact of the covert and absent over the overt and present. The reference to translation as a metaphor for the relationship between a prior 'virtual' text and the actual text of a hybrid novel is but another expression of this dialogic relationship between the covert and absent, on the one hand, and the overt and present, on the other. Language, whether subliminal, virtual or real, is at the heart of this relationship, which may be characterised as one of 'contact' or 'collision', not just between languages, but also between their ideologies and the cultural politics that they serve to enunciate, in line with Bakhtin's characterisation of hybridisation as a: 'mixture of two *social* languages within the limits of a single utterance, an encounter within the arena of an utterance, between two different linguistic consciousnesses',[39] as this is clearly represented in the excerpts from Ahdaf Soueif (above).

Ideology and cultural politics are writ large in the above discussion, and literature, as Berger rightly observes, is an: 'exemplary site for the study of the politics of language . . . since it [literature] can never be far away when language is at stake'.[40] Ideology is concerned with generating meaning, both descriptively and normatively. The concern with the identity of hybrid texts mixes these two forces in generating ideological meanings: the one describes the objective facts of the hybrid text, its form and content, while the other places interpretations on these facts, which serve two antithetical political ends: keeping the core of hegemonic culture intact or coherent against

39 Mikhail Mikhaĭlovich Bakhtin, *The Dialogic Imagination: Four Essays*, Michael Holquist (ed.) and trans. Caryl Emerson and Michael Holquist (Austin, TX: University of Texas Press, 1981), p. 358.

40 Berger adds two further sites: 'the field of political discourse and policy-making, [but], however, the foremost site is "popular" discourse, heterogeneous as it is'. See Anne-Emmanuelle Berger, 'Introduction', in Anne-Emmanuelle Berger (ed.), *Algeria in Others' Languages* (Ithaca and London: Cornell University Press, 2002), p. 11. Berger does not tell us why the last site is the most important one – I believe this is because of its ideological nature as a meaning-making field in society among competing interests – but she rightly points to the multiplicity of perspectives that are needed to study these sites, which are well represented in this book: 'historical (political and cultural history), anthropological, philosophical and literary'. To these, we can add sociology of language and sociolinguistics. The present study approaches these data mainly from the perspective that I have dubbed as language in the social world.

external intrusion[41] by using the centrifugal force of classification, and preventing cultural leakage or betrayal, in the metaphorical sense, by using the centripetal force of classification to claim writers as 'tokens of achievement' of, and for, a given culture.[42] Here, culture and politics meet through literature, with language standing at the nexus of contact. In the French or Arabic writings of the Algerian Rachid Boujedra, the two languages exist in a state of tension, but without one excluding the other.[43] In the case of Bouazza, Willemsen relates the reaction to his stylistic innovations among Dutch critics to the concern with, or about, multiculturalism, in which categorising literary texts has the effect of claiming the hybrid writer, whilst simultaneously distancing him from the mainstream, thus: '[acknowledging] him as self and "other" simultaneously'.[44]

Changes in classifying hybrid texts – for example, as in the case of George Shehadé's poems and plays or the one applied by Rukaybi in Algeria – reflect changes in political sensibilities, revealing the ideological nature of these classifications in the process. The above discussion has also revealed how the classification of hybrid works is used in the defence or promotion of nation-state identity. Ghanim's view of Lebanon as a multilingual country and the concomitant treatment of all works by Lebanese writers as equally Lebanese enables him to achieve three objectives: (1) eliminating the hybrid as a description of literature in French by Lebanese writers, effectively moving Lebanon from the third category of Francophone countries to the second category (as explained above); (2) decentring literature in Arabic by

41 Jack comments on the issue of 'coherence' as follows in the context of Francophone literatures: 'The complexities of the linguistic and cultural spaces in which the Francophone texts are written, published, criticised, and read, are thus necessarily bound up in, and in part constitutive of, the complexities and ferment of contemporary literary, cultural and social theory, described . . . in terms of the threat to cultural coherence . . .' See Jack, *Francophone Literatures: An Introductory Survey*, p. 16. This is not unlinked to the confluence of literature and national identity in the imperial project, as Jack points out (Ibid. p. 1): 'The institutionalisation of the study of national literatures and their displacement of the classics as the principal "humane" discipline occurred at a particular historical moment; the growth of empire and the rise of national literary disciplines happened simultaneously'.

42 Khaled Mattawa, 'Four uneasy pieces', *Alif: Journal of Contemporary Poetics* (2000), 20: 271.

43 Serrano comments on this aspect of Boujedra's novels as follows: 'Whether written in French or Arabic, his novels always acknowledge a tension between the two languages . . . It is not entirely clear that Boujedra composes a francophone novel exclusively in French or an Arabophone novel exclusively in Arabic, since he seems to work with both languages simultaneously. Even in his earliest novels the Arabic language sometimes breaks through the francophone surface'. See Serrano, 'Translation and the interlingual text in the novels of Rachid Boudjedra', p. 29.

44 Willemsen, 'Dutch authors from the Arab world: a relief to the multilingual society', p. 68.

Lebanese writers and making it one type of literary expression – albeit the dominant one – among others; and (3) arguing for a Lebanese political and cultural nationalism that challenges the political and cultural hegemony of (pan-)Arab nationalism, in which Arabic is treated as the primary, if not the exclusive, marker of identity in the Arab sphere. Ghanim does not reject the role of Arabic as a marker of identity through cultural production in Lebanon, but he argues that it is one marker among others, including French, thus linking this multiplicity of markers to the 'civilising mission' of Lebanon as a Mediterranean country that looks both West and East from its position in the Middle East. Ghanim's thesis is supremely ideological: it uses culture as a proxy to talk about politics as a field of meaning-making and power relations between competing visions of identity: those of the nation-state versus pan-Arab nationalism. Ideology and cultural politics are explicitly expressed here, but this does not have to be the case in absolute terms. Most of the time, these two interlinked forces apply in subtle ways that do not draw attention to themselves, as, for example, in the classifications that one finds hidden in anthologies, literary encyclopaedias or literary biographical dictionaries, to which reference has been made above.

The Language of Hybrid Texts: Between Choice and Necessity

Whether a matter of conscious or deliberate choice, accident[45] or necessity, the language of hybrid texts are an issue of great ideological and political significance in their evaluation. After independence, most North African writers resorted to French, because it was the only language they could use in writing fiction. French colonial policy, especially in Algeria, promoted French at the expense of Arabic (and Berber), as part of French attempts at (elite) assimilation and acculturation. As mentioned above, the Moroccan writer Taher Ben Jelloun captured this point well when, in the 1960s, he

[45] The Algerian writer Rachid Boujedra ascribes his use of French in his early novels to accident; this is why I refer to it here. Serrano says that: 'in remarks at a 1992 conference on autobiography and the avante-garde in Montreal, [Boujedra] claimed that his writing in French was at first accidental and then was necessitated by the contract he signed with his publisher Denoël . . . Because he was then an unknown writer, he had promised them multiple books in French to get his first novel published'. See Serrano, 'Translation and the interlingual text in the novels of Rachid Boudjedra', p. 29. Serrano (Ibid. p. 29) casts doubt on this claim: 'This comment would seem to imply that [Boujedra] would have always preferred to write in Arabic. His latest novel, again in French, was published by Grasset and not by Denoël, which suggests that he recognises a different set of obligations now [1990s] that Algeria has been wracked by nearly a decade of civil war'. We may add to this the fact that the term 'accident' leaves unexplained why the first novel Boujedra wrote was in French. This is also true of Ahdaf Soueif's statement that her choice of English as a language of literary expression was a 'pure accident' (*maḥḍ ṣudfa*). See Mihriz, 'Khāriṭat al-kitāba: ḥiwār ma' Ahdāf Suwayf', p. 182.

commented: 'writing in French is not a choice: it is the result of colonial violence'.[46] Writing during this period, the Algerian writer Malek Haddad expresses the same point when he says that French was, for him, the language of involuntary exile.[47] The Palestinian writer Soraya Antonius – the product of a foreign schooling system – never questioned her choice of English as the language of writing,[48] such is the power of education and acculturation in determining language choice. Etel Adnan – a Lebanese-American poet writing in English – describes how her French schooling in Lebanon made speaking Arabic the: 'equivalent of sin' (*al-taḥadduth bi-l-'arabiyya kāna mu'ādilan li-fikrat al-ithm*).[49] As a result, Adnan grew up as an outsider (*gharība*), instrumentally, but an insider (*muwāṭina*) in symbolic terms, being, in this way, an exile from Arabic, which she describes as a 'forbidden paradise' (*janna muḥarrama*).[50] But instead of writing in French – the language of her early schooling and literary sensibility – Adnan chose to write in the American language (*al-lugha al-amrīkiyya*), as she calls English in the United States[51] – the language of her higher education and daily life – but a language that she symbolically considers to be 'foreign' to her, as the title of her essay 'Writing in a foreign language' (*al-kitāba bi-lugha ajnabiyya*), to which I am referring here, signals. This choice, she tells us, was initially motivated by an anti-French feeling, owing to the violence used by France in the Algerian War of Independence (*wa-qad ista't min iḍṭirārī ilā al-ta'bīr 'an nafsī bi-l-faransiyya* . . . [*wa*] *adrakt annanī lā astaṭī' al-kitāba bi-ḥuriyya bi-lugha tuwājihunī bi-mithl hādhā al-ṣirā' al-'amīq*).[52] This reaction against French is interesting, because it openly acknowledges the political nature of language choice, while revealing the feelings of solidarity that the Algerian War of Independence generated in the Arabic-speaking world during the heyday of Arab nationalism, in which language played an important part. If a writer is unable to write in his native language (*al-lugha al-umm*), he or she may opt for a language other than the one that is heavily involved in colonial oppression. Adnan's reference to English in America as the American language is significant in this regard: it eliminates the connotations of colonialism from English that accrue to it in its British inflection.

But what kind of Arabic is Adnan talking about here? Spoken or written Arabic? For a writer like Adnan (and, one assumes, most North African Francophone writers), written Arabic must be the language that they have in

46 Serrano, 'Translation and the interlingual text in the novels of Rachid Boudjedra', p. 28.
47 Ibid. p. 28.
48 Antonius, 'The day of outside education', p. 257.
49 Etel 'Adnān, 'al-Kitāba bi-lugha ajnabiyya', trans. Dalia Said Mustafa, *Alif: Journal of Contemporary Poetics* (2002), 20: 133.
50 Ibid. p. 143.
51 Ibid. p. 138.
52 Ibid. p. 139.

mind, since in the diglossic Arabic language situation, proficiency in spoken Arabic does not automatically translate into proficiency in the literary language, with its intricate grammatical rules and stylistic conventions which have to be formally learned. This point is made by Ahdaf Soueif when she says that her competence in Arabic as a language of daily communication is of a different order, in terms of technical ability, from the kind of language competence that the writer needs in creative writing.[53] Although Soueif initially set out to write in Arabic, she quickly discovered that she had a stark choice: either to write in English, the language of her formal education and literary sensibility, or not to write at all.[54] She expresses this point by saying that: 'in the end [I] decided to write, even though in English' (*wa-fī al-nihāya, ikhtart an aktub . . . wa-law bi-l-inglīziyya*),[55] expressing, in this way, the factor of necessity that is under discussion here. The Palestinian-Israeli writer Sayed Kashua faced the same stark choice for the same reasons – either write in Hebrew or don't write at all.[56] This point is hinted at in a piece Sayed Kashua published in the Israeli newspaper *Haaretz* (28 June 2012).[57]

It is not easy to distinguish between conscious choice and necessity as motivating factors behind the language of hybrid texts. A good example of necessity that I could find, albeit of a somewhat different kind, involves the fiction of the Iraqi writers in Israel[58] who switched from Arabic to Hebrew as a language of literary expression – for example, Shalom Darwish, Shimon Ballas and Sami Michael. Although this fiction in Hebrew displays many of the features of hybrid literature – for example, the subversive use of Arabic material in the original or calqued form, Iraqi settings, characters and worldviews, and so forth – [59] and in spite of the fact that some of these authors continue to describe themselves as Arab Jews,[60] to the best of my knowledge, their novels are classified and received as Hebrew Israeli literature by the Israeli literary establishment and reading public, rather than as Hebrewphone literature, as may be the case with Palestinian writers writing in Hebrew.[61] The reason for this discrepancy in categorisation is the

53 Miḥriẓ, 'Khāriṭat al-kitāba: ḥiwār ma' Ahdāf Suwayf', p. 183.

54 Ibid. pp. 175–6.

55 Ibid. p. 176.

56 Personal Interview, 27 September 2012, West Jerusalem.

57 See: http://www.haaretz.com/weekend/magazine/every-writer-loves-to-recount-a-wretched-childhood-except-this-one.premium-1.444714 (accessed 21 August 2012).

58 See Reuven Snir, '"We were like those who dream": Iraqi-Jewish writers in Israel in the 1950s', *Prooftexts* (1991), 11: 153–73.

59 See Nancy E. Berg, *Exile from Exile: Israeli Writers from Iraq* (Albany, NY: State University of New York Press, 1996), pp. 59–62.

60 Personal interviews with Shimon Ballas (18 June 2012, Tel Aviv), Sasson Somekh (18 June 2012, Tel Aviv) and Sami Michael (20 June 2012, Haifa).

61 Hanan Hever is one of the few Israeli critics who proposed treating these writers as 'Hebrewphone'. I am indebted to Yuval Evri for pointing this out to me.

difference in nationality in the two cases, with Jewishness (as religion and ethnicity), the Hebrew language and Israeli nationality being aligned with each other in one case, but being out of kilter in the other, as will be discussed further later. Ramras-Rauch confirms this when she says:

> in the case of [Sami] Michael and [Shimon] Ballas we have two writers raised in the Arabic language and culture but who are Israeli writers now, not only by virtue of their present residence [in Israel] and language [Hebrew] but also because they are *Jews* in Israel.[62]

Be that as it may, these Hebrew Israeli writers explain the switch to Hebrew as a matter of necessity in three ways. First, there is the matter of wanting to become integrated as fully as possible in the target culture, including its language, as an expression of their newly acquired identity.[63] Second, these writers refer to the vastly reduced number of readers of their works in Israel as a result of the switch to Hebrew – the primary target being Jews of Iraqi heritage with active competence in Arabic. Shalom Darwish expresses this point when he says: 'If I write in Arabic no one will read it. There is no market at all. The people who read me in Iraq crossed over to Hebrew. Arabs are not interested in reading a Jew'.[64] In this context, the relative obscurity in the Israeli literary scene of Samir Naqqash, who continued to write until the end of his life in a heavily inflected Iraqi-Jewish Arabic, is offered as an example of the fate of a writer who refuses to write in, or is unable to make the switch to, Hebrew. What is at stake here is not the inadequacy of Arabic as a medium of expression,[65] but the inadequacy of its

[62] Ramras-Rauch, *The Arab in Israeli Literature*, p. 193 [emphasis in the original]. It should be noted here that, for the majority of these writers, the switch to Hebrew did not imply support for Zionist ideology. Shimon Ballas and Sami Michael are, to this day, implacable opponents of this ideology. This paradoxically explains the initial reluctance of these two writers to switch to Hebrew. Shimon Ballas' first Hebrew novel was published in 1964. Sami Michael's first Hebrew novel was published a decade later in 1974.

[63] In an interview with Nancy Berg in 1989, Shimon Ballas expressed this point as follows: 'When one lives in a certain reality, in a certain society, then one must be part of [that] society. To be part of the society is a matter of language, (it means) it is impossible to be in exile . . . You arrive, you become integrated in the society somehow, you take a new identity. If you take a new identity, you must take it fully, including the language'. See Nancy E. Berg, *Exile from Exile: Israeli Writers from Iraq*, p. 65. Shimon Ballas reiterated this view to me when I interviewed him in Tel Aviv (18 June 2012), adding the important role of family in making the shift seem irreversible.

[64] Berg, *Exile from Exile: Israeli Writers from Iraq*, p. 57.

[65] Samir Naqqash wrote most of his works in the Jewish dialect of Baghdad out of a desire to document this dialect and, more importantly, because of the close fit between this dialect and the subject matter that he explored in his fiction. We may therefore argue that this dialect is supremely adequate for the purpose, but it had a

reach to the reading public. Furthermore, the reduction in the Israeli Jewish readership constitutes an acute problem, because it is aligned with negative images of Arabic among Israeli Jews as an inferior[66] and backward language, as well as the language of the enemy.[67] From the Arab side, these writers would have struggled to attract readers in sufficient numbers to compensate for the lost readership in Israel, because by immigrating to Israel and owing to their Israeli-accented Jewish ethnicity, they were perceived to have joined the enemy. Squeezed from both sides, these writers had to switch to Hebrew if they wanted to continue to write. Third, these writers ascribe the switch to Hebrew to the need to choose a language that matches their new reality in Israel, in terms of subject matter, characterisation, settings, themes and worldviews, and so forth. However, the switch to Hebrew was not an easy one: these writers continue to feel that they are not fully at home in their new language. Sami Michael expresses this point when he writes:

very restricted reach. Samir Naqqash was aware of this, as evidenced by his use of glosses to open up his fiction to wider readership.

[66] The inferiority of Arabic among Israeli Jews is described by Hanna Biran (1994) – an Oriental Jew in Israel – from her own personal experience: 'My parents' mother tongue was Arabic and in my childhood, Arabic was the second language spoken at home. The sound of the language always made me ashamed. The world outside brought home to me that reading and writing in Arabic were inferior. I never thought or felt that I possessed an important asset, an instrument of communication with the East. [This] subtle and indirect message permeated so deeply within me that, fearing to be similar to the Arabs and identified with them, I was eventually unable to take in a single word of Arabic'. See Hanna Biran, 'Fear of the Other', *Palestine-Israel Journal* (1994), 4: 48. See also: http://www.pij.org/details.php?id=698 (accessed 23 August 2012).

[67] The image of Arabic as the language of the enemy was mentioned by the young Israeli writer of Moroccan descent Galit Dahan-Karlibach (Personal Interview, 20 June 2012, West Jerusalem). This image, in her case, is not unlinked to her being from Sderot in southern Israel, which was targeted in cross-border shellings by Hamas. Galit Dahan-Karlibach linked Arabic to the sound of Qassam rockets – after the Palestinian national hero Izz al-Din al-Qassam – which Hamas fighters and others in Gaza used in shelling Sderot. This following reflection on Arabic in Israel by Anton Shammas confirms this image of Arabic as the language of the enemy: '[A] ghost . . . followed me for thirteen years without being noticed – the fear that language, as such, is at the same time, a threat that has to be evaded and a fragile secret that has to be protected. When I used to live in Jerusalem, reading an Arabic newspaper in a [West] Jerusalem café would invite hostile looks on a good day but, more often than not, merit a frisking and a violent encounter with the Israeli police. That's when the trivial, the mundane, the absent-minded act of reading a newspaper in public would be interpreted as a potential threat. And I remembered that one of the most gratifying features of living in Ann Arbor, Michigan, had been the sheer pleasure of sitting in a ghost-free café and reading an Arabic newspaper without generating hostile looks of strangers'. See Shammas, 'The drowned library: reflections on found, lost and translated books and languages', pp. 126–7.

> I still envy people who were born into the Hebrew language. They can castrate words on purpose or distort them. They are free to take the language, to make a dough of it, and play with it as they like. They have a legitimate right to do this. I feel as if I am not entitled to do this.[68]

However, it is often the case that once a writer switches to or adopts a particular language as his medium of expression, he will continue to use it in preference to his native language in writing fiction, either out of habit or even acculturation, if nothing else.[69] Examples where a writer rescinds his choice of a language of hybridity in favour of the native language are, to the best of my knowledge, non-existent or very rare,[70] but examples do exist of two languages co-existing in the output of a particular writer – for example, in the use of Arabic and French in the work of the Algerian's Katib Yacine (dialectal Arabic) and Rachid Boujedra (standard Arabic), who started their literary careers in French and later added Arabic.

The argument of matching language to subject matter is a starting point that is often balanced against the purpose(s) of the hybrid text in the target culture.[71] The fact that most hybrid works describe a reality that is lived in one language by means of another language suggests that matching subject matter or reality to language is not a deciding factor in language choice.[72] It would, according to this criterion, be more suitable to choose the native language (Arabic or Iraqi Arabic) to describe the native reality (Jewish life in Iraq), which is something that Samir Naqqash argued for and practised throughout his career, making him an almost unknown writer among Israeli Jews. A recurrent argument in discussions of hybrid texts is the deployment

68 See also Sami Michael, 'On being an Iraqi-Jewish writer in Israel', *Prooftexts* (1984), 4: 58.

69 Sami Michael confirmed this when I asked him if he could return to writing in Arabic (Personal Interview, 20 June 2012, Haifa).

70 This may be another reason for considering the fiction of Iraqi Jewish writers in Israel as hybrid. Ramras-Rauch quotes Sami Michael describing the switch to Hebrew as a: 'divorce from Arabic', likening it to the: 'amputation of a limb'. See Ramras-Rauch, *The Arab in Israeli Literature*, p. 179. Ramras-Rauch says that, despite this 'divorce': 'Michael admits to the influence of Arabic on his Hebrew fiction, a blending of what he calls the pictoriality of Arabic with the modern functionality of Hebrew'.

71 The question of matching language to subject matter is ultimately a question about authenticity. This has been the case for Indian English writers. Sadana expresses this as follows: 'The question of choosing which language to write in has often been a loaded one for Indian English writers, raising issues of which language might be an authentic representation of Indian-ness'. See Rashmi Sadana, 'Two tales of a city: the place of English and the limits of postcolonial critique', *Interventions* (2009), 11: 5–6.

72 Edward Said comments on this point in his memoir *Out of Place*. See Said, *Out of Place*, pp. xiii–ivx.

of these texts to take the battle back to the colonial culture by explaining or defending national causes.[73] Ahdaf Soueif expresses this very point when she asks:

> What is the harm if one of us wrote in English? What is the harm in communicating the feelings/sentiments (*wijdān*) of the Egyptians and the Arab vision (*ru'ya*) to the Western reader directly, without the mediation of translation and without a literary work being cut-down to size as translated literature [in the target culture]? Is this not one way of exercising influence, of storming (*iqtiḥām*) [the target culture]?[74]

The Algerian writer Mouloud Feraoun expresses a similar point when he says: 'what forced me to write was the desire to make our [Algerian] reality known'.[75]

Atallah Mansour, the author of the first novel in Hebrew by a Palestinian writer in Israel – *In a New Light* (*Be-Or Ḥadash*, 1966) – relates this work to the desire to present a Palestinian narrative as an alternative to the hegemonic Zionist narrative to highlight the problems facing Palestinians, especially discrimination, with the aim of influencing the views of Israeli Jews.[76] This aim is encoded in the following statement, in which Mansour sets out the intention behind his novel:

> As an Arab writer who writes in Hebrew, who lives in Arab society and writes *for* the Jewish community, conditions compel me to act as bridge between the two nations . . . I feel that to annoy readers means, in many cases, to prompt them to think. If I have managed to do so, my purpose has been accomplished.[77]

Mansour is clear about his identity as an Arab writer writing in Hebrew, with the aim of presenting the case of his nation in the court of public appeal of another, hegemonic and dominating nation, so as to bring about a change in power relations between the two. Mansour is also aware of the writerly impact of his work, making the bridge that he talks about a one-way crossing over the troubled waters of Israeli-Palestinian relations.

Hybrid writers, therefore, are writers with a mission, and the choice of language cannot, for this reason, be divorced from this mission. In their hands, hybrid literature is an instrument of decolonisation,[78] a matter of

73 Sāmya Miḥriz, 'Khāriṭat al-kitāba: ḥiwār ma' Ahdāf Suwayf', *Alif: Journal of Contemporary Poetics* (2000), 20: 183 (Arabic section).

74 Ibid. p. 182 [inserts in the original].

75 Mortimer, 'Introduction', p. 3.

76 Personal interview (24 September 2011, Nazareth).

77 Rachel Feldhay Brenner, *Inextricably Bonded: Israeli Arab and Jewish Writers Re-Visioning Culture* (Madison, WI: University of Wisconsin Press, 2003), p. 132 [emphasis added].

78 The instrumentality of the colonial language in the decolonisation project is aimed at both the coloniser and the colonised. Katib Yacine expresses this in talking about

writing back, to use the subtitle of one of the most famous texts on postcolonial literature.[79] One of the weapons in this enterprise is the subversion, deterritorialisation or de-ethnicisation and appropriation of the language of colonisation and hegemony. Subversion is expressed in different ways as a matter of violating the target language norms, bending its rules, breaking its stylistic conventions and remoulding it as a tool of counter hegemony by making it sound foreign and strange to the target culture. Although the means of this kind of subversion are instrumental, the aim is symbolic: it seeks to achieve estrangement[80] between the text and its language, on the one hand, and the target reader, on the other – of getting him, in the words of the Tunisian writer Abdelwahab Meddeb, to be lost in the: 'narrow streets of the [linguistic] *casbah*'.[81] In the words of Belinda Jack, the ultimate aim is more far-reaching: 'the subversion of *la langue* (the tongue) is subversive of a *national* language, related to, if not synonymous with the subversion of the nation and its interests'.[82] This subversion operates in the symbolic realm of language signification, since, in instrumental terms, it is of no great consequence in impairing the comprehensibility of a hybrid text or significantly rupturing its language. If the colonial language is, in figurative terms, booty of colonialism,[83] then the hybrid writer is entitled to use it to suit his ends.

Let us examine this theme briefly by looking at the language question in Anton Shammas' *Arabesques*. Anton Shammas expresses this sense of mission when he says: 'as an Arab it is important to say what I want to say *to*

pre-independence Algeria as follows: '[French] is simply a tool by which we can transmit our ideals to Algerian intellectuals, who are unable to understand literary Arabic. It is also a tool by which we reach world opinion in order to assist in our cause'. See Kamal Salihi, 'French words, authentic voice', in Kamal Salihi (ed.), *Francophone Voices* (Exeter: Elm Bank Publications, 1999), p. 42. Reflecting on the identity of the literature from this decolonising perspective, Yacine (Ibid. p. 42) says that: 'it is independent of the language it uses, and has no emotional or racial relationship [to it]. It expresses its own conditions, and its spirit has the wisdom of the Algerian people with its revolutionary determination to free itself from imperialism'.

79 See Ashcroft et al., *The Empire Writes Back: Theory and Practice in Postcolonial Literatures.*

80 The Moroccan writer Abdelkebir Khatibi describes the use of French in Francophone literature as: 'an instrument of catharsis . . . by which one could render the French reader a stranger to his language'. See Armitage, 'The debate over literary writing in a foreign language', p. 57.

81 Mehrez, 'The subversive poetics of radical bilingualism', p. 269.

82 Jack, *Francophone Literatures: An Introductory Survey*, p. 13 [emphasis in the original].

83 This is a variant of Assia Djebar's description of French in Algeria as the: 'booty of colonial war'. See Armitage, 'The debate over literary writing in a foreign language', p. 52.

the [Israeli] Jews',[84] echoing, in this regard, the statement made by Atallah Mansour. Since the vast majority of Israeli Jews cannot speak or read Arabic, it is inevitable that a writer with a mission would choose their language (Hebrew) to address them. The target readership determines the language that a hybrid writer uses. In line with the practice of other hybrid writers, Shammas inscribes Hebrew with features of his absent language, Arabic, but he is reluctant to treat this as a matter of subversion in the postcolonial sense.[85] Adel Shakour lists (and exemplifies) the following intrusions from Arabic into Hebrew in Sahmmas' Hebrew works:

> the use of words and phrases borrowed from spoken Arabic in the Hebrew text, translated borrowings, [calques], use of neologisms in Hebrew [under the influence of Arabic], reviving biblical collocations and Hebrew words by loading them with different supplementary meanings under the influence of Arabic, and a preference for certain verbs due to the etymological influence of their Arabic parallels.

However, none of these intrusions make a dint in the instrumental armoury of Hebrew.[86] The aim, therefore, must be different when operating in a different domain – the domain of language symbolism, which is one of the main themes of this book. As I will explain below in discussing the collision between language ideologies in hybrid texts, Shammas' main mission in writing in Hebrew is to un-Jew the language by making it inclusive of both Jews and Palestinians in Israel, instead of it being exclusively linked to the former in national identity terms. Here, language is treated as a metonymy of the nation in symbolic terms, with *Arabesques* being received as an act of cultural and political 'trespass', for which Shammas: 'might, one day, be

84 Reuven Snir, '"Hebrew as the language of grace": Arab Palestinian writers in Hebrew', *Prooftexts* (1995), 15: 167 [emphasis added].

85 In an interview with Muhammad Siddīq, Shammas seems to downplay the issue of subversion in his work: 'Was I thinking at the time of writing *Arabesques* that the act of writing in Hebrew is, inevitably, a plot (*bi-l-ḍarūra amr ta'āmurī*) whose aim is to explode the language of the new colonisers (*al-musta'mir al-jadīd*) from the inside, as postmodern theory tells us? I don't think so because writing in any language, even if it was the language of the coloniser, is a kind of love/infatuation (*bāb min abwāb al-'ishq*)'. See Muhammad Ṣiddīq, 'al-Kitāba bi-l-'ibriyya al-fuṣḥā: taqdīm riwāyat 'arabisk wa-ḥiwār ma' Aṭūn Shammās', *Alif: Journal of Contemporary Poetics* (2000), 20: 163. Shammas does not say that he set out to subvert Hebrew, but, at the same time, he does not reject the possibility that his Arabic-inflected use of Hebrew in places might be read as a matter of subversion. His use of 'at the time of writing' leaves the door open to the possibility that, with hindsight, subversion may (have) be(en) a feature of the novel. Considering his aim of wanting to un-Jew Hebrew, it is very likely that subversion would be part of his de-Zionisation and de-Judaisation project.

86 Adel Shakour concurs with this view (Personal Interview, 20 June 2102, Haifa).

punished for';[87] a 'hidden transcript' in the 'infrapolitics' of the Palestinians as a dominated group in Israel;[88] a 'semiotic revolt' that seizes the 'means of representation';[89] 'an ideological weapon which aims to break up the monologic, dogmatic message of the politics of difference [between Palestinian and Jew in Israel] that [Hebrew] both reflects and articulates';[90] as a means of forcible entry to: '[break] into the linguistic and literary citadel of the Israeli Jews';[91] and as a 'perfect revenge' against Zionist ideology, although as Shammas reminds us: 'every perfect revenge is already on the verge of love'.[92]

The futility of achieving this decoupling of language and identity – let alone its reconstitution to express an inclusive identity involving the Palestinians in Israel on an equal footing in a state that exclusively belongs, without discrimination, to all of its citizens – does fail, owing to the resilience of the bond between Hebrew and Jewishness in the Zionist project. This failure is recorded in the following exchange between Shammas and the Israeli critic Amnon Shamush, who is of Syrian origin and who wrote a review of *Arabesques*. Referring to himself as: 'a guest in the [Hebrew] language', Shammas wrote:

> With what might have been destructive cynicism I compared myself to the Harold Pinter type of character who appears suddenly in one's house, remains for dinner, washes the dishes, and stays the night, and the next morning he is already starting to take over. And I said, but I will try to be well-mannered. I arrive in the house of the Hebrew language under the banner of good manners.[93]

[87] Snir, '"Hebrew as the language of grace": Arab Palestinian writers in Hebrew', p. 167.

[88] Brenner, 'The search for identity in Israeli Arab fiction', p. 94.

[89] Yael S. Feldman, 'Postcolonial memory, postmodern intertextuality: Anton Shammas's *Arabesques* revisited', *Modern Language Association* (*MLA*) (1999): 373–4.

[90] Brenner, 'In search of identity', p. 437.

[91] Hever and Gensler, 'Hebrew in Israeli Arab hand', p. 74.

[92] Avraham Balaban, 'Anton Shammas: torn between two languages', *World Literature Today* (1989), 63: 421.

[93] Cited in David Grossman, *Sleeping on a Wire: Conversations with Palestinians in Israel*, trans. Haim Watzman (London: Jonathan Cape, 1993), p. 252. An earlier (1985) rendition of this point appears to be weaker about Shammas' actions and intentions as a guest (See Snir, '"Hebrew as the language of grace": Arab Palestinian writers in Hebrew', p. 167): he describes himself as: 'a guest who comes to you to dinner, and at the end of the meal you find him in the kitchen, washing dishes, with almost Harold-Pinterish joy, of one that may, unintentionally, break any beautiful piece. This also means that maybe, maybe, he will stay the night'. The subtle differences between the two renditions may suggest a change of intentions or purpose, but we should not read too much into this, as the core message remains more or less the same.

Playing on the metaphor of the guest to offer a riposte, Shamush wrote in his review: 'One makes up a bed for the guest, Anton my friend, my brother, and one hosts him in the good tradition of good hospitality; but one never gives him the keys to the house or the deed to it'.[94] Shammas' less than assertive statement of intent draws a more assertive response: Shammas – a metaphorical friend and brother – can be a guest in the house of the Hebrew language, but he cannot take ownership of it. Shammas may have thought of *Arabesque* as his key to enter this house, but ownership of the lock is not his. Shammas may cross the border constructed by language, but he will not have the right to indefinite occupation or the acquisition of (linguistic) citizenship. Israeli Jewish readers may marvel at the linguistic virtuosity which Shammas displays so richly in *Arabesques*,[95] but he cannot have right of ownership over the means of linguistic production; he may have rights over the performance, but he does not own the score. This is the essence of the politics of unbridgeable difference, which Said characterises by saying that: 'in a Jewish state . . . created by and for the Jewish people . . . non-Jews [i.e. Palestinians] are posited as radically other, fundamentally and constitutively different'.[96] I will pursue this point further in dealing with language ideologies below.

Shammas draws our attention to the fact that using the language of the 'Other' in creative writing involves more than just the political objective of serving a particular mission or achieving a defined purpose, in spite of its supreme importance. It also involves infatuation (*iftinān*), curiosity (*ḥub al-istiṭlā'*), quarrelsome playfulness (*al-mushākasa*), a desire to embarrass or put the 'Other' into a tight corner (*iḥrāj al-ākhar*), parading one's linguistic muscles (*isti'rāḍ al-'aḍalāt al-lughawiyya*), the conceit of youth (*ghurūr al-shabāb*) and a sense of wondrous/Sinbad-like adventure (*mughāmara sindibādiyya*).[97] Most of these motivations are inseparable from the language of the hybrid text, to which the writer comes as an outsider, with the challenge of proving himself to the target readers and literary establishment.

94 Ibid. p. 253.

95 Ṣiddīq offers this assessment of *Arabesques* (See Ṣiddīq, 'al-Kitāba bi-l-'ibriyya al-fuṣḥā: taqdīm riwāyat 'arabisk wa-ḥiwār ma' Aṭūn Shammās', pp. 157–8): 'First and foremost [*Arabesques*] is different from other works [in Hebrew by Palestinian writers in Israel] because of its superb literary qualities. It is, by any standards, a unique (*fadhdh*) work that merits great interest, regardless of the language in which it is written or the standards used to judge it . . . *Arabesques* has harnessed the power of Hebrew (*ṭawwa'a*) and energised (*fajjara*) its stylistic [storehouse] with expressive ways of meaning (*ab'ādan wa-ẓilālan ta'bīriyya*) that have rarely been witnessed before, even among the best of Jewish writers. The distinguished literary calibre of *Arabesques* warrants calling it the Hebrew novel *par excellence* (*al-kitāb al-'ibrī bi-imtiyāz*)'.

96 Edward Said, 'An ideology of difference', in Henry Louis Gates, Jr (ed.), *'Race', Writing and Difference* (Chicago, IL: University of Chicago Press, 1986), p. 42.

97 See Siddīq, 'al-Kitāba bi-l-'ibriyya al-fuṣḥā: taqdīm riwāyat 'arabisk wa-ḥiwār ma' Aṭūn Shammās', p.163.

This set of motivations points to the complexity of language choice in hybrid texts, mixing, as it does, the pragmatic with the personal at different levels and, we assume, in different measures; it is therefore important not to streamline every aspect of language choice into a postcolonial framework, with subversion writ large over the creative process, for political purposes, such as cultural resistance or countering hegemony. And it is also important not to treat the language of the coloniser from the perspective of totalising animosity, as the Algerian Francophone writer Rachid Boujedra reminds us:

> As an Algerian, I did not choose French. It chose me, or rather it was imposed on me throughout centuries of blood and tears and during a long and painful colonial history. Yet, it is thanks to the celebrated French writers that I feel at peace with this language, with which I have established a passionate relationship that can only add to its beauty as far as I am concerned.[98]

Therefore, it is important not to view languages in situations of conflict as always standing in a relation of (absolute) animosity to each other, at least at the individual level.[99]

The passage from imposition to positive acceptance or 'peace' in using the language of hybridity that is hinted at here points to the dynamic relation between writer and language; and it calls for recognising the synchronic and diachronic complexity of language choice. This complexity is recognised by Assia Djebar, who refers to French in the early stages of her career as a 'veil': 'I have used the French language as a *veil*. A veil over my individual self, a veil over my woman's body; I could almost say a veil over my own voice'.[100] I interpret the reference to 'voice' to imply a voice in the *absent* language, with which the *present* voice in the language of hybridity is in dialogic relation to express the individual self. A veil draws attention to the 'veilee', to coin a term, and to itself, enacting a communion between the absent and covert, on the one hand, and the present and overt, on the other. Later in her career, Djebar describes French as a 'welcoming home', over which she has some permanent rights of residence, but no right of ownership:

98 Cited in Armitage, 'The debate over literary writing in a foreign language', p. 52.

99 This is typified by the following reflection from the famous Palestinian poet Maḥmūd Darwīsh (cited in Brenner, 'The search for identity in Israeli Arab fiction', pp. 91–2): 'In this language [Hebrew] I spoke with the stranger, with the policeman, with the military governor, with the teacher, with the jailer and with my lover. Hebrew does not signify for me the language of the occupier, because it was the language of love and friendship . . . It opened for me the door to European literature . . . It is the language of my childhood memories. When I read in Hebrew, I remember the land; Hebrew brings back the landscape'.

100 Assia Djebar, 'Writing in the language of the Other', in Isaebelle de Courtivron (ed.), *Lives in Translation: Bilingual Writers on Identity and Creativity* (New York, NY: Palgrave Macmillan, 2003), p. 21 [emphasis in the original].

> French was truly becoming for me a welcoming home, maybe even a permanent place where each day the ephemeral nature of dwelling is sensed. Finally I crossed the threshold freely, no longer submitting to a colonial gaze . . . this language seems to me a house that I will inhabit henceforth and that I will try to put my mark on every day – knowing all the while that over the soil that supports it I have no direct rights.[101]

Continuing with the property metaphor, whereas in her early novels, Djebar felt like a tenant in the French language, as a mature writer, she now feels like a 'lease holder', but not a 'free holder'. French is hers and not hers at the same time; she owns the keys, but does not own the lock, as I have similarly referred to Shammas' relationship with Hebrew above. The use of both the 'veil' and 'home' metaphors in Djebar to express her relationship with French signals the complexity of this relationship; metaphors are always attempts at approximating a meaning which direct language cannot capture well or, at least, economically. In addition, the move from the 'veil' to the 'home' metaphor is expressed as a mode of 'becoming', rather than 'being', thus directing our attention to the diachronic nature of this process and, in theory, to its open-endedness.

The above motivations mentioned by Shammas may be linked to the sense of freedom and experimentation that the *present* language of hybridity affords the writer, as opposed to the pervading feeling of constraint that the *absent* language of his native culture may generate, especially in a diglossic language situation. Although Shammas does not mention diglossia in this context, his statement that: 'the native language (*al-lugha al-umm*) imposes on the writer, without him being aware of this, ready-made modes of expression (*qawālib ta'bīriyya jāhiza*) and an instinctive acquiescence (*ṭā'a fiṭriyya*) to conventional/traditional linguistic patterns (*anmāṭ lughawiyya taqlīdiyya*)' seems to be particularly relevant in this context.[102] This same point of using a language of hybridity to gain freedom is made by Mattawa when he says: 'writing in another language is sometimes the only way to pose certain questions or to take certain attitudes',[103] which view makes sense only if pitched against an absent language – the native language. I will return to this point later. However, Mattawa goes on to say that all languages impose a sense of constraint on their users, but they can equally lead the writer into unfamiliar linguistic paths, which, we take it, are full of discovery and adventure.[104] It is therefore important to take what Shammas says about Arabic with some

[101] Ibid. pp. 21–2.
[102] Ibid. pp. 21–2.
[103] Mattawa, 'Four uneasy pieces', p. 271.
[104] This is what Mattawa (Ibid. p. 271) says on this matter: 'Languages are rationales and when we use them we think along the grooves they make for us by the force of their histories and their intellectual output. They can lead us to paths we have not travelled before, not because of a necessarily unavoidable ideological logic,

caution, without, however, casting doubt on the influence of the language of hybridity on the writer.

The sense of freedom that the language of hybridity offers is often linked to the distancing space – a third space, twilight zone or no-man's land –[105] that it provides the writer to explore sensitive topics by blurring the boundaries between cultural spaces. Shammas tells us that he started to write *Arabesques* in Arabic – which text is generally recognised as a semi-autobiographical novel that tells the history of the Shammas family, since the middle of the nineteenth century – but that he quickly avoided the project and turned to Hebrew instead, so as to avoid hurting his family's feelings. Writing in Arabic would have made the novel available to members of the older generation in the family. According to this, Hebrew could afford Shammas cover, because of limited facility in the language capacity of the older members of the family.[106] Siddīq takes this explanation with a 'pinch of salt', arguing that the novel had to be written in Hebrew, considering, we assume, the sense of mission that it embodies and the target readership at which it is aimed.[107] It is not the Palestinians in Israel, but the Israeli Jews who needed to be convinced of the importance of un-Jewing Hebrew and turning Israel into a (fully democratic) state for *all* its citizens, be they Jews or Palestinians. However,

but rather by the sheer reality of their irrational technicalities and their random signification and metaphorical formations'.

105 See Kayyal, 'Arabs dancing in a new light of *Arabesques*'. The term 'no-man's land' carries in 'modern Hebrew a distinctive geopolitical significance, referring to the areas between Israel and its Arab neighbours which no party was allowed to enter' (See Balaban, 'Anton Shammas: torn between two languages', p. 418). The Arabic term for this is even more expressive: *'al-arḍ al-ḥarām'* (forbidden land), which combines the notion of the forbidden with the hidden invitation to explore.

106 Shammas expressed this as follows (quoted in Kayyal, 'Arabs dancing in a new light of *Arabesques*', p. 35): 'I write about my village in Hebrew, of course. I'm quite sure how the story would turn out if I were to write in Arabic. First of all, I'd certainly be more careful. Paradoxically, the Hebrew language provides me with some sort of apparent security, a kind of freedom which I wouldn't have if I were to write in Arabic, and put all my family into a story . . . And what will my aunt say, and what will my uncle and my cousins and all my extended family say? So this is a conscious act; I use Hebrew as a kind of camouflage net'. Paradoxically, this act of inscribing the story in Hebrew may be read as an act of silencing the story in Arabic, thereby silencing the language itself. Brenner ('The search for identity in Israeli Arab fiction', p. 103) makes a similar point when he says that the: 'determination to tell the story [of the Shammas family in Hebrew] breaks the silence imposed on it [among Israeli Jews], [but at the same time] it reinforces the silence imposed on its language [Arabic]'. This is another example of what I mean by dialogism in hybrid texts. What Shammas says in the above quotation may in some way explain why he has so far refused to allow the novel to be translated into Arabic.

107 See Siddīq, 'al-Kitāba bi-l-'ibriyya al-fuṣḥā: taqdīm riwāyat 'arabisk wa-ḥiwār ma' Aṭūn Shammās'.

the question of using a language of hybridity to gain critical space is cited as a reason behind this choice by various other writers. Zahia Qundus – a young Palestinian writer from Jaffa in Israel – gave this point as one of the rationales behind her choice of Hebrew in some of her short stories: 'when I write about topics that may upset my family, or when I want to have a dig at one of my annoying neighbours, I turn to Hebrew instead of Arabic'.[108]

The desire to avoid embarrassing one's family or community is a form of self-censorship, not, strictly speaking, of subject matter – for the matter to be censored ends up being publicly aired through another linguistic medium and can get back to those concerned through translation or hearsay – but of language. However, we may, if we relax what censorship means a little, still honour this notion in the way that Shammas, Qundus and Kittana apply it in describing their work. Censorship, here, is not about preventing the subject matter from being publicly aired, but about making it less accessible to those for whom it might be an issue of concern. Silencing a language in its capacity as a carrier of a meaning with which it is socially or anthropologically connected reflects the power of talk and its absence in maintaining the fabric of a community. Censorship as the absence of language may therefore be read as an expression of belonging, of marking the Self of the hybrid writer as a member of the absent-language community.

Tackling cultural taboos in the native language culture is considered another advantage that the colonial language affords the hybrid writer. Taher Ben Jelloun comments on the cathartic use of French, because it: 'makes it possible to break all taboos'[109] and allows one to speak the unspeakable. The Egyptian novelist Sunallah Ibrahim ascribes the: 'great margin of freedom' (*masāḥat al-ḥurriya al-wāsi'a*) that Ahdaf Soueif had in dealing with the inner life of the protagonist in *In the Eye of the Sun* to the fact that she wrote the novel in a different language (English *not* Arabic) and thus addressed herself to a reading public that: 'does not bury its head in the sand' (*lā yadfin ra'sah fī al-rimāl*).[110] Commenting on the same phenomenon, Malak says that English provided Soueif with a: 'liberating lexical storehouse and semantic sanctuary' and that it allowed her: 'to infiltrate taboo terrains, both sexual and political, that might be inaccessible when handled in Arabic'.[111] The same phenomenon is noted in North African Francophone writings, especially when published in France, rather than at home, where, in the latter circumstances, freedoms can be heavily circumscribed.[112] The reference to

[108] Personal interview (27 September 2011, Jaffa). The use of Hebrew as cover was also cited by Tamima Kittana (Personal Interview, 26 September 2011, Baqa Al-Gharbiyya).

[109] Armitage, 'The debate over literary writing in a foreign language', p. 49.

[110] See Mihriz, 'Khāriṭat al-kitāba: ḥiwār ma' Ahdāf Suwayf', p. 170.

[111] Malak, 'Arab-Muslim feminism and the narrative of hybridity', p. 161.

[112] See Mortimer, 'Introduction', p. 5; Abu-Haidar, 'Inscribing a Maghrebian identity in French', p. 15.

place of publication in the preceding sentence allows us to modify the statement that the colonial language affords the writer more freedom than the native language. It is not language per se that provides or denies freedom of expression to the writer, but the culture that underpins it that has the final word in this regard. Arabic is capable of expressing all taboo subjects – sexual, political or religious – as it had done in the past, but it is the social, religious and political culture in present-day Arab society that impedes the realisation of this potential. However, talk about taboos and the role of language in maintaining or breaking these constraints highlights the braiding of language and culture in society, as well as their ability to be deployed in the pursuit of political ends.

Discussions of hybrid literature further ascribe the use of hegemonic language to it being the language of modernisation,[113] progress and social liberation, in comparison to Arabic, as the language of tradition, conservatism and conformism.[114] This is a recurring theme in discussions of the language question in North African Francophone literature, which is indirectly linked to the issue of censorship discussed above. Armitage says that: 'overall, the use of French for many Francophone writers has represented escape from the past, from a backward society still dominated by tradition and history and ruled by harsh religious precepts'.[115] Escaping Arabic is often claimed to be most rewarding for women writers who need to free themselves from the constraints placed on them by male-dominated Arabic – *fuṣḥā* Arabic, which lacks the dynamism and flexibility of the spoken language or French. This charge is rebutted by Algerian Francophone novelist Rachid Boujedra, who, after a period of writing in French, returned to Arabic and used it in fiction writing. Some of his novels appear in two non-identical versions, both Arabic and French, and the Arabic version appears as innovative in its style of writing as its French counterpart. Abu-Haidar offers the following comparative assessment of these Arabic novels, in order to make this point:

> Not afraid of taking liberties with the sometimes rigidly structured and rhetoric–ridden Arabic language, [Rachid Boujedra] began by coining new words and

[113] Modernisation here refers to social and cultural modernisation, including literary modernisation. The point about cultural and literary modernisation was raised by all of the Palestinian writers in Israel who write in Hebrew: Naim Araidi (Personal Interview, 23 September 2011, Al-Maghar), Oudeh Bisharat (Personal Interview, 22 September 2011, Nazareth), Altayyib Ghanayim (Personal Interview, 26 September 2011, Baqa Al-Gharbiyya), Ala Hlehel (Personal Interview, 25 September 2011, Acre), Tamima Kittana (Personal Interview, 26 September 2011, Baqa Al-Gharbiyya), Sayed Kashua (Personal Interview, 27 September 2011), Nida Khury (Personal Interview, 25 September 2011, Acre), Atallah Mansour (Personal Interview, 24 September 2011, Nazareth) and Zahia Qundus (Personal Interview, 27 September 2011, Jaffa).

[114] See Jack, *Francophone Literatures: An Introductory Survey*, p. 7.

[115] Armitage, 'The debate over literary writing in a foreign language', p. 57.

> concepts novel to Arab experience. Throughout his Arabic works he has shown an almost unique mastery in twisting words into far-reaching nuances and drawing on the different sounds of Arabic phonology to create the images he wants.[116]

Based on this evidence, we may say that the issues of traditionalism, conservatism or conformism are ones of culture, rather than language *per se*, although, as has been pointed out above, the braiding of the two makes it impossible to separate them out from each other. The crucial point for us here is the realisation that the choice of the *present* language in the hybrid text is always made in relation to contrasting attitudes and stereotypes about the *absent* language of that text. This is why the language of a hybrid text is never monologic: it always exists in a state of dialogic conversation with the absent language; hence my reference to the notion of communion and the treatment of these texts as zones of contact between languages and their associated ideologies, as I will discuss further below.

Writing in the hegemonic language is further linked to a host of factors, most of which pertain to literature as a cultural product. In this connection, North African Francophone writers cite the global readership that French affords them,[117] whether directly to the French-reading public worldwide or indirectly through translation into other languages. They also mention the active involvement of various channels of patronage in disseminating their work through promotion, organisation of talks and interviews and reviews in the press or specialised outlets, which publishers undertake on their behalf.[118] The involvement of editors and copy-editors in shaping their work and ensuring that it is well-designed and mistake free (as much as possible) guarantees that the finished product conforms to high standards.[119] This is true of Palestinian Hebrewphone writers in Israel.[120] In comparison, the Arab publishing industry is in a pitiful state and cannot match the professionalism of English, French

116 Abu-Haidar, 'Inscribing a Maghrebian identity in French', p. 16.

117 Ibid. p. 13. Berg (*Exile from Exile: Israeli Writers from Iraq*, p. 29) specifies the 'cultural community' as the 'large potential readership' that French offers the Francophone writer.

118 See Kayyal ('Arabs dancing in a new light of *Arabesques*', pp. 35–6) for similar views by Sayed Kahua and Naim Araidi.

119 Berg (*Exile from Exile: Israeli Writers from Iraq*, pp. 62–4) mentions how Iraqi Jewish writers in Israel initially resented the involvement of Israeli editors in their works, but later came to appreciate this aspect of publishing. The initial reaction was no doubt conditioned by the absence of similar input in publishing their works in Iraq.

120 This point was made by Sayed Kashua (Personal Interview, 27 September 2011, West Jerusalem) and Salman Natour (Personal Interview, 24 September 2011, Dalyat Al-Karmil). Dror Mishani – one of the top Israeli Jewish critics of the young generation and a friend of Sayed Kahua – confirmed this when I interviewed him (Personal Interview, 17 June 2012, Tel Aviv).

or Israeli publishers. While this constellation of differential factors in the cultural market may play a role in choosing the language of hegemony for writing hybrid texts, these factors are no more than post hoc justifications.

According to some writers and critics, the issue of language choice in hybrid texts is a red herring. They justify this argument in two ways. On the one hand, Israel and North Africa are not monolingual countries (we have seen this argument applied to Lebanon above), so writing in the language of hegemony is not writing in the language of the 'Other', by virtue of the fact that this language, no matter which one, is part of the linguistic repertoire of a hybrid writer's cultural space. For writers from these backgrounds, Hebrew and French are not foreign languages; rather, they are part of the bilingual or multilingual landscape in which the hybrid writers operate. These languages are: 'languages of work'.[121] In short, for these writers and critics, the language of the 'Other' can have an 'Othered' status, if the cultural space in which a hybrid writer works is monolingual.[122] On the other hand, some writers and critics question the issue of language ownership.[123] Armitage refers to the Algerian Francophone writer Mourad Bourboune, who dealt with this matter in a functional and instrumental way, to the effect that no one has exclusive or universal rights over a language, and ownership of a language is always temporary or provisional, belonging, as it does, to the 'person using it'.[124]

For the young Palestinian Hebrewphone writer Zahia Qundus, the question of language ownership is contextual. When I asked her how she viewed Hebrew, she first said she considered it a 'native language' in which she was educated and which she uses for different purposes in her daily life – for example, when visiting the doctor or talking to her Jewish friends. She then modified her answer, saying that, in contact with the security apparatus of the Israeli state (for example, the Ministry of the Interior or even the passport authority), this ownership is compromised, turning Hebrew into the language of the 'Other' and causing her to speak in a halting manner (involuntarily). Furthermore, if she was near a military checkpoint inside Israel or if she was in the Occupied Territories, Hebrew acquires a different meaning to her: it becomes the language of hegemony or the language of

121 Assia Djebar, cited in Abu-Haidar, 'Inscribing a Maghrebian identity in French', p. 13.

122 Djebar rejects the premise of monolingualism for North African Francophone writers. She exemplifies this by referring to the linguistic environment in which the Tunisian writer Taos Amrouche grew up (cited in Abu-Haidar, 'Inscribing a Maghrebian identity in French', p. 14): 'Taos has bathed from the start in the bath of languages: those of the street, Sicilian, the dialectal Arabic of Tunis, the language of school, French, of course, which she reads and writes, and finally the language of exile and family secrets, Kabyle Berber'.

123 See Berger, *Algeria in Others' Languages*, p. 9.

124 Armitage, 'The debate over literary writing in a foreign language', p. 53.

occupation and oppression, as the case may be. If this points to anything, it tells us two significant things. First, it tells us that language ownership is not based on instrumentality or the degree to which one knows a language, but on the symbolic power of language to signal an identity border that marks who is in, who is out and, maybe, who is in a form of twilight zone (hence the correlation of the border with frontier as interchangeable notions in this chapter). Second, Zahia Qundus tells us that language ownership, or lack of this ownership, is contextual, with conflict, whether overt or covert, playing a determining factor.

The above discussion reveals that language choice in hybrid and postcolonial literature is a multifaceted issue that cannot, and should not, be abstracted to one dimension, no matter how important this dimension may be. Although deterritorialisation/de-ethnicisation, reterritorialisation or re-ethnicisation and appropriation are important factors as aspects of subversion in talk about language choice, the visibility that this rationale has been given in the literature has tended to downplay other factors, including quotidian ones, such as those involved in the notion of the cultural market. Placing the choice of language in a framework of an inter-nation or intercultural encounter cannot capture the synchronic and diachronic complexity inherent in this issue, as I have argued above. While there are cross-cultural or regional and cross-individual commonalities at work in language choice or its evaluation, the above discussion reveals the existence of variation and difference in this matter and highlights the importance of context in creating these commonalities (variations and differences). The discussion of language choice has also revealed the dialogic nature of hybrid texts, in which a covert/absent language is always in communion with the overt/present language of that text in symbolic terms. The problematisation of language choice cannot make sense without this dialogism. Put differently, it is only through the contrast between both a present and an absent language, together with their ideologies, as I will explain below, that the matter of language choice is deserving of public or scholarly attention. Finally, the above discussion reveals what it means to do politics through culture in the social world – in other words, what I have called 'cultural politics' in the subtitle of this book. As an ideological matter, language choice is a zone for meaning-making in which claims are made about ownership, hegemony, resistance, exile, belonging, modernisation, progress, liberation, traditionalism, conservatism, conformism and identity. Language is a productive site within this zone. It is braided with culture and vice versa, and the two are used directly, but mostly as proxies, to fight symbolically over history in all its ambiguities. There is no blood here, but this does not mean that the fight is not serious.

The Language of Hybrid Texts: A Question of Ideology

One of the premises upon which this chapter is based is that of *dialogism*: the idea that hybrid texts are zones of contact in which languages (the present/overt versus the absent/covert) and language ideologies interact with each other, mostly in conflict in varying degrees of tension or collision. Subversion is the major strategy for enacting tension or expressing collision in this conflictual model, as I have tried to show above. The language of a hybrid text is always judged in relation to another code, as if to imply that the text in this code could have existed or may have even subliminally existed in a covert indigenous language. I have further tried to ascribe this interest in the language of hybrid texts to the interest in identity, which has long been recognised as a site for ideological meaning-making and contestation in the literature. *Identity*, which is another premise in this study, is linked directly here not to language instrumentality, but to *language symbolism*, which constitutes a fundamental principle of this study. Linked to these premises is the idea of language as *proxy*. According to this principle, the symbolic power of language and its connection with identity marking and differentiation enables the dialogism of hybrid texts to be deployed and read politically in conflictual models of inter-group relations. The following discussion of the clash of language ideologies is based on the confluence of these concepts, wherein ideology, as has been mentioned above, is understood as a: 'a cultural [amalgam] of ideas about social and linguistic relationships, together with their loadings of moral and political interests'.[125] We are directly interested here in the political dimension of ideology, insofar as this is an expression of counter-domination and as a meaning-making strategy that seeks to undermine the power of colonial and postcolonial hegemony.

Let us explore this nexus of ideas by reflecting upon the clash of ideologies between French and Arabic in the Francophone literature of North Africa in its early stages, both before and in the period immediately after independence in 1962. The socio-political history of French during the past few centuries is inseparable from its deployment as an instrument of French nation-building. To do this, the French of Paris, as the language of elite education, government administration, the judiciary and diplomacy, had to assert itself over regional dialects, as well as the other languages in its political sphere – for example, Breton and Basque – with the effect that it is less tolerant of regional variations and other linguistic 'impurities' than, say, English or Spanish, even to this day. This process of linguistic-cum-political consolidation coincided with the reinvigoration of the French colonial endeavour in the nineteenth and twentieth centuries. It is therefore not surprising that France extended to its colonies and protectorates the same centrist socio-political processes, culturally and politically, that surrounded French at home, albeit in varying degrees in different North African countries, depending on their colonial status and the length of time that they came under French rule. In its pursuit of (elite) assimilation and acculturation, France promoted French as

125 Judith T. Irvine, 'When talk isn't cheap: language and political economy', *American Ethnologist* (1989), 16: 255.

a means of power consolidation, but to do this, it had to sideline, undermine or coerce any indigenous language that might compete with it, either instrumentally or symbolically in terms of prestige. The relationship between French and Arabic in North Africa, especially Algeria, during the colonial period answered to this hegemonic framework. French was promoted at the expense of Arabic, both in education and administration sectors, turning it (French) into a cultural resource of greater value in the eyes of the local elite. Those who submitted to it in the colonial period by being: '[thrown] into the open mouth of a wolf', to use Katib Yacine's words in describing his situation, experienced a rupture of various degrees in their lives by losing: 'at the same time [their] mother and her language'.[126]

Therefore, it is not surprising that the Algerian struggle for independence was envisaged as a clash of ideologies, in which language was an important component.[127] This is best summed up in Ibn Badis' famous statement: 'Islam is our religion, Arabic is our language, Algeria is our country'.[128] The importance of Arabic as an instrument of resistance was reflected in the institution of Arabisation/Arabicisation in Algeria as a priority of national policy after independence,[129] although, in practice, it met with uneven success.[130] Arabic was drawn into the domain of ideological and political contestation in two distinct ways. First, the logocentric nature of French colonial

[126] Isaac Yetiv, 'The crisis of identity of the native North African writer', in George Stambolian (ed.), *Twentieth Century French Fiction* (New Brunswick, NJ: Rutgers University Press, 1975), p. 126. Students in rural areas had to leave home to join French-speaking schools in urban centres, hence the reference to the 'loss of mother'.

[127] Berger's (*Algeria in Others' Languages*, p. 1) comment on the situation in Algeria fits this description: '[Modern nation-states and colonial enterprises have functioned [in this way]: in contrast to old dynastic states and empires, they have made language a primary tool and coercive agent of national or colonial cohesion, whatever the grounds – ethnic or political – of their claim. The role of French in the discourse of the revolutionary proponents of modern France is well known; the process of "nationalising" the French language initiated by the Revolution is well known . . . The role Arabic has played and continues to play in shaping Arabophone nations has been equally decisive, if not more so'.

[128] Berger, *Algeria in Others' Languages*, p. 3.

[129] Berger (Ibid. p. 2) explains the instrumental rationale behind Arabisation/Arabicisation as follows: 'By the time Algeria became independent, the language of its administration and judicial system was French, as was that of its school system, where only an extremely restricted number of indigenous Algerians were educated. "Arabisation", then, was a matter of cultural decolonisation and social equity, since those educated in French had access to positions barred to the majority of the population, which remained illiterate'. To this instrumental purpose of Arabisation, we must add its symbolic role as a project for 'doing politics through language'.

[130] Arabisation failed to achieve full linguistic decolonisation for a variety of reasons, which will not detain us here.

policy was bound to elicit a logocentric response, in the sense that, for the response to be effective, it had to match its challenge on the same ontological level (language) and by using equal epistemological force (traditions of language election, linguistic excellence, linguistic pedigree, and so forth). Second, Arabic was well-placed to serve as the locus of counter logocentric resistance. As the language of Islam and the Arabic-based intellectual heritage, the language was itself endowed with historically rooted prestige and cultural value. During the war of independence, what ensued was a clash of language ideologies, each of which sought to counter the political force of the other. Although the situation was somewhat different in Morocco and Tunisia, elements of this same encounter were played out in different degrees in these countries. In North Africa, especially in Algeria, the Arabic language was conscripted into the fight against French colonialism, which itself had enlisted the French language in the service of the colonial cause. This is a clear example of how languages and their associated ideological narratives are used as instruments of domination and counter-domination or hegemony and counter-hegemony in power relations between groups in conflict situations.

The use of French in North African Francophone writing in the colonial period must be read against this background. This is also true of hybrid literature in the period following independence, although its meaning has changed in myriad ways in the last two to three decades, especially in Algeria, which suffered internal political strife in the 1990s. As the overt and present language of the hybrid text, French carries in its social and cultural DNA, so to speak, a set of ideological meanings and historical experiences of domination and hegemony that clash with the ideological meanings of Arabic as a covert or absent language. And by virtue of being endowed with symbolic meaning, language choice acts as proxy for accessing the hidden myths of the two languages concerned, wherein, as mentioned above, notions of linguistic excellence and superiority are read metonymically as indices for the excellence and superiority of the nation, whether this has to be asserted or resisted. The use of Arabic to subvert French in the Francophone novel must therefore be read as an attack against the set of ideological meanings that French carries in its capacity as a metonym of the nation, as I have pointed out earlier. Also, as an act of linguistic border crossing from a covert language to an overt one, hybrid literature constitutes a border infringement, which aims to counterbalance the earlier colonial infringement in the opposite direction. I have given many examples to substantiate this point in earlier parts of this chapter.

But this is only one ideological reading of this hybrid literature. Another reading treats it as an act of 'cultural betrayal' that continues to favour the colonial language out of choice, rather than necessity, instead of championing the covert language and the set of ideological meanings that it carries culturally and politically in nation-building. Earlier, I referred to Rukaybi, who reads Francophone Algerian literature in the 1980s and 1990s in this way.[131] 'Cultural betrayal' is also one of the interpretations that Brenner applies to understanding Shammas' *Arabesques*; applying Richard Coe's work on autobiography,[132] Brenner says that Shammas': 'necessary adoption of the coloniser's language . . .' amounts to an acknowledgement: 'that the writer has . . . betrayed his own national and cultural authenticity and accepted the superior idiom of the coloniser'.[133] The notion of betrayal has also been raised (and dismissed) in a discussion by the Anglophone Libyan poet Khaled Mattawa, who describes accusations of betrayal as: 'allegories of the cave, revelations [and] epiphanies'.[134] Mattawa is right to rebut the notion of linguistic betrayal in hybrid literature, which he clearly reads as an act of meaning-making that is ideologically driven by a nationalist monolingualism. Yet the notion of betrayal seems to linger on for some, manifesting itself in rationalisations, such as the: 'continuation of a Francophone literature would inevitably undermine the emergence of a national literature in Arabic'[135] or: 'writing in French, rather than in the native idiom, [creates] a rupture between the [Francophone] writers and their compatriots'.[136] Cultural betrayal is linked to some deep-seated suspicion of the 'Other' and, by extension, to the hybrid writer as a 'Self Othered', leading to a feeling that the: 'more successful a writer is in the West, and in France in particular, the more he is treated with caution in his home country',[137] at least by some. Inbetweeness and the twilight zone are 'liquid' places where the borders are blurred between groups in conflict situations, leading to intensive contact, but also suspicion and, according to the Palestinian Israeli writer Naim Araidi: 'the great fear of a person in whom two different cultures cross'.[138]

131 This notion has been applied elsewhere – for example, in English writings in India. See Sadana, 'A suitable text for a vegetarian audience'.

132 Richard N. Coe, *When the Grass was Taller: Autobiography and the Experience of Childhood* (New Haven, CT: Yale University Press, 1984), p. 226.

133 Brenner, 'In search of identity', p. 434.

134 Mattawa, 'Four uneasy pieces', p. 271.

135 Armitage, 'The debate over literary writing in a foreign language', p. 48.

136 Ibid. p. 40.

137 Ibid. p. 40.

138 Snir, '"Hebrew as the language of grace": Arab Palestinian writers in Hebrew', p. 166. Anton Shammas provides the following insightful reflection on the linguistic twilight zone through the prism of multilingualism in, we take it, conflict situations ('The drowned library: reflections on found, lost and translated books and languages', p. 124): 'Borders are no longer there because they cannot be seen and deciphered from within [the] twilight zone that we refer to as bilingualism, or trilingualism for that matter, where the edges of any given language are filed down, blurred, cannibalised, metabolised and then assimilated into the two intersections where the two languages overlap'. When languages overlap, they clearly come into contact and, in conflict situations, collision with each other, together with their associated language ideologies.

The ideological reading of Hebrewphone literature provides another example of the play of language ideologies in conflictual situations where languages 'intersect' and 'overlap'. This is particularly true of Anton Shammas' *Arabesques* and the debate that it ignited in Israel. I have referred above to Shammas' statement of purpose, mission or intent, following the publication of *Arabesques* in 1986, as trying to un-Jew the Hebrew language, which mission he described in the following manner:

> What I'm trying to do – mulishly, it seems – is to un-Jew the Hebrew language . . . to make it more Israeli and less Jewish, thus bringing it back to its Semitic origins, to its place. This is parallel to what I believe the state should be. As English is the language of those who speak it, so is Hebrew; and so the state should be the state of those who live in it.[139]

Put differently, Shammas' intent through *Arabesques* is to argue for 'dismantling' the exclusive relationship between Hebrew and Jewishness in the Israeli body-politic, turning Hebrew into the language of all Israelis, Palestinian Arabs and Israeli Jews alike in a state that belongs equally to both national groups or is equi-distant from all of its citizens, regardless of nationality, ethnicity or religion. What makes this aim intellectually credible is the fact that: (1) *Arabesques* forces on the Israeli Jewish public a Palestinian tale of dispossession, in which they are complicit through commission or omission, in the sense that, in the latter case, Zionist ideology has silenced this tale or tried to erase it; (2) the very act of telling the story declares it to be a narrative worthy of telling and worthy of the attention of the Israeli Jewish public, who can no longer continue to ignore it; (3) the story is told in Hebrew of great virtuosity, what Hever and Gensler call: 'a kind of synthetic Hebrew wielded so able by Shammas . . . to build a new-old language as a bridge toward the creation of an old-new nation';[140] and (4) the story trades on the symbolic configuration of Hebrew as a metonymy of Israel as a Jewish state, using it as proxy to enact a political dialogue with the 'Other'.

This objective of de-Zionisation, denationalisation or de-ethnicisation of the language elicited different responses from Israeli Jews. It was celebrated by some scholars – for example, Hever and Gensler,[141] who treated the novel as perhaps the: 'most truly Israeli novel ever written', because it exposed the discriminatory contradictions in the Zionist project and offered a 'utopia' to eliminate those contradictions – the point here being that pre-state Zionism as a 'national liberation' movement was no longer serviceable in a post-state political reality where 'liberation' had been achieved. The fact that this utopian vision was offered by a Palestinian – belonging to a Christian

[139] Snir, '"Hebrew as the language of grace": Arab Palestinian writers in Hebrew', p. 165.
[140] Hever and Gensler, 'Hebrew in Israeli Arab hand', p. 74.
[141] It seems that Gensler's contribution was mainly to translate Hever into English.

minority in an Arab minority within a state which thinks and acts like a minority in respect to the larger Middle East – adds to the power of the call to un-Jew the Hebrew language. Un-Jewing Hebrew within a newly reconfigured Israeli state is different from the ideology of the Cannanite movement, which wanted to return to a pre-biblical Hebrew past, which is not connected to Judaism or Zionism, hence the positive reception of writers like Shammas and Araidi by members of this group. As a small literary-cum-political movement in Israel, the Canaanites wanted to suspend the competing claims over the holy land in a larger Middle East in which Hebrew will serve as the *lingua franca*, much as it did in the past.[142] This, it must be said, is a forlorn hope, as it is extremely unlikely that the Arab Christians and Muslims will relinquish their language, because of deep-rooted cultural and political loadings.

This reception of *Arabesques* was rejected by Rueven Snir, who – rightly in my view – considered the link between Hebrew and Israeli Jewish identity to be immune to the kind of attack mounted against it by Shammas. From its inception, Zionist ideology was based on the premise that Jewish national identity would not be possible without a double return: to the land (roughly, historical Palestine) and to the original Jewish language (Hebrew). This ideological formation in Israel has reached a state of solidification, which makes the separation of identity from language and vice versa to be well-nigh impossible to accomplish. That is why Hebrew acts as a perfect metonymy for Israeli Zionist/Jewish national identity –this being the reason why Shammas aimed his proxy attack against it through *Arabesques*. Snir is supportive of Shammas' argument for equality among all Israeli citizens, regardless of their nationality, ethnicity or faith background, but he does not believe that Shammas' project of un-Jewing the Hebrew language can achieve this result. When I interviewed him on 17 June 2012, Snir told me that his views were validated by two facts: (1) Shammas has not written any novels since the publication of *Arabesques* in 1986, taking this as an admission of defeat in regards to his project; and (2) he left Israel completely to live and work in the United States, making very few journeys back to Israel, which journeys were mainly personal visits. Snir considered these (sad) facts as an inevitable admission of failure of the Shammasian project and the dream-like talk about the utopian vision that Hever used in its reception.[143]

Snir went further and suggested, as he did in his writings on the topic, that

142 For information on the Canaanite movement, see Ramras-Rauch (*The Arab in Israeli Literature*, pp. 113–17).

143 Hever, a leading Israeli literary critic and Professor of Hebrew literature, lamented the death of this utopian vision when I interviewed him in Tel Aviv on 18 June 2012. He considered the failure of the Shammasian project to be a body blow to Zionism, which is still riddled with discriminatory contradictions as a result of its inability to make the move from an exclusive pre-state ideology to an inclusive post-state one. Yehouda Shenhav, a highly respected Israeli sociologist of Iraqi origin, shared this sense of dismay when I interviewed him on the same day.

the positive reception of Shammas in (the Left-dominated) Israeli literary establishment was not based on any real support for his alternative, post-Zionist ideological vision of un-Jewing the Hebrew language or even on the excellence of his writing, but on his being a member of a minority, even a minority within a minority,[144] in relation to a dominant culture that wishes to validate its liberal credentials. Snir considers this stance as tokenistic.[145] The fact that a writer like Shammas attracted a lot of media attention in Israel does not, according to Snir, change the tokenism with which he was received. He cites as evidence for this the attention accorded to Israeli Jewish writers who published under Arab pseudonyms and notes how this attention fizzled out when their covers were eventually blown. The poet Israel Eliraz is a case in point. This poet points out how the poems that he wrote under the (Christian) Arab name George Mathias Ibrahim received a lot of attention from the Hebrew literary establishment, unlike his poems in Hebrew, which he published under his real name.[146]

In spite of their different reactions to *Arabesques*, both Hever and Snir agree as to the need to make Israeli identity equally inclusive of Palestinians and Jews. This is a different position from that taken by the leading Israeli writer A. B. Yehoshua, who, in a famous debate with Anton Shammas following the publication of *Arabesques* with its un-Jewing of Hebrew thesis, told him (Shammas was living in West Jerusalem at the time):

> I say to Anton Shammas – if you want your full identity, if you want to live in a country that has an independent Palestinian personality, that possesses an original Palestinian culture [the implication here being that Palestinian culture in Israel cannot be original because it exists in an Israeli state], rise up, take your belongings, and move 100 meters to the east, to the independent Palestinian state that will lie beside Israel.[147]

Yehoshua refuses to include Shammas in the Israeli nation, on par with Israeli Jews, because he is Palestinian. But what does Israeliness represent for Yehoshua to make it impossible to include Shammas and the Palestinians in it? The problematic notion for Hever and Snir is not Israeliness, which, as a notion of civic belonging, can be made to be inclusive, but Judaism or Jewishness and Zionism as a related political ideology that excludes

144 Referring to Shammas and Araidi, see Snir ('"Hebrew as the language of grace": Arab Palestinian writers in Hebrew', p. 173): '[In] Hebrew literature [Shammas and Araidi] are unique not only in their being outsiders, but because their activities in it is made possible precisely by their being representatives of a minority'.

145 See Brenner (2003) for an insightful discussion of what she calls the 'codes of reception' of Palestinian writings in Hebrew in Israel.

146 See Snir, '"Hebrew as the language of grace": Arab Palestinian writers in Hebrew', p. 174.

147 Grossman, *Sleeping on a Wire*, p. 250.

non-Jews. For Yehoshua, the primary concept of identity linked to the Hebrew language, among other things, is not Jewishness, but Israeliness, which he describes as follows:

> For me, 'Israeli' is the authentic, complete, and consummate word for the concept 'Jewish'! Israeliness is the total, perfect and original Judaism, one that should provide answers in all areas of life. The term 'Jewish,' after all, came into being a thousand years after the concept 'Israeli' existed in practice, and it was created to describe a fraction, what remained after everything the Israeli lost in the diaspora, until he turned into a 'Jew.' That whole mess has no connection to the Palestinian or Arab issue; even if there were no Arabs here there would still be the problem between the two concepts 'Jewish' and 'Israeli.'[148]

This description of Israeli identity demands that, as a category, it cease to be a legal notion coterminous with citizenship, but that it must be established as an essentialist unit of definition with a primordial nature, which cannot but exclude the Palestinians in Israel. A Palestinian in Israel remains a Palestinian, not an Israeli, and his participation in Hebrew as an index of identity would therefore have to remain instrumental, rather than symbolic. He can use Hebrew, but he cannot claim it as a sign of his identity, because such a claim would infringe upon the very notion of Israeliness.

When I interviewed Yehoushu on 17 June 2012, I asked him if Shammas was a Hebrew or Palestinian writer; his answer was that he considered him to be a Palestinian writer of Hebrew literature. When I pressed him as to whether he preferred Shammas to write in Hebrew or Arabic, he answered that Shammas and all Palestinian writers of Hebrew should write in Arabic, in the same way that all Israeli writers should write in Hebrew. Yehoshua justified this by saying that Palestinian Arabic literature needs its own Palestinian writers to enrich its canon, in the same way that Hebrew literature needed its Israeli writers to enrich its canon. Translation can then take care of transferring the literature of one group to the other.

This is a curious argument, because it refuses to recognise the consequences of multilingualism and its political implications within a state, but it makes sense when set in the context of Yehoshua's essentialist understanding of identity. As indices of identity, languages create borders between groups. The essentialist understanding of language requires that borders are not infringed or blurred – a fact that Shammas, Araidi and other Palestinian writers of Hebrew do not acknowledge. Legal cultural traffic through the recognised channel of translation is acceptable as a means of transfer between Israelis and Palestinians, but the expression of the content of one group directly in the language of the other is not permissible, because it blurs the border between them. This was reflected in the consistent way in which Yehoshua used the term 'Israeli', without the qualifying descriptors of

[148] Ibid. pp. 253–4.

'Jew', as in Israeli Jew, or 'Jewish', as in Jewish Israelis, throughout the interview, in order to exclude Palestinians in Israel, since such a concatenated usage would constitute semantic redundancy. Yehoshua remained terminologically consistent, even when I tried to induce him otherwise by using the term Israeli Palestinians to demark them from Palestinians in the Occupied Territories or outside the borders of historical Palestine.

For Yehoshua, an Israeli is a Jew, and a Palestinian is a Palestinian or an Arab (the two terms may be interchangeable for him). The following quotation sums up his position well:

> Do the Arabs [Palestinians in Israel] interfere with defining our identity [as Israelis]? It seems to me only in a certain sense, but not in the long run. That is, at first Israeliness as an identity is infringed upon, because we need to apply it to Arabs as well. So when Anton comes, or the Druze [in Israel], and they say, 'we're Israeli, too', it complicates matters, and something in that identity becomes foggy.[149]

According to Yehoshua, the Arabs/Palestinians in Israel have a place, but only as a minority, which is not Israeli in the sense that he describes. Therefore, it is not surprising that Yehoshua rejects the thesis of un-Jewing Hebrew, because it means for him un-Israelising it to allow into the category of the nation 'foreign' or, more correctly, minority elements, which, strictly speaking, do not belong to it, but are one of its: 'components [like] the scent of the citrus fruit and the special air of Jerusalem, and the goats, and the cactuses'.[150] Palestinians in Israel are a flavour of the land or an expression of its landscape with the rights of a minority, but certainly not the same rights as those that accrue to Israelis as members of the nation. Un-Jewing Hebrew challenges the concepts of Israel and Israeliness and must therefore be rejected as, in fact, it has been.

The debate between Shammas and Yehoshua as ideological brokers does not affect language instrumentality and the entitlement to it at that level by the Palestinians in Israel. What is at stake here is language symbolism and the ideological meanings it carries vis-à-vis inclusion and exclusion, borders and their infringements and the very definition of the nation and its identity. Yehoshua believes that the infringement of Hebrew as a symbolic resource is an infringement of the nation. Shammas believes that changing the ideological loadings of Hebrew is tantamount to changing the ethnocratic nature of the Israeli state, turning it into a real liberal democracy that speaks on behalf of all its citizens, without ethnic, religious or linguistic privilege being accorded to some over others. This discussion would not have been possible if language did not have symbolic power and could not act as a proxy for ideological debates of great consequence. But language, as we have seen

149 Ibid. p. 259.
150 Ibid. p. 260.

throughout this chapter, does have symbolic power and acts as a proxy, allowing for (acrimonious) debates of the kind under consideration here to take place in the public sphere. 'Doing politics through culture' is possible precisely because of language symbolism and its capacity to act as proxy in ideological debates. Language instrumentality has an important place in the study of language, but it cannot replace the meanings that language symbolism carries.

But where does Arabic language ideology come into this? Hever and Yehoshua do not allude to it, but Snir does. He rightly points out that the 'high status of the Arabic language in Arab culture and religious heritage, especially among Muslims, makes it undesirable to write in a language that is regarded as inferior'.[151] This assessment is true of the reception of Hebrewphone literature outside Israel in the Arabic-speaking Middle East, but not representative of opinion among Israeli Palestinians, as my field interviews in September 2011 and June 2012 revealed. Palestinians in Israel face a different reality, and, for them, Hebrew is not an inferior language: it is the language of power and social modernisation. In the Arab world at large, the response to Hebrewphone literature was conditioned by an Arabic language ideology of the kind we have seen at work in Algeria and which I have described at length in Chapter 3. However, in the case of Hebrewphone literature, the possibilities of ideological clash in the Arab world were considerably magnified, because of the high intensity of the Arab-Israeli conflict. In this respect, writing in Hebrew – a language that few Arabs outside Israel know – acquires heightened political meanings, with associated feelings of estrangement and suspicion. Furthermore, writing in Hebrew cannot be compared to writing in French or English. These are considered to be major world languages, unlike Hebrew, which has no more than a limited reach that cannot compare with the reach of Arabic internationally – this being a factor in the perception of inferiority surrounding it, which Snir mentions above. And there is a qualitative ideological difference between these languages and Hebrew: they were or are colonial languages; however, Hebrew is the language of settler colonialism, which, in the scale of things, is a lot worse than its parent enterprise, as represented by French and English.

The reception of Hebrewphone literature in the Arab world cannot escape these ideological meanings and the socio-political conditions that give rise to them.[152] But even inside Israel, the ideologies of Arabic and Hebrew are never far from the surface of the inter-cultural encounter as this is enacted in hybrid texts. Shammas, who has been at the centre of the language debate through *Arabesques*, acknowledges this when he says that Hebrew, for the

[151] Snir, '"Hebrew as the language of grace": Arab Palestinian writers in Hebrew', p. 173.

[152] See Kayyal ('Arabs dancing in a new light of *Arabesques*') for the critical reception of Anton Shammas by Arab critics.

Palestinians, has been: 'the language of power and deterritorialisation, of dispossession, of lethal interrogations, of bloody occupation', and that for the Israeli, it has been the: 'language of the locked-up ghost inside the closet, the suppressed language of Caliban, the muffled language of the landscapes . . . and, for the average Israeli, the language of "terrorism"'.[153] The reception of Hebrewphone literature has been affected by these ideologies, at least on the Arab side.

On the Hebrew side, it is the threat to Hebrew language ideology that has been uppermost in discussions of this literature. Hebrewphone literature cannot, therefore, but bring the covert and overt languages of the text, each with its distinct language ideology, into interaction with each other. Naim Araidi, who is most accommodating of Hebrew and its ideology among Palestinian writers writing in the language, hints at this when he says that, in his case, the problem has not been: 'learning the new language [Hebrew], but forgetting the old one [Arabic]'.[154] This statement gives credence to Brenner's dialogic interpretation of Shammas' *Arabesques* as enacting a communion between the overt language of the writing self and the silenced one of the self-recalled: 'to elucidate his Hebrew speaking self, the writer must confront the political and psychological implications of his painful severance from his Arabic-speaking formative self'.[155] Considered from the other perspective – that of a Hebrew writer of Iraqi descent – Almog Behar's poem 'My Arabic is Mute' provides an excellent statement of the play of languages in the writings of those who consider themselves to be, or who are classified as, belonging to a third space or twilight zone between cultures in conflict (and perhaps even in non-conflict situations).

Conclusion: Hybrid Literature, Language Ideology and Cultural Politics

It should be clear from the above discussion that hybrid literature as a body of texts in its own right or as a site for second-order ideological reflections on inter-cultural relations in situations of conflict, whether real or symbolic is a productive arena for investigating language in the social world – the overarching theme of this book. In doing so, I have approached the subject by examining three major themes: the identity of hybrid texts, language choice in hybrid texts and the language ideologies of these texts. These nested themes are braided together through a number of notions, including dialogism, language symbolism and the use of language as proxy in 'doing politics through culture' or cultural politics, as the subtitle of this book renders this practice. Language stands at the crossroad of all of these themes and

153 Shammas, 'The drowned library: reflections on found, lost and translated books and languages', p. 126.

154 Cited in Snir, '"Hebrew as the language of grace": Arab Palestinian writers in Hebrew', p. 175 [inserts added].

155 Brenner, 'In search of identity', p. 433.

notions, revealing its ability to convey meaning over and above the meanings which it can communicate through its instrumentality.

The concern with identity is linked to issues of importance in society and group cohesion. The link with notions of inclusion and exclusion, border control and border crossing or infringement, ethnic purity, cultural leakage and cultural betrayal may be related to an essentialist and, in some cases, primordialist understanding of identity that does not tolerate inbetweeness. A set of arguments are deployed to defend these ideological constructs, as attempts at meaning-making in society that are always enacted in relation to the 'Other'. Form is pitted against content, monolingualism against bilingualism or multilingualism and descent against notions of civil belonging within the legal or constitutional parameters of the nation-state. Through its symbolic function, language stands at the heart of this melange of means and ends, revealing its fettle in domination and counter-domination manoeuvres in different settings that, while related, show marked differences.

Language choice in hybrid literature has been shown to be more complex than it is sometimes made out to be in postcolonial theory. While language choice is linked to the notions of subversion, deterritorialisation and reterritorialisation, de-ethnicisation and appropriation, this set of related notions cannot encompass its complexity. The political is important in language choice, but a host of other factors that are related to notions such as modernisation, liberation, breaking taboos, fighting conformism, conservatism or traditionalism also play a part. One of the recurring themes in language choice is how adopting a language other than one's native language for literary expression can lead to exploring different ways of formulating content and expressing aesthetic and cultural sensibilities that are not hemmed in by the norms of the native culture or its conventional ways of linguistic expression. These factors in language use are ideological in the sense that they are intended to do politics through culture. Other factors relate to literature as a product of, and in, a cultural market. Hybrid writers mention how the colonial language and its associated channels of patronage and organisational capacity provide them with greater readership in primary and, through translation, secondary markets, which are not available through the native language. Writers write because they want to be read by as many readers as possible; language choice cannot be divorced, for pragmatic reasons at least, from this legitimate desire for circulation.

The third theme is the clash of language ideologies in hybrid texts. There are two sides to this theme. The first is that hybrid texts are contact zones or third spaces, in which borders are blurred in an area characterised by conflict and, as a result, the imperatives of separation. The second is that the overt or present language of the hybrid text clashes with its covert or absent counterpart in conflict situations. The intensity of this ideological clash concerns notions of group superiority, the intellectual excellence of the group – both synchronically and diachronically – the moral loadings of cultural values on both sides of the language divide and the extent to which language has been constructed as a metonymy of the nation. These concerns are myths of language, but, as such, they represent taken-for-granted cultural attitudes in folk-linguistic thinking that signal group worth, in relation to other groups. As ideological stereotypes, these myths or traditions can be traded and activated to valorise societal norms.

Language ideologies are further implicated in asymmetrical power relations inside the state and between states. Francophone literature reflects the asymmetry in cross-state power relations, but it may also signal power differences within the same society along lines drawn by education, sex, religion, ethnicity or economic power. Hebrewphone literature operates first and foremost at the level of the state, locating the imbalance in power distribution, materially and symbolically, between Israeli Jews and Israeli Palestinians; it is primarily an intra-state, rather than a cross-state, phenomenon. It signals, but only marginally, ideological clashes with the Arabic-speaking world. In fact, the reaction from the Arab world is not so much directed at Israeli Jews, but at the Palestinian Hebrew writers, whose choice of language runs counter to the political imperatives of the Arab–Israeli conflict, that demand privileging Arabic over Hebrew as a marker of identity for both the group and its literary products. The fact that Palestinians in Israel face this conflict from a different geopolitical position is rarely acknowledged in the Arab world; the negative reaction to Emile Habiby's acceptance of the Israeli State Prize for Literature for his *translated* works from Arabic into Hebrew (1992) is an expression of this same attitude against any accommodation within the Israeli state in the cultural domain. It is no wonder that culture, far more so than politics or commerce, has proved to be the most resilient instrument in the boycott movement against Israel to this day.

Appendix

My Arabic is Mute
Almog Behar[156]
Translated from the Hebrew by Dimi Reider

My Arabic is mute
strangled at the throat
Cursing itself
Without uttering a word
Sleeps in the airless shelters of my soul
Hiding
From relatives
Behind the Hebrew blinds

And my Hebrew is raging
Running between rooms and neighbours' balconies
Making its voice heard in public
Prophesying the coming of God
and of bullodzers
And then it holes up in the living room
Thinking itself so open in the language of its skin
So hidden between the pages of its flesh
A moment naked, a moment later dressed
It curls up into the armchair
And begs itself for forgiveness

My Arabic is petrified
It quietly pretends to be Hebrew
And whispers to friends
Whenever somebody knocks at her gate
'Ahlan Ahlan, welcome'
And whenever a policeman passes it in the street
It produces an ID card
And points out the protective clause
'Ana min al-yahud, ana min al-yahud' – 'I am a Jew, I am a Jew'.
And My Hebrew is deaf
Sometimes very deaf.

156 I am grateful to Almog Behar for giving me permission to use his poem in this book.

CHAPTER

5

THROUGH THE LOOKING GLASS: ARABIC, THOUGHT AND REALITY

This chapter continues the exploration of the symbolic function of language by considering an important text that marks the transition from the pre-modern to the modern period. It then moves to explore the cognitive role that Arabic plays in connecting thought with reality. This chapter examines two modes of performing this task: the behaviour-centred and the structure-centred approaches, with emphasis on the former, owing to its dominance in attempts to study Arabic from a cognitive perspective. The data for this analysis are a set of texts in Arabic and English, which, in spite of their differences, exhibit similarities in terms of method, as reflected in the use of cross-cultural comparisons and literal translation. The loose nature of the behaviour-centred approach brings many of the findings based on it close to ideological advocacy. This proximity invites language symbolism into the cognitive domain through the back door, in a way that blurs the difference between them. As a result, the overall effect is not one of looking at Arabic through a cognitive prism, but through an ideological gaze that uses the power of language as a proxy to construct a largely negative view of Arab culture. Both Arab and non-Arab authors participate in this mode of doing politics through language as a cultural product.

Introduction: Language Symbolism and Language Cognition

I have referred earlier to the instrumental and symbolic roles of language and used the symbolic as a prism through which to probe into issues of identity and conflict in the modern and pre-modern periods of Arab history. Under this rubric, I have dealt with the construction of languages and scripts as markers of identity; the inimitability of the Qur'an principle as a location for ethnic identity marking and divine selection in the early Islamic period; the (un)translatability of the Qur'an debate during this period, which continues to this day; the linguistic component in the inter-ethnic *shu'ūbiyya* 'movement' in early Islamic society and its echoes and applications in modern times; language ideology and cultural politics with their recurrent motifs of language endangerment and culture wars, in which external and internal actors and factors play an important part; and issues of identity, language choice and the clash of language ideologies in hybrid texts. The use of language as proxy is an integral part of this symbolic role: the latter is a condition for the occurrence of the former. Language serves as a leitmotif, through which the social world speaks extra-linguistically about a host of concerns in a given society, exploiting, in this regard, the symbolic role of this medium in both intra- and inter-cultural communication.

In this chapter, I will deal with another role of language: its ability to serve as a window through which readings of thought and reality in a given society can be *enacted*. I will call this role of language 'cognitive', for want of a better term. This perspective on language is of interest to a wide constituency of scholars and practitioners: anthropologists, educationalists, linguists, cognitive and social psychologists, cultural studies students, public policymakers and media specialists more generally. The use of the word 'enacted' is intended to suggest that this role of language is not entirely based on empirical evidence or strict scientific experimentation, as will later become clear, but is more often than not subject to construction and deployment, either overtly or covertly, in ideologically driven articulations. When this ideologisation happens, the cognitive role of language starts to border on its symbolic function in a manner that makes it difficult to separate the one from the other in some cases. We may, however, disentangle them from each other by deciphering the extent to which a given reading of a language claims to be about thought as a kind of mental category that configures and shapes reality, as happens, for example, in what some authors refer to as the 'Arab mind' or an 'Arab worldview' when talking about Arabic, as I will show.[1] In principle, readings of this kind are cognitive, not symbolic, although, in reality, the two may mix in different ways under different extra-linguistic conditions.

However, before delving into this cognitive role, I would like to consider the symbolic role of language further. The context for this is the reference in the opening paragraph of this chapter in regards to the deployment of this role in modern and pre-modern times in the Arabic-speaking world. Although any separation of these two categories in periodisation is bound to be somewhat artificial, there is common agreement among those who use this distinction to treat the French campaign in Egypt between 1798 and 1801 as marking the beginning of the transition from pre-modern to modern times in Arab history. This campaign constituted a turning point in the relationship between the Arabic-speaking lands in the Middle East and

[1] The term 'Arabic' is used in this chapter to refer to *fuṣḥā* Arabic in its classical and modern forms, unless otherwise stated.

Europe,[2] leading to the beginning of a 'modern' form of nation-building in Egypt under Muhammad Ali (1805–49). As has been pointed out in several places earlier, the symbolic role of language comes into full effect during times of acute stress in society or when there is conflict or hostility involving external actors. The French campaign in Egypt constituted such an event. It is fortuitous, but also in line with the symbolic role of language, that, in reporting on the first seven months of the French occupation of Egypt between 15 June and December 1798, the historian al-Jabarti (1753–1825) deploys Arabic as a socio-political motif to comment on this invasion; in short, using the language as a proxy to signal extra-linguistic views. Being at the threshold between the pre-modern and modern worlds – in spite of the fact that they were treated separately in Chapter 2, 3 and 4 – I will dwell on this use of language as a proxy at this defining moment in modern Arab Egyptian history, in order to show the continuity between the pre-modern and the modern in Arab social and political life.

Upon their arrival in Egypt, the French issued[3] a printed proclamation in Arabic in which they sought to gain the confidence of the Egyptians.[4]

[2] Moreh comments on this encounter between Egypt and Europe as follows: 'al-Jabarti was the first Arab to experience and write about the first and greatest confrontation between Christendom and Islam in the Mediterranean littoral on a military and cultural level since the campaigns of the Crusaders ... This confrontation between East and West occurred not only after the atrophy of the military power and culture of Islam, but after a period in which European science and technology had developed to an extent that the Islamic world could not imagine'. See Samuel Moreh (ed. and trans.), *Al-Jabartī's Chronicle of the First Seven Months of the French Occupation of Egypt* (Leiden: Brill, 1975), p. 23. He later adds (Ibid. pp. 24–5): 'The French brought with them to Egypt ideas and concepts which were revolutionary among other European nations and furthermore attempted to introduce these into an Egypt which had stagnated in terms of its own Islamic culture for centuries ... The French occupation was riddle to the Egyptians, for it had no precedent in their world-view. They could understand the invasions of the Crusaders, for they represented a battle between two conflicting religions engaged in holy war. But the French invasion of 1798 was different. Her armies came not bearing the cross, but accompanied by scholars and orientalists of a high standard who had come to study Egypt as well as to introduce a Western secular civilisation ... They showed respect for the *'ulamā'* and integrated them into their ruling system'.

[3] Mitchell says that this proclamation was: 'prepared in Arabic by French Orientalists'. See Timothy Mitchell, *Colonising Egypt* (Cambridge: Cambridge University Press, 1988), p. 133. Moreh (*Al-Jabartī's Chronicle of the First Seven Months of the French Occupation of Egypt*, p. 25) says that this proclamation was: 'probably translated [from the French] by Syrian Christian dragomans or translators who had accompanied the French'. Regardless of the route through which the proclamation found its way into Arabic, the following analysis still applies.

[4] Al-Jabarti describes this proclamation as follows: '[The French] printed a large proclamation in Arabic, calling on the people to obey them and to raise their

Content aside, this proclamation must have appeared as a new mode of communication to the Egyptians, representing a departure from the past, where the content of such a communication, if it existed, would have been communicated in handwritten, not printed, form, and would have most probably been conveyed orally through longstanding channels of communication, as represented by the mosque or town crier. Al-Jabarti reproduces this proclamation verbatim – as he tells us – in his chronicle on the French occupation, merely a few pages into the text. Placing the proclamation near the start of the text is consistent with the order of the narrative that one expects in a linearly constructed chronicle, in addition to showing the importance that al-Jabarti ascribes to this text. What is surprising, however, is the decision – in the middle of what must have been a momentous event in Egypt – to follow this proclamation with a detailed linguistic analysis, in which al-Jabarti provides a list of the mistakes that it contains on morphological, syntactic, semantic and stylistic levels. It is as if in providing this analysis, al-Jabarti shifts from being a historian to that of a grammarian and language teacher. But is this the case? Or can we interpret this shift in a way which shows that the exercise in grammar is still, at some deeper level, a continuation of history writing through other means?

At one level, Al-Jabarti's analysis reads like an exercise in language instrumentality – an attempt at mending a broken instrument to make it fit for purpose again. Al-Jabarti was an Azhari scholar, and this exercise in language correction could not have been an alien practice to him. However, what is somewhat surprising is that al-Jabarti commits the same kinds of mistakes that he criticises the proclamation for throughout his chronicle. In his edition of this work, Moreh comments on al-Jabarti's defective language and points to the plethora of mistakes in the text:

> [Al-Jabarti] is harshly critical of the 'corrupted style' and grammatical errors in the first French proclamation . . . Yet he himself frequently violated the elementary principles of classical Arabic grammar and syntax in spite of the fact that he was an Azhari scholar.[5]

In addition to 'a proliferation of colloquial terms, expressions and linguistic patterns',[6] al-Jabarti makes elementary errors in, among other things, verb-subject number agreement, subject-adjective number agreement, use of the masculine where the feminine is grammatically required, pronominal number marking, case marking, gender marking of cardinal numbers

"Bandiera". In this proclamation were inducements, warnings, all manner of wiliness and stipulations. Some copies were sent from the provinces to Cairo' (Moreh, *Al-Jabartī's Chronicle of the First Seven Months of the French Occupation of Egypt*, p. 39).

5 Ibid. p. 25.

6 Ibid. p. 26.

and the forms of the verb.[7] This disjunction between grammatical sensibility and defective linguistic practice may be because al-Jabarti's chronicle was intended as a draft text for private use, as Moreh suggests, to be later subjected to stringent language correction to eliminate all errors before its publication. It may be pointed out, in support of this view, that this text is at variance with al-Jabarti's other historical writings, which were intended for public circulation and are largely free of the kinds of language mistakes noted above. While this may be true, the question remains as to why al-Jabarti decided to engage in grammatical analysis in a text devoted to history. Could it be that his *immediate* aim was the efficacy of language as an instrument, but that his *ulterior* motive was engaging its symbolic role to comment on the momentous events unfolding before him from the position of the historian? Put differently, can we make the argument that by attending to the linguistic order, al-Jabarti was, in effect, continuing his work as a historian through grammatical means?

The answer to the above questions may, in fact, lie in some deeper level of language signification. Commenting on this part of the chronicle, Mitchell says that:

> Phrase by phrase [al-Jabarti] pointed out the colloquialisms, misspellings, ellipses, inconsistencies, morphological inaccuracies and errors of syntax of the French Orientalists, drawing from these incorrect usages a picture of the corruptions, deceptions, misunderstandings and ignorance of the French.[8]

What is interesting about Mitchell's comment is that it does not read linguistic errors instrumentally, but symbolically, thus pointing to an ulterior motive behind al-Jabarti's exercise in instrumentality, this being encoded in the reference to: 'deception, misunderstandings and ignorance'. Instrumentality, in this case, is not an end in itself, but a means to a symbolically oriented end, the aim of which is a complex one. On the one hand, al-Jabarti's seems to want to correlate the military penetration of Egypt with the penetration of its language at the hands of the French occupiers: both are acts of occupation, in which the normal order of things is fractured and plunged into a state of disorder. Mitchell's comment on Marsafi's treatise on political vocabulary – *The Essay on Eight Words*, published in 1881 – to the effect that its author: 'understood the political crisis [in Egypt at the time] . . . in terms of the breakdown of . . . textual authority' seems to apply here, too. In spite of all of the assurances that it seeks to offer ordinary Egyptians, the proclamation is read by al-Jabarti as a sinister act of appropriation, in which the breakdown in the linguistic order/authority is symbolic of the breakdown in political and

[7] Ibid. pp. 26–8 (see here for a list of these mistakes, along with examples from al-Jabarti's chronicle).

[8] Mitchell, *Colonising Egypt*, p. 133.

moral authority. Pointing out the mistakes in the former may therefore be read as a proxy reading for signalling the latter.

In doing this, al-Jabarti may, additionally, have aimed at reclaiming textual authority over language as a measure of resistance to the French occupiers, who could not be resisted on the 'battlefield'; here, political impotence does not necessarily translate into linguistic impotence. In addition, al-Jabarti seems to have wanted to tell his readers that an occupier who breaks the linguistic code cannot be trusted not to break the promises he makes in the proclamation, nor can this enemy be trusted to actually believe what he says he believes in, as regards matters of faith. There are two kinds of evidence in the analysis of the proclamation which support this reading. First, al-Jabarti treats the opening statement in the proclamation as deception: 'In the name of God, the Merciful, the Compassionate. There is no God but God. He has no son, nor has He an associate in His Dominion'.[9] On the surface, this statement seems to indicate that the French subscribe to a Muslim view in matters of faith, but the absence of any assertion or declaration of faith in Islam (*shahādatayn*) or of Muhammad's position as an Apostle of God (*jaḥd al-risāla*) in the proclamation suggests that they do not fully agree with the Muslims in matters of faith. Clearly, Al-Jabarti reads the text for what it does not say, as much as for what it says, to point to what he regards as deception on the part of the French. Although al-Jabarti does not put it this way, the French, for him, are guilty of omission by commission: no one can be considered Muslim without uttering the *shahādatayn* (declaration of faith) in its full form – something that the proclamation does not do. Put differently, the message seems to be that even when the French are not guilty of defective language, what they say cannot be trusted or read at face value. Accuracy in language is no guarantee of accuracy in matters of faith.

Second, al-Jabarti uses his analysis of the errors in the proclamation to curse the French, sometimes in general terms or through the (unidentified) person who composed it. Pointing out the redundancy in the use of the adverb of time *al-ān* (now) in one of the constructions in the text,[10] al-Jabarti adds: 'may Gold afflict [the French occupiers] with every calamity'.[11] The

[9] The original formulation reads as follows (Moreh, *Al-Jabartī's Chronicle of the First Seven Months of the French Occupation of Egypt*, pp. 10–11 [Arabic text]): '*Bismillāhi al-raḥmāni al-raḥim, lā ilāha illā Allāh lā walada lahu wa-lā sharīka fī mulkihi*'. There is no assertion of faith in this formulation (*ashhadu an* . . .) and no reference to Muhammad as His Apostle (*ashhadu anna Muhammadan rasūlu Allāh*).

[10] The original Arabic text reads as follows (Ibid. p. 7): '*fa-ḥaḍara al-ān sā'at 'uqūbatihim*'. Al-Jabarti comments on this, as follows (Ibid. p. 44 [English translation]): 'The words *al-ān* (now) is in the accusative, being an adverb modifying the verb *ḥaḍara* (has come) and *sā'a* (the hour) is a subject. So the meaning is: "the hour of their punishment has come now". It is much better to delete the word "now" (*al-ān*), the adverb being redundant, because *al-ān* is a noun denoting present time, and it is the same as the hour of punishment'.

[11] Ibid. p. 7.

connection between the curse and the word that occasions it is not clear here, but this is not the case in the following examples, where incorrect language acts as an occasion to declare moral outrage. Commenting on the expression *wā ḥasratan* (Woe! Unfortunately), al-Jabarti says that it is redundant in the proclamation: '*wā ḥasratan* is a word expressing affliction and the context doesn't permit it here'.[12] The moral outrage in the analysis follows immediately: 'Its occurrence here is like animal droppings on the road or a boulder in a mountain pass, may God afflict the man who composed it with break-bone fever and may God expose him to all sorts of destruction'.[13] The comparison of this misplaced word with 'animal droppings' expresses al-Jabarti's moral outrage well. Similarly, his reference to a 'boulder in a mountain pass' signals his reading of the mistakes in the proclamation as an act of banditry that is designed to impede the correct navigation of meaning.

Another example in which the lexical meaning of a term, even when correctly used, acts as an occasion to malign the moral character of the French occupiers is *muftarīn* (slanderers, liars) in the expression *wa-qūlū li-l-muftarīn* (tell the slanderers). Al-Jabarti comments here: 'how worthy of [this] description [the French occupiers] are'.[14] A similar example – although linguistically incorrect in the proclamation – of what may be called lexical bridging in the analysis occurs when al-Jabarti says that *al-muslimīn* (Muslims) in the expression '*hum ayḍan muslimīn*' (They are also Muslims) should be *muslimūn* in the nominative, instead of in the accusative (*naṣb*), as it is rendered in the proclamation. Referring to a similar example he corrected in the proclamation earlier, al-Jabarti says: 'The point of putting the word in *naṣb* (accusative) has already been mentioned. There is another point namely: that their Islam is *naṣb* (fraud)'.[15] Al-Jabarti plays here on the lexical and semantic multivalency of the term (*naṣb*) – it signifies fraud and the accusative – to link his correction of the grammar to what he considers as the moral degeneracy of the French in their expressions of Islamic faith, which, as we have seen earlier, are said to be made formulaically, rather than as a matter of true belief.

In a similar vein, the following example underscores al-Jabarti's moral outrage at the defective Arabic in the proclamation. Commenting on the colloquial expression *btā' al-Mamālīk* (belonging to the Mamluks, the rulers of Egypt at the time of the French occupation), al-Jabarti says that it is 'despicable and banal and trite',[16] owing to its status as a colloquial expression (*kalima 'āmmiyya*), although he himself uses such an expression in his chronicle. This

[12] Ibid. p. 44.

[13] Ibid. p. 44. The Arabic original reads as follows (Ibid. p. 13 [Arabic text]): '*li-anna wā-ḥasratan kalima tūji' wa-l-siyāq yā'bāhā fa-wujūduhā ka-mithl al-ba'ra fī al-ṭarīq aw al-mijdāl fī al-maḍīq, ramā Allāhu munshīh bi-waja' al-rukab wa-yassara lahu asbāb al-'aṭab*'.

[14] Ibid. p. 45.

[15] Ibid. p. 47.

[16] The Arabic expression reads as follows (Ibid. p. 16 [Arabic text]): '*kalima 'āmmiyya marzūla wa lafẓa muntahaka mabdhūla*'.

is followed by an interesting example of what I have called lexical bridging in the commentary. Al-Jabarti comments on the use of the word *muṭma'inn* in the expression 'every countryman shall remain peaceably in his dwelling',[17] saying that: 'it should be *muṭma'innan* because it is *ḥāl* [circumstantial expression in Arabic grammar]'.[18] Al-Jabarti then adds that: 'converting [*muṭma'inn*] to the nominative (*raf'*) incorrectly is an indication of their state [*ḥāl*], and their insignificance'.[19] The second part of this statement is cryptic, but I read it as follows: converting what should be in the accusative (*naṣb*) to nominative *raf'* (nominative) is fraud (*naṣb*, in the lexical, not the grammatical sense), this being part of the moral composition or the state (*ḥāl*, in the lexical, not the grammatical sense) of the French occupiers. The reference to 'insignificance' plays on the desire of the French to hide their fraud by elevating it to the nominative (*raf'*); this, again, is another deception, which shows their insignificance (absence of genuine elevation). Al-Jabarti then rounds off his attack on the French with the following invocation: 'May God hurry their misfortune and punishment upon them, may He strike their tongues with dumbness, may He scatter their hosts, and disperse them, confound their intelligence and cause their breath to cease'.[20] The reference to the striking of tongues and dumbness brings the analysis at its point of closure back to the importance of language, not just as a means of communication, but as the instrument of verbal action, too.

The above discussion provides examples in support of my view that the instrumental intent of al-Jabarti's analysis of the proclamation hides a deeper meaning, which works through, among other things, language symbolism. Moreh's translation of the opening statement in this commentary: 'here is an explanation of the incoherent words and vulgar constructions which [the French] put into this miserable letter',[21] does not, in my view, capture this precise point, because it makes the object of al-Jabarti's analysis to be exclusively the: 'incoherent words and vulgar constructions' in the text. A better translation would be: '[Here is the] explanation or interpretation of this wretched and miserable proclamation with its disjointed words and crooked

[17] The Arabic original reads as follows (Ibid. p. 10 [Arabic text]): *'kull wāḥad min ahālī al-balad annahu yabqā fī maskanihi muṭma'inn'*.

[18] Ibid. p. 10. The Arabic original reads as follows (Ibid. p. 16 [Arabic text]): *'ṣawābuhu muṭma'innan li-annahu ḥāl'*.

[19] The Arabic original reads as follows (Ibid. pp. 16–17 [Arabic text]): *'fa-'udūluhu ilā al-raf' fī ghayr mawḍi'ih ishāratun li-ḥālihim wa-khafḍi sha'nihim'*.

[20] Ibid. p. 47. The Arabic original is as follows (Ibid. p. 17 [Arabic text]): *''ajjala Allāhu lahum al-wabāl wa-l-nikāl wa-akhrasa minhum 'uḍwa al-maqāl wa farraqa jam'ahum wa shattata shamlahum wa-afsada ra'yahum wa akhmada anfāsahum'*.

[21] Ibid. p. 42. The Arabic original reads as follows (Ibid. p. 10 [Arabic text]): *'tafsīr mā awda'ahu hadhā al-maktūb al-mankūb mina al-kalimāt al-mufakkaka wa-l-tarākīb al-mula'baka'*. The English does not convey the assonance between *al-maktūb al-mankūb* and *al-mufakkaka* and *al-mula'baka'*, which, for the modern ear, seems to poke fun at the French.

expressions and constructions'. The key term here is the word *tafsīr* (explanation or interpretation) in the Arabic, which indicates that the proclamation could not be taken at face value, but that it needed, in modern parlance, a hermeneutic intervention to decipher its content, including pointing out and correcting the grammatical and other linguistic errors it contains. This, in fact, is reflected in the interpretations that al-Jabarti offers of non-linguistic issues in the proclamation, as we have seen above. It is also reflected in his commentary on the correct usage in the proclamation to express moral outrage or on omitted linguistic material that the Muslim reader expects to be given to highlight French fraud or economy in telling the truth. The linkages between defective grammar and the moral degeneracy of the French were made possible because of the symbolic meanings that the language can carry. Language instrumentality is the gateway to this world of political and moral signification, but it cannot capture this world on its own, without invoking the symbolism that language has in the social world.

In doing this work, al-Jabarti exploits the lexical meanings of grammatical terms – for example, the use of the terms *naṣb* (accusative) and *raf'* (nominative) in their lexical sense of 'fraud' and 'elevation' to link instrumentality to moral degeneracy through the overall function of language as a symbol with political and moral moorings. This combination of the moral with the political, occasioned by language as subject, is embedded in an analysis that, in culmination, conveys the flavour of a sermon. The use of the expressions *farraqa jam'ahum wa-shattata shamlahum* (May He scatter their hosts and disperse them) are still heard to this day in Friday prayers to refer to the enemies of Islam, whenever Muslims feel under threat. There is no doubt that al-Jabarti's readers would have been able to understand this message and use it to contextualise the intent of his analysis, part of which being that an occupier's corrupt language indexes or references his corruption in other domains of social life. In fact, Al-Jabarti lists some of these in his analysis of the proclamation; the following is part of what he says on this topic:

> Their [French] women do not veil themselves and have no modesty; they do not care whether they uncover their private parts. Whenever a Frenchman has to perform an act of nature he does so wherever he happens to be, even in full view of people, and he goes away as he is, without washing his private parts after defecation. If he is a man of taste and refinement he wipes himself with whatever he finds, even with a paper with writing on it, otherwise he remains as he is. They have intercourse with any woman who pleases them and vice versa. Sometimes one of their women goes into a barber's shop, and invites him to shave her pubic hair. If he wishes he can take his fee in kind.[22]

[22] Ibid. p. 43. This is the Arabic original of this translation (Ibid. p. 12 [Arabic text]): *'wa nisā'uhum lā yastatirūn wa-lā yaḥtashimūn wa-lā yubālūn bi-kashf al-'awrāt, wa-matā da'athu ḍarūrat al-ḥāja qaḍāhā fī ayy makān ittafaq wa-law bi-mar'ā min al-nās wa-yadhhab kamā huwa min ghayr istinjā fa-in kāna ṣāḥib ṭabī'a masaḥa bimā yajiduhu*

I have dwelt at some length on al-Jabarti's analysis and interpretation of the French proclamation because of its timing: it stands at the transition between the pre-modern and modern worlds in Arab history. Instead of marking their discontinuity, this analysis and interpretation signals the continuity of the past or pre-modern into the present and the foreshadowing of the present or modern in the past. This is possible because of language symbolism and of the importance of Arabic in social life. I have dealt with this role of Arabic in the preceding chapters – allocating the past or pre-modern to Chapter 2 and the present or modern to Chapter 3 and Chapter 4, respectively – as if they were distinct or disconnected trajectories in Arab social history, language ideology and cultural politics. I have delayed the discussion of al-Jabarti until now, as this is the best place to highlight the connectivity of the past or pre-modern to the present or modern in Arab history in a way which shows the perennial significance of Arabic as a symbol in society.

The Cognitive Role of Language

The cognitive role of language – its ability to connect thought with reality by marking the former to configure or shape the way that the latter is experienced by speakers – is categorially distinct from language instrumentality, in spite of the fact that cognition is intertwined with this instrumentality, as it (instrumentality) is enacted through language as a system of communication.[23] This cognitive role is also distinct from language symbolism, although the two come into contact and feed into each other when language ideology in the formal sense intervenes as a factor, as I shall explain below. Discussions of this cognitive role are dealt with under the rubric of linguistic relativity in linguistics and anthropology. Lucy characterises the relationship between language, thought and reality under this cognitive role as follows:

> They [linguistic relativity proposals] all claim that certain properties of a given *language* have consequences for patterns of *thought* about *reality*. The properties of language at issue are usually morpho-syntactic (but may be phonological or pragmatic) and are taken to vary in important respects. The pattern of *thought*

wa-law waraqa maktūba wa-illā baqiya 'alā ḥālihi. Wa-yaṭa'ūn mā ṭāb lahum min al-nisā wa-bi-l-'aks wa rubbamā dakhalat al-marā minhum ilā ḥānūt al-ḥallāq wa-da'athu li-ḥalq 'anatihā wa-in shā akhadha ujratahu minh'. I have kept the text as given in Moreh without correction, except for inserting the *hamza* in *nisā'uhum* to give the reader a flavour of al-Jabarti's style and the errors that he has made in the text.

23 In previous research on language and identity in the Arabic-speaking world, I have given attention to the instrumental and, more specifically, symbolic roles of language only. This chapter offers a corrective to this limitation of language roles, but see Yasir Suleiman, '"Under the spell of language": Arabic between linguistic determinism and linguistic reality', in Ian R. Netton (ed.), *Studies in Honour of Clifford Edmund Bosworth, Vol I: Hunter of the East: Arabic and Semitic Studies* (Leiden: Brill, 2000), pp. 113–37.

> may have to do with immediate perception and attention, with personal and social cultural systems of classification, inference, memory or with aesthetic judgment and creativity. The reality may be the world of every day experience, of specialised contexts, or of ideational tradition. The three key elements are linked by two relations: Language embodies *an interpretation* of reality and language can *influence* thought about that reality. The interpretation arises from the selection of substantive aspects of experience and their formal arrangements in the verbal code.[24]

The use of the 'looking glass' metaphor in the title of this chapter is an approximation or refraction of this triadic relationship among language, thought and reality: a looking glass does not offer an accurate reflection of the objects or bodies that stand in front of it, but, to use Lucy's formulation, an 'interpretation' – not without some kind of distortion – of those objects and the relations that hold them together. In other words, this metaphor is not intended to mean that thought copies the structural and pragmatic imprint of the language that gives expression to it, nor is it intended to say that reality without language is formless. This interpretation of the cognitive role of language differs from the kind of *linguistic determinism* in which language is said to *determine* thought, not just *influence* it, in Lucy's formulation above, conforming, in this regard, to what Dufrenne describes as a: 'kind of linguistic destiny' for the speakers of a language.[25] It is also different, on the other side of the cognitive triad (from language to reality), from Whorf's statement that speakers: '*dissect* nature [rather than *interpret* it in Lucy's formulation] along the lines laid down by [their] native languages', although Whorf's position tends to be more nuanced when considered in its totality.[26] Cognitive readings of the Arabic language veer between linguistic determinism and linguistic relativity, although it is not possible to ascertain in every case where the boundary lies between them, as will become clear later in this chapter.

However, before moving on to explain, in brief, the various approaches to investigating the cognitive role of language, it is important to remind the reader of three caveats that Lucy[27] enters in this connection, all of which

[24] John A. Lucy, 'Linguistic relativity', *Annual Review of Anthropology* (1997), 26: 294 (original emphasis).

[25] See Robert B. Kaplan, 'Cultural thought patterns in inter-cultural education', *Language Learning* (1966), 26: 2. The following statement by Dufrenne sets out his views more fully (Ibid. p. 2): 'If one admits that a language represents a kind of a destiny, so far as human thought is concerned, [the] diversity of languages leads to a radical relativism. As Pierce said, if Aristotle had been Mexican, his logic would have been different; and perhaps, by the same token, the whole of our philosophy and our science would have been different'.

[26] Benjamin Whorf, 'Linguistic relativity and the relation of linguistic processes to perception and cognition', in Sol Saporta (ed.), *Psycholinguistics: A Book of Readings* (New York, NY: Holt, Reinhart and Winston, 1961), p. 464 (emphasis added).

[27] Lucy, 'Linguistic relativity'.

apply to the discussion of Arabic below: (1) the cognitive role of language is premised on linguistic diversity, but it is not the same as diversity; (2) the cognitive role of language depends on the existence of differences between languages in structural, pragmatic or behavioural terms, whether these differences are overtly acknowledged or covertly signalled; and (3) the cognitive role of language acknowledges that differences exist between cultures, but it does not consider those differences to be isomorphic with the differences languages exercise in relating thought to reality, according to the triadic relationship described above: linguistic and cultural differences criss-cross each other, but cultural difference can exist outside the realms that are influenced by language differences.[28] I should also add here a fourth caveat of my own: I am not, in fact, interested in investigating empirically the relationship between thought and reality as this is mediated through language, but in assessing a corpus of readings that connect with this relationship from different sources in both Arabic and English, although the latter will be dominant.

Before giving some examples to illustrate the above, it would be useful to provide a general characterisation of the approaches used to investigate the cognitive role of language. Lucy cites three general approaches.[29] First, Lucy cites the structure-centred approach, which begins by noting the differences between languages in matters pertaining to structure and pragmatics as a prelude to correlating them with differences in speakers' behaviour. Differences in tense and aspect or number marking between languages, together with their behavioural correlates – assuming that these can be unequivocally identified – may be suitable candidates for study under this kind of approach. Studies of the differences in patterns of repetition between Arabic and English and their correlation with persuasion or otherwise may serve as examples of this approach. The second approach is domain-centred. Studies of this kind start with a well-circumscribed experiential domain – for example, colour recognition or cognition – and seek to establish how this domain is encoded in different languages. This approach will not figure in this study, owing to its absence from the corpus of writings that I have collected. The third approach, which will predominate in this chapter, is behaviour-centred. It starts from observations of differences in behaviour

[28] This is not an uncontested view. Hill and Mannheim argue that it is not possible to separate behaviour into 'linguistic' and 'cultural' forms: 'There is no prima facie way to identify certain behaviours – or better, certain forms of social action – as linguistic and others as cultural . . . Even the most formal and minute aspect of phonetics-syllable timing – completely interpenetrates the most identifiably nonolinguistic, unconscious part of behaviour . . . Thus "language" and "culture" cannot be neatly separated by distinctions like "structure" versus "practice"'. See Jane H. Hill and Bruce Mannheim, 'Language and world view', *Annual Review of Anthropology* (1992), 21: 382.

[29] Lucy, 'Linguistic relativity', p. 382.

among the speakers of different languages and seeks to locate the source of these differences in differences between the languages that they speak, either through small-scale comparisons or broad-brush comparative strokes. Comparison is an important component in all of these approaches – this being a consequence of the existence of difference in diversity – which has deep roots in literate cultures, which may be ignited when these cultures come into contact with each other.[30]

However, while the first two approaches aim to provide fine-tuned analyses of linguistic structure in constructing the cognitive triad above, the behaviour-centred approach tends to be less stringent about this task. This initial observation, as I shall point out below, is in line with Lucy's comment on this approach:

> Essentially this approach 'selects' structural features of the language according to a criterion of presumed relevance to a practical behaviour at issue. Often no formal analysis of the language is undertaken and no comparison with other languages is attempted. When they are, both follow the same pattern of devoting attention only to elements that seem patently relevant regardless of their broader structural place and significance.[31]

Lucy's comment on the 'comparison with other' languages is worthy of discussion. Previously, I have referred to both overt and covert comparisons. In some cases, the comparisons are made overtly and in abundance. And in some discussions of the cognitive role of Arabic, comparisons with English through translation abide, as we shall see below. In other cases, comparisons are encoded covertly, but the context can still offer us clues as to which languages might be intended in the enactment of these comparisons. Examples of this will be given below.

Lucy reminds us that throughout most of the twentieth century:

> interest and controversy [concerning the view that 'the particular language we speak influences the way we think about reality'] have not given rise to

[30] Lucy offers the following contextualisation for this kind of interest in language in the European context ('Linguistic relativity', p. 293): 'Interest in the intellectual significance of the diversity of language categories has deep roots in the European tradition ... [Formulations] recognisably related to our contemporary ones were stimulated by theoretical concerns (opposition to the tenets of universal grammarians regarding the origin and status of different languages), methodological concerns (the reliability of language-based knowledge in religion and science), and practical social concerns (European efforts to consolidate national identities and cope with colonial expansion)'. Similar interest in linguistic differences between Arabic and other languages are 'recognisably related', to use Lucy's formulation, to our concern with the cognitive role of language as understood here, as will be discussed below.

[31] Ibid. p. 302.

> sustained programmes of empirical research in any of the concerned disciplines and, as a result, the validity of the proposal has remained largely in the realm of speculation.[32]

This is particularly true of the behaviour-centred approach and its loose application to Arabic, wherein it dominates the other approaches. The fact that this approach, in its mostly speculative mode, lends itself to manipulation has made it an effective tool in ideological advocacy or contestation among groups. In some cases, one cannot help but detect a kind of 'racism' in studies belonging to this approach, which reminds us of the belief in a universal grammar and evolutionary anthropology that are tied to European superiority, as these had started to emerge in the late eighteenth and early nineteenth centuries. This is clear, as will be explained below, from the totalising and essentialising tone of some of these studies, whether in their full or nascent form in the Arab context.

Let us exemplify some of the above points by referring to a few examples from the Arab intellectual tradition. A good place to start is al-Arsuzi – one of the founders of pan-Arab nationalism in the twentieth century. Writing in the middle of the twentieth century, during the heyday of Arab nationalism, when it was thought that Arab political unity was possible, al-Arsuzi coins the phrase: 'the genius of the Arabs resides in their language'. To explain how this works, he mines the Arabic lexicon to show how the programme of Arab nationalism is foreshadowed by the Arabic language as a mediating code between thought and reality, though this is more desired than real. The following quotation illustrates this:

> The word for nation in Arabic is *umma*, which signifies the ideas of motherhood and goal-orientation – by virtue of its root: *umm* (mother) and *amm* (to lead the way) – at one and the same time, as if to capture the views of common historical ancestry [through *umm*] and shared aspiration [through *amm*]. . . And, since the relationship between brothers, sisters and other members of the extended Arab family is designated by the term *'alāqat raḥm*, literally 'womb relationship', an additional meaning is added to the signification of *umma* [through umm] and the root *r-ḥ-m* (to be compassionate, the Compassionate as an attribute of God), to reveal at one and the same time the ideas of compassion and godlinness which [this] root signifies. In a similar vein, the word which signifies the meaning of solidarity between members of the same nation is *ukhuwwa*, the meaning of whose stem *akh* (brother) captures this relation by virtue of its phonetic similarity to the interjection of pain (*ākh*).[33] On the basis of [the above network of meanings, extracted using sound symbolism and word morphology], the nation [in

32 Ibid. pp. 291–2.
33 The connection between *akh* and *ākh* is part of popular etymology. I remember my mother making this connection whenever she wanted to impress on us the need for sibling solidarity as brothers and sisters.

> its original meaning in the Arab world view signifies] a familial, goal-oriented community among whose members relations of compassion and solidarity obtain by virtue of divine intervention and action.[34]

According to this quote, three components of Arab nationalism as a political ideal can be derived from the meanings of a small set of words and the relations between them: these are the notions of: (1) common origin, derived from the words *umm* (mother), *akh* (brother) and *raḥm* (womb); (2) solidarity, derived from the words *ukhuwwa* (brotherhood) and *'alāqat raḥm* (familial relations); and (3) common purpose, derived from the word *amma* (to move forward with a purpose). Here we have an example of how language can or may (be made to) influence or shape thought and, in the context of the time, how 'political reality' can or may be interpreted and acted upon by language. The fact that the project of pan-Arab unity has not succeeded shows the contingency and precariousness of this interpretation of language, thought and reality on the political front, although some Arab intellectuals still argue that this project is not devoid of cultural relevance; from this, it would not be difficult to argue that al-Arsuzi's cognitive reading of Arabic is still endowed with some force for this constituency. Finally, although al-Arsuzi's discussions of the cognitive role of Arabic do not offer a comparative perspective, they are, rather covertly, pitched against the claim, in the first decades of the Turkish Republic, that Turkish is the original language, in what came to be called the 'Sun-Language Theory'.[35] As a native of what is now called Hatay in Turkey – the region from which he descended and continued to consider as part of Syria – al-Arsuzi was offering his cognitive construction of Arabic in rebuttal of the Turkish claim. This is not the same as providing a comparative perspective, but it has hidden elements of comparison in it drawn against a conflictual ideological canvas; this is what I meant above when referring to broad-brush comparative strokes between languages. The comparisons are purely ideological in intent, but, in al-Arsuzi's case, they are premised on the facts of the Arabic lexicon, as he interprets it through the nationalist domain of signification.

Although pre-shadowed earlier (for example, in the dissolution of political unity between Egypt and Syria in 1962), the (official) failure of the Arab nationalist project after the defeat of Egypt, Syria and Jordan in the 1967 war with Israel and the death of Nasser in September 1970 coincided with readings of the cognitive role of Arabic, which implicate the language as one of the culprits in this defeat. This antithetical reading points to the historical

[34] See Yasir Suleiman, 'Ideology, grammar-making and the standardisation of Arabic', in Bilal Orfali (ed.), *In the Shadow of Arabic: The Centrality of Language to Arabic Culture* (Studies Presented to Ramzi Baalbaki on the Occasion of his Sixtieth Birthday) (Leiden and Boston, MA: Brill, 2011b), p. 22.

[35] See Yasir Suleiman, *The Arabic Language and National Identity: A Study in Ideology* (Washington, DC: Georgetown University Press, 2003).

contingency and contextuality of the cognitive readings of Arabic in the Arabic-speaking world, as well as pointing to the ideological impregnation of these readings. Lucy's comment about speculation applies here with full force. In spite of this, the continued exploitation of Arabic as a 'cognitive resource' testifies to the continued importance of the language in the Arab socio-political sphere.

An example of a critical cognitive reading of Arabic is provided by Sharabi.[36] In his post-1967 publications, Sharabi, who spent his academic career at Georgetown University until his retirement in the 1990s, developed a critique of Arab society based around the notion of 'neopatriarchy', in which language was an important element. Sharabi declares, with little hesitation, that: 'if language structures thought, classical Arabic [*fuṣḥā*] structures it in a decisive way'.[37] This is an expression of linguistic determinism – a strong one, in fact – in which Arabic, cognitively speaking, represents a 'linguistic destiny' for its users. Sharabi explains his position as follows:

> Classical Arabic produces a sort of discourse that mediates reality through a double ideology: the ideology inherent in the 'trance of language' – produced and reproduced by the magic of catchwords, incantations, verbal stereotypes and internal referents – and the ideology supplied by the 'encratic' language – produced and disseminated under the protection of political or religious orthodoxy.[38]

Sharabi's view of the cognitive role of Arabic is richer than what we meant by this role (above): it gives prominence to language ideology as a form of tyranny, in which language itself, through habituated practice, and the power of its protectors and defenders dictates precisely how it mediates the relationship between thought and reality. The reference to the hypnotic power of language or the 'trance' that it exercises on its speakers sums up the former point. However, at no point does Sharabi provide concrete examples of how this mediation is actually done through language. This makes it difficult to interrogate, on a level close to the world of concrete reality and examples, what Sharabi says, but there is no doubt that he subscribes to a strong deterministic view of the cognitive role of Arabic and that through the comparisons he makes with other languages, including the Arabic colloquials, he

[36] Hisham Sharabi, *Neopatriarchy: A Theory of Distorted Change in Arab Society* (New York, NY: Oxford University Press, 1988); Hishām Sharābī, *al-Naqd al-ḥaḍārī li-wāqiʿ al-mujtamaʿ al-ʿarabī al-muʿāṣir* (Beirut: Dār Nilsun, 2000).

[37] Sharabi, *Neopatriarchy*, p. 86. This view is opposed by Adonis, who believes that although language influences thought, it is not correct to say that it constrains or subjugates the mind: 'While it is true that Arabic has its own structure (*binyatuhā al-khāṣṣa*) that influences Arab thought (*al-niẓām al-maʿrifī al-ʿarabī*) . . . it is not true to say that . . . it constrains/subjugates (*taqsir*) the Arab mind'. See ʿAlī Aḥmad Saʿīd (Adonis) *Kalām al-bidāyāt* (Beirut: Dār al-Ādāb, 1989a), p. 120.

[38] Ibid. p. 120.

believes that *fuṣḥā* Arabic is *sui generis* in this determinism, relating this to the fact that it is used: 'practically unchanged [from ancient times] as [the] basic means of bureaucratic communication and formal discourse'.[39]

Central to Sharabi's views of the cognitive role of Arabic is the notion of the monologue in Arab neopatriarchal discourse. Sharabi seems to model this on the uni-directional nature of divine traffic – through revelation – in Islam, as will be remarked later. Sharabi explains his view of this mode of speaking as follows:

> The monological mode of discourse manifests itself . . . in the tendency of speakers persistently to exclude or ignore other speakers. But this mode also appears in the very structure of the discourse itself: not just authority produces the monological discourse, but also the language itself, in that it privileges rhetoric and discourages dialogue.[40]

This point is glossed on the following page:

> This [monologic] discourse derives its perceived sense of signification from the structure of language itself rather than from the individual utterance. While the structure reinforces authority, hierarchy and the relations of dependency, it also produces oppositional forms typical of the neopatrarichal discourse: gossip, back-biting, storytelling and silence.[41]

The references to the 'structure of discourse' and the 'structure of language' are never explained, nor are the influences they are said to have on thought, or the interpretations they make of reality, exemplified. We are therefore at a loss as to how language mediates the relationship between thought and reality in Sharabi's scheme, in spite of his insistent assertions that it does. The connection between monologic and neopatriarchal discourse, on the one hand, and the practice of 'gossip, back-biting, story-telling and silence', on the other, is asserted as if it was a given of the Arabic-dominated social world.

There is no doubt, as I have mentioned above, that Sharabi subscribes to a radical form of linguistic determinism in conceptualising the cognitive role of Arabic to such an extent, in fact, that we may combine the reference to 'linguistic destiny' above with 'language tyranny', in order to describe his position. This seems to be consistent with the following iteration of Sharabi's view of the monologue:

> All monologues, in insisting on agreement, exclude difference, questioning and qualification. Hence monological speech (and writing) typically never exhibits hesitation and doubt – attributes that delimit or undermine monological

39 Ibid. p. 85.
40 Ibid. p. 87.
41 Ibid. p. 88.

> authority – but relies on general and unqualified affirmation. The fundamental type of monological truth is absolute truth and its ultimate ground is revelation. Clearly, the monological discourse is, by its very structure, a negation of dialogue and of the assumption on which it is based: the assumption, for example, that no discourse is itself final or closed, that only free questioning can yield true knowledge, or that truth is constituted not by authority but by discussion, exchange and criticism.[42]

Sharabi's treatment of the relationship between language, thought and reality exemplifies Lucy's point about the speculative nature of discussions of the cognitive role of language – in this case, Arabic. The references to linguistic and discursive structure are offered as though they were primitive terms that need no definition. There is no doubt that Sharabi believes that these structures act as strict regimes that shape thought and, through thought, impose a structure on reality. But we are not told how. Sharabi also seems to apply an essentialising ontology that conceives of the influence of Arabic on thought and, through that reality, to be static, the assumption here being that classical Arabic has not changed to any significant degree, as he tells us, throughout its history. There is, under this ontology, no chance of any real change in the Arab worldview without the wholesale ditching of classical Arabic in Arab social life. Language tyranny does not fail, nor can it be disposed of easily, because it reproduces itself recursively as structure and regime of authority from generation to generation. Because of the above, Sharabi's views of the cognitive role of Arabic turn into a form of ideological advocacy, in spite of the fact that they are intended to eschew ideology. This exemplifies the reference I made above to the adjacency of discussions of the cognitive role of Arabic to its symbolic role through language ideology.

This same trend of mixing ideology with a loose interpretation of the cognitive role of language characterises al-Qasimi's views on Arabic in his book *al-'Arab ẓāhira ṣawtiyya*. The reference to the cognitive role of Arabic here will need some qualification. Al-Qasimi's book contains over 700 pages of relentless prose, which must have been written over a long period of time. As a result, al-Qasimi is not consistent in respect to how he conceptualises the relation between Arabic, thought and reality. In some places, he seems to suggest that Arabic determines thought and culture. In others, he inverses the relation, making culture the determinant of language. Towards the end of the book, he speaks of reciprocal influences between the two: 'People live in the languages they speak . . . and their languages live in them. Yes, they live in each other'.[43] He expands this view on the following page:

[42] Ibid. p. 88.

[43] 'Abdallah al-Qaṣīmī, *al-'Arab ẓāhira ṣawtiyya* (Cologne: Manshūrāt al-Jamal, [2002] 2006), p. 579. The Arabic original is as follows: *'inna al-nās ya'īshūn fi al-lugha allatī yata'allamūnahā . . . kamā ta'īshu lughātuhim fīhim. Na'am ta'īshu fīhim wa-ya'īshūna fīhā'*.

> Language, any language, is not something that is more or less, better or worse, more or less intelligent than the people who speak it. They are one and the same (*innahā hiya hum*): letters that are spoken, heard, written and read. People, throughout history, are their languages.[44]

This conflation of people with language exaggerates the extent to which language influences its speakers, making it a straightjacket from which they cannot escape.

Al-Qasimi's book is a trenchant attack on many aspects of Arab life, including the role of language in society. The title of the book and the image on the front cover of a howling man are both intended to allure, entice and shock the public and readers at the same time, in line with my comments on this matter in Chapter 4 (See Figure 5.1). On first encounter, the title creates dissonance in the public and readers. Describing the Arabs as *ẓāhira* (phenomenon) objectifies them in a way which denudes them from part or all of their humanity. This is consistent with the content and tone of the book, which is the best example of Arab exceptionalism – the Arabs are outside history – I have read. This sense of dissonance is continued through the use of the term *ṣawtiyya* (from *ṣawt*: sound, noise). It is not easy to translate this term, but it may be best rendered as 'acoustic', in line with the content of the book, but also because this rendering accords with the objectification of the Arabs, as conveyed by the term 'phenomenon'. Translating the title as *The Arabs: An Acoustic Phenomenon* would convey the same sense of enticement and shock to the English reader: the Arabs verbalise, but they do not mean. To understand the significance of the title, al-Qasimi makes a distinction between *ẓāhira kalāmiyya* (verbal phenomenon) and *ẓāhira ṣawtiyya* (acoustic phenomenon), glossing the latter as 'less than verbal' (*aqall min kalāmiyya*)[45] or 'the Arabs have not yet reached the stage of being a verbal or linguistic phenomenon' (*ayy annahum lam yablughū an yakūnū ẓāhira kalāmiyya aw lughawiyya*),[46] thus making them similar to the category of the *'a'jam* creatures that Jahiz talks about, as we have seen in Chapter 2. Al-Qasimi expands on this distinction by telling us that:

> speaking/speech is thinking, morality, planning, problem solving, finding solutions or searching for solutions. As for acoustication (*taswīt*), it is vomit and lies. It (acoustication) is state not action. Speaking is action not state. Speaking is (purposeful) walking, going up or coming down. Acoustication is rolling along,

[44] Ibid. p. 580. The Arabic original reads as follows: *'al-lugha, ayyat lugha laysat shay'an akthar aw aqall, afḍal aw arda', adhkā aw aghbā mimman yatakallamūnahā, innahā hiya hum jā'ū ḥurūfan manṭūqatan wa-masmū'atan wa-maktūbatan wa-maqrū'atan. Inna al-bashar fī kull tārīkhihim laysū illā lughātahim . . .'*

[45] Ibid. p. 114.

[46] Ibid. p. 115.

slipping or falling down; that is, it is not planned movement that is subject to careful calculations.[47]

This explanation of the difference between verbalisation and acoustication is characteristic of the metaphorical way in which al-Qasimi writes, making it difficult to pin his writing down, although we can somehow guess what he wants to say.

Al-Qasimi's view that the Arabs are an acoustic phenomenon springs from his belief that they say a lot, but do very little – something I have heard ordinary Arabs, who have not come across al-Qasimi's work, say. The first time that he refers to this, he singles out Arab 'leaders, rulers, chiefs, teachers and writers'[48] for criticism, before expanding the circle of referents to: 'poets, orators, preachers, thinkers / intellectuals, broadcasters . . . journalists and military readers'.[49] This deficit between action and speech is no doubt related to the general feeling of impotence (*'ajz*)[50] in the Arab world on many fronts, politically, economically, militarily, educationally and culturally, hence the singling out of the above members of Arab society for: (1) their failure to lead; and (2) their use of acoustication as a response to the speech of the others (non-Arabs, Westerners) in a way that leads to a failure in communication. It is also related to the sense of defeatism (*hazīma*)[51] that pervades significant parts of Arab life, which has roots in the colonial experience. Al-Qasimi believes that the problem is much deeper, in fact. It goes back to pre-Islamic and early Islamic times, hence his treatment of the pre-Islamic odes (*mu'allaqāt*) as the earliest known examples of Arab acoustication (*taṣwīt*).

The Qur'an is placed within the same trajectory: al-Qasimi treats it as an acoustication of the Lord to a people who have fallen in love with their language, as, though they do not know it, an exercise in acoustication, not speech or communication, as found in other cultures. This, al-Qasimi daringly states, is why the inimitability of the Qur'an was not made to reside in its meanings, but in its form, as has been explained at length in Chapter 2. Although he does not state this overtly, al-Qasimi seems to believe that the text of the Qur'an and the way it is deployed in Arab life (recitation, rote learning and as a corpus of proofs) is a form of acoustication: 'the genius of

47 Ibid. p. 134. This is the Arabic original: *'inna al-kalām tafkīr wa-akhlāq wa-takhṭīṭ wa-mu'ālaja wa-waḍ' ḥulūl aw baḥth 'an ḥulūl. Ammā al-taṣwīt fa-innahu istifrāgh wa qadhf. Innahu ḥāla wa-laysa 'amalan. Ammā al-kalām fa-innahu 'amalan wa-lays ḥāla. Al-kalām sayr aw ṣu'ūd aw nuzūl. Ammā al-taṣwīt fa-innahu tadaḥruj aw inzilāq aw -suqūṭ'*.

48 Ibid. p. 113. This is the Arabic original: *'zu'amā'uhum, wa-ḥukkāmuhum, wa-qādātuhum, wa-kuttābuhum . . .'*

49 Ibid. p. 119. This is the Arabic original: *'shā'iran aw khaṭīban aw wā'iẓan aw mufakirran aw mu'alliman aw mudhī'an aw ṣaḥafiyyan aw qā'idan 'askariyyan . . .'*

50 Ibid. p. 162.

51 Ibid. p. 162.

the Qur'an is derived from the genius of the Arabic language and it is an imitation of that language'.[52] If Arabic is a matter of acoustication – *taṣwīt* – the Qur'an must be, too. Al-Qasimi encodes this with one of his trademark metaphors: 'Why does the ear/auditorisation come before the brain/mind in Qur'anic rhetoric?'[53] He then links the auditory nature of the Qur'an to the endemic obedience and acquiescence to authority and power that characterises social, political and intellectual life in the Arab world (*al-sam' wa-l-ṭā'a*).[54] When form is what counts, meaning is thrown out of the window: repetition, rote learning and acquiescence become the dominant norms.

At no point does al-Qasimi offer any arguments or provide any examples as to how his expression 'the Arabs are an acoustic phenomenon' applies in relating language to thought, on the one hand, and to reality, on the other. This expression and the idea behind it are repeated *ad nauseam* in al-Qasimi's book, as if it is sufficient to state and restate the point repeatedly for it to be proven. Johnstone, whose work on repetition in Arabic will be dealt with below, calls this mode of argumentation proof by presentation or presentation as proof – a form of 'browbeating' the interlocutor until 'he drops dead' through sheer exhaustion or utter boredom.[55] There is, however, no doubt that al-Qasimi believes that Arabic is an important factor in construing the social world as a set of acoustic signs with little meaning. Arabic moulds thought and is moulded by it, both interpreting reality – by which is primarily meant the social world – in a way that empties it from any coherent meaning. Under this essentialising view, the Arabs are said to be doomed to failure, because of their inability to engage with the word as a set of signs with meanings.

A conclusion of this kind is possible in al-Qasimi's schema, only because of the ideological nature of his view of the cognitive role of Arabic. Here again, as with Sharabi, we have an example of language ideology masquerading as a representation of the cognitive role of Arabic. Both Sharabi and al-Qasimi are driven by trying to make sense of the political modalities of their time in an age of Arab defeat and impotence on many fronts. Both writers see language as one of the prisms through which they can explain this defeat and impotence, although they fail to do so, because of the obscurantist nature of their writing, the lack of substantiation of their arguments and mixing ideology with language cognition in a manner that seems to privilege the former.

Al-Qasimi reserves some of his most trenchant criticisms for the Arab grammarians, because of the complexity of their grammars and the unfounded

52 Ibid. p. 592. This is the Arabic original: '[*inna*] '*abqariyyat al-qur'ān laysat illā akhdhan min 'abqariyyat al-lugha al-'arabiyya wa-taqlīdan lahā*'.

53 Ibid. p. 307. This is the Arabic original: '*li-mādhā al-udhn qabl al-'aql fī balāghat al-qur'ān*?'

54 Ibid. p. 309.

55 Barbara Johnstone, *Repetition in Arabic Discourse: Paradigms, Syntagms and the Ecology of Language* (Amsterdam and Philadelphia, PA: John Benjamins, 1991).

adulation they express for Arabic – a topic with which I have dealt with in Chapter 2 and, less so, in Chapter 3. He disparagingly calls them: 'language priests' (*kuhhān al-lugha*),[56] the 'Caesars' of Arabic (*qayāṣira*),[57] the Prophets of language and its Sultans (*anbiyā' al-lugh wa-salāṭīnuhā*)[58] and the makers of shackles and coffins (*ṣāni'ū al-quyūd wa-l-akfān*).[59] He considers them partly responsible for why the Arabs cannot take the next step up on the ladder towards speaking, away from acoustication. Clearly, al-Qasimi associates grammar with coercive power, false religious order, torture and death, as the above descriptions of the language defenders indicate. These are metaphorical ways of speaking, to which no real argument or proof is attached, even though the presumed difficulty of Arabic grammar is a well-trodden topic, which is supported by evidence from pedagogy and has been subject to critical comments in the past, as Jahiz's remark on the topic, quoted in Chapter 2, amply testifies. Al-Qasimi's point of departure is ideological, not empirical; this explains his constant eschewing of evidence and non-rhetorical argumentation.

Like Sharabi, al-Qasimi is probably not troubled by his obscurantist mode of writing. Sharabi expresses this attitude openly when he reflects on the Arabic translation of his book *Neopatriarchy*, to which I referred earlier. In his book *al-Naqd al-ḥaḍārī*,[60] Sharabi refers to how readers of the Arabic translation of neopatriarchy, including educated ones, found it 'difficult to understand' and suggested that a more accessible translation might be produced. Sharabi rejects the charge of the incomprehensibility of the text, which he ascribes to the occlusive intervention of Arab consciousness, which makes new ideas difficult to decipher. Patriarchal language and the thought structure to which they are related, Sharabi wants to tell us, condition the Arab mind to such an extent that makes it resistant to new and challenging ideas of the kind that he is offering. This is a damning statement of Arabic and Arab culture, but it serves to show the extent of Sharabi's belief in linguistic determinism in reading the cognitive role of Arabic.

The Arabic Language and the Arab Mind: Al-Jabiri as an Example

As a term, the 'Arab mind' occurs in discussions of the state of backwardness (*wāqi' al-takhalluf al-'arabī*) of Arab society in the Arab media. This term is linked to another, *al-'aqliyya al-'arabiyya* (Arab mentality), which is used disparagingly to refer to an ossified Arab mind and culture that are backward and resistant to change. The two terms must not, however, be confused with each other, not least because of the essentialist nature and overwhelmingly

56 al-Qaṣīmī, *al-'Arab ẓāhira ṣawtiyya*, p. 592.
57 Ibid. p. 592.
58 Ibid. p. 596.
59 Ibid. p. 596.
60 Sharābī, *al-Naqd al-ḥaḍārī li-wāqi' al-mujtama' al-'arabī al-mu'āṣir*.

negative connotations of the latter in Arabic discourse, although the former does not completely escape this essentialist connotation completely in common parlance in Arabic either. Al-Jabiri expresses this understanding of the term 'Arab mentality' by saying that it: 'refers to a static and innate mental state that moulds individual and collective understanding (*naẓra*) in the same way as biological inheritance moulds the behaviour of the two'.[61] In this section, we will use the first term only, which occurs in two studies that link the 'Arab mind' to the Arabic language in a way that qualifies including their content under the cognitive role of Arabic. The first is al-Jabiri's well-known work in the Arab world *Takwīn al-'aql al-'arabī* (*The Making/Make up of the Arab Mind*, 1998) and Patai's book *The Arab Mind* (1973). These two books use the term 'Arab mind' in different ways. I will therefore examine this term as it is applied in each case, linking each application to the cognitive role of Arabic.

Al-Jabiri links the Arab mind to thought, treating the former as the instrument that produces the latter. He makes this distinction by using the two terms *adāt* (instrument, tool) and *muḥtawā* or *maḍmūn* (content) to refer to mind and thought, respectively. Both mind and thought are moulded by their intellectual and social context in a way that configures reality in a culture-bound manner. The incorporation of context has two consequences. On the one hand, it recognises that different cultural frameworks mould the relation between mind, thought and reality differently. Al-Jabiri exemplifies this by considering how this relationship is marked, in what he calls the Greek and Arabic sentences.[62] The Arabic sentence, he tells us, is declarative; by contrast, the Greek sentence is evaluative. In this regard, the Arabic sentence is linked to the normative perspective (*naẓra mi'yāriyya*)[63] of the Arab mind, which links meaning to the set of socially determined values to which the speaker subscribes. In this sense, the Arab mind may be described as inward-looking or subjective. In the other case, the Greek mind works in an analytical-cum-synthetic manner (*naẓra taḥlīliyya tarkībiyya*),[64] which directs the speaker's attention to the outside world and the objective features of the topic of conversation.[65] The fact that al-Jabiri does not provide concrete

[61] Muḥammad 'Ābid al-Jābirī, *Takwīn al-'aql al-'arabī* (Beirut: Markaz Dirāsāt al-Waḥda al-'Arabiyya, 1998), p. 26. The Arabic original reads as follows: '*ḥāla dhihniyya fiṭriyya wa-ṭabī'iyya wa-qārra taḥkum naẓrat al-fard wa-l-jamā'a kamā taḥkum al-'awāmil al-bayūlūjiyya al-mawrūtha sulūkahumā wa-taṣarrufātihimā*'.

[62] Muḥammad 'Ābid al-Jābirī, *al-Turāth wa-l-ḥadātha: Dirāsāt wa munāqashāt* (Beirut: Markaz Dirāsāt al-Waḥda al-'Arabiyya, 1991), p. 148. Al-Jabiri expresses this distinction as follows: '*inna al-amr yata'allaq fī al-jumla al-'arabiyya, ismiyya kānat aw fi'liyya, bi-iṣdār bayān, lā iṣdār ḥukm kamā huwa l-ḥāl fī al-jumla al-yūnāniyya wa fī al-lughāt al-āriyya bi ṣūra 'āmma*'.

[63] Al-Jābirī, *Takwīn al-'aql al-'arabī*, p. 32.

[64] Ibid. p. 32.

[65] Al-Jābirī (Ibid. p. 32) expresses this differences as follows: '*inna al-naẓra al-mi'yāriyya* [Arabic] *naẓra ikhtizāliyya, takhtaṣir al-shay' fī qīmatih, wa-bi-l-tāli fī al-ma'nā alladhī*

examples to support this comparison makes it difficult to know exactly what he means here. In this respect, his comparison continues the obscurantist tradition of Arab discussions of the cognitive role of the Arabic language. On the other hand, the recognition of context in understanding the relation between mind, thought and, ultimately, language and reality implies that this relationship changes when the context changes. The historicity of this relation counters the essentialist trend in reading the cognitive role of Arabic, examples of which were given above.

Al-Jabiri places language at the centre of the above relational complex; in the opening chapter of his study of the making or make-up of the Arab mind, he declares that he: 'started [his task] by approaching the elements that form, or help form, the specific character of the Arab mind through the language/vocabularies that the Arab lexica have preserved and that constitute the language of the pre-Islamic Arabs'.[66] Having said this, al-Jabiri asks the important question as to whether the Arab mind is still hemmed in by the pre-Islamic culture that helped form it and, thus, is still reflected in Arabic lexica. To answer this question, al-Jabiri defines context historically in a manner that frees it from the tyranny of chronology. Chronological time, he says, is different from 'cultural time' (*al-zaman al-thaqāfī*).[67] He expands this later by saying that: 'cultural time does not conform to natural, political or social time: it has its own criteria'.[68] He then declares, with little hesitation, that Arab cultural time has remained static since its early inception in pre-Islamic Arabic, in spite of all the 'movements' (*taḥarrukāt*), 'tremors' (*ihtizāzāt*) and 'convulsions' (*hazzāt*) to which it was exposed, the reason being that it depends on other cultures, rather than on internally generated shifts, to propel it forward from within (*ḥarakat i'timād lā ḥarakat naqla*).[69]

Al-Jabiri clearly believes that the division of Arab cultural time into successive periods, based on major political ruptures as the principle of classification, is not valid, since the tool (the Arab mind) used in each period is still the same, and, as a result, there is no significant variation in the resulting

yuḍfih 'alayh al-shakhṣ (wa-l-mujtam' wa-l-thaqāfa) ṣāḥib tilka al-naẓra. Ammā al-naẓra al-mawḍū'iyya [Greek] fa-hiya naẓra taḥlīliyya tarkībiyya: tuḥallil al-shay' ilā 'anāṣirih al-asāsiyya li-tu'īd binā'ah bi-shakl yubriz mā huwa jawhariyy fīh'.

66 The Arabic original reads as follows (Ibid. p. 33): *'la-qad inṭalaqnā fī talammus ba'ḍ al-'anāṣir allatī tushakkil aw tusāhim fī tashkīl, khuṣuṣiyyat 'al-'aql al-'arabī' min al-lugha allatī taḥtafiẓ lanā bihā al-ma'ājim, lughat 'arab al-jāhiliyya'.*

67 Ibid. p. 37.

68 The Arabic original reads as follows (Ibid. p. 39): *'inna al-zaman al-thaqāfī lā yakhḍa' li-maqāyīs al-waqt wa-l-tawqīt al-ṭabī'ī wa-l-siyāsī wa-l-ijtimā'ī, li-anna lahu maqāyīsuhu al-khāssa'.*

69 This is how al-Jābirī expresses this point (Ibid. p. 42): *'wa-akādu an uqarrir anna al-ḥaraka fī althaqāfa al-'arabiyya kānat wa-mā tazāl ḥarakat i'timād lā ḥarakat naqla wa-bi-l-tālī fa-zamanuhā mudda yaḥidduhā al-sukūn lā al-ḥaraka, wa hādhā 'alā al-raghm min jamī' al-taḥarrukāt wa-l-ihtizāzāt wa-l-hazzāt alllatī 'arafathā'.*

thought. This raises the question as to whether al-Jabiri is offering an essentialist interpretation of the Arab mind – something he previously seemed to reject, as I pointed out earlier. The answer is that he is not, in principle, doing so. Al-Jabiri does not rule out the possibility of norm-breaking change in the Arab mind, but, at the same time, he believes that such a change has not yet materialised. This justifies his assertion that little has changed in the Arab mind since pre-Islamic times, as was stated above. The question he faces at this stage in the argument is one of validation: what kind of support can he provide to back up this contention? It is at this point that language enters into the fray to provide the basis for the conclusion that the Arab mind has remained locked into its pre-Islamic past.

Al-Jabiri says that there are four reasons why Arabic can be considered the primary constituent in making up the Arab mind. First, the Arab sanctifies his language (*fa-l-'arabiyy yuḥibb laughatahu ilā darajat al-taqdīs*).[70] The Arab submits willingly to the authority that the language has over him, because it is an expression of his own authority as the only human being who can respond to the exquisite eloquence it can communicate. This, al-Jabiri tells us, is consistent with the image of the Arab as the 'eloquent animal' (*fa-l-'arabiyy hayawān faṣīḥ*),[71] putting him on a level above other human beings, which are assigned to the species of 'verbal / speaking animal' (*ḥayawān nāṭiq*). This view of eloquence as a criterion of classification is consistent with my interpretation of al-Jahiz's work in Chapter 2, in which *bayān* (eloquence) was established as a principle of classification. Second, since the Arabs' contribution to Islamic civilisation, which inherited the other civilisations that preceded it, revolved around the Arabic language and Islam and since Islam, through the text of the Qur'an, is rooted in Arabic (*fa-l-'arabiyya juz' min māhiyyatihi*),[72] it follows that Arabic constitutes the very substance of this civilisational contribution. Third, since the first of the Arabic sciences revolved around the collection of the language and the writing up of grammars for it, it is reasonable to assume that this activity provided a model for the development of other Islamic sciences, although reciprocity among these intellectual enterprises became a norm later. This again reflects the importance of Arabic in Arab life and culture. Finally, Arabic must have played a formative role in configuring the Arab mind, since it is in line with the view that attributes a role to all human languages in forming their speakers understanding of their universe. This reference to linguistic determinism and relativity is aligned with the preceding factors, not just to give them theoretical validity, but to show that, in this respect, Arabic is in line with other languages in the cognitive domain: Arabic is now conceptualised as a specific or culturally determined application of this universal principle. Al-Jabiri concludes this part of his argument

70 Ibid. p. 75.
71 Ibid. p. 75.
72 Ibid. p. 75.

by saying that: 'if philosophy was the miracle (*mu'jiza*) of the Greeks, the sciences of Arabic (*'ulūm al-'arabiyya*) were the miracle of the Arabs'.[73]

Playing on the root meaning of the term 'miracle' in Arabic, al-Jabiri tells us that the attempt to codify Arabic by the grammarians have made it 'incapable' (*'ājiza*)[74] of serving as an instrument of renewal and development in Arab life. Treating all permutations of Arabic lexical roots as Arabic words, be they real or virtual, in early treatments of the language has, according to al-Jabiri, made it not only a frozen medium of communication, but also an overly regulated one that lacks malleability and historicity (*lugha lā-tārīkhiyya*): 'it is a language that does not keep pace with the times nor does it evolve with them'.[75] Another reason why Arabic constrains the Arab mind to its ancient roots is the Bedouin nature of its lexicon. According to the Arabic grammatical tradition, the Arabic lexicon was collected from desert Arabs (*'a'rāb*), who had little contact with other nations, so as to avoid linguistic contamination. The primitive nature of the lives that these desert Arabs must have lived left its imprint on their language and thought, which were more engrossed with sensory experience than abstract thought. As a result, Arabic suffers from the double malaise of 'civilisational malnutrition' (*faqr ḥadārī*)[76] and 'Bedouin wealth' (*ghinā badawī*)[77] in the lexical domain, which, as I pointed out in Chapter 3, has caused some modern scholars to describe Arabic as a 'Bedouin language' (*lugha badawiyya*). These 'facts' – indeed, this is how they are presented to us – lead al-Jabiri to the conclusion that the: 'old Bedouins of Arabia are the real makers of the Arab world today': '[*inna*] *al-a'rābiyy huwa fi'lan ṣāni' 'al-'ālam al-'arabiyy'*.[78] The Arab mind now, as it has been in the past, is moulded by Arabic, just as it has been created by the grammarians of old.[79] This has led to the following syndrome of the Arab mind: evaluating what is new according to the old [norms]: *'al-ḥukm 'alā al-jadīd bimā yarāh al-qadīm'*.[80]

According to this web of ideas, the Arab cultural time is language-defined and rooted in an ancient past. Since Arabic is moulded in material terms by the desert ethos that affects Arab thought, the language is unable to serve as an instrument that can produce a genuine indigenous change in Arab reality. Influenced by Arabic, Arab thought cannot change the reality in which it is

73 Ibid. p. 75. This is the Arabic original (Ibid. p. 80): *'idhā kānat al-falsafa hiya 'mu'jizat' al-yūnān fa-inna'ulūm al-'arabiyya hiya 'mu'jizat' al-'arab'*.

74 Ibid. p. 82.

75 This is the Arabic original (Ibid. p. 83): *'innahā lā tatajaddad bi-tajaddud al-aḥwāl wa-lā tataṭawwar bi-tataṭuwwur al-'uṣūr'*.

76 Ibid. p. 87.

77 Ibid. p. 88.

78 Ibid. p. 88.

79 Al-Jābirī (Ibid. p. 89) expresses this conclusion as follows: *'fa-inna ṣinā'at al-lughawiyyīn wa-l-nuḥā qad qawlabat bi-dawrihā al-'aql al-'arabī alladhī yumāris fa'āliyyatahu fi hādhhi al-lugha wa-bi-wāsiṭatihā'*.

80 Ibid. p. 93.

embedded or upon which it seeks to act. Here, language and thought do no more than interpret the present by reference to the past. The failure of the Arabs to modernise in modern times is now projected as the result of a language-based cognitive deficit. Only when the Arabs can override the imperatives of this deficit will they be able to configure reality as it is and modernise accordingly.[81] Until then, their interpretations of reality will remain rooted in a 'cultural time', in which their Bedouin language plays a defining role.[82]

Al-Jabiri arrives at these far-reaching conclusions through a series of arguments that are, in some parts, based on aspects of the Arabic grammatical tradition. The importance of Arabic in Arab life and the role of the desert Arabs as language informants in setting up grammatical theory are both established aspects of this tradition. The idea that language, thought and reality are interconnected is another building block in al-Jabiri's argument. Al-Jabiri's style is sober and controlled when compared with the rampant barrage of prose offered by al-Qasimi or the terse and clipped presentation of the same relationship that we find in Sharabi's work. However, al-Jabiri does not overcome the obscurantism of both Sharabi and al-Qasimi. His concept of an invariant Arab 'cultural time', which is crucial to his arguments, is presented with insufficient proof. The idea that the Arab mind, based on the Arabic language, is still using the same tools to interpret reality that have been utilised since pre-Islamic times is a major proposition in need of in-depth theoretical and empirical validation to make it work. This, al-Jabiri does not provide. His approach and, therefore, his findings are more suggestive than fully grounded in empirical research. However, unlike al-Qasimi and Sharabi, al-Jabiri recognises the importance of keeping ideology and the kind of epistemological project in which he is engaged separate from each other. This gives his work a feeling of greater integrity and detachment, as far as the role of Arabic in influencing thought and interpreting reality is concerned. Al-Qasimi comes across as an angry writer, who is lashing out at anything and everything in Arab life and culture, including the cognitive

81 A similar conclusion is arrived at by Patai when he says: 'Before Arabic can become a medium adequate for the requirements of modern life, including those of scholarly and scientific discourse, it will have to undergo [some developments]. It will have to become more factual, rid itself of its traditional rhetoricism, its exaggeration and over assertion, and transform its perfect and imperfect verb forms into semantic equivalents of the past and future tenses respectively of Standard Average European'. See Raphael Patai, *The Arab Mind* (New York, NY: Charles Scribner's Son, 1973), p. 72. I will comment on this in the following section.

82 Patai (Ibid. p. 75) refers to the continuity between legal rulings in Islam and Bedouin precedents, as well as the reliance of the Arabic grammarians on Bedouin usage in constructing Arabic grammar. These two facts seem to underlie the conclusion (p. 74) of the a-historicity of the timeless desert in defining a heroic age for the modern Arabs: 'While the desert and its Bedouins are very far removed from the great majority of the Arabs, in ideology and scale of values both still loom large; in fact, they still hold the undisputed first place'.

role of language. Sharabi's critical attitude of much of Arab culture, including the role of language, is given to us as though it was a matter-of-fact issue that needs little validation. Al-Jabiri recognises that the discussion of the cognitive role of Arabic needs careful argumentation. Although he does not completely succeed in providing this, there is no doubt that he provides one of the best treatments of this topic that I know of by an Arab author. In principle, al-Jabiri conceives of the cognitive role of Arabic from a linguistic relativity perspective. In practice, he articulates this role in terms of linguistic determinism.

The Arabic Language and the Arab Mind: Patai as an Example

Patai's concept of the 'Arab mind' differs considerably from al-Jabiri's, although both believe in the role of language in mediating thought and reality. Patai deals with this concept in his book *The Arab Mind*, which is written against the background of the pan-Arab nationalism that held sway in Arab political and cultural life up to the 1970s of the twentieth century. Arabic, according to Patai, is the only criterion capable of defining who an Arab is.[83] This places Arabic in a privileged position, in terms of the mediat-

[83] The following quotation from Patai explains the basis of this conclusion (Ibid. p. 13): 'Numerous scholars, both Arab and Western, have struggled to answer the question, who is an Arab? The answers usually include one or more of the following criteria: Arabs are those who speak Arabic, are brought up in Arab culture, live in an Arab country, believe in Muhammad's teachings, cherish the memory of the Arab Empire, are members of any of the Arab nations. A moment's reflection will suffice to show that of all these criteria, only the linguistic one holds good for all Arabs and almost for nobody else but Arabs. Persons whose mother tongue is Arabic may be brought up in a non-Arab culture . . . and still consider themselves Arabs and be so considered by others. They may live in a non-Arab country – witness the many Arabs who live in France, the United States, Latin America, and elsewhere – and still be Arabs. They may not believe in Muhammad – the hundreds of thousands of Christian Arabs do not – and yet are as intensely Arab in their feelings and national orientations as any Muslim Arab. Many Arabs do not "cherish" in particular the memory of the Arab Empire because they are communists, or for any of several other reasons. And, finally, there are numerous Arabs who emigrated to other countries, acquired citizenship there, and have become members of other nations, without thereby losing their Arab identity'. This position is amplified later, as follows (Ibid. pp. 41–2): 'When the inhabitants of two or more countries speak the same language, the common tongue constitutes a bond among them, affinity and a sympathy that transcends diverse political boundaries ... However, the sense of affinity created by a common language is invariably limited. It does not blur national considerations and interests, which remain primary in the consciousness of each nation . . . Not so with Arabic among the Arabs. In the Arab countries, there is at present a pervading consciousness of being one nation, the Arab nation, irrespective of the number of political units into which the nation is broken up. This does not mean, of course, that there are no differences, or even enmities and

ing role that it plays between thought and reality. However, the move from the socio-politically constructed role of Arabic as a marker of the nation to its cognitive role is methodologically problematic. This move constitutes an abrupt jump between two ontological realms. There is no doubt that the social and the cognitive interact with each other in matters of language, but the connection between them is not seamless: it requires the intervention of some bridging notions to make the arguments from the socio-political realm appear relevant to the cognitive one.

Patai is aware of the difficulty of defining the 'Arab mind'. However, he considers this mind as an abstraction by generalisation, based on the fact that the speakers of Arabic exhibit strong, common personality factors based on sharing a common sociocultural environment. These factors constitute what Patai calls 'modal personality', which he equates with national character in its capacity as the: '*sum total of the motives, traits, beliefs and values shared by the plurality in a national population*'.[84] Patai points out that in: 'contemporary large-scale industrial societies . . . there may be several modal personality structures'.[85] This is not the case with the Arabs:

> If the national population . . . is fairly homogeneous as far as its ethnic composition is concerned, one will find the modal personalities of any two or more sample groups will be sufficiently similar to warrant extrapolation from them to the character of the national population at large.[86]

He then adds that: 'as a preliminary tentative estimate . . . one can state that the Muslim Arabs, who form the overwhelming majority of the population in the Arab world, are definitely closer to this homogeneous type of cultural and personality configuration than to the disparate variety'[87] found in large-scale industrialised societies. In spite of the note of caution that Patai strikes through the expression 'tentative estimate', his study of the 'Arab mind' proceeds with little hesitation, in spite of some of the caveats he enters in his work.

In several places in his book, Patai highlights the decisive influence of language on thought in the Arab world. He captures this influence in the

fiery denunciations, among Arab states. But even in the midst of fratricidal wars, the feeling persists that, however painful the conflict, it is merely a temporary disagreement which sooner or later will be settled and which, even while it lasts, in no way infringes upon the principle of Arab brotherhood and the ideal of all-Arab national unity. There can be no doubt that the Arabic language is the most potent factor in both the creation and maintenance of this overriding myth of Arab nation, Arab unity, Arab brotherhood'.

84 Ibid. p. 18 (emphasis in the original).

85 Ibid. p. 19.

86 Ibid. p. 19.

87 Ibid. p. 19.

title of the chapter that he dedicates to this topic, picturing the Arabs to be 'Under the Spell of Language'. The 'spell' metaphor is correlated to the 'lure of Arabic'[88] as a language that works its magic on its speakers, who view it with veneration for its beauty, logicality, precision and mystique; Patai designates this feature of the Arab modal personality as 'rhetoricism'.[89] The 'lure' and 'spell' that the language works on its speakers are connected to what Patai considers as: 'the exceptional suitability [of the language] to rhetoric and hyperbole'.[90] To support this description of Arabic, Patai quotes a number of writers of Arab background – all of whom are of Lebanese origin – as if to say that their pronouncements constitute internal evidence, rather than the imposition of an outsider. Edward Attiyah's views on this matter will suffice as an illustration; he is quoted as saying that: 'it is characteristic of the Arab mind to be swayed more by words than by ideas, and more by ideas than by facts'.[91] Patai further links his views on rhetoricism and hyperbole to the Arabic word for rhetoric – *balāgha* – whose root meaning conveys the idea of exaggeration, in addition to those of eloquence, achievement and male maturity. However, Patai warns us that, although to the Arab mind 'eloquence is related to exaggeration', the latter (exaggeration) is 'not meant to be taken literally',[92] but encoded as a matter of effect.

Having linked Arabic to exaggeration, Patai then links it to over-assertion and over-emphasis (*tawkīd*).[93] He tells us that:

> It is almost inevitable that people who are used to expressing their thoughts in [complex] ready-made phraseology, to which must be added the frequent use of innumerable proverbs and sayings, *should be led* by their language into exaggeration and over-assertion.[94]

[88] Ibid. p. 44.
[89] Ibid. p. 48.
[90] Ibid. p. 48.
[91] Ibid. p. 48.
[92] Ibid. p. 49.
[93] Exaggeration is also dealt with in Shouby, which provides the following devices for expressing it in Arabic: 'The is the common *n*, ending words that are meant to be emphasised [emphatic *nūn*]; there is also the doubling of the sounds of some consonants to create the desirable stronger effect [gemination]; there are the frequent words *inna* [lit. verily] and *qad* [lit. indeed], used to emphasise a large number of sentences; and there are such forms of assertion as the repetition of pronouns and certain other words to get across their meanings or significance. Besides these grammatical types of over-assertion are the numerous stylistic and rhetorical devices to achieve even further exaggeration. Fantastic metaphors and similes are used in abundance, and long arrays of adjectives to modify the same word are quite frequent'. See E. Shouby, 'The influence of the Arabic language on the psychology of the Arabs', *The Middle East Journal* (1951), 5: 298–9.
[94] Patai, *The Arab Mind*, p. 50 (emphasis added).

Patai establishes this exaggeration and over-emphasis through comparison with English. Comparing the English expression 'speedy recovery' with the Arabic equivalent *'mā 'alāk illā al-'āfye in shā' Allāh'* (lit. May there be upon you nothing but health, if Allah wills) or 'Thank you!' in English with the equivalent Arabic expression *'Allāh yukaththir khyrak'* (lit. May Allah increase your well-being), he points to the florid Arabic style in these expressions, which, to the English ear, sounds exaggerated and overemphatic, but, to the Arab ear, sounds 'quite ordinary'.[95] I will comment on the use of translation in this and other contexts later. This tendency for exaggeration is also said to characterise Arabic political speeches and discussions, which, as we shall see later, are said to be prone to verbal excess, because, we are told, words can replace action in the Arab mind. The Arab is acculturated to these practises and uses them in a reflexive fashion, without too much reflection. It is in this sense that the lure of Arabic puts the Arab under the spell of his language, producing what the late Princeton Lebanese Professor Philip Hitti calls: 'lawful magic'.[96] Patai[97] expresses this point by saying that the Arabs' predilection for exaggeration and over-emphasis is anchored in the Arabic language itself or that it (exaggeration and over-emphasis) is one of the: 'numerous inducements . . . that [Arabic] offers to the Arab mind'.[98] The hold that these stylistic tropes have on the Arab mind is said to be exhibited in the inability of Arab bilinguals to rid themselves of exaggeration: 'even when writing in a European tongue'.[99] This predilection to exaggeration and over-emphasis is linked by Patai to the importance of 'face' in Arab culture. This is particularly relevant in the political arena, where modern Arab leaders consistently turn defeats into victories to save face.[100]

According to Patai, the use of exaggeration and over-emphasis leads to communication breakdowns between Arabs and non-Arabs.[101] Thus, an

95 Ibid. p. 50.

96 Ibid. p. 49. Bengio uses the following generic quotation from Ernst Cassirer, *Language and Myth* (New York, NY: Dover Publications, 1946), to talk about this kind of magic in Arabic: 'Language draws a magic circle around a people from which there is no escape save by stepping out of it into another' (p. 9). See Ofra Bengio, *Saddam's Word: Political Discourse in Iraq* (New York and Oxford: Oxford University Press, 1998), p. 4.

97 Patai, *The Arab Mind*, p. 52.

98 Ibid. p. 53.

99 Ibid. p. 55.

100 See Patai (Ibid. pp. 101–6) for a discussion of face and how it links to exaggeration in the political field. Another interesting study of face in a comparative context is Katriel, in which she deals with two styles of speaking in Israel involving young Israeli-born Jews and Palestinians: *dugri* speech (pp. 9–33) and *musāyara*, respectively (pp. 111–15). See Tamar Katriel, *Talking Straight: Dugri Speech in Israeli Sabra Culture* (Cambridge: Cambridge University Press, 1986).

101 Shouby ('The influence of the Arabic language on the psychology of the Arabs', p. 298) links this breakdown in communication between Arabs and non-Arabs

unembellished statement of truth or assent in another language sounds neutral and non-committal to the Arab ear. To a non-Arab ear, the embellished statements of an Arab sound exaggerated, when, in fact, they are not intended to be so in their Arab context.[102] Patai cites a study by Prothro (1955) to support this conclusion. In his study of 60 Arabic-English bilingual students from the American University of Beirut, Prothro compared their reactions to 46 general statements on a well-known test instrument at the time – the Grice-Remmers generalised attitude scale – in terms of favourableness and unfavourableness using an 11-point scale. In view of the empirical nature of this study, I will quote Prothro's conclusions below:

> It seems justified to infer from our results that Arab students . . . are more prone to over-assertion than American students, that American students are more given to understatement than are Arab students. There are cognitive differences between the two groups of students with respect to the manner in which they respond to written messages. These differences would seem to be of considerable importance to anyone interested in written communication between Arabs and Americans. Persons interested in fostering information campaigns to present the Arab point of view to Americans should keep in mind that statements which seem to Arabs to be mere statements of fact will seem to Americans to be extreme or even violent assertions. Statements which Arabs view as showing firmness and strength on a negative or positive issue may sound to Americans as exaggerated. On the other hand, those persons interested in presenting the American point of view to literate Arabs should note that a statement which seems to be a firm assertion to the Americans may sound weak and even doubtful to the Arabs who read it.[103]

to the 'emotivity and impulsiveness' that Arabic imprints on the minds of its speakers, even when they speak other languages: 'Even when he speaks a foreign language, an Arab shows signs of emotivity and impulsiveness of which he may not even be aware. This naturally creates a great deal of misunderstanding. A foreigner may think an Arab from his manner of speaking excited, or angry, or affectionate when in fact he is not. One the other hand, an Arab may think a foreigner calm and serene when he is already mildly upset or annoyed'.

102 Shouby (Ibid. p. 300) expresses this point as follows: 'If an Arab says exactly what he means without the expected exaggeration, other Arabs may still think that he means the opposite. This fact leads to misunderstanding on the part of non-Arabs who do not realise that the Arab speaker is merely following a linguistic tradition . . . We [also] have the corollary of the [preceding point]: the failure of the Arabs to realise that others mean exactly what they say if it is put in a simple, unelaborated manner; even repetition may not be enough for an Arab to realise that the communication cannot perhaps mean the opposite of what the speaker intends'.

103 Terry Prothro, 'Arab-American differences in the judgment of written messages', *The Journal of Social Psychology* (1955), 42: 9–10.

The above conclusion seems to offer empirical support to Patai's views on exaggeration and over-emphasis as features of the Arab mind. However, for Prothro, his conclusions are more nuanced, as is obvious from his answer to the following question: 'What do our results tell us about modal personality differences between members of the two cultures?'[104] In response, he says: 'The answer to this question is: very little'.[105] Prothro explains this by saying that:

> Studies of individual differences within a culture cannot be generalised to apply to differences in modal personality between cultures, contradicting the very basis upon which Patai's study is based. At best such studies can suggest hypothesis for investigation. From this study it would seem worthwhile to examine the hypothesis that students in the Arab world are either more emotional than those in America, or that they are more emotional with respect to judgements about peoples.[106]

Clearly, Prothro is aware of the limitations of his study, empirical though it was, and, although he later says that the hypothesis about over-assertion seemed to be confirmed in his study, he is careful to contextualise this by saying that this is only the case: 'when compared with [results for American students]', which are judged to be neutral (in other words, free from over-assertion). I will examine the use of this comparative method, alongside the use of translation below.

Another claim about the Arab mind in the language domain is the substitution of 'words for action'.[107] According to Patai, this feature is linked to child-rearing practices in Arab society in two ways. The first concerns breastfeeding:

> A connection may exist between the custom of the nursing mother yielding her breast to her son at his verbal demand and the expectation, formed and reinforced in the mind of the child as a result of this experience, that whenever he utters emphatic verbal demand it would unfailingly be fulfilled, as well as with the adult Arab's proclivity for emphatically uttering demands and intentions without following them with actions.[108]

The second concerns the mother's practice of issuing verbal threats to her children, especially sons, which are not followed by action in child-rearing practices. Patai explains this as follows:

104 Ibid. p. 10.
105 Ibid. p. 10.
106 Ibid. p. 10.
107 Patai, *The Arab Mind*, p. 59.
108 Ibid. p. 59. For a fuller explanation of this point, see pp. 31–2.

> Conditioned by the childhood experiences of frequent threats often not carried out, the adult Arab makes statements which express threats, demands, or intentions which he does not intend to carry out but which, once uttered, relax emotional tension, give psychological relief and at the same time reduce the pressure to engage in any act aimed at realising the verbal goal.[109]

Patai later tells us that it is in: 'this sense that in the Arab mentality [not mind] *words often can and do* serve as substitutes for acts'.[110] Patai is careful not to say that the Arabs confuse words with their referents in the objective world. However, he continues to apply the comparative method, which, in this case, leads him to make even bolder generalisations of a dichotomous kind:

> In a pragmatically oriented community, the modal personality is strongly influenced by reality and his verbal expression even more so. At the other end of the scale we find societies where reality does not exercise a high degree of influence on thinking and speech. Western peoples stand at one end of the scale, the Arabs near the other end. In the Arab world, thought and verbal expression can be relatively uncorrelated with what the circumstances actually allow.[111]

According to this view, language influences thought, but the two fail to impact upon reality, although, at this stage in the argument, Patai seems to blame reality for failing to penetrate language and thought sufficiently. Put differently, under this interpretation, language and thought are impervious to reality. It is not that they do not impact it, but that they fail to interpret it correctly.

Patai dwells on another feature of the cognitive role of Arabic: the indeterminate or vague interpretation of time, whose behavioural consequences, we are told, include a lack of punctuality and resistance to the: 'introduction

[109] Ibid. p. 60.

[110] Ibid. p. 64 (emphasis added).

[111] Ibid. p. 163. Patai refers (Ibid. p. 164) to the: 'insufficiently strong hold that factual realities have on the Arab psyche'. He explains this as follows (Ibid. pp. 164–5): 'A psyche that has well internalised reality factors does not have to indulge in emotional outbursts which bear no relationship to reality, outbursts qualitatively akin to the "impotent rage" expressed by infantile temper tantrums. It will instead try to deal with the inevitable frustrations of life by rational and purposive reactions. Similarly, the gap between thought and speech, on the other hand, and action, on the other, can be seen as the result of the failure of reality to penetrate sufficiently. A person who entertains thoughts and makes utterances which cannot be translated into action indulges in a flight into a fantasy world for the sake of its emotional satisfaction. While this satisfaction is not as intense as that obtained from emotional outbursts, it is of longer duration and fulfils a basically similar function: both obliterate the objectionable world of reality, and allow the individual to live, for a shorter or longer spell, in a world that is the creation of his wishes'.

of rigorous time schedules [that are] demanded by modernisation'.[112] Patai ascribes this 'nonchalant' attitude to time to the 'cavalier' way in which the Arabic verb system treats time.[113] In pursuing this point, Patai compares the Arabic and English verb systems, which are organised around the grammatical categories of aspect and tense, respectively. According to this distinction, the English tenses correlate with the neat division of chronological time into past, present and future. The case in Arabic is different. For example, in Arabic: 'the imperfect form can stand for present, future, and past; the perfect can also mean pluperfect, future and . . . past participle'.[114] Patai gives other examples of this 'cavalier' marking of time in Arabic to support the conclusion that: 'for people speaking a language in which the verb [is aspectually organised] time cannot have the same definite, ordered and sequential connotation that it has for people speaking a strictly time-structured language'.[115] Patai also adds that, owing to this, Arabic cannot: 'easily lend itself to verbal distinction between two different past time periods',[116] as a result, the past appears to the Arabs to be: 'one huge undifferentiated entity . . . [that] merges into the present and continues into the future'.[117]

Referring to the cognitive role of language, Patai paints a sinister picture of the Arab modal personality – the Arab mind. In spite of its length, I will give the following rendition of this picture, offered in the conclusion of Patai's study, to convey the full flavour of his views:

> While Arab conduct is of the conforming type, requiring the individual to behave in a manner approved by his social environment, Arab culture provides a vent through which suppressed emotions can, at least occasionally, break into the open [no doubt owing to exaggeration, over-emphasis and the substitution of words for action]. This culturally approved outlet is the flare up of temper, flashes of anger, aggression and violence, which are condoned by society and readily forgiven. This type of behaviour tends to veer from one extreme to the other, being polarised between the two contrasting syndromes of self-control and wild outbursts of aggressivity. While these seizures last, Arab temperament goes on a rampage and hostility can be easily become irrational. Once they pass, sincere contrition follows, accompanied by bafflement and a total lack of comprehension of what one has done and how one could have done it.
>
> It would appear that there is some connections between this disjointed type of behaviour and the relative lack of correlation among the three functional planes of human existence: thoughts, words and action. Arab thought processes are relatively autonomous, that is, more independent of reality, than the thought

[112] Ibid. p. 66.
[113] Ibid. p. 66.
[114] Ibid. p. 67.
[115] Ibid. p. 68.
[116] Ibid. p. 70.
[117] Ibid. p. 70.

> processes of the typical Western man. Nor is the verbal formulation influenced by reality to the degree to which it is in the West. Arab thought tends more to move on an ideal level, divorced from the Procrustean bed of reality. Arab speech likewise tends to express ideal thoughts, and to represent that which is desired or hoped for as if it were an actual fact in evidence, rather than cleave to the limitations of the real. There is thus among Arabs a relatively [why relatively? This should read 'massively' if we follow Patai's logic] greater discrepancy between thought and speech on the one hand and action of the other. In action, one is hemmed in by reality; thought and words, however, manage to retain a relative independence from reality.[118]

The above quotation presents a damning picture of the Arab modal personality or the Arab mind. It is, however, necessary to say here that the content of the above extract borders on cultural racism. To test this, I invite the reader to replace the word 'Arab' by the word 'Jewish' and to test the impact of this substitution on their reaction to the extract. There is no doubt that this substitution would immediately reveal the cultural racism that this extract, based on earlier arguments in the book, articulates. Anti-Jewish racism or anti-Semitism is the litmus test of all racisms, and it is legitimate to use it to probe into other forms of cultural racism. By turning the above extract into a text about Jews and Jewish culture, we can clearly decipher the deeply racist treatise that Patai presents to us. Linguistic racism is a well-known phenomenon in the history of modern linguistics. It was used in the nineteenth century as an aid to European colonialism. Renan's well-known pronouncements about the Semitic mind were based on his pseudo-scientific analysis of the Semitic languages and used for political advantage in the prosecution of colonialism. Patai's views of the Arab modal personality – the Arab mind – is little different, in spite of the different context, from Renan's. The cognitive role of language has been used in different contexts as a portal through which cultural racism can be expressed. Its application here is no exception.

Patai seems to start from aspects of Arab behaviour, which are then assumed to be the result of the influence of language on thought, and, of these two, on how reality is configured and navigated (or not) through action. This is in line with the behaviour-centred approach to the cognitive role of language mentioned above. For example, the lack of punctuality in Arab society or the presumed influence of the past on the present – as if the two merge with each other – are considered to be the result of the aspectual morphology of Arabic. The inability to modernise in Arab society is connected with the substitution of words for action. Breakdowns in communication with non-Arabs are considered to be the result of the proclivity and predilection of the Arabs for exaggeration and over-emphasis. The influence of the language on thought is not restricted to the structural features of Arabic, mainly its morphology and syntax, but to stylistic practices, which Patai seems to put on a

[118] Ibid. pp. 310–11.

par with linguistic structure in discussing the cognitive role of Arabic. Style here seems to be part of the language, rather than the creation of writers who mould the language to suit their aims and aesthetic preferences across genres and time periods.

Patai uses the comparative method to press his arguments. He constantly compares the Arabic language, thought and culture to its Western counterparts, mainly English. We have seen examples of this earlier. In some cases, the two sides of the comparison are presented as though they were parts of an irreconcilable dichotomy and as if they exhibited little or no significant internal variation, particularly on the Arab side. The reference to homogeneity in establishing the Arab modal personality, to which reference was made above, is an example of this tendency. The reference to the '*typical* Western man'[119] in talking about the relative autonomy of Arab thought processes is another example of this tendency. The concept of a 'Standard Average European' language[120] is an abstraction, even fiction, which Patai resorts to for comparative purposes. Reification is an operative feature of all these comparisons. In addition, whenever these comparisons are made, one gets the impression that Western languages, thought and culture are the unmarked category, in terms of which the Arabic language, thought and culture are to be assessed as the marked category.

Exaggeration in Arabic is exaggeration in categorial terms, because it looks and feels like exaggeration, when compared with English or other Western languages. Since, we are told: 'the Arabic language has no *literal equivalent* to the English word "child"',[121] the concept of childhood is said not to exist in Arabic. Patai explains this further, as follows:

> Since there are no 'children' in the Arabic language but only 'sons' and 'daughters', there are no 'children' in the Arab consciousness either, but only either 'sons' or 'daughters'. And, accordingly, there are no child rearing practices in the Arab world, but only 'boy' rearing practices on the one hand, and 'girl' rearing practices on the other.[122]

Here we have an example of how the English language, comparatively speaking, is used as the yardstick, in terms of which Arabic is judged, as well as how this judgement is extended to apply to Arab 'consciousness' and culture. At no point, however, does Patai interrogate the validity of this comparative approach, which privileges Western languages (mainly English in his book) and cultures over Arabic. Arabic is found wanting, because it does not behave like English or does not have 'literal equivalents' to English. The Arabic word *raḍīʿ* does convey the gender-undifferentiated sense of the

119 Ibid. p. 311 (emphasis added).
120 Ibid. p. 72.
121 Ibid. p. 27 (emphasis added).
122 Ibid. p. 28.

word 'child' in English. Patai does not mention this word as an argument against his comparison in arguing for the non-existence of childhood (*ṭufūla*; a perfectly acceptable abstract noun in Arabic); 'literalness' here refers to the marking of the meanings of morphological constituents of a word in a language. In addition to presenting a reductive, even defective, view of how language is processed in ordinary communication, this interpretation of the anatomy of meaning ignores the global way in which meanings are processed, as I will discuss below. Hans Wehr's well-known *A Dictionary of Modern Arabic* glosses the word *raḍī'* as 'child' and 'baby'. Although the following is not strictly speaking relevant here, one may wish to argue that Arabic provides one of the best un-gendered definitions of 'child' and 'childhood' that a language can offer (as parents the world over may agree). According to *A Dictionary of Modern Arabic*, the root (*ṭ-f-l*) meaning of the words for child and childhood in Arabic covers the following senses: 'to intrude, obtrude, impose oneself; to sponge . . ., live at other people's expense; to arrive uninvited or at an inconvenient time, disturb, intrude; to be obtrusive'. Some may use this lexical information wrongly, in my view, to argue the opposite point to Patai's, pointing to the ingenious way in which Arabic captures and describes reality.

While it is legitimate to use 'extrapolation'[123] in moving from the particular to the general when studying the cognitive role of language, it is, however, important, when doing so, to rely on a sufficiently robust basis, so as to ensure that the generalisations or abstractions that we extrapolate can enjoy some validity. This is clearly not the case in Patai. Saying that Arabic culture lacks a concept of childhood on the basis of one comparative example that privileges English over Arabic – dubious though this example is – is an example that supports the above criticism. Treating style – in the case of so-called exaggeration and over-emphasis – as though it was a structural property of Arabic, rather than a matter of personal choice that can change to suit the demands that a genre makes or suit the changes in aesthetic sensibility in a literate culture over time, is not consistent with established understandings of how language works. This understanding of style leads to statements that endow Arabic with properties that do not accrue to other languages – for example, that it is characterised by an: 'exceptional suitability to rhetoric and hyperbole'.[124] How this is the case, we are not told. People may be drawn to 'rhetoric and hyperbole', but this is not something that can be said of languages, as though this was an unproblematic statement to make. In matters of style, *a language does not do, rather, the users of a language do things with it.*

The view that the past appears to the Arabs to be 'one huge undifferentiated entity . . . [that] merges into the present and continues into the future'[125] is offered by Patai on the basis of a few comparative examples of aspect and

[123] Ibid. p. 19.
[124] Ibid. p. 42.
[125] Ibid. p. 70.

tense in Arabic and English, respectively. A statement of this kind requires extensive validation before it can be tendered in academic discourse. The same applies to the conclusion about punctuality, which was mentioned above. The fact that no language can exhibit a pure tense or aspect system to mark time is an established fact in modern linguistic theory.[126] Awareness of time in Arabic is, in fact, marked in the use of the terms *māḍī*, *ḥāḍir* and *mutsaqbal* in Arabic grammar to designate the past, present and future respectively, terms which every Arab child reiteratively learns at school at different stages in their progression in the educational system. While punctuality may be an issue in Arab societies, it is perhaps more productive to look to other socio-economic factors to explain it, instead of ascribing it exclusively to the influence of language on thought and, transitively, the interpretation of reality. A language-based explanation of the lack of punctuality, what Patai calls a 'nonchalant' attitude to time, would preclude improvements in punctuality levels in Arab society. Although I have no figures to prove it, there is no doubt that socio-economic changes affecting work practices during the past five decades (since the publication of Patai's book) in Arab society have led to improvements in punctuality levels, which, if true, suggests that Arabs are able to override the limitations of the aspectual morphology of their language.

The claim that the Arabs substitute words for action is equally problematic. This claim creates a disjunction between language and thought, on the one hand, and action and reality, on the other, in a way which runs against the cognitive role of language – a role that Patai invokes several times in his book.[127] Before a claim such as this can be made, it is important to establish whether speech itself can be a form of action. It is a principle of Arabic grammatical theory that speaking is action (*al-kalāmu fi'lun min af'āl al-mutakallim*). This principle provides a view of language that posits action both in and outside the verbal domain. It would also be important to establish whether utterances that do not end in action were, in fact, intended as expressions of the intent to act. An appeal to the pragmatics of the situation, rather than a reading of the literal meaning of an utterance, can sometimes help to decipher whether verbal or non-verbal action is intended. Speech-act theory, which I tangentially invoked in Chapter 3, can offer us clues in this regard.

Let me now turn to the use of literal translation by Patai. I have provided some examples above as to why this is a problematic method in drawing particular conclusions regarding the cognitive role of Arabic. Reflecting on this issue in ethnolinguistic research, Lenneberg reminds us that it: 'makes no sense to equate the global meaning of an utterance with the sequence of abstracted, general meanings of the morphemes that occur in that

[126] See Bernard Comrie, *Aspect: An Introduction to the Study of Verbal Aspect and Related Problems* (Cambridge: Cambridge University Press, 1976), pp. 78–82.

[127] Patai, *The Arab Mind*, pp. 69–70.

utterance'.[128] The constituent morphemes of an utterance can give us the grammatical meaning of that utterance, but are no blueprints as to how the utterance is, in fact, understood by native speakers. It is therefore a fallacy to think that native speakers do what the grammarian does in recovering the grammatical meaning of an utterance through segmental analysis. Patai's comments about 'childhood' in Arabic do not consider this mismatch between the parsing of the grammarian and language processing by native speakers. Applying the same point, it is unlikely that the morphological parsing of 'speedy recovery' (below) maps onto the way in which the native speaker processes this expression. Based on the *Shorter Oxford Dictionary*, the literal meaning of the phrase 'speedy recovery' may be segmented as follows:

> *speed*, 'success, superiority, good fortune'; -y, an adjectival morpheme which denotes quality; *re-*, a morpheme which denotes repetition of what the stem denotes; *cover*, 'to overlay, over spread with something so as to hide or protect'; *-y*, a nominalising morpheme which denotes a state.

The same applies to extracting the meaning of an utterance in an additive fashion, which aggregates the meanings of its segmental parts. A simple example will suffice to show why this is a mistaken view of computing meaning. The two utterances 'John hit Paul' and 'Paul hit John' give different meanings, in spite of the fact that they share the same words. A lexically additive approach to meaning ignores the semantic contribution of the syntactic relations that hold in these utterances and therefore fails to account for the differences in meaning between them. Patai's explanation of the Arabic expression '*mā 'alāk illā al-'āfye in shā' Allāh*' as, literally: 'May there be upon you nothing but health, if Allah wills',[129] is an example of this literal and additive approach to establishing the meaning of an utterance. The problem is compounded by the fact that this utterance is, in fact, a fossilised expression, whose meaning cannot be recovered from its constituent parts. The same is true of the fossilised expression '*Awḥashtena*', which Patai, using literal translation, tells us that it means: 'you made us desolate'.[130] The global meaning of this in Arabic is the more prosaic: 'We missed you!', which, I believe, is how most Arab speakers would globally understand it. But such a translation into English would not offer the validation that Patai seems to be looking for to support his exaggeration thesis. The meanings of fossilised expressions, like those of dead or frequent metaphors, cannot be computed additively from the sum total of their lexical parts. Lenneberg is aware of this when he states that: 'the literal meaning of many metaphors, especially the most frequent ones, never penetrates consciousness'.[131] Steinberg offers

128 Eric H. Lenneberg, 'Cognition in ethnolinguistics', *Language* (1953), 29: 465.
129 Patai, *The Arab Mind*, p. 50.
130 Ibid. p. 50.
131 Lenneberg, 'Cognition in ethnolinguistics', pp. 465–6.

a similar assessment when he says that speakers of a language: 'can believe something quite different from what their language literally specifies'.[132] The English expression 'kick the bucket' does not mean that English speakers believe that: 'kicking the bucket is what death is all about'.[133]

This same procedure of resorting to literal translation in discussing the cognitive role of Arabic is applied by Sharabi, who tells us:

> In political life Arabic is a most effective instrument of influence and persuasion. When translated into another tongue, however, it loses much of its spell [witness the use of the term *spell* here too]. Although meaning may be faithfully reproduced, hidden implications and psychological associations are often lost.[134]

Commenting on the 'elusive character of the language as an instrument of political influence', Sharabi applies literal translation as a method to comment on a speech by Nasser, which, in English: 'appear[s] colourless, almost without meaning or issue'.[135] However, Sharabi continues, speaking to the ears of his Arab listeners in Damascus, to whom this was addressed: 'each phrase was highly significant', thus making them 'cheer with great excitement'.[136] Instead of reading the influence of the Arabic language on Arab thought in an unmediated way or through a translation method that meets the criterion of functional or dynamic equivalence, where impact, not propositional content, is the issue in hand, discussions of the cognitive role of Arabic tend to apply literal translation; this translation method skews comparisons between Arabic and other languages when drawing conclusions of the kind we have seen above. It is as if those who use literal translation as a method have never heard of the adage that 'translation is treason', not because of the transfer of content from one culture to another, but because of (the inevitable) translation loss in this transfer. The idea, established through literal translation, that 'hidden implications'[137] in Arabic discourse are lost in translation into English seems to be linked to the following un-validated series of conclusions that Sharabi offers concerning Arabic in the political arena, as if it was *sui generis* in this respect, as the term 'eminently suitable' seems to suggest:

> Arabic is eminently suitable for diplomacy;[138] behind the formulas of politeness and ceremony, intention is easily concealed and meaning only obliquely

[132] Danny D. Steinberg, *Psycholinguistics: Language, Mind and World* (London and New York, NY: Longman, 1982), p. 110.
[133] Ibid. p. 110.
[134] Sharabi, *Neopatriarchy*, p. 93.
[135] Ibid. p. 93.
[136] Ibid. pp. 93–4. See Sharabi for this literal translation.
[137] Ibid. pp. 93–4.
[138] In the context of Arabic diplomatic discourse, Edzard (1998: 53) seems to think that Arabic is outside the norm in this field: 'While euphemistic style is a universal

revealed. By the same token, it is often incapable of precision and clarity and provides for long-windedness and, often, misunderstanding. This is probably one reason why political discussions in the Arab world are usually extremely prolonged and seem never to be quite conclusive.[139]

Repetition and Persuasion

Patai considers repetition to be one of the features of the Arab modal personality.[140] He exemplifies this by saying that:

> If an Arab wishes to impress his interlocutor with having definitely made up his mind to embark on a certain course of action, he will state several times what he intends to do, using a series of repetitious asseverations, often with increasing emphasis, and always with slight stylistic variations.[141]

Patai considers this practice to be part of a broader cultural syndrome in art, music and literature. For the Arab artist, the decorative field, as the world of the ideal, rather than reality or nature with all their imperfections, is his preferred domain of representation. Iconically, this preference correlates with the substitution of words for action in the Arab modal personality. Furthermore, as with speech or writing, Arab art is said to be characterised

feature of diplomatic language, certain elements of euphemistic and metaphorical language are specific to Arabic. In the Gulf war between Iraq and Iran, the term *ahdāf baḥriyya* "naval targets" was the common euphemism for attacked super tankers in the Persian Gulf. When foreigners were being held hostage in Iraq prior to "Operation Desert Storm" [in 1991], this detention was officially labelled *istiḍāfa* "invitation to hospitality". Sometimes a pompous phrase has to be narrowed down in an accurate translation, as in the case *al-injāzāt allatī taḥaqqaqat fī ẓill qiyādat ḥukūmat al-ḥizb wa-al-thawra*, literally "the achievements carried out under the leadership of the Government of the Party and Revolution". A historical example of euphemistic language was the Ottoman term *waq'i' ḫayrīya* "beneficiary events", as used by a massacre committed by janissary armies. It is not clear to this writer why Arabic is a special case in the use of euphemism. Are not the English terms "ethnic cleansing" and "collateral damage" euphemisms for the massacre and death of innocent people in war? And why is the reference about the achievement of the Iraqi Government euphemistic? It may be untrue or that some people do not believe it to be true, but this does not make the expression a form of euphemism. And in what sense is the reference to an Ottoman term applicable to Arabic? Finally, although the term *istidāfa* in Arabic may be considered euphemistic, it is so blatantly not the case that Arabs reacted to it at the time as if it was a joke that rebounded on the user. The same view is still valid to this day.'

139 Sharabi, *Neopatriarchy*, p. 94.

140 I have not dealt with this in the preceding section to link Patai's views on this matter to those of Johnstone's, which will constitute the main part of this section.

141 Patai, *The Arab Mind*, pp. 53–4.

by the: 'constant recourse to repetition of [a set of units which it uses] to achieve . . . total artistic effect'.[142]

The same phenomenon is said to apply to Arabic music, architecture and literature. Patai concludes his discussion of these art forms as follows:

> Insight into the working of the Arab mind can be gained from a consideration of the Arab arts, music and literature. In the visual field, the Arabs have focused on decorative arts, which can be interpreted as an inclination to adhere to ideal constructs and a concomitant neglect or disregard of, even disdain for, visible reality as expressed in natural forms. In music the same tendency exists but does not strike us so strongly because music is in Western culture too the one art form which is least correlated with reality.[143]

Here, again, we see the same two tendencies I mentioned above in Patai's study of the Arab mind and culture. On the one hand, he reaches conclusions – for example, the reference to 'neglect', 'disregard' and 'disdain' – which go far beyond what the evidence, flimsy as it is, can support. On the other hand, he resorts to cultural comparisons to prove his reading of Arab culture. However, the comparison on this occasion comes with a twist, which shows the suspect nature of this method. Initially, we are told that Arabic music 'neglects', 'disregards' and looks with 'disdain' on 'natural forms'.[144] But soon after telling us this, Patai undermines his conclusion by saying that in the final analysis, this is not 'so strongly'[145] the case in terms of Arabic music, because Western music has a weak correlation with nature. In methodological terms, this is a case of 'having one's cake and eating it'. Western culture is the norm against which Arab culture is to be judged. But even when Western culture seems to be similar to Arab culture, difference is still somehow posited between them, in a way which establishes the latter as a deviation from the norm in relation to the former.

I have referred to Barbara Johnstone's work on repetition in commenting on al-Qasimi's ideas on Arab acoustication above. Al-Qasimi's use of repetition and paraphrase may be interpreted by using what Johnstone says on these two phenomena in Arabic discourse. As a form of 'accumulating and insisting',[146] repetition and paraphrase – according to Johnstone's framework – serve a rhetorical function: the creation of presence in discourse as a mode of substantiation, argumentation and persuasion. In line with this approach, repetition and paraphrase in al-Qasimi's work may be further described

142 Ibid. p. 168.
143 Ibid. p. 311.
144 Ibid. p. 311.
145 Ibid. p. 311.
146 Barbara Johnstone, '"Orality" and discourse structure in Modern Standard Arabic', in Mushira Eid (ed.), *Perspectives on Arabic Linguistics I* (Amsterdam and Philadelphia, PA: John Benjamins, 1990), p. 93.

as a form of persuasion.[147] This sounds like a convincing argument, except that al-Qasimi's *ad nauseam* repetitions and paraphrases may, in fact, create the opposite effect of haranguing and alienating the reader and, more significantly, drawing attention to the fact that the repetitions and paraphrases are not associated with any proof whatsoever. Making a point once in some elegant or intriguing way would create less material presence in discourse, but, at the same time, it may have a greater effect in terms of shaping a reader's thoughts about reality, because of its memorable quality, if it has one. I am therefore unable to agree with Johnstone when she says that:

> persuasion [in Arabic] is a result as much, or more, of the sheer number of times an idea is stated and the balanced, elaborate ways in which it is stated as it is a result of syllogistic or enthymematic 'logical' organisation.[148]

Later, the reference to logic is associated with Western culture, in order to contrast it with Arab culture – the implication being that the latter pays scant attention to it.

Let us examine in more detail Johnstone's views on repetition from the perspective of the cognitive role of Arabic. Johnstone's views on this appear in similar iterations in a number of her publications.[149] Her approach is a structure-based one (according to Lucy's taxonomy), which tracks the occurrence of repetitions and paraphrases in a small corpus of Arabic texts, referencing this phenomenon to English for comparative purposes from time to time. Johnstone starts from the observation that repetition in Arabic occurs at the phonological, morphological, syntactic and lexico-semantic levels. Repetition on the first two levels is linked to the root system of the language, being, in this case, indubitably structural in nature. Syntactic repetition – for

147 In this case, repetition may be in line with what Shouby says about this phenomenon: 'When people are not clear about their own thoughts, they compensate by repeating themselves several times though in different words [i.e. use paraphrase] . . . The repetitions are, in a sense, attempts at clarifications for the self as well as for others'. See Shouby, 'The influence of the Arabic language on the psychology of the Arabs', p. 299. Shouby relates repetition in Arabic discourse to the general vagueness of thought that Arabic induces. I will allude to this below.

148 Barbara Johnstone Koch, 'Presentation as proof: the language of Arabic rhetoric', *Anthropological Linguistics* (1983b), 25: 52.

149 See Barbara Johnstone, 'Arguments with Khomeini: rhetorical situation and persuasive style in cross-cultural perspective', *Text* (1986), 6: 171–87; Barbara Johnstone, 'Parataxis in Arabic: modification as a model for persuasion', *Studies in Language* (1987), 11: 85–98; Barbara Johnstone, '"Orality" and discourse structure in Modern Standard Arabic'; Barbara Johnstone, *Repetition in Arabic Discourse*; Barbara Johnstone Koch, 'Arabic lexical couplets and the evolution of synonymy', *General Linguistics* (1983a), 23: 51–61; Barbara Johnstone Koch, 'Presentation as proof: the language of Arabic rhetoric', *Anthropological Linguistics* (1983b), 25: 47–60.

example, the use of the absolute accusative (*maf'ūl muṭlaq*) for emphasis – is also indubitably structural. The use of lexical couplets that are near-synonyms may count as repetition of sorts, but treating this phenomenon as structural, as Johnstone does, is problematic. There may be a tendency among some users of the language to use couplets – the late Egyptian writer Taha Husayn is one example – but this is a matter of aesthetic choice and taste, rather than something that is structurally (or paradigmatically) demanded by the language, as Johnstone says. It would, of course, be possible to find writers who do not use lexical couplets with the same intensity and accumulation as Taha Husayn or the writers that Johnstone examines in her corpus. Put differently, if there is pressure to use lexical couplets in discourse, this is not pressure stemming from language structure, but stemming from personal style or the result of acquiescence to the dominant aesthetic sensibility at a given time.

The same is true of paraphrasing at the sentential and para-sentential levels. This is a matter of choice and aesthetic sensibility, not structural pressure, although it seems that Johnstone considers this phenomenon as structural in nature. Al-Qasimi's and al-Jabiri's writings about Arabic, which I have discussed above, are not the same, vis-à-vis repetition. The former is repetitive, while the latter is not. Yet both writers use the same root system of the language, which pervades its phonology and morphology. Phonological and morphological repetition becomes salient – that is, rhetorically relevant – only when patterns employing these resources of the language are purposefully reiterated – for example, through the same verb forms (*awzān*) or through stylistic embellishments, such as rhyme and alliteration or assonance (*saj'*) in Arabic poetry and prose. The same is true of syntactic repetition, as it may occur through parallel structures: syntactic frames that exhibit the same slots or positions, but different lexical fillers. For this writer, repetition is linked to choice. Where there is no choice, as in root repetition or the use of the absolute accusative, there is only formal, not rhetorical, repetition. Rhetorical repetition is marked; formal repetition is unmarked in rhetorical terms. Marked repetition is ornamental, may serve as a cohesive device in texts and can be used for persuasion in argumentative texts. In contrast, unmarked repetition cannot serve in these specific capacities or, at least, it cannot do so with any degree of efficacy. By not making these distinctions, Johnstone approaches repetition in Arabic in what strikes this writer as a unitary manner, saying that: 'it is called for by the structure of Arabic'.[150] She treats all types of repetition as the same and reads them with the same totalising prism in functional terms.

Johnstone links her ideas about repetition in Arabic with the socio-political structures in Arab society, using the comparative approach to press her point. She starts from the premise that: 'there is a difference between

150 Johnstone, *Repetition in Arabic Discourse: Paradigms, Syntagms and the Ecology of Language*, p. 113.

argumentative discourse of the Arabic sort and Western argumentation'.[151] Argumentation, for her, is linked to truth: 'argument rests on established truths, and truths emerge through argument'.[152] When truths are considered as established, argumentation relies on the *presentation* of these truths in discourse, using repetition as a strategy to make them salient and, therefore, persuasive. When truths are in doubt, a different method of syllogistic reasoning is used to persuade the target of the argument; this method relies on *proof*, not on presentation. Repetition loses its rhetorical value. Having established this as background, Johnstone then tells us that:

> presentation is the dominant mode of argumentation in hierarchical societies, where truths are not matters for individual decision. In a democracy, there is room for doubt about the truth, and thus for proof; in a more autocratic society there is not.[153]

Argumentation in Arab society follows the first pattern; in Western societies, it follows the second pattern, reflecting the difference between autocracy and democracy between the two societies, respectively. This paves the way in Johnstone's framework to link argumentation by presentation with the macro socio-political structures of Arab society:

> Argument by presentation has its roots in the history of Arab society, in the ultimate, universal truths of the Qur'an, and in hierarchical societies autocratically ruled by caliphs who were not only secular rulers but also the leaders of the faith, and, later until very recently, by colonial powers. Arabic argumentation is structured by the notion that it is the presentation of an idea . . . that is persuasive, not the logical structure of proof which Westerners see behind the words.[154]

The jump from repetition in discourse to macro structures in society is accomplished, without proof or the deployment of mediating steps that take us from the one to the other through tightly controlled moves. What is the nature of the relationship between repetition, as a method of arguing through presentation in language, and autocracy? Is it a causal relation? Does autocracy produce repetition in language, because it demands argumentation by presentation? Is this a causal relation? Or is the relationship between autocracy and repetition one of non-causal co-existence or correlation? If, as Johnstone tells us, repetition is demanded by the structure of the language, does this mean that the language is responsible for autocracy in society? It seems, following Johnstone's argument, that this is an inescapable conclusion. Here, language determines thought, and thought determines

[151] Ibid. p. 115.
[152] Ibid. p. 115.
[153] Ibid. p. 117.
[154] Ibid. p. 117.

reality or, because Arabic demands repetition, and repetition is a method of argumentation through presentation (where the truth is stated, rather than syllogistically arrived at), Arabic seems to demand autocratic rulers, so that it can continue to work in the way that its structures demand. This is obviously an odd conclusion, but an inevitable one, if we follow the logic of Johnstone's argument. Equally odd is the conclusion that autocracy will be the norm of political power and governance in Arab society, because the Arabic language requires it to continue to deliver its communicative function.

It is one thing to say that there is repetition in Arabic, but quite another to say that repetition is a method of argumentation by presentation in Arabic discourse. And it is one thing to say that presentation is a dominant method of argumentation in Arabic discourse, but another to say that autocracy is an outcome or cause of this mode of argumentation. The chain holding repetition with presentation, argumentation and autocracy is, to use two of Johnstone's operative terms, presented, but not proven, in her work. There is no doubt that language influences thought and that both configure reality. However, as in the preceding sections, language in Johnstone's framework is made to carry a significant cognitive load, which the evidence, even if it were unproblematic, does not seem to justify.

The Arabic Language and the Psychology of the Arabs

One of the earliest attempts at investigating the cognitive role of Arabic is Shouby's article 'The influence of the Arabic language on the psychology of the Arabs'.[155] Many of the ideas that we find in Sharabi, Patai and Johnstone are foreshadowed by Shouby in kernel or more developed form – for example, the discussions of exaggeration, over-emphasis, repetition and vagueness of thought. Shouby's reliance on literal or, what he sometimes calls, exact translation foreshadows the use of this method by these writers. Shouby points to the interdependence of language, psychology and culture in any society, but he chooses to concentrate, in this article – which he calls a theoretical study only – on the influence of language on psychology and culture. For the purposes of this study, psychology here is treated as a rendition or variant of the Arab modal personality – the 'Arab mind', as Patai calls it in his work and Shouby uses once in his article.

Shouby does not limit the influence of Arabic on Arab psychology to matters of linguistic structure. He also includes the effect of diglossia as a sociolinguistic phenomenon on Arab psychology. The existence of two varieties of the language, *fuṣḥā* and the colloquials, are said to lead to two modes of the self for the Arab: the ideal self, associated with the former variety, and the real-world self, associated with the latter variety. Shouby explains the psychological consequences of this differentiation, linking them to the diglossia-centred modes of the self, as follows:

155 Shouby, 'The influence of the Arabic language on the psychology of the Arabs'.

> While an Arab may express himself in the loftiest moral tone, he may also under the proper circumstances freely descend to a low stratum of moral behaviour – and what is significant, feel all the time little contradiction between the two modes of action.[156]

Shouby highlights another consequence of diglossia in influencing the Arab modal personality. The main point, in this regard, is how diglossia endows *fuṣḥā* Arabic with high status in society, turning it into a coveted symbol and model that is to be adhered to, but, in reality, is hardly ever mastered by literate Arabs – his target constituency in the article under consideration. The difficulty of achieving full mastery over *fuṣḥā* Arabic leads to anxiety and a tendency to: 'over-emphasise the significance of words [for their formal properties] . . ., [and] paying less regard to their meaning than is usually the case in Western cultures and languages'.[157] This tendency of substituting words for thoughts, established through comparison, reminds us of Patai's view of the substitution of words for action in Arabic, although the two are very different from each other. Shouby further links this tendency to what he calls the general vagueness of thought that the language creates in Arab culture, as I will discuss below. This tendency, Shouby says, is aided and abetted by the musicality and rhythmic quality of Arabic words, which derives from their form, rather than from what they mean.

Patai's discussion of the influence of diglossia and bilingualism on the Arab modal personality offers further insights as to the cognitive readings of Arabic in the literature. We are told, following Shouby, that educated and literate Arabs live in 'two language-worlds':[158] those of the *fuṣḥā* and the colloquial(s). As a result, the educated Arabs are: 'saddled with psychological problems'.[159] Although these speakers are not always proficient users of *fuṣḥā,* they still internalise a feeling of superiority towards the uneducated Arabs, who feel inferior to them because of their total reliance on the colloquial. However, because educated Arabs do not have full functional competence in the language, they end up living with a: 'seed of doubt [about their] own superiority'.[160] Arabic-Western bilinguals are at a further disadvantage, because of their shaky mastery of Western languages and cultures, producing in them what Patai calls a feeling of marginality, even inferiority. These feelings increase their load of language-induced psychological problems and anxieties, making the bilingual marginal to even his own society.

The above discussion is based on a reductive understanding of linguistic status and prestige in the Arabic language situation. *Fuṣḥā* Arabic, no doubt, has its own domain-defined prestige, which it does not (fully) retain in other

156 Ibid. pp. 301–2.
157 Ibid. p. 295.
158 Patai, *The Arab Mind*, p. 186.
159 Ibid. p. 188.
160 Ibid. p. 188.

domains; in fact, it may, and often does, lose it when it is used out of context, as in a situation that demands informality. The colloquials, or some varieties of them, also have their own domain-defined prestige, which is not (fully) retained outside these domains. The major domain-definitions in these cases run across two axes of differentiation, which are drawn in pencil, not in ink, as it were: writing-orality and formality-informality. Patai and Shouby allocate prestige and status to *fuṣḥā* and the lack of prestige to the colloquial(s), without recognising the complexity and malleability of the Arabic language situation, as I have outlined it above. Their dichotomous approach therefore leads them to exaggerated conclusions about irreconcilable superiorities and inferiorities or ideal and real selves that diglossia cannot empirically support. Being more textured than they think, the Arabic language situation cannot be made to do the cognitive work that Shouby and Patai place on it.

Let us now deal with another feature of the Arab modal personality according to Shouby: the language-linked 'general vagueness of thought' in Arab life, as he calls it.[161] Shouby begins his presentation of this feature through using cultural and linguistic comparisons as method:

> Any Westerner who has attempted to comprehend Arabic will agree that thoughts expressed in that language are generally vague and hard to pin down. It is possible to understand an ordinary Arabic sentence as a whole, but when it comes to understanding it in a manner that fits all the details into a clear and well-integrated picture, then it is a different matter.[162]

This feature can also be established by attempting an 'exact translation'[163] of an Arabic sentence, wherein it becomes clear that the global meaning of this sentence cannot be recovered unequivocally from the meaning of its component parts. The reason for this, Shouby tells us, is: 'due mainly to the fact that Arabic is constituted by diffuse, undifferentiated and rigid units and structures'.[164] It is not clear what this means in practice or concrete terms – Shouby does not offer a single example to support this description of Arabic – but we are later told, in explanation, it seems, that Arabic is: 'an extra-complex conglomeration of intricate rules and regulations which certainly restricts the freedom of the Arab thinker'.[165] Again, it is important to note that not a shred of evidence is given to support this contention. In spite of this, Shouby goes on to tell us that: 'instead of manipulating the linguistic tools to make them convey his thoughts and ideas in an appropriate manner, [the educated Arab] forces his thoughts to accommodate themselves to the ready-made

161 Shouby, 'The influence of the Arabic language on the psychology of the Arabs', p. 291.
162 Ibid. p. 291.
163 Ibid. p. 292.
164 Ibid. p. 292.
165 Ibid. p. 292.

linguistic structures which he borrows from general use'.[166] Shouby believes that this linguistic vagueness results in a 'lax' frame of mind,[167] on the reality side, to: 'the general lack of organisation governing life in the Arab world today'.[168] Linked to the emphasis on words for their own sake (the tendency to substitute words for thought) and the associated 'musicality' and 'emotivity' of the language, the vagueness of Arabic and its associated thought is said to lead to an affective mood that, together with 'subliminal linguistic habits reduces the ability to think clearly'.[169] And since this 'emotivity is contagious' in Arabic, it can lead to: 'a vicious spiral of rising emotivity which finally reduces reasoning and thinking to a minimum and contributes to controversy and quarrelling'.[170] These are far-reaching conclusions, but they are offered without any substantiation. The idea that Arabic forces the Arab's thinking to follow pre-set linguistic patterns that seem to act as straightjackets, rather than as free means of expression, may be true of certain situations in any language where language rituals are common practice – for example, condolences, birthdays, and so on.

Like Patai and Johnstone, Shouby uses comparison and literal translation to set out his views concerning the cognitive role of Arabic. As has been pointed out earlier, this method makes Western languages, normally English and its associated culture, as the measure in terms of which Arabic is to be judged. In all of these cases, Arabic and its associated culture are not judged on their own terms, and they are invariably found wanting. Communication breakdowns between Arabs and non-Arabs are therefore blamed on the Arabs, rather than on the non-Arabs, instead of more realistically considering the two groups be responsible for this breakdown in equal or differential measures. Shouby provides little to no evidence for most of his views here. The idea that Arab life is vague because Arabic is vague cannot, in all seriousness, be offered without considerable evidence and a tight chain of arguments that allow this conclusion to emerge in a publicly assessable manner. The fact that Shouby intended his views to be 'theoretical', as he says, may explain the absence of evidence and the concomitant absence of the required validation. To the best of my knowledge, no studies with empirical evidence were ever produced by Shouby in order to support the conclusions discussed here, although there is a suggestion in a footnote in Shouby's paper that these would be made available soon after the publication of this writer's paper. As a result, it is hard to assess the validity of the conclusions that Shouby offers, much harder, in fact, than in the case of Patai and Johnstone, particularly the latter, who, to her credit, provides some interesting examples for the reader to think about. In spite of this, direct references to Shouby, as in Patai, or

166 Ibid. p. 293.
167 Ibid. p. 293.
168 Ibid. p. 294.
169 Ibid. p. 298.
170 Ibid. p. 298.

echoes of his ideas, as in Sharabi, are found in the literature. Shoubi's references to over-exaggeration, over-assertion and over-emphasis, repetition and vagueness seem to have circulated in talk about the cognitive role of Arabic. These readings of the cognitive role of Arabic may coincide with stereotypical views about Arabs in the West or among Arabs themselves, but this is not enough to give credibility to these readings. Generalisations about a people on the basis of vague statements concerning their language and its influence on thought need to be undertaken with one eye on the evidence and the other fixed firmly on the limits of generalisation that this evidence can support. By failing to keep his gaze fixed on hard evidence, Shouby provides a set of sweeping generalisations, which are unfortunately then used or echoed by others, uncritically, to pursue similar narratives.

Conclusion

Language symbolism is markedly different from language cognition. Chapter 2, 3 and 4 provided case studies of how language symbolism works: Chapter 2 dealt with the pre-modern period and Chapter 3 and 4 focused on the modern period. This chapter started by providing a case study of the symbolic role of language at a significant moment of historical transition from the pre-modern to the modern world, showing the seamless continuity of this role through a situation of conflict and political crisis. As was pointed out, language symbolism as an analytical category is separate from language instrumentality, and both are categorially different from language cognition. Instrumentality can express ideology, but language ideology constitutes the very substance from which language symbolism is fashioned. Language cognition depends on language instrumentality, but it tends to be mixed with language ideology in a manner that opens language to linguistic racism, as we have seen.

The cognitive role of Arabic has been used to express a variety of perspectives on the mediating role that the language plays in influencing thought and interpreting reality. In one case (mentioned above) – that of al-Arsuzi – Arabic was viewed as a mirror through which the Arabs can gain insight into their genius, using this to develop a home-grown understanding of their destiny to chart a way towards their legitimate political goals. Here, Arabic is used as an instrument that points to a cognitive self-sufficiency that is not in need of external props for validation or as the basis of action. On a different level, this cognitive reading of Arabic is intended, in part, to contest the claims made by Turkish nationalism, against the background of competing claims over al-Iskandarun/Hatay in modern-day Turkey between Syrians/Arabs and Turks. This political motive underlines the dominant practice in discussing the cognitive role of Arabic in the Arab sphere, whereby cognition and ideology live cheek-by-jowl. The close connection between the two often appears as a case of ideology masquerading as cognition. In the case of al-Arsuzi, this conflation is offered with a celebratory note redolent of the ambitions of confident pan-Arab nationalism, harking back to postcolonialism and pre-dating the crushing Arab defeat at the hands of the Israelis in 1967.

This defeat marked a turning point in modern Arab history and self-evaluation. Pan-Arabism as a political paradigm was found to be wanting. The sense of optimism that pervaded this period promptly dissipated and was replaced by a critical attitude that set out to investigate the reasons behind this defeat in a new phase of the Arab renaissance project. Culture became an arena for this line of investigation in Arab thought. Language, as we have seen, was brought into this arena, and, for some writers, it was considered to be a cause for the deep malaise in Arab life. Al-Qasimi's erratic treatise on Arab acoustication is an example of this approach. Although it is not clear where the fault in Arab culture lies exactly, Al-Qasimi believes that language, to a great extent, is responsible for the ossification in Arab cultural and political life. He goes even further and suggests that, effectively, the Arabs will not be able to develop if they do not institute a break with their past and with cultural icons, such as their language. Al-Qasimi does not put it this way, but the vehemence of his claims about acoustication suggests that he does not believe that the Arabs are capable of making this break, such is the hold of the language on their thought and culture through its association with the Qur'an as a paradigm example of one-way communication between God and the Muslims and, also, such is the intense accoustication, through formulaic recitations, that the text of the Qur'an is said to exercise on the Arabs. In this sense, al-Qasimi adopts an extreme form of linguistic determinism, in which Arabic is viewed as a procrustean form of linguistic destiny, from which there is little room, if any, for escape. Sharabi reaches a similar conclusion, but he does not push it to the extreme limits of al-Qasimi's treatise. For Sharabi, Arabic is intertwined with neopatriarchy in an indissoluble way, and the two, together, are primary causes of Arab backwardness. Sharabi believes that Arabic has a defining influence on Arab culture and the Arab mind and that these, in turn, are unable to shape or change reality in a way that can effect a significant transformation of the Arabs' fortunes in the world.

Both al-Qasimi's and Sharabi's views of the cognitive role of Arabic are part of the search for Arab regeneration in the modern world. And both seem to strike a pessimistic note in this regard, although al-Qasimi excels in the vehemence of his prose and the *ad nauseam* repetitions of his claims. Both writers offer no evidence – empirical or otherwise – to support their claims, but seem to be convinced of their veracity as if they were axioms of the social world. Their readings of Arabic and Arab life are therefore ideological and, by implication, political. For both writers, culture is infused with ideology and politics, and, as part of Arab culture, Arabic carries responsibility for the pitiful state of this culture. Overcoming the deficit in Arab life, as part of any regeneration programme, one must, therefore, begin by tackling the state of the language to affect the prism through which reality is tackled. The irony, however, is that the success of such an approach seems to be doomed to failure; such is the strength of the linguistic determinism to which these two writers subscribe. Al-Jabiri's views on the cognitive role of Arabic and the notion of an invariant Arab cultural time lead in the same direction, in spite of the fact that he seems to be more measured in the way that he argues the point concerning the hold that Arabic has on the Arab mind. Al-Jabiri's distinguished intellectual project has been built around the concept of the renewal of Arab thought, but his deterministic views of the cognitive role of Arabic seem to block the possibility of that renewal. It is intuitively difficult to believe that language can hold the destiny of any group to ransom in the way that Arabic is projected to be able to.

This deterministic perspective on language must therefore be regarded as a case of overstatement that is in need of explanation. I believe the explanation lies in the traumatic effect of the 1967 defeat on the Arabs, which must have affected these three writers deeply. I dealt with the linguistic manifestations of this trauma in my book *Arabic, Self and Identity*.[171] The depth of this trauma seems to have been translated in al-Qasimi's, Sharabi's and al-Jabiri's case into an equally deep imprinting of the language as a traumatising cognitive endowment. If true, Arab traumas of the 1967 kind must be considered as reflexes of a cognitive order, in which language is a central component. Such a conclusion of far-reaching proportions, both biologically and psychologically, cannot be entertained lightly, yet it is promulgated here as if it were given fact, as far as Arabic and the Arabs are concerned. This is the Achilles heel of all attempts to read into Arabic such a defining role in creating the Arab malaise, as Arab intellectuals in the post-1967 world see it. Language is made to carry a heavier burden than what it seems to be able to deliver, and this is done, for the most part, though speculation, rather than empirical evidence. With the exception of Johnstone's work, which is structure-based, most readings of the Arab mind are behaviour-oriented: they attempt to explain differences in practice and behaviour between the Arabs and other nations or groups of people using language as a looking glass through which this can be made.

Shouby's and Patai's readings of the cognitive role of Arabic move in a cognate orbit to those of al-Qasimi's, Sharabi's and, to a lesser extent, al-Jabiri's. Shouby and Patai consider Arabic to be responsible for influencing Arab thought and behaviour in ways in which exaggeration, overstatement, repetition and empty talk play a major part. Patai links these practices to Arab-rearing practices. Arabic is said to be well-suited to exaggeration and repetition, although we are not told how this is the case. What is it that makes Arabic well-suited to these kinds of linguistic practices? Is this a matter of grammatical structure, lexicon or both? Language behaviour is not behaviour by language, but by language users. So if exaggeration and repetition

[171] Yasir Suleiman, *Arabic, Self and Identity: A Study in Conflict and Displacement* (New York and Oxford: Oxford University Press, 2011a), pp. 108–21.

are features of language behaviour in Arabic, then they must be ascribed not to Arabic per se, but to its users. By attributing to the Arabic language properties that are better treated as speech patterns that pertain to its users, Patai eliminates the ontological distance between Arabic and its users. The language and its users fuse into each other. Shouby falls into the same logical error of eliminating the ontological distinction between a language and its speakers, falling foul of the Arabic linguistic dictum that speech is an act of the speaker (*al-kalām fi'l min af'āl al-mutakallim*). A similar conclusion may be applied to Johnstone's view of repetition in Arabic: it turns what is essentially a matter of style and, therefore, language behaviour into one of structure. Repetition now emerges as a matter that is built into the very recesses of the language itself and, on a social level, is linked to autocracy in Arab society. This chaining of language to autocracy seems to acquire a deterministic force in Johnstone's framework, but the precise mechanics of how this is done are left unexplained.

Patai, Shouby, Johnstone and, to a lesser extent, Sharabi all rely on comparison and translation to make their points. I have criticised the uncritical use of these two methods, which turn Western languages and cultures as the norms from which Arabic deviates. The idea that one culture and its products are to be judged by another, as the norm, is problematic. What makes a norm a norm? Is this a matter of structure, culture or power? Are there standards of language and cultural behaviour that can help us decide what can count as norm and what is a deviation? In the absence of these criteria, norm-making must be a matter of differential power: a question of politics, rather than linguistic structure. The culture and language of the powerful are treated as the norm, because they are powerful. Normativity, therefore, is a matter of construction, which is defined by non-linguistic factors. The danger in views of the kind offered by Patai and Shouby, in particular, is that they can be exploited for blatant cultural racism or even worse.[172] As the quotation

[172] In a piece on the way that Arabs and Jews have been treated in the US, James Zogby – the founder and President of the Arab American Institute in Washington, DC – has commented on the ways in which anti-Arab feelings in America are made and sustained in the public sphere, including policymaking. He refers to Patai's book as one of the items that are used in this area (*The Jordan Times*, 26 June 2012): 'Racist books like Raphael Patai's *The Arab Mind* continued to be used to train our [US] military through the end of the Iraq war'. A Wikipedia article on the book says that it: 'came to public attention in 2004 after investigative journalist Seymour Hersh, writing for the New Yorker magazine, revealed that the book was "the bible of the neocons on Arab behaviour" to the effect that it was the source of the idea held by the US military officials responsible for the Abu Ghraib scandal that "Arabs are particularly vulnerable to sexual humiliation"' (see: http://en.wikipedia.org/wiki/The_Arab_Mind [accessed 4 September 2012]). Free copies of the latest edition of the book were distributed in 2006 at the Middle Eastern Studies Association conference – the premier academic conference on the Middle East internationally. The introduction to the new reprint (2002) by Col.

below shows, the transition from what is considered to be academic research on the cognitive role of Arabic to popularising and 'racist' knowledge seems to be almost seamless:

- To the Arab there may be several truths about one situation, depending on the type of language he is using.
- [For the Arab] A linguistic truth over-rides a perceptual one; that is, what language can be made to say about a situation has more validity than what they eyes or reason might say. Language is not used to reason but to persuade, but on analysis it can be seen that the greater the rhetoric the lesser the substance. Among Arabs the value of words is often assessed by quantity but at the same time meanings are not constant from one person to another. Language creates violence, justifies and excuses it; indeed words can justify or rationalise anything.
- No foreigner should assume that because an Arab does not say 'No' that he means 'Yes'.[173]

I have suggested applying a substitution test to establish the linguistic racism of such views. Replacing Arab by Jew in the above text is sufficient to show

(res.) Norvell B. De Atkine – an instructor in Middle East Studies at the John F. Kennedy Special Warfare School – explains the modern relevance of the book as follows (see: http://www.meforum.org/636/the-arab-mind-revisited [accessed 4 September 2012]): 'It is a particular pleasure to write a foreword to this much-needed reprint of Raphael Patai's classic analysis of Arab culture and society. In view of the events of 2001 – including another bloody year of heightened conflict between Palestinians and Israelis and the horrendous terrorist assault on the United States on September 11 – there is a critical need to bring this seminal study of the modal Arab personality to the attention of policymakers, scholars, and the general public. In the wake of the September 11 attack, there was a torrent of commentary on "why" such an assault took place, and on the motivation and mindset of the terrorists. Much of this commentary was either ill-informed or agenda-driven. A number of U.S. Middle East scholars attributed the attack to a simple matter of imbalance in the American approach to the perennial Arab-Israeli conflict. This facile explanation did nothing to improve the credibility of the community of Middle East scholars in the United States, already much diminished by their misreading of the Arab world and their reaction to the U.S. response to the Iraqi invasion of Kuwait in 1990. To begin a process of understanding the seemingly irrational hatred that motivated the World Trade Centre attackers, one must understand the social and cultural environment in which they lived and the modal personality traits that make them susceptible to engaging in terrorist actions. This book does a great deal to further that understanding. In fact, it is essential reading. At the institution where I teach military officers, *The Arab Mind* forms the basis of my cultural instruction, complemented by my own experiences of some twenty-five years living in, studying, or teaching about the Middle East'.

173 John Laffin, *Know the Middle East* (Gloucester: Alan Sutton, 1985), pp. 78, 79, 80 (respectively).

the racism that Laffin harbours against the Arabs. The cognitive role of Arabic has been used and abused to offer interpretations of Arab modal personality or thought for purposes that seem to lie outside language. A more extensive study might reveal the factors that animate this approach, but for some writers, politics, conflict and ideology must be paramount. Under the cognitive role of Arabic, the language acts as a looking glass through which Arab thought can be refracted. It seems that because of the intervention of extraneous factors, the looking glass is made to act as a distorting mirror of the kind that one finds in the fairground. Based on the evidence so far, if Arabic were to see itself in this looking glass, it may not recognise itself. Or might it?

It is, however, important to acknowledge, as I have done above, that extremist views on the influence of Arabic on the Arab psyche or mind are not restricted to non-Arabs. Fawaz Turki,[174] a Palestinian-American, provides one of the most scathing attacks on Modern Standard Arabic (which he calls Formal Arabic) and the colloquials (which he calls Oral Arabic). In what follows, I will give snippets of Turki's views without commentary, as most of the critique of similar studies above applies to what he has to say:

> Formal Arabic is a bastard, the offspring of the times of neobackwardness. Its ambiguous jargon, stock similes, mechanical habits of expression and complex rhetoric . . . lend no sense of spontaneity or style. It lacks directness and intensity of feeling. Like the ruling class that uses it, the language blunts and stultifies. It communicates but creates no communion. Formal Arabic neither lives nor is lived; rather, it is a lingo reflecting the deadness of spirit of a society and a class that possesses informality but no form, rhetoric but no style, dissimulation but no grace . . . It has the function of perpetuating the backwardness of Arab society, enforcing the brutalities of the regimes, and justifying the debauchery, waste, corruption and decadence of the ruling elite. Used generation after generation by the ruling elite to intimidate, deceive and control, its syntax has long since come to interact with and support the various instruments of domination in society . . . The use of masculine gender [in formal Arabic] asserts the unlimited power wielded by the male in Arab society.[175]

And:

> The politics of terror in Arab society . . . press the individual to guard and stylise his words and to adopt the same convention of constraints in his speech as he does in his lifestyle. That is why the very hinge of Oral Arabic is evasion, conspiracy, ambiguity and opacity. The Oral Arab has to take refuge in double-speak, for he knows that, in coercive society, if he were to speak openly, he would stand in mortal peril. Hence Oral Arabs have become skilled dissemblers. Language is no less a weapon of assault and vengeance in the hands of the Oral Arab than the

[174] Fawaz Turki, *Exile's Return: The Making of a Palestinian American* (New York, NY: The Free Press, 1994).

[175] Ibid. pp. 121–2.

state party and the government newspaper . . . The forced politeness, even theatricality, evident in Arab manners is in fact a calculated ruse by Oral Arabs who hope to survive by dissembling and masking their anxieties . . . Oral Arabs will say 'no' when they mean 'yes'; tell you that they have eaten enough when they are still hungry; explain how much they have missed your company when they mean the opposite; boast of their prowess when they are helpless; value pomposity over modesty. They exaggerate and boast and lie as a matter of course, in a way that is commensurate with the counterfactuals of their society.[176]

Figure 5.1 *The Arabs: An Acoustic Phenomenon*

[176] Ibid. pp. 124–6.

CONCLUSION

Arabic in the fray (*al-'Arabiyyutu fī al-maydān*) is an apt description of the fields of meta-linguistic data that have been examined in this book. These data were considered for what they say about *fuṣḥā* Arabic to decipher the language ideology that they encode, as well as to show how Arabic, both as a symbolic resource and ideological site, is used to do politics, with a small *p*, in society. These themes run throughout the book, although some are better illustrated in some sites than others. Language ideology has been closely examined in Chapter 3, dealing with paratexts and the various tropes that are used in Arab culture to talk about the state of Arabic in modern times. Doing politics through culture, via language symbolism, is best illustrated in Chapter 4, wherein hybrid literature has been read as an inter-cultural phenomenon, in which language dialogism plays an important part. Both themes of ideology and cultural politics are encoded in other sites: the role of language and script in constructing national identities, the (in)imitability and (un)translatability of the Qur'an and their link to *shu'ūbiyya* and, finally, the use of Arabic to generate readings of the Arab mind. In all of these sites, the notion of the 'fray' is ever present, whether directly or indirectly, as a contextual factor that points to conflict. The best illustration of this notion occurs in al-Jabarti's analysis of, and commentary on, the French proclamation to the Egyptians following the invasion of Egypt in 1798. Here, al-Jabarti uses Arabic to do politics through language symbolism, treating the corruptions in the language of this proclamation as indicative of the corruptions of the moral order of the invaders. Through this, al-Jabarti wants to tell his readers that the French invaders cannot be trusted to uphold their promises: an invader who cannot respect the integrity of the language of those whom he is invading must be judged by the form of his message, not just its content. Here, form, as the locus of language symbolism in al-Jabarti's analysis, is treated as more important than content, as the domain of instrumentality at which the proclamation is aimed.

The introduction set out the methodological principles underlying this book, focusing on constructivism, language symbolism, language as proxy and methodological complementarity. Constructivism is directly linked to the meta-linguistic data upon which this book is based. These data stand at the interface of language and the extra-linguistic world, wherein what is done *through* language is the subject of interest, hence the notion of contestation that is an integral part of the overarching theme of the 'fray' in studying Arabic in the social world. Traditional sociolinguistics of the correlational kind eschews these data, not because they lack information on how Arabic is positioned in society (and important information, at that), but because it lacks the tools that can handle these data. Ever since the first volume in my project on Arabic in the social world, *The Arabic Language and National Identity* (2003), I have argued for the importance of mining data of the kind used in this book and the application of a composite gaze to analyse them in a way that resonates with students of language, politics, anthropology, sociology and cultural studies. Such a perspective will rescue Arabic from the isolation that traditional sociolinguistics imposes on it by 'dismissing' what cannot be accommodated under this approach as marginal or out of bounds.

In pursuing its objectives, this book aims to link the pre-modern to the modern world. Language ideology in the pre-modern world is shown to reside in one of the most seminal debates about the Qur'an that links theology to ethnic (s)election. The (in)imitability of the Qur'an and its (un)translatability are rooted in this link. Jahiz's theory of communication is linked to this debate, too. This theory is distinguished by treating language as a semiological system that shares the task of communication with other semiological systems. The extra-linguistic purpose of this theory is to provide a basis for a vision of ethnic (s)election that gives special status to the Arabs, whose eloquence and linguistic virtuosity is said to be second to none. This vision makes full sense only when linked to the notion of the inimitability of the Qur'an and the *shu'ūbiyya*. These two facts – one theological and the other political – provide the context for this theory. The fact that claims about language and ethnic (s)election continued to exist in treatises on grammar after the embers of *shu'ūbiyya* had been more or less completely extinguished in pre-modern time signals the iconisation of this movement into a kind of trope that is linked to the war trope of Arabic language ideology in modern times. This is what makes *shu'ūbiyya* susceptible to resuscitation in modern Arab political culture to point to enemies of the language, be they insiders or outsiders.

Tropes of modern Arabic language ideology continue the notion of the 'fray' noted above, but they add an additional meaning through the trope of fossilisation, according to which Arabic is wearing away or is threadbare, in instrumental terms, thus reflecting, in this regard, one of the lexical meanings of 'fray' in English. In these tropes, Arabic is constructed to exist in a situation of conflict and endangerment, which is marked in book titles, dedications, epigraphs, forewords, jacket copies and poetic compositions. This book investigated these tropes at length. The choice of paratexts to pursue Arabic language ideology is intended to highlight the interfacing of language and the extra-linguistic world at various thresholds in texts. Paratexts reflect and refract language ideology and disseminate it throughout society in ways that their textual materials cannot. To the best of my knowledge, this is the first time that paratexts have been deployed at length in studying Arabic in the social world; their inclusion here is therefore intended to highlight the importance of opening up the empirical domain to include unorthodox phenomena in studying the positioning of language in society in the Arab context. In addition, by linking language ideology tropes to canonical texts (whether in poetry and prose) in Arab culture, we can expand the kinds of data available to us in investigating language in the social world. The picture that emerges is a one of a web of domains, through which language ideology circulates in society in a way that leads to greater exposure for this ideology.

Hybrid texts add to the tally of empirical domains that are available to the study of Arabic in the social world. The question of language choice is at the heart of these texts. This choice is motivated by a variety of factors, which are shaped by conflict. Reading this choice in a dialogic manner, this study reveals the interfacing of language with the extra-linguistic world, in which emergent valuations of this choice are subject to contextual factors. This is true of the classification of literary works in French by writers from a Middle Eastern or North African background. A writer who is classified as a French writer at one stage may be classified as a Francophone writer at another for exactly the same oeuvre, reflecting, in this regard, changes in the political context. The shift from Arabic to Hebrew by Jewish writers in Israel is valued differently from the adoption of Hebrew as the language of literary expression by Israeli Palestinian writers. This difference in valuation reflects the importance of ethnicity and nationality in scoping language in the social world. Hybrid texts act as a bridge between cultures, but, more importantly, they also reveal the tensions between cultures by bringing language ideologies into contact with each other in ways that impact on the conduct of cultural politics. This aspect of hybrid texts is most clearly illustrated in A. B. Yehoshua's evaluation of the work of Israeli Palestinian writers in Hebrew, especially his reaction to Anton Shammas' project of un-Jewing the Hebrew language.

Cognitive readings of Arabic, aimed at mediating the relationship between thought and reality, offer another field for investigating language in the social world. Arab and non-Arab writers have participated in providing readings of the 'Arab mind' through language. These readings ascribe to the Arabs behavioural traits that seem to be at odds with those that are believed to obtain in Western cultures. These readings are conducted in a way that verges, in some cases, on linguistic racism. Often relying on literal translations from Arabic into a Western language, these cognitive readings of the Arab mind make the language responsible for inter-cultural communication failures, cultural ossification and political autocracy. By failing to provide robust evidence in support of these conclusions, cognitive readings of Arabic emerge as ideological, in the sense of being attempts at framing the Arabs and their culture for political purposes, whether out of genuine concern over the Arabs' place in history or out of ill-intent. Here again, we have an example of how Arabic is used in cultural politics. The use of Patai's book *The Arab Mind* as a guide in dealing with the Arabs in post-9/11 America is an example of the interfacing of cognitive readings of Arabic (among other things) with politics in a direct way.

The use of meta-linguistic materials to understand the role that Arabic plays in the social world is one of the most important features of my project on this topic. This choice is linked to constructivism, language symbolism, language as proxy and methodological complementarity. The four volumes on this topic so far reveal the productive ways in which this set of ideas have expanded our understanding of Arabic in the social world, both at the individual and collective levels. These volumes have covered issues of identity, conflict and a lot more in ways that are beyond the scope of traditional Arabic sociolinguistics in its correlationist incarnation. Although some champions of this approach may read this project as a major (unsanctioned) departure from the normative approach to studying Arabic in its social context, my intention here is not to offer an alternative to this approach that seeks its demise, so to speak, but a complementary one, which opens up new terrains for investigation at the empirical and methodological levels. The next volume, which will deal with language policy in the Arabic-speaking world, will continue with this trajectory.

BIBLIOGRAPHY

References Cited in Arabic

'Abd al-Raḥmān, 'Ā'isha (bint al-Shāṭi'), *Lughatunā wa-l-ḥayā* (Cairo: Dār al-Ma'ārif, n.d.)

'Abd al-Raḥmān, 'Ā'isha (bint al-Shāṭi'), *al-I'jāz al-bayānī li-l-qur'ān wa masā'il ibn al-azraq: dirāsa qur'āniyya lughawiyya wa-bayāniyya* (Cairo: Dār al-Ma'ārif, 1950).

'Abd al-Raḥmān, Ṭālib, *al-'Arabiyya tuwājih al-taḥaddiyāt* (Qatar: Wazārat al-Awqāf, 2006).

'Adnān, Etel, 'al-Kitāba bi-lugha ajnabiyya', trans. Dalia Said Mustafa, *Alif: Journal of Contemporary Poetics* (2000), 20: 133–43.

Adonis ('Alī Aḥmad Sa'īd), *Kalām al-bidāyāt* (Beirut: Dār al-Ādāb, 1989a).

Adonis ('Alī Aḥmad Sa'īd), *al-Shi'riyya al-'arabiyya* (Beirut: Dār al-Ādāb, [2nd printing] 1989b).

Adonis ('Alī Aḥmad Sa'īd), *al-Naṣṣ al-qur'ānī wa-āfāq al-kitāba* (Beirut: Dār al-Ādāb, 1993).

al-Afghānī, Sa'īd, *Min ḥāḍir al-lugha al-'arabiyya* (Damascus: Dār al-Fikr, 1971).

al-'Alawī, Hādī, *al-Mu'jam al-'arabī al-jadīd: muqaddima* (Latakiyya: Dār al-Ḥiwār, 1983).

al-'Alāylī, 'Abdallah, *Dustūr al-'arab al-qawmī* (Beirut: Dār al-Jadīd, [1938] 1996).

al-Alfī, Usāma, *al-Lugha al-'arabiyya wa-kayfa nanhaḍ bihā nuṭqan wa-ktiābatan* (Cairo: al-Hay'a al-Miṣriyya al-'Āmma li-l-Kitāb, 2004).

al-'Ālim, Maḥmūd Amīn (ed.), *Qaḍāyā fikriyya: lughtatunā al-'arabiyya fī ma'rakat al-ḥaḍāra (Vols 17 and 18)* (Cairo: Qaḍāyā Fikriyya li-l-Nashr wa-l-Tawzī', 1997).

Anīs, Ibrāhīm, 'hal al-lugha al-'arabiyya badawiyya?', *Majallat Majma' al-Lugha al-'Arabiyya* (1969), 24: 172–80.

al-Ashtar, 'Abd al-Karīm, *al-'Arabiyya fī muwājahat al-makhāṭir* (Beirut: al-Maktab al-Islāmī, 2006).

'Aṭṭār, Aḥmad 'Abd al-Ghafūr, *al-Zaḥf 'alā lughat al-qur'ān* (Beirut: no publisher, 1966).

al-A'ẓamī, 'Abd al-Ḥaqq, *al-'Arab wa-l-'arabiyya bihimā ṣalāh al-umma al-'arabiyya wa jamī' al-umam al-bashariyya* (Dayr al-Zūr: al-Maktaba al-'Urūbiyya, 1983).
al-Barāzī, Majd Muḥammad al-Bākīr, *Mushkilāt al-lugha al-'arabiyya al-mu'āṣira* (Amman: Maktabat al-Risāla, 1989).
Baybars, Aḥmad Samīr, *al-Wāqi' al-lughawī wa-l-huwiyya al-'arabiyya* (Cairo: Dār al-Fikr al-'Arabī, n.d.).
Bayyūmī, Sa'īd Aḥmad, *Umm al-lughāt: dirāsa fī khaṣā'iṣ al-lugha al-'arabiyya wa-l-nuhūḍ bihā* (Cairo: Maktabat al-Ādāb, 2002).
Darwīsh, Mahmūd, 'Inqāẓ al-lugha min aydī al-nuḥā', in Maḥmūd Amīn al-'Ālim (ed.), *Qaḍāyā fikriyya: lughatunā fī ma'rakat al-ḥaḍāra (Vols 17–18: 81–91)* (Cairo: Qaḍāyā Fikriyya li-l-Nashr wa-l-Tawzī', 1997).
Darwīsh, Mahmūd, *Inqāẓ al-lugha, inqāẓ al-huwiyya: taṭwīr al-lugha al-'arabiyya* (Cairo: Nahḍat Miṣr, 2006).
al-Ḍubayb, Aḥmad bin Muḥammad, *al-Lugha al-'arabiyya fī 'aṣr al-'awlama* (Riyadh: Maktabat al-'Ubaykān, 2001).
al-Dūrī, 'Abd al-'Azīz, *al-Judhūr al-tārīkhiyya li-l-shu'ūbiyya* (Beirut: Dār al-Ṭalī'a, [3rd printing] 1981).
Fahmī, 'Abd al-'Azīz, *al-Ḥurūf al-lātīniyya li-kitābat al-'arabiyya* (Egypt: Dār al-'Arab, n.d.).
al-Faraḥ, Wajīh, 'Khaṭa' dārij yajib taṣḥīḥuh: li-mādhā kalimat al-rūm wa-naḥnu 'arab ūrdhudux?', *Al-Nashra* (2004), 32: 30–2 (The Royal Institute of Religious Studies, Jordan).
Farrūkh, 'Umar, *al-Qawmiyya al-fuṣḥā* (Beirut: Dār al-'Ilm li-l-Malāyīn, 1961).
al-Fihrī, al-Fāsī 'Abd al-Qādir, *Azmat al-lugha al-'arabiyya fī al-maghrib: bayna ikhtilālāt al-ta'addudiyya wa-ta'aththurāt 'al-tarjama* (Rabat: Manshūrāt Zāwiya, 2005).
al-Fikāykī, 'Abd al-Hādī, *al-Shu'ūbiyya wa-l-qawmiyya al-'arabiyya* (Beirut: Dār al-Ādāb, 1961).
Frayḥa, Anīs, *Fī al-lugha al-'arabiyya wa-ba'ḍ mushkilātihā* (Beirut: Dār al-Nahār, 1980).
Ghānim, Ghālib, *Shi'r al-lubnāniyyīn bi-l-lugha al-faransiyya: 1903–1968* (Beirut: Manshūrāt al-Jāmi'a al-Lubnāniyya, 1981).
Ghānim, Ghālib, 'al-Adab al-lubnānī 'alā imtidād al-qarn al-'ishrīn', *Al-'Arabī* (2001), 515: 80–3.
al-Ḥājj, Kamāl Yūsuf, *Difā'an 'an al-'arabiyya* (Beirut: Manshūrāt 'Uwaydāt, 1959a).
al-Ḥājj, Kamāl Yūsuf, *Fī al-qawmiyya wa-l-insāniyya* (Beirut: Manshūrāt 'Uwaydāt, 1959b).
al-Ḥājj, Kamāl Yūsuf, *al-Qawmiyya laysat marḥala* (Beirut: Manshūrāt 'Uwaydāt, 1959c).
al-Ḥājj, Kamāl Yūsuf, *Fī ghurrat al-ḥaqīqa* (Beirut: Manshūrāt 'Uwaydāt, 1966).
al-Ḥājj, Kamāl Yūsuf, *Fī falsafat al-lugha* (Beirut: Dār al-Nahār, [1956] 1978).
Ḥārib, Sa'īd, *al-Ta'rīb wa-l-ta'līm al-'ālī* (Sharjah: Jam'iyyat Ḥimāyat al-Lugha al-'Arabiyya, 2000).
al-Ḥasanī, Bahīja Bāqir, 'al-Zamakhsharī wa-l-shu'ūbiyya', *Majallat majma' al-lugha al-'arabiyya al-urdunnī* (1989), 37: 177–211.
Ḥusayn, Ṭaha, *Mustaqbal al-thaqāfa fī miṣr* (Cairo: Maṭba'at al-Ma'ārif, [1938] 1944).

al-Ḥuṣrī, Sāṭi', *al-'Urūba awwalan* (Beirut: Markiz Dirāsāt al-Waḥda al-'Arabiyya, 1985).

al-Jābirī, Muḥammad 'Ābid, *al-Turāth wa-l-ḥadātha: Dirāsāt wa munāqashāt* (Beirut: Markaz Dirāsāt al-Waḥda al-'Arabiyya, 1991).

al-Jābirī, Muḥammad 'Ābid, *Takwīn al-'aql al-'arabī* (Beirut: Markaz Dirāsāt al-Waḥda al-'Arabiyya, [1984] 1998).

al-Jāḥiẓ, Abū 'Uthmān 'Amr Ibn Baḥr, *Kitāb al-Bayān wa-l-tabyīn (3 Vols)*, Ḥasan al-Sandūbī (ed.) (Cairo: no publisher, 1932).

al-Jāḥiẓ, Abū 'Uthmān 'Amr Ibn Baḥr, *al-Ḥayawān (6 Vols)*, 'Abd al-Salām Hārūn (ed.) (Cairo: Maktabat Muṣṭafā al-Bābī al-Ḥalabī wa-Awlāduh, 1945).

al-Jāḥiẓ, Abū 'Uthmān 'Amr Ibn Baḥr, *al-Bukhalā'*, Aḥmad al-'Awāmirī and 'Alī al-Jārim (eds) (Beirut: Dār al-Kutub al-'Ilmiyya, 1983) (Trans. R. B. Serjeant (Reading: Garnet Publishing, 1997)).

al-Jamālī, Fāḍil, *Difā'an 'an al-'arabiyya* (Tunis: Mu'assassāt 'Abd al-Karīm Bin 'Abdallah, 1996).

Jubrān, Sulaymān, *'Alā hāmish al-tajdīd wa-l-taqyīd fī al-lugha al-'arabiyya al-mu'āṣira* (Haifa: Majma' al-Lugha al-'Arabiyya, 2009).

al-Kattānī, Idrīs, *Thamānūna 'āman mina al-ḥarb al-frakūfūniyya ḍidd al-islām wa-l-lugha al-'arabiyya* (Rabat: Manshūrāt Nādī al-Fikr al-Islāmī, 2000).

al-Khafājī, Ibn Sinān Abū Muḥammad 'Abdallah Ibn Muḥammad Ibn Sa'īd, *Sirr al-faṣāḥa* (Beirut: Dār al-Kutub al-'Ilmiyya, 1982).

Khalīfa, 'Abd al-Karīm, *Taysīr al-'arabiyya bayna al-qadīm wa-l-ḥadīth* (Amman: Manshūrāt Majma' al-Lugha al-'Arabiyya al-Urdunnī, 1986).

Khalīfa, al-Junaydī, *Naḥwa 'arabiyya afḍal* (Beirut: Manshūrāt Dār al-Ḥayāt, n.d.).

al-Kharrāṭ, Edwār, 'Miṣriyyūn qalban ... frankūfūniyyūn qāliban: shahāda shakhṣiyya', *Alif: Journal of Contemporary Poetics* (2000), 20: 8–24 (Arabic section).

al-Kharrāṭ, Edwār, 'Fī al-baḥth 'an huwyyat al-adab al-frankūfūnī', *Al-'Arabī* (2001), 515: 76–9.

al-Khashshāb, Walīd, 'al-Iflāt min mu'assasat al-huwiyya wa-l-thaqāfa: George Shehadé musāfiran', *Alif: Journal of Contemporary Poetics* (2000), 20: 54–76 (Arabic section).

Khashshāsh, Muḥammad, *'Ilal al-lisān wa-amrāḍ al-lugha* (Sidon and Beirut: al-Maktaba al-'Aṣriyya li-l-Ṭibā'a wa-l-Nashr, 1998).

al-Khuḍarī, Muḥammad al-Amīn, 'Malāmih nazariyyat al-'i'jāz', *Majallat al-'ulūm al-'insāniyya wa-l-'ijtimā'iyya* (2005), 21: 3–54.

al-Khūlī, Amīn, *Min hady al-qur'ān: mushkilāt ḥayātinā al-lughawiyya* (Cairo: al-Hay'a al-Miṣriyya al-'Āmma li-l-Kiṭāb, 1987).

al-Kindī, Ya'qūb, 'Risālat ya'qūb al-kindī fī al-lugha', Muḥammad Ḥasan al-Tayyān (ed.), *Majallat majma' al-lugha al-'arabiyya bi-dimashq* (1985), 60: 515–32.

Laḥḥūd, 'Abdallah, *Lubnān: 'arabiyy al-wajh, 'arabiyy al-lisān* (Beirut: Dār al-'Ilm li-l-Malāyīn, 1993).

Luṭfī al-Sayyid, Aḥmad, *al-Muntakhabāt (2 Vols)* (Cairo: Maṭba'at al-Anglū al-Miṣriyya, 1945).

Maḥmūd, Sa'd Ḥāfiẓ, 'al-Ḥawal al-lughawī: ta'ammulāt fī ẓāhirat inḥirāf wa-inḥiṭāṭ al-lugha', in Maḥmūd Amīn al-'Ālim (ed.), *Qaḍāyā fikriyya: lughatunā fī ma'rakat al-ḥaḍāra* (*Vols 17–18*) (Cairo: Qaḍāyā Fikriyya li-l-Nashr wa-l-Tawzī', 1997), pp. 131–4.

Miḥriz, Sāmya, 'Khāriṭat al-kitāba: ḥiwār ma' Ahdāf Suwayf', *Alif: Journal of Contemporary Poetics* (2000), 20: 168–75 (Arabic section).

al-Mināwī, Muḥammad Fawzī, *Azmat al-ta'rīb* (Cairo: Markiz al-Ahrām li-l-Tarjama wa-l-Nashr, 2003).

al-Misaddī, 'Abd al-Salām, *al-'Arab wa-l-intiḥār al-lughawī* (Beirut: Dār al-Kitāb al-Jadīd al-Muttaḥida, 2011).

Moreh, Shmuel and Maḥmūd 'Abbāsī, *Tarājim wa-āthār fi al-adab al-'arabī fi isrā'īl* (Shfa'amr: Dar al-Mashriq, 1998).

al-Mūsā, Nihād, *Qaḍiyyat al-taḥawull ilā al-fuṣḥā fi al-'ālam al-arabī al-ḥadīth* (Amman: Dār al-Fikr li-l-Nashr wa-l-Tawzī', 1978).

al-Mūsā, Nihād, *al-Asālīb: manāhij wa-namādhij fi ta'līm al-lugha al-'arabiyya* (Amman: Dār al-Shurūq li-l-Nashr wa-l-Tawzī', 2003).

Nahr, Hādī, *al-Lisāniyyāt al-ijtimā'iyya 'ind al-'arab* (Irbid: 'Ālam Al-Kutub al-Ḥadīth, 1998).

Nahr, Hādī, *al-Lugha al-'arabiyya wa-taḥaddiyāt al-'awlama* (Irbid: 'Ālam al-Kutub al-Ḥadīth, 2010).

al-Naḥwī, 'Adnān 'Alī Riḍā, *Limādhā al-lugha al-'arabiyya?* (Riyadh: Dār al-Naḥwī li-l-Nashr wa-l-Tawzī', 1998).

al-Naqqāsh, Rajā', *hal tantaḥir al-lugha al-'arabiyya?* (Cairo: Nahḍat Miṣr, 2009).

Naṣr, Marlyne, *al-Ghurabā' fi khiṭāb al-lubnāniyyīn 'an al-ḥarb al-ahliyya* (Beirut: Dār Al-Sāqī, 1996).

Nu'aymī, Ṣādiq Muḥammad, *al-Tārīkh al-fikrī li-azmat al-lugha al-'arabiyya* (Rabat: Ifrīqyā al-Sharq, 2008).

Nu'mān, Aḥmad Bin, *al-Ta'rīb byana al-mabda' wa-l-taṭbīq fi al-jazā'ir wa-l-'ālam al-'arabī* (Algiers: al-Sharika al-Waṭaniyya li-l-Nashr wa-l-Tawzī', 1981).

Qaddūra, Zāhiya, *al-Shu'ūbiyya wa-atharuhā al-ijtimā'ī wa-l-siyāsī fi al-ḥayāt al-islāmiyya fi al-'aṣr al-'abbāsī al-awwal* (Beirut: Dār al-Kitāb al-Lunbānī, 1972).

Qāsim, Maḥmūd, *al-Adab al-'arabī al-maktūb bi-l-faransiyya* (Cairo: al-Hay'a al-Miṣriyya al-'Āmma li-l-Kitāb, 1996).

Qāsim, Maḥmūd, 'al-Sīnimā al-'arabiyya al-nāṭiqa bi-l-faransiyya: ḥālat Mahdī Sharaf', *Alif: Journal of Contemporary Poetics* (2000), 20: 117–32 (Arabic section).

Qaṣṣāb, Walīd Ibrāhīm, 'Jināyat al-ḥadātha al-mu'āṣira 'alā al-lugha al-'arabiyya', *Majallat Kulliyat al-Dirāsāt al-Islāmiyya wa-l-'Arabiyya (United Arab Emirates)* (1994), 9: 201–22.

al-Qaṣīmī, 'Abdallah, *al-'Arab ẓāhira ṣawtiyya* (Cologne: Manshūrāt al-Jamal, [2002] 2006).

al-Rāfi'ī, Muṣṭafā Ṣādiq, *I'jāz al-qur'ān wa-l-balāgha al-nabawiyya* (Beirut: Dār al-Fikr al-'Arabī, n.d.).

Rukaybī, 'Abdallah, *al-Frankūfūniyya mashriqan wa-magriban* (Beirut: al-Ruwwād li-l-Nashr wa-l-Tawzī', 1992).

Sa'āda, Anṭūn, *Nushū' al-umam* (No place of publication: no publisher, 1994).

Sallūm, 'Abdallah, *al-Shu'ūbiyya ḥaraka muḍādda li-l-islām wa-l-umma al-'arabiyya* (Baghdad: Manshūrat Wazārat al-Thqāfa, 1980).

Salmān, Shurūq Muḥammad, *Durar bahiyya fī madḥ al-'arabiyya* (United Arab Emirates: no publisher, 2007).

Sawwā'ī, Muḥammad, *Azmat al-muṣṭalaḥ al-'arabī fī al-qarn al-tāsi' 'ashar: muqaddima tārīkhiyya 'āmma* (Damascus: al-Ma'had al-Faransī li-l-Dirāsāt al-'Arabiyya bi-Dimashq, 1999).

al-Sayyid, Maḥmūd Aḥmad, *Fī qaḍāyā al-lugha al-tarbawiyya* (Kuwait: Wakālat al-Maṭbū'āt, n.d.).

al-Sayyid, Maḥmūd Aḥmad, *Shu'ūn lughawiyya* (Beirut: Dār al-Fikr al-Mu'āṣir, 1989).

Sharābī, Hishām, *al-Naqd al-ḥaḍārī li-wāqi' al-mujtama' al-'arabī al-mu'āṣir* (Beirut: Dār Nilsun, 2000).

al-Shūbāshī, Sharīf, *Li-taḥyā al-lugha al-'arabiyya: yasquṭ Sībawayhi* (Cairo: Madbūlī al-Ṣaghīr, [3rd printing] 2004).

Ṣiddīq, Muḥammad, 'al-Kitāba bi-l-'ibriyya al-fuṣḥā: taqdīm riwāyat 'arabisk wa-ḥiwār ma' Aṭūn Shammās', *Alif: Journal of Contemporary Poetics* (2000), 20: 155–67 (Arabic section).

al-Tūnusī, Muḥammad Khalīfa, *Aḍwā' 'alā lughatinā al-samḥa* (Kuwait: Dār al-'Arabī, 1985).

al-'Ubaydī, Rashīd 'Abd al-Raḥmān, 'Uyūb al-lisān wa-l-lahajāt al-madhmūma', *Majallat al-majma' al-'ilmī al-'Irāqī* (1985), 36: 236–300.

'Umar, Aḥmad Mukhtār, 'Azmat al-lugha al-'arabiyya wa-l-ḥāja ilā ḥulūl ghayr taqlīdiyya', in Amīn Maḥmūd al-'Ālim (ed.), *Qaḍāyā fikriyya: lughtatunā al-'arabiyya fī ma'rakat al-ḥaḍāra (Vols 17 and 18)* (Cairo: Qaḍāyā Fikriyya li-l-Nashr wa-l-Tawzī', 1997), pp. 65–80.

'Umar, Muḥammad Ṣāliḥ, 'Mu'āmarat istibdāl al-ḥurūf al-'arabiyya bi-l-ḥurūf al-lātīniyya fī 'ahd al-ḥimāya fī tūnis', *Al-Mustaqbal al-'Arabī* (1987), 99: 65–76.

'Uways, Muḥammad, *al-Mujtama' al-'abbāsī min khilāl kitābāt al-jāḥiẓ* (Cairo: Dār al-Thaqāfa li-l-Ṭibā'a wa-l-Nashr, 1977).

Ūzūn, Zakariyyā, *Jināyat Sībawayhi: al-rafḍ al-tāmm li-mā fī al-naḥw min awhām* (Beirut: Riyād al-Rayyis li-l-Kutub wa-l-Nashr, 2002).

al-Zamakhshrī, Abū al-Qāsim Muḥammad Ibn 'Umar, *al-Mufaṣṣal fī al-naḥw* (Alexandria: Maṭba'at al-Kawkab al-Sharqī, [1291] 1874).

References Cited in Other Languages

Abdul-Raof, Hussein, *Qur'an Translation: Discourse, Texture and Exegesis* (Richmond: Curzon Press, 2001).

Aberbach, David, 'The poetry of nationalism', *Nations and Nationalism* (2003), 9: 255–75.

Aberbach, David, 'Nationalism and the Hebrew Bible', *Nations and Nationalism* (2005), 11: 223–42.

Abu-Haidar, Farida, 'Inscribing a Maghrebian identity in French', in Mildred Mortimer (ed.), *Maghrebian Mosaic: A Literature in Transition* (Boulder and London: Lynne Rienner Publishers, 2001), pp. 13–25.

Achebe, Chinua, 'The African writer and the English language', in Patrick Williams and Laura Chrisman (eds), *Colonial Discourse and Postcolonial Theory: A Reader* (New York, NY: Columbia University Press, 1994), pp. 428–34.

Ager, Dennis, *'Francophonie' in the 1990s: Problems and Opportunities* (Cleveland, OH: Multilingual Matters, 1996).

Aleem, Abdul, 'I'jazul-Qur'an', *Islamic Culture* (1933), 7: 215–33.

Anderson, Benedict, *Imagined Communities: Reflections on the Origin and Spread of Nationalism* (London and New York, NY: Verso, 1991).

Antonius, Soraya, 'The day of outside education', *Alif: Journal of Contemporary Poetics* (2000), 20: 257–68.

Armitage, Anne, 'The debate over literary writing in a foreign language: an overview of Francophonie in the Magreb', *Alif: Journal of Contemporary Poetics* (2000), 20: 39–67.

Ashcroft, Bill, Gareth Griffiths and Helen Tiffin, *The Empire Writes Back: Theory and Practice in Postcolonial Literatures*, 2nd edn (London and New York, NY: Routledge, 2002).

Aytürk, İlker, 'Turkish linguists against the West: the origins of linguistic nationalism in Ataturk's Turkey', *Middle Eastern Studies* (2004), 40: 1–25.

Baalbaki, Ramzi, 'The historic relevance of poetry in the Arab grammatical tradition', in Ramzi Baalbaki, Salih Said Agha and Tarif Khalidi (eds), *Poetry and History: The Value of Poetry in Reconstructing Arab History* (Beirut: American University of Beirut Press, 2011), pp. 95–120.

Bakhtin, M. M. (Mikhail Mikhaĭlovich), *The Dialogic Imagination: Four Essays*, Michael Holquist (ed.), trans. Caryl Emerson and Michael Holquist (Austin, TX: University of Texas Press, 1981).

Balaban, Avraham, 'Anton Shammas: torn between two languages', *World Literature Today* (1989), 63: 418–21.

Bauer, Laurie and Peter Trudgill (eds), *Language Myths* (London: Routledge, 1998).

Bauman, Zygmut, *Identity* (Cambridge: Polity, 2004).

Bender, Margaret, 'Indexicality, voice and context in the distribution of Cherokee script', *International Journal of the Sociology of Language* (2008), 192: 91–103.

Bengio, Ofra, *Saddam's Word: Political Discourse in Iraq* (New York and Oxford: Oxford University Press, 1998).

Ben-Rafael, E., E. Shohamy, M. A. Amara and N. Trumper-Hecht, *Linguistic Landscape and Multiculturalism: A Jewish-Arab Comparative Study* (Tel Aviv University: The Tami Steinmetz Centre for Peace Research, 2004).

Benson, Phil, *Ethnocentricism and the English Dictionary* (London and New York, NY: Routledge, 2001).

Berg, Nancy E., *Exile from Exile: Israeli Writers from Iraq* (Albany, NY: State University of New York Press, 1996).

Berger, Anne-Emmanuelle, 'Introduction', in Anne-Emmanuelle Berger (ed.), *Algeria in Others' Languages* (Ithaca and London: Cornell University Press, 2002), pp. 1–16.

Berque, Jaques, *Cultural Expression in Arab Society Today*, trans. Robert W. Stookey (Austin, TX: University of Texas Press, 1978).

Billig, Michael, 'Methodology and scholarship in understanding ideological explanation', in Charles Antaki (ed.), *Analysing Everyday Explanation: A Casebook of Methods* (London: Sage Publications, 1988), pp. 199–215.

Biran, Hanna, 'Fear of the Other', *Palestine–Israel Journal* (1994), 4: 44–52. Accessed online at http://www.pij.org/details.php?id=698.

Blommaert, Jan, 'Language and nationalism: comparing Flanders with Tanzania', *Nations and Nationalism* (1996), 2: 235–56.

Blommaert, Jan, 'The debate is open', in Jan Blommaert (ed.), *Language Ideological Debates* (Berlin and New York, NY: Mouton de Gruyter, 1999), pp. 1–38.

Blumer, Herbert, 'Sociological analysis and the "variable"', *American Sociological Review* (1956), 21: 683–90.

Boullata, Issa J., 'The rhetorical interpretation of the Qur'an: *I'jāz* and related topics', in Andrew Rippin (ed.), *Approaches to the History of the Interpretation of the Qur'ān* (Oxford: Clarendon Press, 1988), pp. 139–57.

Brenner, Rachel Feldhay, 'In search of identity: the Israeli Arab artist in Anton Shammas's *Arabesques*', *Modern Language Association* (*MLA*) (1993), 108: 431–45.

Brenner, Rachel Feldhay, 'The search for identity in Israeli Arab fiction: Atallah Mansour, Emile Habiby and Anton Shammas', *Israeli Studies* (2001), 6: 91–112.

Brenner, Rachel Feldhay, *Inextricably Bonded: Israeli Arab and Jewish Writers Re-Visioning Culture* (Madison, WI: University of Wisconsin Press, 2003).

Bryman, Alan, 'The debate about quantitative and qualitative research: a question of method or epistemology?', *The British Journal of Sociology* (1984), 35: 75–92.

Carmichael, Cathie, 'A people exists and that people has its language: language and nationalism in the Balkans', in Stephen Barbour and Cathie Carmichael (eds), *Language and Nationalism in Europe* (Oxford: Oxford University Press, 2000), pp. 221–39.

Carter, Michael G. (ed.), *Arab Linguistics: An Introductory Classical Text with Translation and Notes* (Amsterdam and Philadelphia, PA: John Benjamins, 1981).

Carter, Michael G., *Sibawayhi* (London: I. B. Tauris, 2004).

Cassirer, Ernst, *Language and Myth* (New York, NY: Dover Publications, 1946).

Cheshin, A. S., B. Hutman and A. Melamed, *Separate and Unequal: The Inside Story of Israeli Rule in East Jerusalem* (Cambridge, MA: Harvard University Press, 1999).

Chilton, Paul, *Analysing Political Discourse: Theory and Practice* (London and New York, NY: Routledge, 2004).

Clement, Victoria, 'Emblems of independence: script choice in post-Soviet Turkmenistan', *International Journal of the Sociology of Language* (2008), 192: 171–85.

Coe, Richard N., *When the Grass was Taller: Autobiography and the Experience of Childhood* (New Haven, CT: Yale University Press, 1984).

Comrie, Bernard, *Aspect: An Introduction to the Study of Verbal Aspect and Related Problems* (Cambridge: Cambridge University Press, 1976).

Conchubhair, Brian, 'The Gaelic font controversy: the Gaelic League's (post-colonial) crux', *Irish University Review: A Journal of Irish Studies* (2003), 33: 46–63.

Cooper, Robert L., *Language Planning and Social Change* (Cambridge: Cambridge University Press, 1996).

Coulmas, Flourian, 'Language policy and language planning: political perspectives', *Annual Review of Applied Linguistics* (1994), 14: 34–52.

Daston, Lorraine and Peter Galison, 'The image of objectivity', *Representations* (1992), 40: 81–128.

Deleuze, Gilles and Félix Guattari, *Kafka: Toward a Minor Literature*, trans. Dana Polan, foreword by Réda Bensamaïa (Minneapolis and London: University of Minnesota Press, 1986).

Djebar, Assia, 'Writing in the language of the Other', in Isaebelle de Courtivron (ed.), *Lives in Translation: Bilingual Writers on Identity and Creativity* (New York, NY: Palgrave Macmillan, 2003), pp. 19–27.

Durand, Jacques, 'Linguistic purification, the French nation-state and the linguist', in Charlotte Hoffmann (ed.), *Language, Culture and Communication in Contemporary Europe* (Clevedon: Multilingual Matters Ltd, 1996), pp. 75–92.

Edwards, John, *Language, Society and Identity* (Oxford and New York, NY: Basil Blackwell, 1988).

Edwards, John, *Language and Identity* (Cambridge: Cambridge University Press, 2009).

Edzard, Lutz, *Language as a Medium of Legal Norms: The Implications of the Use of Arabic as a Language in the United Nations System* (Berlin: Duncker and Humblot, 1998).

Ergun, Ayça, 'Politics of Romanisation in Azerbaijan (1921–1992)', *Journal of the Royal Asiatic Society* (2010), 20: 23–48.

Feldman, Yael S., 'Postcolonial memory, postmodern intertextuality: Anton Shammas's *Arabesques* revisited', *Modern Language Association (MLA)* (1999): 373–89.

Fishman, Joshua, *Language and Nationalism: Two Integrative Essays* (Rowley, MA: Newbury House Publishers, 1972).

Gal, Susan, 'Multiplicity and contention among language ideologies', in Bambi B. Schieffelin, Kathryn A. Woolard and Paul V. Kroskrity (eds), *Language Ideologies: Practice and Theory* (New York and Oxford: Oxford University Press, 1998), pp. 317–331.

Gellner, Ernest, *Nations and Nationalism* (Oxford: Basil Blackwell, 1983).

Genette, Gerard, *Paratexts: Thresholds of Interpretation* (Cambridge: Cambridge University Press, 1997).

Gershoni, Israel and James Jankowski, *Egypt, Islam and the Arabs: The Search for Egyptian Nationalism 1900–1930* (New York and Oxford: Oxford University Press, 1986).

Gibb, Hamilton A. R., *Studies on the Civilisation of Islam* (London: Routledge & Kegan Paul, 1962).

Gilson, Erika H., 'Introduction of new writing systems: the Turkish case', in Nancy Schweda-Nicholson (ed.), *Languages in the International Perspective* (Norwood, NJ: Ablex Publishing Corporation, 1986), pp. 23–40.

Githiora, Chege, 'Kenya: language and the search for a coherent national identity', in Andrew Simpson (ed.), *Language and National Identity in Africa* (Oxford: Oxford University Press, 2008), pp. 235–51.

Goldziher, Ignaz, *Muslim Studies (Vol. I)*, trans. C. R. Barber and S. M. Stern (London: Allen & Unwin, 1967).

Gramsci, Antonio, *Selections from Cultural Writings*, trans. W. Boelhower (London: Lawrence & Wishart, 1985).

Greenberg, Robert D., *Language and Identity in the Balkans: Serbo-Croatian and its Disintegration* (Oxford: Oxford University Press, 2004).

Grice, Herbert Paul, 'Logic and conversation', in Peter Cole and Jerry L. Morgan (eds), *Syntax and Semantic 3: Speech Acts* (New York, NY: Academic Press, 1975), pp. 41–58.

Grossman, David, *Sleeping on a Wire: Conversations with Palestinians in Israel*, trans. Haim Watzman (London: Jonathan Cape, 1993).

Hanna, Sami and George H. Gradner, *Arab Socialism: A Documentary Survey* (Leiden: Brill, 1969).

Hargreaves, Alec G., 'Writers of Maghrebian immigrant origin in France: French, Francophone, Maghrebian or Beur?', in Laila Ibnifassi and Nicki Hitchcott (eds), *African Francophone Writing: A Critical Introduction* (Oxford and Washington, DC: Berg, 1996), pp. 33–43.

Hargreaves, Alec G., 'Francophonie and globalisation: France at the crossroads', in Kamal Salhi (ed.), *Francophone Voices* (Exeter: Elm Bank Publications, 1999), pp. 49–57.

Hatcher, Lynley, 'Script change in Azerbaijan', *International Journal of the Sociology of Language* (2008), 192: 105–16.

Heller, Monica, 'Code-switching and the politics of language', in Lesley Milroy and Pieter Muysken (eds), *One Speaker, Two Languages: Cross-Disciplinary Perspectives on Code-Switching* (Cambridge: Cambridge University Press, 1995), pp. 158–74.

Hever, Hanan and Orlin D. Gensler, 'Hebrew in Israeli Arab hand: six miniatures on Anton Shammas's *Arabesques*', *Cultural Critique* (1987), 7: 47–76.

Hill, Jane H. and Bruce Mannheim, 'Language and world view', *Annual Review of Anthropology* (1992), 21: 381–406.

Hobsbawm, Eric, *Nations and Nationalism since 1870* (Cambridge: Cambridge University Press, 1990).

Hodges, Adam, *The 'War on Terror' Narrative: Discourse and Intertextuality in the Construction and Contestation of Sociopolitical Reality* (Cambridge: Cambridge University Press, 2011).

Howell, Robert B., 'The low countries: a study in sharply contrasting nationalisms', in Stephen Barbour and Cathie Carmichael (eds), *Language and Nationalism in Europe* (Oxford: Oxford University Press, 2000), pp. 130–50.

Hsiau, A-chin, 'Language ideology in Taiwan: the KMT's language policy, the Tai-yü language movement, and ethnic politics', *Journal of Multilingual and Multicultural Development* (1997), 18: 302–15.

Irvine, Judith T., 'When talk isn't cheap: language and political economy', *American Ethnologist* (1989), 16: 248–67.

Ivanić, Roz, *Writing and Identity: The Discoursal Construction of Identity in Academic Writing* (Amsterdam and Philadelphia, PA: John Benjamins, 1998).

Jack, Belinda, *Francophone Literatures: An Introductory Survey* (New York and Oxford: Oxford University Press, 1996).

Jayyusi, Salma Khadra (ed.), *An Anthology of Modern Palestinian Literature* (New York, NY: University of Columbia Press, 1992).

Johnstone, Barbara, 'Arguments with Khomeini: rhetorical situation and persuasive style in cross-cultural perspective', *Text* (1986), 6: 171–87.

Johnstone, Barbara, 'Parataxis in Arabic: modification as a model for persuasion', *Studies in Language* (1987), 11: 85–98.

Johnstone, Barbara, '"Orality" and discourse structure in Modern Standard Arabic', in Mushira Eid (ed.), *Perspectives on Arabic Linguistics I* (Amsterdam and Philadelphia, PA: John Benjamins, 1990), pp. 215–31.

Johnstone, Barbara, *Repetition in Arabic Discourse: Paradigms, Syntagms and the Ecology of Language* (Amsterdam and Philadelphia, PA: John Benjamins, 1991).

Joyaux, Georges J., 'Driss Chräibi, Mohammed Dib, Kateb Yacine, and indigenous North African literature', in Issa J. Boullata (ed.), *Critical Perspectives on Modern Arabic Literature 1945–1980* (Washington, DC: Three Continents Press, 1980), pp. 117–27.

Judge, Anne, 'The institutional framework of *la Francophonie*', in Laila Ibnfassi and Nicki Hitchcot (eds), *African Francophone Writing: A Critical Introduction* (Oxford and Washington, DC: Berg, 1996), pp. 11–30.

Kamusella, Tomasz D. I., 'Language as an instrument of nationalism in Central Europe', *Nations and Nationalism* (2001), 7: 235–51.

Kaplan, Robert B., 'Cultural thought patterns in inter-cultural education', *Language Learning* (1966), 26: 1–20.

Katriel, Tamar, *Talking Straight: Dugri Speech in Israeli Sabra Culture* (Cambridge: Cambridge University Press, 1986).

Kayyal, Mahmoud, 'Arabs dancing in a new light of *Arabesques*': minor Hebrew works of Palestinian authors in the eyes of critics', *Middle Eastern Literatures* (2008), 11: 31–51.

Kedourie, Elie, *Nationalism* (London: Hutchinson University Library, 1966).

Khadduri, Majid, *Islamic Jurisprudence: Shāfi'ī's Risāla* (Baltimore, MD: The Johns Hopkins University Press, 1961).

Kilpatrick, Hilary, 'Arab fiction in English: a case of dual nationality', *New Comparisons* (1992), 13: 46–55.

King, Robert D., *Nehru and the Language Politics of India* (Delhi: Oxford University Press, 1998).

King, Robert D., 'The poisonous potency of script: Hindi and Urdu', *International Journal of the Sociology of Language* (2001), 150: 43–59.

Koch, Barbara Johnstone, 'Arabic lexical couplets and the evolution of synonymy', *General Linguistics* (1983a), 23: 51–61.

Koch, Barbara Johnstone, 'Presentation as proof: the language of Arabic rhetoric', *Anthropological Linguistics* (1983b), 25: 47–60.

Labov, William, *The Social Stratification of English in New York City* (Washington, DC: Centre for Applied Linguistics, 1966).

Labov, William, 'The reflection of social processes in linguistic structures', in Joshua Fishman (ed.), *Readings in the Sociology of Language* (Mouton: The Hague, 1968), pp. 240–51.

Laffin, John, *Know the Middle East* (Gloucester: Alan Sutton, 1985).

Lakoff, Robin Tolmach, *The Language War* (Berkeley, CA: The University of California Press, 2000).

Landau, Jacob M., 'Alphabet reform in the six independent ex-Soviet Muslim republics', *Journal of the Royal Asiatic Society* (2010), 20: 25–32.

Landau, Jacob M. and Barbara Kellner-Heinkele, *Politics of Language in the ex-Soviet Muslim States* (London: Hurst, 2001).

Landry, R and R. Y. Bourhis, 'Linguistic landscape and ethnolinguistic vitality: an empirical study', *Journal of Language and Social Psychology* (1997), 16: 23–49.

Lane, Edward William, *Arabic–English Lexicon* (Beirut: Librairie du Liban, 1980).

Larkin, Margaret, 'The inimitability of the Qur'an: two perspectives', *Religion & Literature* (1988), 20: 31–47.

Lenneberg, Eric H., 'Cognition in ethnolinguistics', *Language* (1953), 29: 463–71.

Le Page, R. B. and A. Tabouret-Keller, 'Models and stereotypes of ethnicity and language', *Journal of Multilingual and Multicultural Development* (1982), 3: 161–92.

Lewis, Bernard, *The Political Language of Islam* (Chicago and London: University of Chicago Press, 1991).

Lewis, Geoffrey, *The Turkish Language Reform: A Catastrophic Success* (Oxford: Oxford University Press, 1999).

Lodge, Anthony, 'French is a logical language', in Laurie Bauer and Peter Trudgill (eds), *Language Myths* (London: Penguin Books, 1998), pp. 23–31.

Lucy, John A., 'Linguistic relativity', *Annual Review of Anthropology* (1997), 26: 291–312.

Maalouf, Amin, *On Identity*, trans. Barbara Bray (London: The Harvill Press, 2000).

Machan, Tim William, *Language Anxiety: Conflict and Change in the History of English* (Oxford: Oxford University Press, 2009).

Mackridge, Peter, *Language and National Identity in Greece, 1766–1967* (Oxford: Oxford University Press, 2009).

Magner, Thomas, F., 'Digraphia in the territories of the Croats and Serbs', *International Journal of the Sociology of Language* (2001), 150: 11–26.

Malak, Amin, 'Arab-Muslim feminism and the narrative of hybridity: the fiction of Ahdaf Soueif', *Alif: Journal of Contemporary Poetics* (2000), 20: 140–65.

Mar-Molinero, Clare, 'The Iberian Peninsula: conflicting linguistic nationalisms', in Stephen Barbour and Cathie Carmichael (eds), *Language and Nationalism in Europe* (Oxford: Oxford University Press, 2000), pp. 83–104.

Martin, Richard C., 'The role of Basrah Mutazillah in formulating the doctrine of the apologetic miracle', *Journal of Near Eastern Studies* (1980), 3: 175–89.

Mattawa, Khaled, 'Four uneasy pieces', *Alif: Journal of Contemporary Poetics* (2000), 20: 269–83.

May, Stephen, *Language and Minority Rights: Ethnicity, Nationalism and the Politics of Language* (Harlow: Longman, 2001).

Mazrui, Ali A. and Alamin M. Mazrui, *The Power of Babel: Language and Governance in the African Experience* (Oxford: James Currey, 1998).

McLellan, David, *Ideology*, 2nd edn (Buckingham: Open University Press, 1995).

Mehrez, Samia, 'The subversive poetics of radical bilingualism: postcolonial Francophone North African literature', in Dominick La Capra (ed.), *The Bounds of Race: Perspectives on Hegemony and Resistance* (Ithaca and London: Cornell University Press, 1991), pp. 255–77.

Meisami, Julie Scott and Paul Starkey (eds), *Encyclopaedia of Arabic Literature (2 Vols)* (London and New York, NY: Routledge, 1998).

Mejdell, Gunvor, 'What is happening to *lughatunā al-jamīla*? Recent media representations and social practice in Egypt', *Journal of Arabic and Islamic Studies* (2008), 8: 108–24.

Michael, Sami, 'On being an Iraqi-Jewish writer in Israel', *Prooftexts* (1984), 4: 23–33.

Mignon, Laurent, 'The literati and letters: a few words on the Turkish alphabet reform', *Journal of the Royal Asiatic Society* (2010), 20: 11.24.

Mitchell, Timothy, *Colonising Egypt* (Cambridge: Cambridge University Press, 1988).

Moreh, Samuel (ed. and trans.), *Al-Jabartī's Chronicle of the First Seven Months of the French Occupation of Egypt* (Leiden: Brill, 1975).

Morris, Nancy, 'Language and identity in twentieth century Puerto Rico', *Journal of Multilingual and Multicultural Development* (1996), 17: 17–32.

Mortimer, Mildred, 'Introduction', in Mildred Mortimer (ed.), *Maghrebian Mosaic: A Literature in Transition* (Boulder and London: Lynne Rienner Publishers, 2001), p. 5.

Mottahedeh, Roy P., 'The *Shu'ūbiyya* controversy and the social history of early Islamic Iran', *International Journal of Middle Eastern Studies* (1976), 7: 161–82.

Munroe, James T., *The Shu'ūbiyya in Al-Andalus: The Risāla of Ibn García and Five Refutations* (Berkeley, CA: University of California Press, 1970).

Ngom, Fallou, 'Linguistic resistance in the Murid speech community in Senegal', *Journal of Multilingual and Multicultural Development* (2002), 23: 214–26.

Norris, Harry T., '*Shu'ūbiyya* in Arabic literature', in Julia Ashtiany, T. M. Johnstone, J. D. Letham, R. B. Serjeant and G. Rex Smith (eds), *'Abbasid Belles-Lettres* (Cambridge: Cambridge University Press, 1990), pp. 31–47.

Patai, Raphael, *The Arab Mind* (New York, NY: Charles Scribner's Son, 1973).

Pellat, Charles, *The Life and Works of Jāḥiẓ: Translations of Selected Texts*, trans. D. M. Hawke (London: Routledge & Kegan Paul, 1969).

Poonawala, Ismail K., 'Translatability of the Qur'an: theological and literary considerations', *Translation and Scripture. A Jewish Quarterly Review Supplement* (1990): 161–92.

Prothro, Terry, 'Arab-American differences in the judgment of written messages', *The Journal of Social Psychology* (1955), 42: 3–11.

Rahman, Fazlur, 'Translating the Qur'an', *Religion & Literature* (1988), 20: 23–30.

Ramras-Rauch, Gila, *The Arab in Israeli Literature* (Bloomington and Indianapolis, IN: Indiana University Press, 1989).

Romaine, Suzanne, 'Signs of identity, signs of discord: glottal goofs and the green grocer's glottal in debates on Hawaiian orthography', *Journal of Linguistic Anthropology* (2002), 12: 189–224.

Ruzza, Carlo, 'Language and nationalism in Italy: language as a weak marker of identity', in Stephen Barbour and Cathie Carmichael (eds), *Language and Nationalism in Europe* (Oxford: Oxford University Press, 2000), pp. 168–82.

Sadana, Rashmi, 'A suitable text for a vegetarian audience: questions of authenticity and the politics of translation', *Public Culture* (2007), 19: 309–28.

Sadana, Rashmi, 'Two tales of a city: the place of English and the limits of postcolonial critique', *Interventions* (2009), 11: 1–15.

Said, Edward, 'An ideology of difference', in Henry Louis Gates, Jr (ed.), *'Race', Writing and Difference* (Chicago, IL: University of Chicago Press, 1986), pp. 38–58.

Said, Edward, *Out of Place: A Memoir* (New York, NY: Alfred A. Knopf, 1999).

Salameh, Franck, *Language, Memory and Identity in the Middle East: The Case of Lebanon* (Lanham, MD: Lexington Books, 2010).

Salihi, Kamal, 'French words, authentic voice', in Kamal Salihi (ed.), *Francophone Voices* (Exeter: Elm Bank Publications, 1999), pp. 27–48.

Sánchez, José Ignacio, 'Ibn Qutayba and Shu'ūbiyya', Masters dissertation, University of Cambridge, 2007.

Sarup, Madan, *Identity, Culture and the Postmodern World* (Edinburgh: Edinburgh University Press, 1996).

Savage, Andrew, 'Writing Tuareg: three script options', *International Journal of the Sociology of Language* (2008), 192: 5–13.

Schieffelin, Bambi B. and Rachelle Charlier Doucet, 'The "real" Haitian Creole: ideology, metalinguistics and orthographic choices', in Bambi B. Schieffelin, Kathryn A. Woolard and Paul V. Kroskrity (eds), *Language Ideologies: Practice and Theory* (New York and Oxford: Oxford University Press, 1998), pp. 285–316.

Schmid, Carol L., *The Politics of Language: Conflict, Identity and Cultural Pluralism in Comparative Perspective* (Oxford: Oxford University Press, 2001).

Schöpflin, George, 'The functions of myth and the taxonomy of myths', in Geoffrey Hosking and George Schöpflin (eds), *Myths and Nationhood* (London: Hurst, 1997), pp. 19–35.

Seliktar, Ofira, 'Ethnic stratification and foreign policy in Israel: the attitudes of Oriental Jews towards the Arabs and the Arab-Israeli conflict', *The Middle East Journal* (1984), 38: 34–50.

Semmerling, Tim Jon, *Israeli and Palestinian Postcards: Presentations of National Self* (Austin, TX: University of Texas Press, 2004).

Sen, Amartya, *Identity and Violence: The Illusion of Destiny* (London: Allen Lane, 2006).

Serrano, Richard, 'Translation and the interlingual text in the novels of Rachid Boudjedra', in Mildred Mortimer (ed.), *Maghrebian Mosaic: A Literature in Transition* (Boulder and London: Lynne Rienner Publishers, 2001), pp. 27–40.

Shabi, Rachel, *Not the Enemy: Israel's Jews from Arab Lands* (New Haven and London: Yale University Press, 2009).

Shakour, Adel, *Explaining the Use of Hebrew Neologisms in the Writings of Anton Shammas* (forthcoming).

Shammas, Anton, *Arabesques*, trans. Vivian Eden (London: Viking, 1988).

Shammas, Anton, 'The drowned library: reflections on found, lost and translated books and languages', in Isaebelle de Courtivron (ed.), *Lives in Translation: Bilingual Writers on Identity and Creativity* (New York, NY: Palgrave Macmillan, 2003), pp. 111–28.

Sharabi, Hisham, *Nationalism and Revolution in the Arab World* (Princeton, NJ: D. Van Nostrand Company, 1966).

Sharabi, Hisham, *Neopatriarchy: A Theory of Distorted Change in Arab Society* (New York, NY: Oxford University Press, 1988).

Sharky, Heather J., *Living with Colonialism: Nationalism and Culture in the Anglo-Egyptian Sudan* (Berkeley, CA: University of California Press, 2003).

Shohamy, Elena and Elena Goldberg, *The Hidden Agendas of Language Policy: An Expanded View* (New York, NY: Routledge, 2006).

Shohamy, Elena and Durk Gorter, *Linguistic Landscape: Expanding the Scenery* (New York and London: Routledge, 2009).

Shouby, E., 'The influence of the Arabic language on the psychology of the Arabs', *The Middle East Journal* (1951), 5: 284–302.

Shraybom-Shivtiel, Shlomit, 'The question of the Romanisation of the script and the emergence of nationalism in the Middle East', *Mediterranean Language Review* (1998), 10: 179–96.

Smith, Anthony D., *National Identity* (London: Penguin, 1991).

Smith, Anthony D., *Nationalism* (Cambridge: Polity, 2001).

Snir, Reuven, '"We were like those who dream": Iraqi–Jewish writers in Israel in the 1950s', *Prooftexts* (1991), 11: 153–73.

Snir, Reuven, '"Hebrew as the language of grace": Arab Palestinian writers in Hebrew', *Prooftexts* (1995), 15: 163–83.

Somekh, Sasson, *Life after Baghdad: Memoirs of an Arab-Jew in Israel, 1950–2000* (Brighton: Sussex Academic Press, 2012).

Soueif, Ahdaf, *In the Eye of the Sun* (London: Bloomsbury, 1994).

Steinberg, Danny D., *Psycholinguistics: Language, Mind and World* (London and New York, NY: Longman, 1982).

Suleiman, Yasir, 'The methodological rules of Arabic grammar', in Kinga Dévényi and Támash Iványi (eds), *Proceedings of the Collouium on Arabic Grammar/The Arabist: Budapest Studies in Arabic* (Budapest: Etövös Loránd University and Csoma De Körös Society, 1991), pp. 351–64.

Suleiman, Yasir, 'Nationalism and the Arabic language: an historical overview', in Yasir Suleiman (ed.), *Arabic Sociolinguistics: Issues and Perspectives* (Richmond: Curzon Press, 1994), pp. 3–23.

Suleiman, Yasir, 'The concept of *Faṣāḥa* in Ibn Sinān al-Khafājī', *New Arabian Studies* (1996), 3: 219–37.

Suleiman, Yasir, *The Arabic Grammatical Tradition: A Study in Ta'līl* (Edinburgh: Edinburgh University Press, 1999).

Suleiman, Yasir, '"Under the spell of language": Arabic between linguistic determinism and linguistic reality', in Ian R. Netton (ed.), *Studies in Honour of Clifford Edmund Bosworth, Vol I: Hunter of the East: Arabic and Semitic Studies* (Leiden: Brill, 2000), pp. 113–37.

Suleiman, Yasir, '*Bayān* as a principle of taxonomy: linguistic elements in Jāḥiẓ's thinking', in John F. Healey and Venetia Porter (eds), *Studies on Arabia in Honour of Professor G. Rex Smith: Journal of Semitic Studies Supplement* (2002), 14: 273–95.

Suleiman, Yasir, *The Arabic Language and National Identity: A Study in Ideology* (Washington, DC: Georgetown University Press, 2003).

Suleiman, Yasir, *A War of Words: Language and Conflict in the Middle East* (Cambridge: Cambridge University Press, 2004).

Suleiman, Yasir, 'The nation speaks: on the poetics of nationalist literature', in Yasir Suleiman and Ibrahim Muhawi (eds), *Literature and Nation in the Middle East* (Edinburgh: Edinburgh University Press, 2006a), pp. 208–31.

Suleiman, Yasir, 'Arabic language reforms, language ideology and the criminalisation of Sībawayhi', in Lutz Edzard and Janet Watson (eds), *Grammar as a Window onto Arabic Humanism: A Collection of Articles in Honour of Michael G. Carter* (Wiesbaden: Harrassowitz Verlag, 2006b), pp. 66–83.

Suleiman, Yasir, 'Egypt: from Egyptian to pan-Arab nationalism', in Andrew Simpson (ed.), *Language and National Identity in Africa* (Oxford: Oxford University Press, 2008), pp. 26–43.

Suleiman, Yasir, 'Nationalist poetry, conflict and meta-linguistic discourse', in Yasir Suleiman (ed.), *Living Islamic History: Studies in Honour of Professor Carole Hillenbrand* (Edinburgh: Edinburgh University Press, 2010), pp. 252–78.

Suleiman, Yasir, *Arabic, Self and Identity: A Study in Conflict and Displacement* (New York and Oxford: Oxford University Press, 2011a).

Suleiman, Yasir, 'Ideology, grammar-making and the standardisation of Arabic', in Bilal Orfali (ed.), *In the Shadow of Arabic: The Centrality of Language to Arabic Culture* (Studies Presented to Ramzi Baalbaki on the Occasion of his Sixtieth Birthday) (Leiden and Boston, MA: Brill, 2011b), pp. 3–30.

Talib, Ismail, *The Language of Postcolonial Literatures: An Introduction* (London and New York, NY: Routledge, 2002).

Thompson, John B., *Studies in the Theory of Ideology* (Cambridge: Polity Press, 1984).

Tibawi, A. L., 'Is the Qur'an translatable? Early Muslim opinion', *The Muslim World* (1962), 52: 4–16.

Topan, Farouk, 'Tanzania: the development of Swahili as a national and official language', in Andrew Simpson (ed.), *Language and National Identity in Africa* (Oxford: Oxford University Press, 2008), pp. 252–66.

Törnquist-Plewa, Barbara, 'Contrasting ethnic nationalisms: Eastern Central Europe', in Stephen Barbour and Cathie Carmichael (eds), *Language and Nationalism in Europe* (Oxford: Oxford University Press, 2000), pp. 183–220.

Trudgill, Peter, 'Greece and European Turkey: from religious to ethnic identity', in Stephen Barbour and Cathie Carmichael (eds), *Language and Nationalism in Europe* (Oxford: Oxford University Press, 2000), pp. 240–63.

Turki, Fawaz, *Exile's Return: The Making of a Palestinian American* (New York, NY: The Free Press, 1994).

van Gelder, Geert Jan, 'Against the Arabic grammarians: some poems', in Bilal Orfali (ed.), *In the Shadow of Arabic: The Centrality of Language to Arabic Culture* (Studies Presented to Ramzi Baalbaki on the Occasion of his Sixtieth Birthday) (Leiden and Boston, MA: Brill, 2011), pp. 249–63.

Vasalou, Sophia, 'The miraculous eloquence of the Qur'an: general trajectories and individual approaches', *Journal of Qur'anic Studies* (2002), 4: 23–53.

Verschueren, Jef, *Ideology in Language Use: Pragmatic Guidelines for Empirical Research* (Cambridge: Cambridge University Press, 2012).

Versteegh, Kees, *The Explanation of Linguistic Causes: Az-Zajjājī's Theory of Grammar* (Amsterdam and Philadelphia, PA: John Benjamins, 1995).

Vikør, Lars S., 'Northern Europe: languages as prime markers of ethnic and national identity', in Stephen Barbour and Cathie Carmichael (eds), *Language and Nationalism in Europe* (Oxford: Oxford University Press, 2000), pp. 105–29.

Von Grunebaum, Gustave, *A Tenth Century Document of Arabic Literary Theory and Criticism* (Chicago, IL: University of Chicago Press, 1950).

Unseth, Peter, 'Sociolinguistic parallels between choosing scripts and languages', *Written Language and Literacy* (2005), 8: 19–42.

Urla, Jacqueline, 'Ethnic protests and social planning: a look at Basque language revival', *Cultural Anthropology* (1988), 1: 379–94.

Urla, Jacqueline, 'Contesting modernities: language standardization and the production of an ancient/modern Basque culture', *Critique of Anthropology* (1993), 13: 101–18.

Uzman, Mehmet, 'Romanisation in Uzbekistan past and present', *Journal of the Royal Asiatic Society* (2010), 20: 49–60.

Wassink, Alicia Beckford and Anne Curzan, 'Addressing ideologies around African American English', *Journal of English Linguistics* (2004), 32: 171–85.

Watson, Cameron, 'Folklore and Basque nationalism: language, myth, reality', *Nations and Nationalism* (1996), 2: 17–34.

Wehr, Hans, *A Dictionary of Modern Written Arabic*, J. Milton Cowan (ed.) (Beirut: Librairie du Liban, 1980).

Weiss, Bernard G., 'Medieval Muslim discussions of the origin of language', *Zeitschrift der Deutschen Morgenländischen Gessellschaft* (1974), 124: 33–41.

Whorf, Benjamin, 'Linguistic relativity and the relation of linguistic processes to perception and cognition', in Sol Saporta (ed.), *Psycholinguistics: A Book of Readings* (New York, NY: Holt, Reinhart and Winston, 1961), pp. 460–8.

Willemsen, Marlous, 'Dutch authors from the Arab world: a relief to the Multilingual Society', *Alif: Journal of Contemporary Poetics* (2000), 20: 68–84.

Wodak, Ruth, R. de Cilla, M. Reisigl and A. H. Liebhart, *The Discursive Construction of National Identity*, trans. Richard Mitten (Edinburgh: Edinburgh University Press, 1999).

Woodhul, Winifred, *Transfigurations of the Maghreb: Feminism, Decolonisation and Literatures* (Minneapolis and London: University of Minnesota Press, 1993).

Woolard, K. A. and B. B. Schieffelin, 'Language ideology', *Annual Review of Anthropology* (1994), 32: 55–82.

Yetiv, Isaac, 'The crisis of identity of the Native North African writer', in George Stambolian (ed.), *Twentieth Century French Fiction* (New Brunswick, NJ: Rutgers University Press, 1975), pp. 123–40.

INDEX

'-j-m root, 69
'-r-b root, 62

a'ājim (animals), 80
'Abbasids, 84
'Abd al-Rahim, Mahmud, 116
'Abd al-Rahman, 'A'isha (Bint al-Shati'), 61
'Abd al-Raḥmān, Ṭālib, *al-'Arabiyya tuwājih al-taḥaddiyāt*, 138, 139, 142–3
Abu-Haidar, Farida, 178n22, 202–3
Abu Hanifa, 63–4
Achebe, Chinua, 173n10
acoustication, Arab, 238–9, 240, 270, 271, *276*
action, Arab substitution of words for, 252–3, 254, 255, 258
aḍdād (homonyms), 87
'Adnān, Etel, 188
Aeschylus, *Orestia*, 21
African American English (AAE), 27–8
African literature, 173n10
a'jam, 68, 69, 70, 74
'ajam (non-Arabs), 67–8, 69, *69*, 70, 80, 84, 90
Akif, Muhammad (Mehmet), 66n47
al-Siyāsa al-usbū'iyya (newspaper), 33
al-'Alayli, Abdullah, 31–2
Algeria, 168, 180–1, 183, 187, 188, 194n78, 207–8
Ali, Muhammad, 222
al-'Ālim, Maḥmūd Amīn, *Lughatunā al-'arabiyya fī ma'rakat al-ḥaḍāra*, 137
alterity, 16–17, 20, 25, 27, 29
amalgam, ideology as an, 6, 54, 103, 144–5, 206
America, anti-Arab feelings, 273–4n172
American language, 188
Americanisation, 43–4
'āmmiyyāt (colloquial Arabic), 54
Amrouche, Marie-Louise, 180
Amrouche, Taos, 204n122
al-Anbari, Abu Bakr, 87
Anderson, Benedict, *Imagined Communities*, 19
Angel Gabriel, 56
Anglophone literature, 171–2, 184, 209
anthologies, 182–3
anti-Semitism, 255
Antonius, Soraya, 176n16, 188
anxiety
  and globalisation, 141
  and identity, 183
  and language, 30, 149, 267
'aqd (counting), 72, 75
'Aql, Sa'id, *Yara*, 42
'arab, 51–2, 68, *69*, 70
Arab Christians, 54, 83n111, 210–11, 212, 247
Arab culture
  cultural politics, 110, 111, 150, 279–80
  epigraphs, 100, 128–9
  importance of 'face', 250
  influence of Arabic on, 214, 271
  ossification of, 270
  Patai on, 254, 261–2
  poetry, 57n18, 100, 112–19, 128–9, 146–7
  repetition and persuasion in, 261–6
  time in, 243–4, 245–6
  vagueness of thought in, 267, 268–70
  see also Sharabi, Hisham
Arab history, 82, 143, 150, 221–2, 228, 229, 271
Arab Jews, 35n67, 183, 189
Arab mind, 241–7, 247–61, 272
Arab Muslims, 5–6, 31, 247, 248
Arab nationalism *see* pan-Arab nationalism
Arab publishing industry, 203–4
Arab society, argumentation in, 265–6
Arab Spring, 47, 133